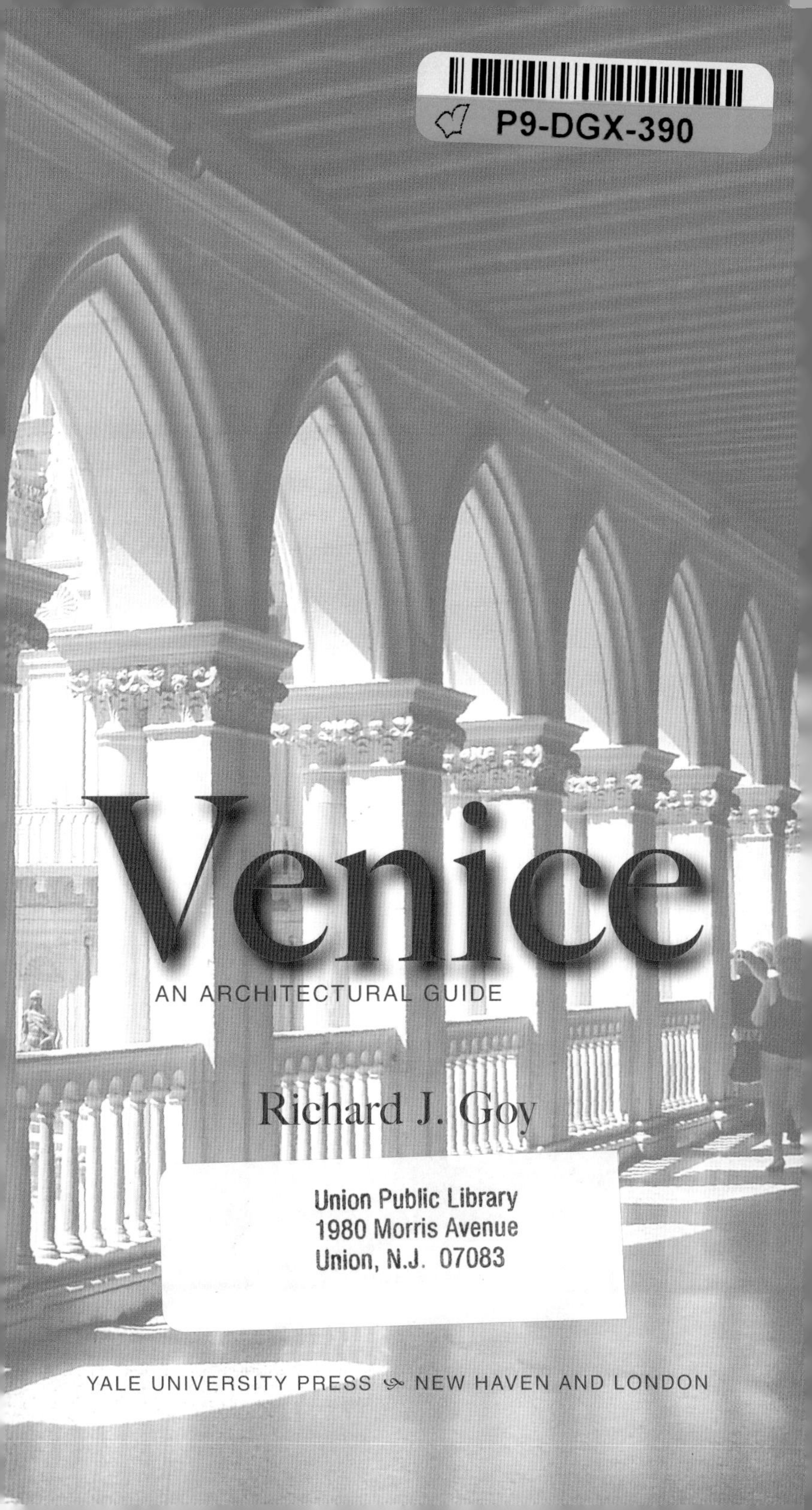

Venice

AN ARCHITECTURAL GUIDE

Richard J. Goy

YALE UNIVERSITY PRESS ❧ NEW HAVEN AND LONDON

VENICE IN PERIL

For every copy sold, a donation from the author's royalties
will be made to Venice in Peril

Designed by Emily Lees

Printed in China

Library of Congress Cataloging-in-Publication Data

Goy, Richard J. (Richard John), 1947–
Venice : city guide / Richard Goy.
p. cm.
Includes bibliographical references and index.
ISBN 978–0–300–14882–4 (cl : alk. paper)
1. Architecture–Italy–Venice–Guidebooks. 2. Venice
(Italy)–Guidebooks. I. Title.
NA1121.V4G679 2010
720.945'311–dc22

2009054058

A catalogue record for this book is available from The British Library

Frontispiece: Palazzo Ducale cortile loggia

VENICE

AN ARCHITECTURAL GUIDE

Contents

Preface

The basic premise behind this book is a simple one: to provide a
comprehensive but concise guide to the architecture of Venice. It
arises from my belief that, despite the astonishing profusion of
popular guides published in ever-greater numbers over the last few
decades, we still do not have such a succinct, authoritative
architectural guide in English. Italian visitors have the estimable
Guida Rossa published by the Touring Club Italiano, but sadly not
yet in any other languages. What we do have in English is the
equally authoritative *Venice and its Lagoon* by Giulio Lorenzetti,
first published in English in 1961 and never out of print since;
unquestionably indispensable though Lorenzetti is, I believe that it
still has a drawback for the modern visitor who is primarily
interested in the city's unparalleled architectural heritage. Lorenzetti
was principally a notable art historian, and his coverage of this aspect
of Venice's cultural legacy is comprehensive; his coverage of
architecture is less so. And this is where I believe the present work
will fulfil a useful role. By concentrating almost exclusively on the
city's architecture, it has been possible, within the limitations of a
reasonably portable and attractive single volume, to provide at least
some coverage of just about every building of architectural
significance in the city.

This guide is thus almost solely concerned with the built heritage,
although I have broadened its scope to include works of art and

sculpture where they are significant to the architecture in question, or have particular intrinsic importance.

The book is therefore intended for a certain type of visitor to Venice; one who seeks rather more detail and depth than is to be found in the numerous popular guides; one who lacks Italian, and yet seeks a guide that is 'user-friendly', attractive, manageable and as comprehensive as space allows.

It is organised following the principle (also adopted by Lorenzetti) of a series of walks through the city. In order to cover the city in a clear, comprehensible manner, they are planned by recognising its division into the six ancient districts or *sestieri*, first established around the end of the twelfth century, and still in use today as administrative subdivisions. The buildings of each *sestiere* are numbered sequentially through the entire district, from one end to the other, so, by simply following this numeration, one will visit every building in that *sestiere*. For example, the *sestiere* of Castello starts at the ancient former cathedral of San Pietro and ends, 6,827 numbers later, in front of the statue of Colleoni at Santi Giovanni e Paolo, having traversed the whole district from east to west. The walks can, of course, be broken at any point, and begun again on another occasion. Within the *sestieri* I have divided each itinerary into 'sub-sections', each of which can be easily accomplished in an hour or so.

In trying to make the guide as comprehensive as possible, I have included a number of secondary (or even 'tertiary') buildings that rarely rate a mention in more popular guides. This is an important distinction, since the city is not defined solely by its great *palazzi* and churches, but also by the urban matrix of numerous other less monumental buildings, many of which, in a less richly endowed context, would receive more attention than they usually do here. I have also mentioned a limited number of lost buildings, some of which had considerable architectural value, and the loss of which draws attention to the fact that – despite popular conceptions – Venice is not a 'preserved' city, but has experienced enormous physical change, particularly over the last two post-Republican centuries. Chronologically, the net is drawn as widely as possible, from the earliest Venetian-Byzantine fragments to the surprisingly numerous significant works of the nineteenth and twentieth centuries.

Brief introductory essays lay the foundations for the guide itself. Venice is unique in so many ways that a basic understanding of the city's political and urban history is essential if one is to gain any real understanding of its extraordinary architectural heritage. I have also briefly discussed the city's condition today, one that rightly continues to attract the world's concern, but in which one needs to appreciate the extraordinary things that have been achieved since the floods of 1966, as well as the formidable challenges for the future.

Topographically, the guide covers the six *sestieri*, followed by a brief summary of the buildings lining the banks of the Grand Canal; the Giudecca and San Giorgio; and finally, short sections on the other islands of the lagoon, from Torcello in the north to the important fishing port of Chioggia in the south.

Unlike most guides, I have omitted such additional information as that pertaining to *vaporetto* lines, hotels, restaurants and so on. There are two reasons: one is that much of this type of information is often obsolete even by the time of publication; the other is that it would take up valuable space better occupied by the guide itself.

The concluding appendices include a glossary of architectural terms, many unique to the city; a chronological list of the doges; and a brief list of the city's principal architects.`

SPELLING, TERMINOLOGY, DATES AND ATTRIBUTIONS

Venice has a rich linguistic heritage, manifested in its dialect, which still flourishes today and is incomprehensible to many other Italians. It includes many purely Venetian words, as well as distinctive versions of Italian words and verb conjugations (and a wonderfully musical intonation in speech). Many buildings in the city are generally known by their Venetian appellations (thus San Trovaso for Santi Gervasio e Protasio; and the widely used *Ca'* for *casa da stazio*, principal residence); street names also use dialect spelling and terminology. These terms are translated in the appendix, but I have retained dialect in the main text. The reasons are both practical and a little didactic: practical in that it will assist the visitor to match the text with the reality on site; didactic in that Venice's dialect is a vital element in its millennial civilisation, and its survival should matter to us in much the same way that its paintings, squares and palaces do.

The issue of dates and attributions is always a minefield in a book such as this; there is little documentary evidence for many of the claimed dates of the earliest events in the city's history, which should really be identified as 'cultural tradition' rather than established fact, often handed down by earlier chroniclers, such as Marin Sanudo and Francesco Sansovino. Numerous architectural attributions are unclear or unsupported by documentary evidence, with many on which a consensus has not yet settled. I have thus had to resort to the usual caveat vocabulary: 'perhaps', 'attributed to' . . . and so on. Research continues daily, however, and it is certain that attributions will be challenged or overturned by new findings and stylistic analysis. I have naturally tried to eliminate straightforward errors of fact, and will be most grateful to those who point out any that they do identify.

In identifying the building numbers in the text, the titles of the *sestieri* have been abbreviated thus: Castello (hereafter CS); Cannaregio (hereafter CN); San Marco (hereafter SM); San Polo (hereafter SP); Santa Croce (hereafter SC); Dorsoduro (hereafter DD); and Giudecca (hereafter GD).

Acknowledgements

Among the many debts accumulated in assembling this guide, the following are particularly important: to Claudio and Giulio Vianello for numerous examples of practical assistance; Nubar Gianighian and Paolina Pavanini for their unfailing kindness and hospitality; Frances Clarke for her inexhaustible knowledge and generous company; Primo and Caterina Zambon and their colleagues for making the Bar all'Orologio my Venetian centre of gravity over very many years. I am very grateful to Martin Brown for producing the book's maps. Particular thanks must be recorded to my colleagues at Yale: to Gillian Malpass, my editor, for her enthusiastic support and encouragement, Emily Lees for her skill and attention in bringing the project to fruition and Emily Angus. Finally, thanks to Barbara and Catherine, who, over the years, have tolerated our extensive tramping around old palaces and churches, interspersed – quite rightly – at their insistence, by numerous breaks for *gelati* and *ombre*.

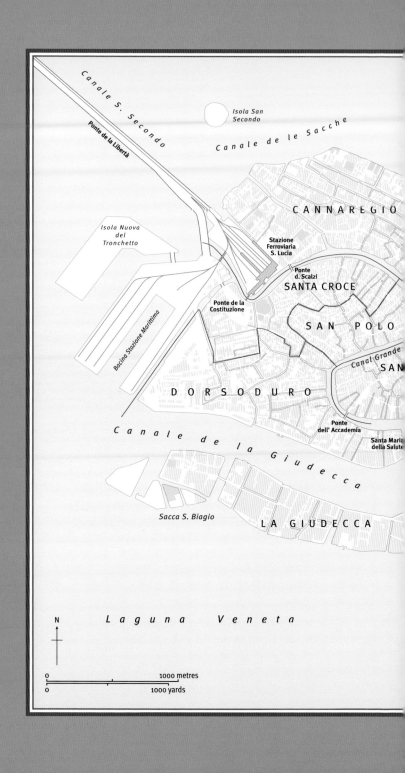

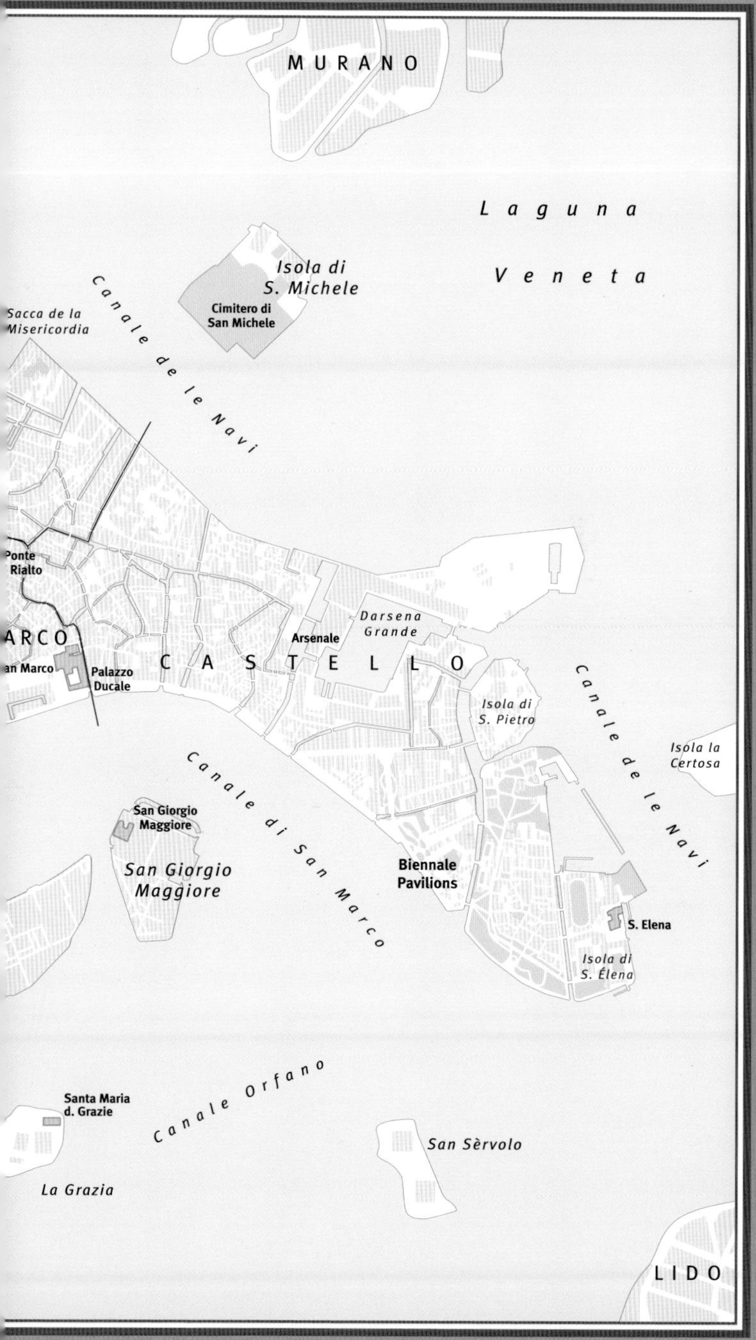

MURANO

Laguna

Veneta

Sacca de la
Misericordia

Isola di
S. Michele

Cimitero di
San Michele

Canale de le Navi

Ponte
Rialto

MARCO

an Marco

Palazzo
Ducale

C A S T E L L O

Arsenale

Darsena
Grande

Isola di
S. Pietro

Canale de le Navi

Isola la
Certosa

Canale di San Marco

San Giorgio
Maggiore

San Giorgio
Maggiore

Biennale
Pavilions

S. Elena

Isola di
S. Elena

Santa Maria
d. Grazie

Canale Orfano

San Sèrvolo

La Grazia

LIDO

VENICE

VENICE

THE MOST SERENE REPUBLIC

Introduction

AN OUTLINE HISTORY OF THE REPUBLIC AND POST-REPUBLICAN VENICE

Over recent decades the traditional view that Venice came into existence only following the 'barbarian' invasions of the fifth and sixth centuries AD has been supplanted by the knowledge that many parts of the lagoon region were well settled in the late Roman era. Torcello and the now abandoned islands to its north, for example, were effectively suburbs of the substantial Roman town of Altino; Chioggia, too, was a significant Roman settlement. The nearby Terraferma was one of the most intensively settled and cultivated parts of Roman Italy, and all the modern cities of the region – Padua, Treviso, Verona – were also major Roman cities. Aquileia, near the present small lagoon town of Grado, was the capital of the Roman tenth region (roughly, the Friuli), and was a large, sprawling city. The Adriatic margins were fished extensively, and the aquatic way of life of this coastal strip, beyond the Roman littoral roads, the Via Popilia and Via Annia, was equally well established. Although Roman traces have been found in Venice itself, the extremely dense nature of the city's fabric has rendered large-scale archaeological investigation extremely difficult.

Venice was founded, according to the ancient chronicles, on 25 March AD 421. There is no historical basis whatsoever for this

Facing page: Statue of Carlo Goldoni (1855) in Campo San Bortolamio by Antonio dal Zotto

precision, although there is no doubt that the invasions of Attila (AD 452) and of the Lombards (AD 569) provoked a migration from the Terraferma towards the relative safety of the lagoons; not solely that of Venice, but also the long chain of lagoons around the coastal strip from Chioggia almost as far as modern Trieste. Twelve sites were definitively settled, and they formed themselves into a loose 'confederation', the first administrative centre of which was at Eraclea. The first doge (*dux*), Paoluccio Anafesto, was elected in 697. Bitter rivalry grew between the members of this confederation, though, and in 742 the seat was transferred to Malamocco; in 810 it was moved once again, this time permanently, to Rivo Alto, Rialto; the acquisition of the body of St Mark in 829 finally set the seal on Venice as the definitive capital of the confederation, which was to evolve into the Most Serene Republic. The littoral strip, the Dogado, was the heartland of this initially largely aquatic empire.

The region lay at the edges of both the European mainland empire of the Franks and of the eastern Byzantine empire, with its capital at Constantinople, and this crucial position, between two great powers, cultures and landmasses, proved decisive in establishing the Republic at the interface between the Christian west and what became the Muslim east. Initially, Venice maintained a formal role as the western outpost of the Eastern Byzantine Christian empire, but slowly increased in wealth, power and trading skills, thereby weakening these formal ties, to achieve de facto independence. In 967 many privileges were formally recognised by Otto, the German emperor, while the Republic's government continued to evolve independently of either great power. In 1085 the Eastern emperor formally recognised Venice's complete independence and rule over the Dalmatian coast, the first element of what was to become an extensive maritime empire. Slowly, a complex, sophisticated form of republican government evolved that was to survive for centuries, until the Napoleonic invasion of 1797. At its head was the doge, elected by the Maggior Consiglio, the 'great council', formally instituted in 1172 and 'locked' in 1297, to comprise all adult male nobles whose names were registered in the 'Golden Book', the Libro d'Oro. The doge also presided over the Collegio or cabinet, as well as the Senate, the upper house; these bodies, too, were elected by secret ballot in the Maggior Consiglio.

Venice's location between east and west was mirrored in its religious affiliations. Ecclesiastical subjection to Constantinople was reflected in the see of Aquileia, and the Terraferma bishoprics were transferred into the lagoons with their congregations; the patriarchate of Grado, established in 766, became the focus of the Byzantine church in the region, and the settlements remained subject to the Eastern Church rather than Rome. For centuries thereafter, the Venetian church maintained a similarly dualistic relationship with both Rome and Byzantium, mirroring the political, cultural and mercantile duality between east and west. On many occasions Venice openly defied Rome, while maintaining its Christian fidelity; the entire Republic was excommunicated in 1309, for example, and again two centuries later, during the League of Cambrai crisis. In 1451 the patriarchate of Venice was established, and survives today, one of only four such 'eastern' titles in the Catholic Church. Relations with Rome remained highly ambivalent, often reflecting political realities as much as doctrinal stances; and although several Venetian cardinals were elected to the papacy, the Venetian church maintained a high degree of independence, both administratively and theologically.

During the early middle ages, the city's wealth, power and population grew dramatically; favourable trading rights with Byzantium resulted in the city becoming a vital centre for Mediterranean trade, and an entrepôt for spices and luxury goods from the Middle East, which were re-exported (often at huge profit) over western Europe. A series of trade wars with Genoa concluded with final victory in 1380, rendering Venice the pre-eminent Mediterranean trading nation; its regular fleets of galleys traversed the sea from Beirut to Spain, from Marseille to north Africa; and beyond, into the Black Sea, and to England and Flanders. They were supported by an equally imposing armed naval force, the most numerous and powerful in Europe. The Republic's wealth thereafter was essentially built on international trade.

The physical overseas empire, too, expanded, from the early acquisition of the Ionian islands (1126) and Istria (1145). The taking of Constantinople in the Fourth Crusade (1204) led to the dismemberment of what remained of the Eastern Empire, three-eighths of which now passed to the Venetians, including most of the Aegean archipelago, Crete and Negroponte (Euboea), with strategic ports in the Morea and a large permanent trading colony in Constantinople; there were trading communities in many other Middle Eastern cities, including Alexandria and Beirut. Finally, in 1470, Cyprus was acquired. The Republic's mainland territories, traditionally confined to the coastal Dogado, also expanded, first with the voluntary secession of Treviso (1338), then a much larger expansion that began with Padua (1373), then Vicenza, Bassano and Belluno (1403), Rovigo (1404), Verona (1405), the Friuli (1415), Brescia (1426) and Bergamo (1427). By the mid-fifteenth century Venice was one of the greatest territorial powers of Italy and almost certainly the wealthiest. The fifteenth and early sixteenth centuries probably represented the peak of the city's and the Republic's power and prestige, reflected in prodigious creativity in the arts and architecture. This was the era, first of Carpaccio and the Bellini, later of Giorgione, Tintoretto, Veronese and Titian, and of the architecture of Codussi and the Lombardo, then of Sansovino, Sanmicheli and Palladio.

The Eastern Christian Empire finally collapsed in 1453, when Constantinople fell to the Muslim Ottoman Turks; henceforth, Venice pursued a difficult double policy in the east, with phases of open hostility interspersed with periods of peace, during which (despite papal condemnation) trade continued to flourish. Eventually, though, its eastern colonies fell to the Turks; Crete was lost in 1669, the Morea in 1718. The mainland empire, however, had survived the crisis of the disastrous battle of Agnadello in 1509, and much of the Terraferma remained subject to the winged lion of St Mark until 1797.

The Republic's constitution had already been fully developed by the fourteenth century, the last body to be established being the Council of Ten, the committee of state security, founded after the abortive Baiamonte Ticpolo plot in 1310, and again chaired by the doge. Thereafter the Republic remained essentially a relatively benevolent oligarchy, ruled by the noble caste and supported by a class of citizenry that included the professions, civil servants and administrators; below the citizenry were the common people, around 80 per cent of the population. The 'myth of Venice' developed chiefly as a result of the Republic's relative democracy and freedom of activity and thought, as well as its extraordinary resilience and stability, surviving throughout Europe's centuries of turbulent change and bloody crisis. As far back as the medieval period, the formerly democratic communes of Italy had become the fiefdoms of individual princely clans, which ruled with varying degrees of tyranny or enlightenment, but in no case did the population have a role in their own government; almost all were inherently, often violently unstable. Venice was also extraordinarily wealthy, and the Republic maintained a carefully sophisticated regime of 'bread and circuses' to dissuade internal dissent; there was almost none, and the city and much of the Republic were remarkably free from civil discord. Its slow relative decline in the seventeenth and early eighteenth centuries owed less to a real deterioration than to the growth of larger nation-states in Europe with which the Republic could no longer compete, in military, economic or political terms. Even in this era the Republic remained extremely wealthy and nurtured a late flowering of the arts – represented by Canaletto, Longhena, Tiepolo, the Guardi – that claimed to rival the 'golden era' of Titian and Veronese in the sixteenth century.

By the later eighteenth century, though, the Republic's decline had become absolute rather than relative, and with Napoleon's invasion of northern Italy in 1797 it was no longer feasible to resist. On 12 May 1797 the Maggior Consiglio sat for the last time and voted the Republic's government out of existence. For the next half-century Venice was a pawn in the hands of the great powers; the city was first ceded to Austria by Napoleon, only to return to France in 1805. In 1814 it was again returned to Austria, and remained its subject until a popular uprising under Daniele Manin in 1848. After valiant resistance and an Austrian siege of the city, it capitulated again on 24 August 1849. Finally, though, in 1866, the city voluntarily joined the recently united Italy. Since then Venice has been the administrative capital of the wealthy, populous region of the Veneto, which corresponds very closely to the former boundaries of the Terraferma empire of the Serenissima, the Most Serene Republic.

SOME NOTES ON THE CITY'S URBAN HISTORY

Venice's site has given rise to a unique urban structure, all based on communication by water. The natural archipelago of around 100 islets that formed the original basis for settlement was slowly consolidated and enlarged over the centuries to result in the densely packed urban mass of today. The form and layout of these original islets were random, lining meandering natural channels and creeks, with firmer islets interspersed with areas of marsh or *barene*, zones that are usually below the water, but which emerge at low tides.

The archipelago lies in the centre of the 50-kilometre-long, crescent-shaped lagoon, separated from the Adriatic Sea by a chain of low, narrow islets, locally known as *lidi*. These *lidi* offered natural protection from storms, as well as physical defence from aggressors approaching by sea. The tidal lagoon was linked to the Adriatic by gaps between the *lidi*, and three of these had (and retain) great importance: the Porto di Lido, at the north end of the Lido; the Porto di Malamocco, between Venice Lido and Pellestrina; and the Porto di Chioggia, between Pellestrina and the lido of Sottomarina (Chioggia).

The larger, firmer islets forming Rivo Alto were naturally the first to be settled, particularly those adjacent to a broad, navigable waterway. The natural winding course of the Grand Canal was the chief of these, and most early settlements lined its banks. They took the form of island parishes, often colonised by a prominent family originally from the Terraferma, and who endowed a parish church as the community focus. The basic elements of these island parishes were therefore a navigable watercourse; a place of worship, with its attendant bell-tower; and a communal square or *campo*, around which were built the houses of the leading citizens. Since the lagoon is tidal, and thus saline, freshwater supply was a vital concern; in the centre of the *campo* was built a large underground cistern, with its characteristic *vera da pozzo* (well-head), collecting rainwater from the surrounding surfaces and filtering it in sand, for domestic consumption. Collectively, these features remain the fundamental 'building blocks' of the city.

The principal early settlements can be traced to specific locations or natural features. San Pietro di Castello, for example, at the east end of the archipelago, had natural defensive advantages, as well as being a firm, substantial islet, well located for access to the sea. San Marco was similarly substantial, with a strategic location overlooking the basin and the entrance to the Grand Canal. Equally prominent was Rivo Alto, the islet that gave its name both to the city and to its ancient market district – another large, firm islet in the centre of the archipelago, at the confluence of natural routes.

As the smaller islets were settled and consolidated, they were divided by numerous narrow canals, *rii*, navigable only by small, specialised boats. Larger, commercial vessels were confined to the broader, deeper channels, and as the great families developed their international trading interests, they required direct water access from their houses and warehouses. From this need arose the noble *palazzo-fontego* (palace-warehouse), still the most prominent typology in the city today. The island parishes were settled in waves, as the city's population grew. Slowly, too, the smaller, lesser islets between the principal island parishes were also colonised.

By the medieval era, Venice was one of the largest, most populous cities in Europe, with perhaps 100,000 inhabitants; and it continued to grow. Its appearance in 1500 is recorded in extraordinarily faithful detail by Jacopo de' Barbari, excerpts from whose famous woodcut *Venetie MD* illustrate the present book. By then the whole historic centre was a fully developed, densely packed urban form, with very little open space other than Piazza San Marco and the parish *campi*. Around the perimeter, the pattern was different, though, and the city was encircled by a ring of monastic houses, most with extensive gardens and orchards. The Piazza is clearly recognisable as the spiritual and administrative heart of the city; the eastern zone is dominated by the great enclosed, fortified naval base, the Arsenale, while San Pietro terminates the east end of the city. The northern and southern limits are not yet fully defined, though, since the reclamations to form the Zattere and the Fondamente Nuove were not begun until the next century. Many other features, however, are clearly visible, including the sinuous course of the Grand Canal, the Cannaregio Canal and the chain of islets forming the Giudecca, as well as San Giorgio just to the east.

The principal developments in the century after de' Barbari were these peripheral reclamations, as well as those of the Tereni Nuovi, near the present Piazzale Roma, all adding much-needed land for expansion. The population increased steadily during the sixteenth century to reach approximately 170,000 by the survey of 1563, probably the highest number in the city's history, but one that was reduced drastically by the devastating plagues of 1575 and 1630.

There were few dramatic alterations to the city's physical form after *circa* 1600 until the post-Republican era. Napoleon imposed radical changes, notably in Castello, with the demolition of monasteries to create the public gardens; and around Piazza San Marco, with the demolition of the granaries and the construction of the Ala Napoleonica. Reclamation also began for the Campo di Marte, at the west end of the city, later converted for industrial uses. There were further radical changes during the nineteenth century, with reclamation of many of the narrow *rii*, and extensive clearances and street-widening programmes, notably the Strada Nova; the Riva degli Schiavoni was also widened considerably. The city's physical isolation from the rest of Italy ended with the construction of the railway causeway in the years 1841–6, while internal communications were improved by the construction of the Accademia and railway station bridges across the Grand Canal. Towards the end of the century there were reclamations at the Giudecca and the creation of the residential island of Sant'Elena was begun. By the end of the century, too, the extensive western docks, the Stazione Marittima, had also been built.

Among the twentieth-century developments were the introduction of the second causeway, bringing road traffic into the edge of the city, and the development of Piazzale Roma as a transport interchange. In conjunction with this, the Rio Novo was cut, to facilitate communication with San Marco, but inflicting further damage on the historic fabric. Popular housing was built in a number of peripheral zones, including the Giudecca, Sacca Fisola, north-west Cannaregio and Sant'Elena. Most recent activity has principally concerned the redevelopment of former industrial backland for additional housing; conversion of former monastic complexes for other uses (often housing); and widespread conversion of palaces into luxury hotels.

VENETIAN ARCHITECTURAL HISTORY: STYLE AND STRUCTURE

Churches

In the earlier centuries Venice's architectural history was strongly influenced by the Muslim east, as well as more subtle influences from elsewhere in Romanesque and early Gothic western Europe. Even the eastern influences were sometimes indirect; there is, for example, a strong stylistic link between the mosaic tradition of San Marco and that of Byzantine Ravenna. The powerful, lasting influence of the basilica church form, too, can be traced back to early Christian examples in Italy and elsewhere, while the other traditional church form, the centralised or Greek-cross plan, can similarly be traced to numerous early Middle Eastern and Balkan examples, many of them reliquary chapels. The basilica plan was probably the first to be used in the lagoons, similar to those that survive from the fifth and sixth centuries at Grado, but after the establishment of the definitive centralised Greek-cross form of San Marco, the two typologies developed side by side, and can be seen coexisting today at Torcello. In the later medieval period, the Greek-cross plan fell from favour, but was revived with great refinement in the early Renaissance by Mauro Codussi at San Giovanni Grisostomo and Santa Maria Formosa; the linear basilica form was developed first into the Latin cross by the insertion of transepts (San Giacomo da l'Orio and the great monastic houses of the Frari and

Santi Giovanni e Paolo), and in the later Renaissance with a number of subtle and ingenious modifications by Palladio at San Giorgio and the Redentore. Liturgical requirements lay behind most of these variants, from the spacious, open preaching halls of the mendicant friars to the musical requirements of the monastic orders (the choir gallery or *barco*) and later of the orphanage churches (the Mendicanti, Pietà, Ospedaleto).

Functionally, almost all Venetian churches can be characterised in one of three ways: first, there are parish foundations, with their familiar liturgical requirements; parish churches are usually fairly small, although numerous, like the island parishes themselves. Second, there are monastic houses, founded by a wide variety of orders, and with their attendant residential and other accommodation. Third, there are votive churches, built either to house a venerated image (the Miracoli) or to celebrate a momentous historic event (the Redentore, the Salute).

Medieval Venetian churches were built of brick; skill in decorative brickwork can be seen at San Donato, Murano, and at Santi Giovanni e Paolo. Stylistically, a characteristic mature Gothic appearance evolved, the apogee of which is the beautiful façade of the Madona de l'Orto, all of brick, but with rich, complex stone detailing.

In the early Renaissance, Codussi brought a refined harmony to church interiors, while their exteriors metamorphosed traditional Gothic façades into the new classical language. At the same time, a richer, more decorative approach was introduced by Pietro Lombardo at the Miracoli, drawing on the traditional Venetian love of colour, fine marble and *chiaroscuro* (light and shade). In the later Renaissance, a new monumentality and theatricality began to be seen, above all in the façades of Palladio, a process that reached its Baroque peak in Longhena's Santa Maria de la Salute. Palladio's long-lasting influence continued in the work of Massari and others (the Gesuati, San Barnaba), but the Baroque was enthusiastically embraced in the city, and several exuberantly complex façades were built (San Moisè, the Scalzi, Santa Maria del Giglio), before the spirit of the Neo-classical reaction took over, for example, at the Tolentini and the Madalena.

Today, although many Venetian churches are of ancient foundation, most are the result either of a complete reconstruction from the sixteenth century onwards, or else of piecemeal modernisation and alteration over the centuries. Many still contain early basilica elements, enveloped by later (usually Renaissance) modernisations.

Palaces and Houses

The history of Venice's secular architecture has one remarkable feature resulting directly from its physical context. From an early period, probably around the eleventh century, the city considered its lagoon site so impregnable to attack that considerations of defence played no part in the development of its architecture thereafter. Even the twelfth-century Doge's Palace (Palazzo Ducale) itself, the seat of government, had rows of large windows, at a time when other capital cities were ruled from behind massive stone defensive walls with arrow-slots and crenellations; by now, Venice's crenellations were purely decorative.

The development of the Venetian *palazzo-fontego* is the city's single most important typology, and results from bringing together under one roof two distinct functions: that of the trading base of the merchant noble, with its waterfront quay, stores and offices, together with that of the residence of the same noble and his family, who thus lived directly 'over the shop'. The early maturation of the typology can be seen in the (largely rebuilt) Fondaco dei Turchi, and at Ca' Loredan and Ca' Farsetti, all distinguished by tall colonnades with stilted arches and broad rows of upper-level windows. What we might call the post-Romanesque style slowly developed into Gothic, and Venetian Gothic itself evolved over the period up to around 1450 in stylistic stages, famously discussed and analysed by Ruskin in *The Stones of Venice* (1851–8). As the city grew in wealth and power, this growth was directly reflected in the size, scale and richness of its palace façades; the final stage of Gothic, known as *gotico fiorito*, after the prominent stylised flower that caps the window heads, is characterised by rich stone tracery and balconies, and symmetrical, elegantly proportioned façades. Dozens of these fine houses were built in the first half of the fifteenth century, and they still define much of the city's character today: Ca' Foscari, Palazzo Pesaro and the magnificent Ca' d'Oro.

In the later fifteenth century this characteristic style, which had taken three centuries to mature, slowly gave way to the Renaissance, first in the innovative façades of Codussi, later in the much more theatrical, monumental work of Sanmicheli and Sansovino. The most prominent Renaissance palaces are characterised by the universal use of stone and rich sculpture, but also in their attempts to retain elements of the traditional, together with a parallel desire to break from its limitations, and to establish a new formal monumentality. The internal planning of the palaces changed little, other than

Sansovino's introduction, at Ca' Corner, of a Roman axial enfilade of spaces from quay to *cortile*.

The Baroque was adopted as enthusiastically for palace façades as it was for churches, and the massive works of Longhena at Ca' Pesaro and Ca' Rezzonico mark a final expansive flourish that was never to be emulated; instead, the swansong of the Venetian *palazzo* is Massari's imposing but restrained Neo-classical Palazzo Grassi, the last great palace built in the city.

Almost inevitably, the design of the houses of the citizenry parallels the history of the noble *palazzo*; often, the citizen's *palazzetto* is a scaled-down *palazzo* in every respect, including its tripartite plan and symmetrical façade. More humble dwellings, though, could not aspire to such refinements, and although the architectural style still emulates those of the larger houses, the detailing is simpler, the symmetry frequently not achievable.

Another important typology resulted from the extremely limited availability of land, and that is the speculative apartment block, built for rent. Examples survive from the early sixteenth century onwards, and most are regular, logical and repetitive, often ingeniously planned, with features such as interlocking staircases. Architecturally, they are usually fairly plain, with limited use of expensive stonework. Many later examples survive, particularly from the seventeenth and eighteenth centuries.

Scuole Grandi and Piccole

The third important typology is the *scuola grande*, together with the far more numerous *scuole piccole*. The *scuole grandi* were voluntary lay confraternities, each of several hundred members, drawn from all orders of society, which gathered for services and meetings, and engaged in a range of social and philanthropic activities. Other than the religious houses, they became the most important non-governmental organisations in the city. There were six *scuole grandi*, and they each required a large central hall for services and assemblies, together with a small hall in which the governing board met. The *scuole grandi* were notable patrons of the arts, and in the fifteenth and sixteenth centuries built lavish new halls, in which their magnificent collections of paintings were housed. Those that survive today were built at various times, from the small Gothic Scuola Vecchia de la Misericordia, to the vast Scuola Nuova nearby, designed by Sansovino but never completed.

Alongside these six *scuole grandi* were dozens of *scuole piccole*, some of them lay devotional bodies, others representing the city's numerous trade guilds; they, too, built halls, and a good number of these also survive, scattered around the city. Most were far more modest in scale than the *scuole grandi*, but were often designed on a similar basis, with two superimposed halls and a small side wing containing the 'board room'.

HOW THE CITY IS BUILT

The site of Venice contains almost no usable building materials, other than the reeds of the marshes, which are used to thatch fishermen's *casoni* (shacks). Venice thus had to import almost all its materials from elsewhere. The three principal materials, all required in huge quantities, were bricks, for the basic structure of almost all Venetian buildings; stone and marble with which to clad and beautify these buildings; and timber for foundations and for staircases, upper floors and roofs. Bricks were produced for centuries on the nearby Terraferma, chiefly around Mestre, but were also sourced from further afield when necessary: from Treviso, Padua or Ferrara. Most Terraferma brickfields lay well within the mainland empire and supplies were thus secure.

The principal source of building stone was the peninsula of Istria, directly across the gulf, and also a Venetian possession for centuries. This hard, dense white limestone was quarried on the coast and brought by boat into the city's masons' yards. Rare marbles for sculpture and decoration came from many sources, some as far as Greece and the Middle East, as well as Tuscany and Brescia. The Roman site of Altino and other towns were also used as 'quarries', to recycle valuable features such as capitals and columns. Timber came mainly from the upland forests of Cadore and the Marca Trevigiana, much of which was also Venetian territory, as well as the forests of Istria.

Contrary to many superficial perceptions, the city is not built on or in the water, but on low, firm islands, below which, a few metres under the surface, there is a stratum of dense clay, known as the *caranto*. All the principal buildings are supported on timber piles, which bear on this clay. Several guiding principles, however, have governed the development of construction techniques in the city: one is the minimisation of loads as much as possible; another is the avoidance of very high concentrated loads; still another is to distribute those loads to facilitate movement and differential settlement. Some smaller, lighter buildings were not supported on piles, but instead rest directly on a strip foundation of large timber planks, buried in the clay, and known as a *zattaron*, or raft. Most, though, are supported by a forest of subterranean stakes, usually of oak or larch, on top of which is laid the same *zattaron*. On the *zattaron*, in turn, there are built three or four diminishing courses of large squared blocks of Istrian stone, forming the principal foundation itself, as well as providing a damp-proofing layer to prevent water rising in the wall. Directly on top of them are constructed, all in brick, the principal load-bearing walls of the building. We can illustrate the structural characteristics of many Venetian buildings by looking at the evolution of the *palazzo-fontego*, the dominant typology in the city. The early examples had a broad transverse hall immediately behind their façades, beyond which was a longitudinal, axial central hall, known as the *androne* on the ground floor and the *portego* on the first. This central hall was flanked on both sides by smaller, square rooms, either for storing goods or offices (on the ground floor) or bedrooms and other domestic accommodation (on the first floor). Slowly, this plan was rationalised, such that the broad waterfront loggia became narrower, and eventually the long hall behind it was extended forward to meet the main façade. At the ground floor it still contained the essential watergate, but on the first floor the *portego* was terminated with a large group of windows, to let as much light as possible into the long space behind. The rationalisation of the plan was reflected in the basic structure, since the long axial hall was now flanked by two side wings, all three being of the same or nearly equal width. The whole house thus consisted of three elements, divided by four parallel brick walls, which carried almost all the structural load of the house, since all the floor beams spanned onto them. And since the spans were the same, the floor-beam sizes, too, could be standardised. The front façade now carried almost no load other than its own weight, and thus it was possible to incorporate large areas of multi-light windows filled with glass (from nearby Murano), and with fine decorative tracery, all emphasising the wealth and prestige of the owner. The two side wings were more solidly constructed, giving a degree of 'bookend' stability to the façade, and since the wings contained smaller, square rooms, they were generally lit by tall single windows, rather than a multi-light one. So here we see the mature Venetian *palazzo*, with its symmetrical, tripartite façade, a direct reflection of the plan behind.

This basic structure incorporated elements that reflected the need to design flexibility in the construction. All the brick structural walls are bedded in soft lime mortar, which allows for movement and settlement, while the floors are of timber, itself inherently flexible, with closely spaced beams to spread the loads. Floors were finished with timber boarding, and then traditional Venetian *terrazzo*, consisting of a highly compressed mixture of decorative marble chippings set in lime mortar, sealed with linseed oil, and all capable of absorbing structural movement. Roofs are timber trusses, on which are laid smaller joists, and finished with a layer of semicircular interlocking 'Roman' tiles.

Several other characteristic features of Venetian secular architecture represent specific responses to local conditions. Pressures on land, for example, led to the widespread use of timber jetties (*barbacani*), supporting projecting upper floors that provided more space, while maintaining the public right of way below. *Sotoporteghi*, or covered passages, achieved a similar result, while the combination of a colonnade supported on piers and timber beams made use of another type of *barbacane*, a timber bracket that reduced the span and deflection of the supported beams. Similar considerations of maximising space gave rise to the *altana* (roof terrace), supported on brick piers directly above the roof and reached by steps; *altane* were both practical (for drying washing) and used for pleasure (taking the air on hot summer nights), as they still are today. And the covered *liagò*, a gallery across the top floor of a palace, had a similar function, but was also protected from the weather.

The principal private rooms were heated with open fires, and the chimneys taken high above the roof, where they terminated in a characteristic inverted cone-shaped chimney pot, its form ingeniously designed to allow smoke to escape, but its 'lid' forming a trap to prevent flying cinders starting fires elsewhere.

Although the evolution of Venetian architecture was skilfully adapted to take account of subsoil conditions, two particular structural issues were almost impossible to resolve safely. One form of construction used only rarely is structural vaulting, which relies for its integrity on solid, immovable piers, and was rightly considered risky. There are a few, the most famous being the brick vaults of San Marco, encrusted with mosaic decoration. Sansovino's salutary experience at the Library of San Marco, however, where a section of vault collapsed soon after work had begun, epitomised the dangers involved; most church roofs are timber trusses, with plastered ceilings beneath them.

The other almost insurmountable difficulty arose with church *campanili*, tall, narrow towers that inevitably exert high compressive stresses on their foundations. The city's history is littered with failures here, from the occasional complete collapse (spectacularly, at San Marco in 1902), to the alarming inclination of some *campanili* that survive (Santo Stefano, the Greci).

VENICE TODAY: PROBLEMS AND POSSIBILITIES

A UNESCO World Heritage Site, and one of the most intensively visited cities in the world, Venice remains home to only 60,000 permanent Venetian residents, who are today overwhelmed by 20 million tourists a year. The city's physical problems, familiar to many, remain a daunting litany: regular and frequent flooding; air pollution; damage from the wake of vessels, particularly the immense modern cruise ships; the steady loss of its resident population, and with it, the loss of daily amenities; the relentless spread of luxury hotels and 'bed and breakfasts'; the general cost of living, still considerably higher than any other city in Italy; the age and needs of its housing stock, the oldest of any major Italian city, as indeed is the age profile of its residents.

Set against these woes, we must record the extraordinary progress in restoring the city's fabric since the disastrous floods of 1966: the hundreds of millions spent on churches, palaces and other monuments, and hundreds of works of art; the equally vast sums spent recently in restoring and augmenting the traditional sea defences; the raising of quays to prevent flooding; the restoration or reconstruction of most of the city's bridges; and the re-excavation of dozens of miles of canals, as well as the reinforcement of their banks. Then there is MOSE, the highly contentious 'permanent' system of flood barriers, which (at the time of writing in 2009) is under construction, again at huge expense (more than €4,000 million, at present estimates), at the three sea gates between the *lidi*. If it is completed, and if it works reliably, MOSE will prevent the most serious floods – but not the lesser ones – for perhaps fifty years, after which (like the Thames barrier) it will need replacement to cope with ever-rising sea levels. Meanwhile, its medium-term effects on the tides and the ecological balance of the lagoon are unknown, as are the costs of its maintenance. It is certain that smaller-scale measures such as the raising of quays and street levels will have to be completed to deal with the much more frequent, and enormously disruptive 'minor' floods.

Other than floods, and various forms of pollution (all of which are, in theory, treatable), by far the largest challenge is that of people: on one hand, the essential support and survival of the Venetian citizens themselves, and on the other, the management of the quite insupportable numbers of tourists – many of them day-trippers – whose demands now rule the city at the expense of the needs and desires of its residents. It seems inevitable that at some point active measures will have to be taken to control and manage their numbers. Tourists, though, are inherently transitory, and can and must be managed. Even more vital is the need to ensure the survival of Venice as a living city. For this to succeed, a fundamental reappraisal of the city's role and functions must be undertaken, which draws not only on its unique physical fabric, but also on the strength and richness of its cultural and intellectual life. Continuous prostitution to mass tourism is at its root the wrong response to the wrong question: the city needs to be reinvented as global exemplar, a hub of culture, ideas, creativity, sustainability and thought, as indeed it was in its period of greatest wealth and power. The various activities of the Biennale are potentially a beacon for such a new Renaissance, as are many other bodies such as the Istituto Veneto, the Fenice, the Fondazione Cini and the Guggenheim, the Accademia, the Archivio di Stato and the Biblioteca Marciana, the two universities, the Church, the *comune* itself; and, lastly, and most important of all, Venice's own citizens. Grand coalitions of such bodies can achieve far more than they can individually, and can regenerate a new sense of purpose into the city. A number of international cultural and research bodies have bases here; there could be more, such that Venice could ultimately attain a special status as a truly international hub of learning, knowledge and research. Even academics need to eat and somewhere to live; a 'service industry' centred on a major expansion of such activities would be infinitely less demeaning – and potentially more rewarding in all senses – than selling to tens of thousands of day-trippers cheap tourist knick-knacks made abroad.

Many claim that Venice is past the point of 'viability' already, and that it is simply a more authentic, scruffier version of the Venice in Las Vegas. I disagree profoundly: as an intermittent long-term resident over more than thirty years, I believe that Venice is still in many ways a model urban environment, one of the most civilised, 'liveable' cities in the world – free from the obscenity of motor traffic and the levels of noise, visual and air pollution that render many of our other cities almost uninhabitable. It is a city that, for its size, has an extraordinarily rich cultural life. It is a city relatively free from crime, in which one can walk safely day or night, and which one can cross from one side to the other, in conversation, in an hour or so. Observing daily life in the *campi*, it is clear that Venice has a great deal to teach us about creating a safe, attractive, high-density and truly civilised urban environment. If mass tourism were managed and controlled more effectively, it could again become a real exemplar of urban civilisation. Its physical fabric represents one of our greatest historic cultures; like its inhabitants, it needs to be properly understood, fully appreciated and given new meaning.

THE BUILDINGS
OF VENICE

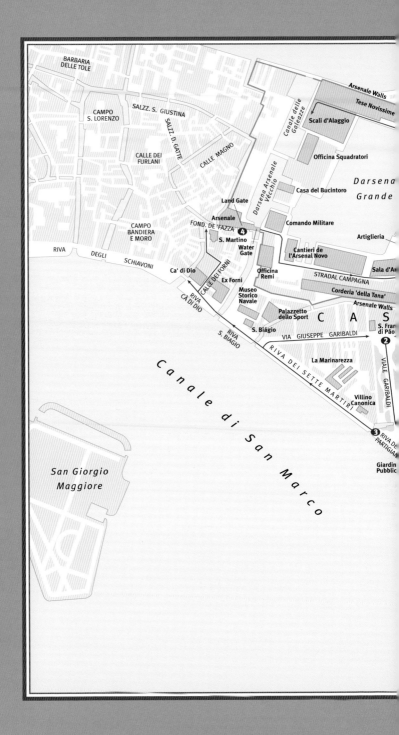

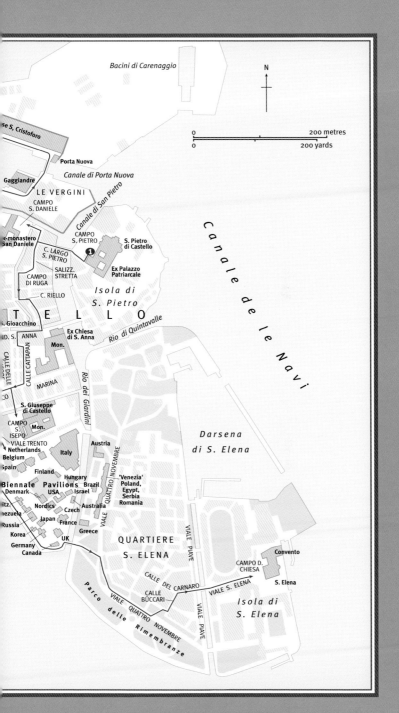

Bacini di Carenaggio

N

| 0 | | 200 metres |
| 0 | | 200 yards |

se S. Cristoforo

Porta Nuova

Gaggiandre

Canale di Porta Nuova

LE VERGINI

CAMPO
S. DANIELE

Canale di San Pietro

x-monastero
San Daniele

CAMPO
S. PIETRO

S. Pietro
di Castello

C. LARGO
S. PIETRO

SALIZZ.
STRETTA

Ex Palazzo
Patriarcale

CAMPO
DI RUGA

C. RIELLO

*Isola di
S. Pietro*

T E L L O

Canale de le Navi

. Gioacchino

Ex Chiesa
di S. Anna

Rio di Quintavalle

ID. S. ANNA

Mon.

CALLE CATTAPAN

MARINA

Rio dei Giardini

CALLE DELLE

S. Giuseppe
di Castello

Mon.

CAMPO
S.
ISEPO

VIALE TRENTO

*Darsena
di S. Elena*

Netherlands

Belgium

Spain

Italy

Austria

Finland

Hungary

VIALE QUATTRO NOVEMBRE

'Venezia'
Poland,
Egypt,
Serbia
Romania

Biennale Pavilions

Denmark

USA

Brazil

Israel

itz.

Nordics

Czech

Australia

ezuela

Japan

France

Russia

Korea

UK

Greece

QUARTIERE
S. ELENA

VIALE PIAVE

Convento

CAMPO D.
CHIESA

S. Elena

Germany

Canada

Parco delle Rimembranze

VIALE QUATTRO NOVEMBRE

CALLE DEL CARNARO

CALLE
BÚCCARI

VIALE S. ELENA

VIALE PIAVE

*Isola di
S. Elena*

Castello East

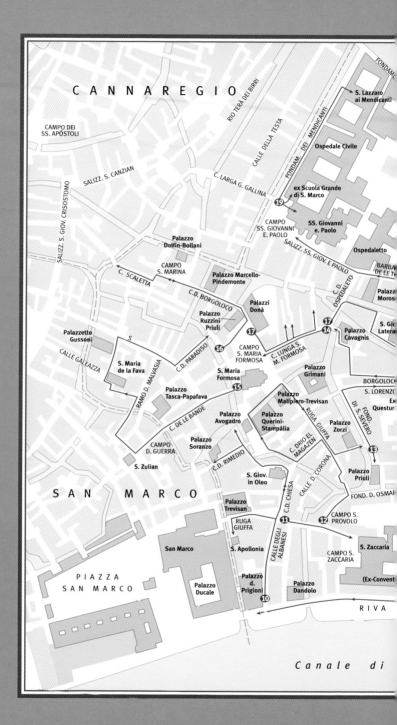

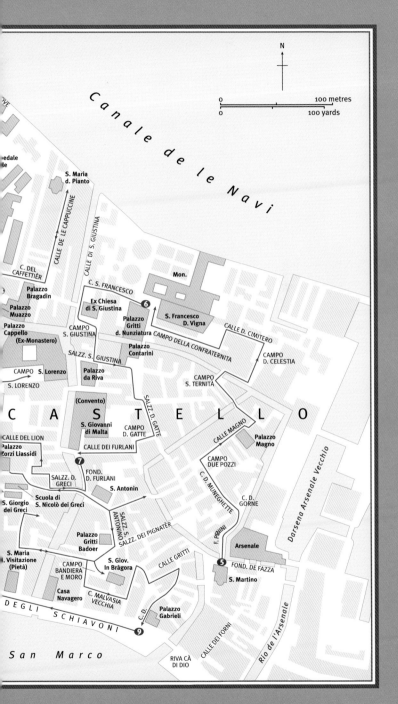

N

0 — 100 metres
0 — 100 yards

Canale de le Navi

S. Maria d. Pianto

CALLE DE LE CAPPUCCINE

CALLE DI S. GIUSTINA

C. DEL CAFFETTIÈR

Palazzo Bragadin

Palazzo Muazzo

Palazzo Cappello (Ex-Monastero)

CAMPO S. Lorenzo

S. LORENZO

CALLE DEL LION

Palazzo Zorzi Liassidi

C. S. FRANCESCO

Mon.

Ex Chiesa di S. Giustina

6

Palazzo Gritti d. Nunziatura

S. Francesco D. Vigna

CALLE D. CIMITERO

CAMPO S. GIUSTINA

CAMPO DELLA CONFRATERNITA

Palazzo Contarini

CAMPO D. CELESTIA

SALZZ. S. GIUSTINA

Palazzo da Riva

CAMPO S. TERNITÀ

SALZZ. D. GATTE

(Convento)

S. Giovanni di Malta

CAMPO D. GATTE

CALLE DEI FURLANI

CALLE MAGNO

Palazzo Magno

C A S T E L L O

CAMPO DUE POZZI

C. D. MUNEGHETTE

C. D. GORNE

7

SALZZ. D. GRECI

FOND. D. FURLANI

S. Antonin

Scuola di S. Nicolò dei Greci

S. Giorgio dei Greci

SALZZ. S. ANTONINO

SALZZ. DEI PIGNATÈR

Palazzo Gritti Badoer

F. PRUINI

Arsenale

5

FOND. DE FAZZA

S. Martino

Darsena Arsenale Vecchio

S. Maria d. Visitazione (Pietà)

CAMPO BANDIERA E MORO

S. Giov. In Bràgora

Casa Navagero

C. MALVASIA VECCHIA

CALLE GRITTI

D E G L I   S C H I A V O N I

C. D.

Palazzo Gabrieli

9

CALLE DEI FORNI

Rio de l'Arsenale

S a n   M a r c o

RIVA CÀ DI DIO

Castello West

Sestiere of Castello

The extensive *sestiere* of Castello covers all the eastern part of the city; its character varies widely, and divides into several distinct zones, extending from west to east. The westernmost zone is densely developed, with a closely packed urban 'grain' characteristic of the *centro storico*. This character extends as far as the walls of the former naval base of the Arsenale, which forms a barrier between the central districts and those beyond. The Arsenale once formed a 'city within the city', and contains numerous important historic naval structures, many built on a large, proto-industrial scale.

To the E and SE of the Arsenale is another densely developed district, centred on the broad Via Garibaldi. Beyond again is a formerly remote peripheral zone, once occupied by monastic houses, but transformed by Napoleon, and today containing the public gardens and the Biennale Gardens. The NE extremity is defined by the islet of San Pietro in Castello, former site of the bishopric and one of the earliest parts of the city to be settled. Finally, at the extreme SE is Sant'Elena, once an isolated monastic house, today an island suburb containing a substantial development of early twentieth-century housing.

We begin at San Pietro, the earliest settlement of the whole district.

Facing page: The Gaggiandre: 16th century wet docks in the Arsenale

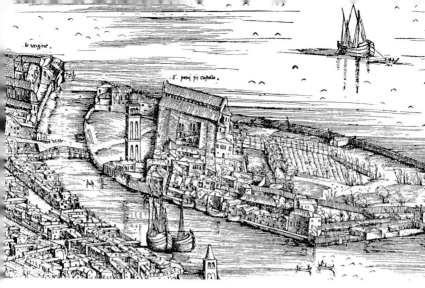

The islet of San Pietro, from de' Barbari's engraving of 1500

1 SAN PIETRO IN CASTELLO, SANT'ANA AND SAN ISEPO

Once also referred to as Olivolo, either from the olive trees that grew here or from the shape of the island, which resembles that of an olive. It is divided from the city by the broad Canale di San Pietro, spanned by two bridges, and was probably first settled in the fifth and sixth centuries AD. The island was also fortified at an early date: hence the title Castello, eventually adopted for the whole *sestiere*. **Campo San Pietro**, in front of the church, is one of few surviving squares in the city that is still grassed.

Ex-cattedrale de San Pietro: said to have been founded in 650; originally dedicated to SS Sergius and Bacchus. One of twelve churches established by St Magnus, but in 774 it was rebuilt and the dedication changed to St Peter the Apostle; a see was established, and the church was completed in 841. The patriarch at Grado had direct jurisdiction over San Pietro, but in 1451 both the patriarchate and the Castello bishopric were suppressed and a new patriarchate of Venice was inaugurated; the first patriarch was Lorenzo Giustinian, later canonised.

Several restorations took place over the centuries, one after 1120, another in 1512–26. In 1556 Patriarch Vincenzo Diedo began reconstruction, but only the façade was begun before his death (1559); it was completed by Francesco Smeraldi (1594–6). Reconstruction of the church itself began in 1619, when Smeraldi was succeeded by Gian Girolamo Grapiglia. Both were close

San Pietro in Castello: west façade, by Francesco
Smeraldi, 1594–6

followers of Palladio; Smeraldi's stone façade is based on Palladio's
original proposal.

It derives from his Redentore. The central bay is crowned by a
pediment, with flanking pairs of giant Corinthian columns on tall
plinths; the portal is also pedimented, while the two side wings are
finished with half-pediments, above which rises a plain parapet. The
overall effect is impressive, although the detailing is a little weak.

The plan is a Latin cross, with a three-bay nave flanked by lower
aisles, each with three side altars. At the crossing is a prominent
cupola, set over a circular drum, supported by plain pendentives. The
large chancel is flanked by side chapels. The interior is cool and
monumental, with light from high-level 'thermal' windows down the
aisles. The order throughout is Corinthian, with a giant order
defining the nave and a smaller one for the side aisles. In the centre
of the chancel is the large free-standing high altar (1649), designed
by Longhena; St Lorenzo Giustinian is buried beneath it.

Several notable altars and paintings: frescoes in the apse vault are
by Girolamo Pellegrini, late seventeenth century. Off the left aisle is
the Vendramin Chapel, also by Longhena, decorated with heavy

The islet of San Pietro in Castello, with the campanile by Mauro Codussi, 1490

sculptures; the altarpiece is by Luca Giordano. Adjacent, on the aisle wall, is a late Veronese, *St John, St Peter and St Paul*. Next to the Vendramin Chapel is the smaller, Gothic, Lando Chapel, 1425, a survivor from the earlier church.

Adjacent to the s side of the church is the substantial **Palazzo Patriarcale** (cs 70), originally Gothic, but modernised in the late sixteenth century, more recently used as a barracks and housing. A large rectangular central cloister, with a simple brick arched colonnade. On the wall adjacent to the campanile is a fine late Gothic tympanum of the Virgin and Child. The **campanile** is the only one in the city faced entirely with Istrian stone; it has a pronounced inclination to the e. The tower was begun in 1463 by Doge Cristoforo Moro, but was badly damaged by lightning, and in 1482 the patriarch, Maffeo Girardi, commissioned Mauro Codussi to restore it. Work was complete by 1490; the tower has a powerful 'Roman' simplicity. In 1670 the cupola was removed and the present octagonal attic added.

Cross the square, take Ponte San Pietro, continue down the Calle Larga and turn right into Salizada Streta. Turning left again, we reach **Campo San Daniele**, site of a church, founded in 820 by the Bragadin and subsequently a Cistercian monastery. It was rebuilt several times before its suppression by Napoleon in 1805. The monastic buildings became a barracks; most survive, and were absorbed by the adjacent naval base, although the church was demolished in 1839.

Immediately N of the square, across the canal, is the site of the former nunnery of **Le Vergini**, surrounded by water on three sides. It was founded by Augustinians in 1224. Like the rest, it was suppressed by Napoleon (1806), and the land given to the navy. The conventual buildings were demolished in 1844; all that remains is the splendid Gothic upper part of the entrance portal, embedded into the Arsenale's external wall.

Return to Salizada Streta and walk S. It is lined with typical small vernacular houses, notably CS 105–8. We enter **Campo Ruga**, an attractive small square. A couple of houses of note: CS 327–8, seventeenth century, with a symmetrical façade, rather heavily detailed, and an elaborate *abbaino*. CS 329–30 is of similar date, but asymmetrical, lacking the left wing.

Turn W out of the square (Calle del Figareto), as far as the quay to **Rielo**. The narrow canal is lined by small picturesque cottages, of considerable value, since few survive in the city today. Back in the square, take Calle Ruga out of the S side, and continue down Crosera. Just before the bridge (left) is a long row of three-storey houses (CS 226–53), with façades to Rio de Sant'Ana. Eighteenth century, a good example of a repetitive terrace development, originally with fine traditional chimneys. Cross the bridge for a

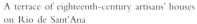

A terrace of eighteenth-century artisans' houses on Rio de Sant'Ana

better view, and then walk w along the quay as far as Ponte San Gioacchino, which we cross, back to the N bank. **San Gioacchino** (CS 455): founded in 1418 as a Franciscan house. It was very modest, and barely survived losses from the plague in 1630; it prospered thereafter, until 1807, when it was closed by Napoleon. In the adjacent *calle* (CS 453) was an *ospizio* dedicated to SS Peter and Paul, founded in the twelfth century. It, too, survived until the suppression. The doorway at CS 450 preserves a good Renaissance relief panel, the *Virgin and Child with SS Peter and Paul.*

Return to Ponte Sant'Ana. Immediately s is the former **Monastero de Sant'Ana** (CS 499). Founded in 1242 by an Augustinian friar, in 1404 it passed to the Benedictines, who remained until the Napoleonic closure in 1807. The church was rebuilt by Francesco Contin (1634–59). Its basic structure has survived, with a spacious, aisle-less nave and a flat ceiling; the last was richly decorated. Down the nave flanks are paired Corinthian pilasters. The chancel was sponsored (and decorated) by craftsmen from the Arsenale. The monastic buildings were restored in 1765, but after its closure they were used for various profane functions; they have recently been converted for housing.

Walking w along the quay, take Calle Correr to its far end; turn right along Seco Marina (the name indicates a reclaimed canal), and left into Corte Soldà, we reach the bridge and Campo San Isepo.

Chiesa e monastero de San Isepo (Giuseppe) (CS 784): established by Senate decree in 1512, and occupied by Augustinians from Verona. The church was completed rapidly, and by 1525 the conventual buildings were also complete; the architect is not known. In 1801 the complex was occupied by Salesian nuns; since 1923 it has been a parish church. The church is a tall, box-like structure, its restrained *campo* façade enlivened by the large stone portico, funded by the Grimani. Above the doorway is an *Adoration of the Magi* by Giulio del Moro. The interior has an aisle-less nave, with a flat, frescoed ceiling, attributed to Pietro Ricchi and Antonio Torri. At the west end is the *barco* (choir gallery), linked to the adjacent conventual buildings. The chancel was also funded by the Grimani, consecrated in 1643. The adjacent family altar has an *Adoration of the Shepherds*, attributed to Alessandro Veronese. The first right nave altar has a *pala* by Tintoretto, *St Michael and the Senator Michele Bon.*

Most of the extensive monastic buildings survive to the SE, built around three cloisters. All have simple arched colonnades, with a single storey of accommodation above.

Return to Corte Soldà; at CS 915 is a substantial house, rare in this part of the city, built in 1560 (plaque) by Alvise Soldà. From Seco Marina, take the long, narrow Calle de le Ancore back to Rio de Sant'Ana. At CS 1036–8: a small row of houses with the date 1544. On the corner of Campielo de le Ancore (CS 1132): a small fifteenth-century Gothic house.

2 THE NAPOLEONIC TRANSFORMATIONS AND THE BIENNALE GARDENS; SANT'ELENA

Much of eastern Castello was radically transformed during the Napoleonic occupation. A considerable area of lagoon was reclaimed to form the Riva dei Sette Martiri, while the decision to set out the public gardens resulted in the demolition of three monastic houses: San Domenico, Sant'Antonio and San Niccolò di Bari. San Domenico stood at the north end of Viale Garibaldi, while Sant'Antonio and San Niccolò both stood in what are now the public gardens. The sole survivor is the Lando Arch, designed by Sanmicheli, formerly part of the family chapel at Sant'Antonio, at the NW end of the gardens.

Viale Garibaldi links the busy Via Garibaldi with the main waterfront; the north gate is by Gianantonio Selva (1810); the Garibaldi monument is by Augusto Benvenuti (1885). At the S end of the avenue of trees, cross the bridge to the Largo Marinai, and walk SE along the Riva dei Partigiani. Near the *vaporetto* stop is the **Monumento alla Partigiana**, dedicated to partisan women of the Second World War; the sculpted figure is by Augusto Murer, the setting by Carlo Scarpa (1968).

The Biennale and its Pavilions

The Biennale was founded by the city council in 1893, under the mayor Riccardo Selvatico; it was formally inaugurated two years later. The emphasis on its international nature gave rise to the development of national pavilions, several by notable architects. Early exhibitions were enormously successful, and the central pavilion was first designed by Mario de' Maria as a classical 'temple of the arts'; it has since been remodelled several times. The first foreign pavilion (Belgium, 1909) was followed by several others; by 1914 there were seven, a number that has steadily increased to the present twenty-seven.

Courtyard by Carlo Scarpa (1968) in the main Italian pavilion, Biennale Gardens

The **Italian pavilion** was the centrepiece for more than a century, and is by far the largest pavilion. It was first modernised in 1914 by Guido Cirilli (in the 'Liberty' style), then in 1932 by Duilio Torres (in a neo-fascist 'white modern' style), and in 1968 by Carlo Scarpa, with a temporary outer screen. Scarpa also added a small internal 'secret garden', with pools and fountains. Today the pavilion broadly retains its 1932 appearance, but there are plans to rebuild it entirely. Inside, the large octagonal entrance hall is a faceted cupola, decorated in 1909 by Galileo Chini.

The **Belgian pavilion** was funded by the Venice municipality, and designed by Leon Sneyers; it was built in 1909 but modernised and enlarged in 1929–30. Further modernisation took place in 1948 under Virgilio Vallot, who reworked the façade. The present appearance is severe and symmetrical. The **British pavilion** is also one of the first group, an adaptation of an existing café. It was modernised in 1909 by Edwin Rickards, and decorated by Frank Brangwyn. The site is prominent, terminating an axis and on a slight eminence, the 'hill of San Antonio'. The pavilion is approached by a long flight of steps, with a deep Doric portico in the centre of the symmetrical façade. The **Hungarian pavilion** was designed by Géza Maróti, and inaugurated in 1909; a radical restoration in 1958 under Agost Benkhard opened the central part to the sky to create a new courtyard. The original entrance has survived, with its mosaic decoration, as have the glazed roof tiles, but much earlier decoration is lost.

The first **German pavilion** (originally Bavarian) was also built in 1909, as a Neo-classical temple. In 1912 the pavilion's scope was widened to artists from all over Germany, but it was closed from 1914 to 1918. In 1938 it was rebuilt by Ernst Haiger. The plan is common to several pavilions, and the design is a diluted fascist style, with square, fluted columns and a heavy entablature. Directly opposite, the third element of this group is the **French pavilion**, by Faust Finzi, inaugurated in 1912. The conventional plan has a large central hall, flanked by smaller rooms; at the front a colonnaded portico, oval on plan, with Ionic *broccatello* columns.

The **Dutch pavilion** was first built in 1912 for the Swedes, but two years later was ceded to the Netherlands. It survived until 1953, when it was replaced by the present work by Gerrit Rietveld. The simple, square plan is divided internally by walls projecting in from the perimeter, with a central circulation space; it is lit from above. The **Russian pavilion** was designed in 1909, and built in 1914 by Aleksej Scusev. After 1924 it displayed works from the whole Soviet Union. The traditional design has eclectic detailing, notably the odd cornice-crenellation. The plan has three volumes arranged in series, with a pyramidal roof over the central space.

The **Spanish pavilion,** by Javier de Luque, was built for the 1922 Biennale. A Baroque façade was added two years later, but in 1952 it was modernised by Joachin Vaquero. The simple façade is almost entirely of brick; the plan resembles that of the British pavilion. The **Czechoslovakian pavilion** was built in 1926 to a design by Otakar Novotný; the simple plan has a large rectangular hall, with two smaller rooms on each side of the entrance.

The **United States pavilion**: by Chester Holmes Aldrich and William Adams Delano, 1932. A neo-colonial villa, in the manner of Jefferson's Monticello. The plan, built around existing trees, takes the form of a C; in the centre is a Doric portico. The entrance hall has a shallow cupola. The **Danish pavilion** has two distinct elements. The first (1932), in a Neo-classical style, is by Carl Brummer. In 1958 it was extended by Peter Koch; a low, restrained Miesian work, carefully incorporating existing trees.

By 1932 most of the original site had been developed, and the gardens now expanded across the Rio dei Giardini onto the adjacent island of Sant'Elena. The layout was symmetrically planned, and is approached by a bridge from the first gardens. The centrepiece is the very long **Venetian pavilion**, by Brenno del Giudice, intended to house the decorative arts, with sections for Poland and Switzerland. The central part was dedicated to Venice, with two pavilions on each side, all united by a long screen-like façade, with pavilions at the far ends. These were added in 1938, and later occupied by Yugoslavia and Romania. In front was an exedra, a fountain and a formal garden, all now lost. The pavilion itself remains as built, in a 'white modern', rather fascist manner, but its axial approach has been destroyed by the insertion of the Brazilian pavilion (see below).

The **Austrian pavilion** is by Josef Hoffmann. It was proposed in 1913, but built only in 1934, following a hurriedly arranged competition. It stands adjacent to the N end of the Venetian pavilion, with a narrow, glazed central hall flanked by two large box-shaped rooms, from which it is divided by tall arches; to the rear are two smaller rooms with a sculpture court between. The main rooms are lit by continous clerestory windows. In 1984 it was restored by Hans Hollein. The **Greek pavilion**, by contrast, at the opposite end of the annexe gardens, is highly traditional, designed by M. Papandreou (1933) in a Balkan Byzantine style, with fine decorative brickwork. The symmetrical façade has a three-bay colonnaded portico; the interior has a T-shaped arrangement of display spaces.

The post-war pavilions were 'slotted in' between existing ones. The **Israeli pavilion** is by Zeev Rechter, 1952. The trapezoidal plan reflects the difficult site; it owes a good deal to the international 'white modern' era, while the interior is planned on three levels.

The Swiss and the Venezuelan pavilions were both built on a small site adjacent to the waterfront entrance. The **Swiss pavilion** is by Bruno Giacometti, 1951; the complex plan has three halls of different sizes, a colonnaded portico and an enclosed sculpture court. The **Venezuelan pavilion**, by Carlo Scarpa, has a more restricted site, and was completed for the 1956 Biennale. There are two main halls, linked by a lobby; the spaces are flexible, with moveable walls. The **Japanese pavilion** was first proposed in 1931, but built only in 1955. The architect was Takamasa Yoshizaka; the basic form is a simple box, raised on pilotis; the central space is lit from above, while the perimeter has a series of smaller display spaces.

The **Finnish pavilion** is one of the smallest, and was intended to be temporary. It was designed by Alvar Aalto, with a wedge-shaped plan, prefabricated in Finland and erected in June 1956. The interior has an open timber truss roof. In 1962 the new 'Nordic' pavilion was complete and Finland moved into it; recently, their former pavilion

The Biennale Gardens: 'Nordic' pavilion by Sverre Fehn, 1961–2

has been used by Iceland. The small **Canadian pavilion** (by BBPR, 1956–7) is located s of the British pavilion; the irregular plan is based on the constraints of existing trees, one rising through the centre. The exterior is faced with brickwork, and the roof is clad with zinc. The **Uruguayan pavilion** is one of the smallest, originally a service structure. It was ceded to Uruguay in 1960. A simple rectangular hall, located behind the USA pavilion.

The **'Nordic' pavilion** was the result of a competition in 1958 for a joint pavilion for Norway, Finland and Sweden. The Norwegian Sverre Fehn won, with a design of great simplicity and refinement, based on a large rectangular hall, two sides fully glazed, with sliding, removable windows. It was planned around several trees, some rising within the pavilion. The roof consists of numerous tall, narrow beams through which diffused light is filtered. The **Brazilian pavilion** was first proposed in 1959, but a new, controversial site was chosen in 1964, directly opposite the bridge to the annexe gardens, obscuring the axial view of the Venetian pavilion. It was designed by the Venetian Amerigo Marchesin, with two halls divided by an entrance hall. The simple, box-like exterior has clerestory lighting. The **Australian pavilion** was first proposed in 1954, but inaugurated only in 1987. By Philip Cox, on a difficult, restricted site, on an embankment adjacent to the canal. The space consists of two rectangular boxes, at different levels, with a light steel frame and a barrel-vaulted roof of corrugated iron.

The Biennale Gardens: Electa Bookshop by James
Stirling, 1991

The **bookshop**: the first bookshop, by Scarpa (1950), was destroyed
by fire, and in 1989 the publishing house Electa commissioned a
new one by James Stirling and Michael Wilford. It was inaugurated
in 1991. Its form is based on that of an upturned boat, with a
prominent tower (or 'funnel') at one end. The exterior is lit by a
long continuous band of glazing, protected by the deep overhang of
the pitched copper roof. The **Korean pavilion**, by Seok Chul Kim, is
the most recent pavilion, completed in 1996. The plan is complex,
and articulated with steel framing, allowing extensive transparency of
the cladding. The structure was fabricated off-site.

Sant'Elena

Linked to the city by two bridges, one behind the Italian pavilion,
the other near the SE corner of the Biennale gardens. It consists of
two islets, divided by the straight Rio de Sant'Elena. On the W
island is a large zone of twentieth-century housing, while on the E
one is the eponymous church and the city's football stadium.

At the s end of the residential district is a public park. The housing, proposed by Duilio Torres in 1911, was begun in 1923, to relieve pressure on the city centre. The principal architect was Paolo Bertanza, and the quarter was laid out on a rectilinear plan, with a small garden near the centre. The housing consists of small blocks of apartments and villas; the styles are a mixture of Venetian Gothic and Byzantine-Moorish, decried at the time as 'pastiche', although they are solidly built, with inventive, eclectic detailing. Near the eastern edge, Calle del Carnaro leads to the bridge to Sant'Elena.

Sant'Elena: the first record dates from 1060, when a church served by Augustinian canons stood on the site. In the thirteenth century the remains of the titular saint were brought here, and in 1407 a Benedictine house was established; the monastic buildings were reconstructed and in the 1430s the church was rebuilt; thereafter it became a place of pilgrimage. In 1807 it was deconsecrated and the campanile demolished. By the 1920s the church was ruinous, but was radically restored in 1927–30, and reopened. Most of the monastic buildings were destroyed after the Napoleonic closure; one cloistered wing remains.

The church has a tall, aisle-less nave, with a faceted apse. The façade is typically fifteenth-century Venetian Gothic, although much restored. The chief feature is the Renaissance portal, transferred from Sant'Aponal in 1929; set into the lunette of the curved pediment is a fine sculpture of Vettor Cappello, the sea-captain, kneeling in front of the titular saint. It is often attributed to Antonio Rizzo, although Schulz attributes it to Niccolò Fiorentino.

The large patronal chapel is to the right of the nave, and has a similar appearance. It was funded by the Borromeo, with several family tombs. Adjacent is the smaller Giustinian family chapel, 1460. The *barco* that stood above the nave was destroyed after 1807; the roof is a modern open timber truss of traditional design.

3   FROM VIA GARIBALDI TO THE ARSENALE

Return to the Riva dei Partigiani, and continue w along the Riva dei Sette Martiri. On the right: a group of buildings known as the **Marinarezza** (cs 1411–68). This originally consisted of three parallel terraces of housing, built by the Republic in the late fifteenth century to accommodate retired mariners who had given distinguished service to the state. The three blocks are orthogonal to

Via Garibaldi: general view from the east, with Rio de Sant'Ana in the foreground

the quay and have three storeys, with a total of twenty-one houses. They were modernised in 1645–61, when a fourth block was added across the front. This block has two large archways giving access to the terraces behind; all the detailing is simple and repetitive, reminiscent of the speculative developments of the same era.

Continuing NW along the quay, we reach Via Garibaldi on the right. This broad street, formerly the Rio de Castelo (reclaimed 1807), forms the social and commercial centre of the district; several

The Marinarezza (1645–61) from San Giorgio Maggiore

buildings of interest. At CS 1310 (S side) is an early fifteenth-century Gothic archway, formerly the entrance to the lost monastery of San Domenico. At CS 1581 is Casa Marcorà, mid-sixteenth century, an attractive four-storey Renaissance *palazzetto*; late Gothic *stemma* above the portal. At CS 1643 a plaque marks the house of the explorers Giovanni and Sebastiano Caboto (John and Sebastian Cabot).

Halfway along the N side is **San Francesco da Paola,** whose origins lie in a hospital founded by Bartolomeo Querini (1296). In 1503 it was ceded to the Minims of San Francesco, who established a convent here. In 1588 the present church was begun, consecrated in 1619. The friary was closed in 1806 and turned into a barracks; it was demolished in 1885, and a school built on the site. The church's late Renaissance façade is simple but imposing. Inside: a single nave, terminating with a deep square chancel, flanked by small chapels. It was modernised in the mid-eighteenth century. The surviving *barco* extends down the sides of the nave, with three small chapels below it on each side. The flat ceiling is divided into panels, with paintings by Giovanni Contarini (late sixteenth century). The right chancel altar has an *Annunciation* by Palma il Giovane; on the left side, a painting of St Francis by Giandomenico Tiepolo.

To the W are two charitable almshouse developments, Calle dei Preti (CS 2066–74) and Corte Nova (CS 2040–52); both originally fifteenth century, but the latter has been much altered.

Return to the W end of Via Garibaldi, and cross Ponte de le Cadene onto Riva San Biagio.

San Biagio was a parish church, founded in 1052; it was also used by the Greeks, before their own church was completed in 1561. It was modernised in the Gothic era, and survived until 1749, when it was rebuilt, perhaps by Filippo Rossi, *proto* of the Arsenale. It was closed in 1810, but reopened in 1817 as a chapel for the naval base. The unusual façade is all in brickwork, with a large central portal and two superimposed orders. Just behind the church is the uncompromisingly modern concrete **Palazzetto dello Sport** (Enrico Capuzzo and Giandomenico Cocco, 1979), built on a highly restricted triangular site. Adjacent is the **Museo Storico Navale** (CS 2148), housed in the former granaries of the Republic, built in 1322. The envelope survives, although the interior was rebuilt in the 1950s to house the extensive collections of the naval history museum. Five storeys, with simple, functional fenestration.

Continuing W over Ponte de l'Arsenale, on the right corner are the former **Forni Militari**, the bakeries of the Venetian navy; two

San Martino: north façade, by Jacopo Sansovino, after
1552, partly remodelled in 1897

adjacent structures, one for storing cereals, the other the bakeries
with their ovens, originally numbering thirty-two. The principal
interest is the rich late Gothic portal (1473). Continuing along the
Riva, just before the next bridge is the **Ca' di Dio**, originally a
hostel for pilgrims to the Holy Land. The earliest record dates from
1272, but later its function changed; by the fifteenth century it had
become a hostel for poor women. In 1544 the procurators of San
Marco decided on its partial reconstruction, to a design by
Sansovino. The three-storey side wing contains residential
accommodation, while the wing onto the quay contains the chapel
(right) and a long central hall or *androne*, both denoted by
Serliane.

Turn inland down Calle dei Forni; near the end, turn left along
Ramo de la Pegola, then along the *fondamenta*. At the end is **San
Martino**, one of the earliest parish foundations in Venice, established
in the seventh or eighth century. For centuries, it was also the
church for the Arsenale workers. It was restored several times prior
to 1540, when it was demolished. Sansovino's reconstruction began in

1553, although the parish was hampered by lack of funds; it was finally consecrated in 1653. The simple brick façade was radically restored in 1897 by Domenico Rupolo and Federico Berchet, and has minimal stone detailing. The plan is a Greek cross, with a large cubical central space surrounded by pairs of smaller, lower chapels at each of the four corners; the spatial arrangement derives from Codussi. A tall clerestory brings light from above. The internal articulation is simple, refined Doric, although obscured by elaborate eighteenth-century paintings to walls and ceiling. The ceiling painting is *St Martin in Glory* by Jacopo Guarana, surrounded by panels by Domenico Bruni. On the right side wall: sumptuous marble monument to Doge Francesco Erizzo (Matteo Carmero, 1633); on the left side wall: modified font by Tullio Lombardo (1484).

Attached to the NW corner is the little oratory of the **Scuola de San Martino**, established in 1335; prominent *barbacani*. Above the doorway is a fifteenth-century relief of St Martin giving his cloak to a beggar. A little further E is the main land gate to the Arsenale.

4   THE ARSENALE

A Historical Note

The Venetian Arsenale was for centuries one of the largest and most important naval bases in Europe. Popular history claims that it was established in 1104; it survived as an active base until very recent times. The Arsenale contains a remarkable collection of historic buildings, many awaiting restoration and new uses. Its story is one of evolution and expansion over the centuries, each stage representing either a response to technological developments or to military challenges from abroad. The mature Arsenale was an extraordinarily efficient 'machine' for building, fitting out, victualling and maintaining the most powerful fleet in the Mediterranean. It was organised in a proto-modern 'production line' manner, with each zone dedicated to a specialised activity, from laying keels to making oars and sails, and the installation of armaments.

The first nucleus is said to have been founded by Doge Ordelaffo Falier (1102–18) on a pair of small rectangular islets (*gemelle* = twins) bisected by a canal. Two rows, each of twelve large sheds, were built down the sides, while the canal gave direct access into the basin of San Marco. The Arsenale was surrounded by a high defensive wall.

The Arsenale, from de' Barbari's engraving of 1500

This small nucleus was first expanded in 1304 by the *proto* Andrea Pisano, while in the same period (*circa* 1320) the first ropeworks (Corderia) was also built. In 1325 a major expansion was begun to the east, the Arsenale Nuovo, more than tripling its original size. Thenceforth, all the Republic's galleys were built and maintained here. Between the ropeworks and this new basin was an area known as the Campagna, where specialist workshops were located, as well as munitions stores and depositories for oars and anchors. In the early fifteenth century the 'production line' system was first developed; the Arsenale Nuovo was able to construct and fit out fifty galleys at a time. From the 1460s, too, the Sala d'Armi was built, halls for making and storing armaments.

The third major expansion began in 1473, but took decades to complete; this was the Arsenale Novissimo, a second large rectangular basin directly N of the Arsenale Nuovo. It is recorded by de' Barbari in 1500, when its perimeter wall was complete, but the sheds were not yet built. These were begun in 1525–8 and completed *circa* 1550. The two basins were divided by a strip of land called the Isolotto. Once complete, the whole complex could now build and maintain a fleet of 100 galleys.

Further sixteenth-century expansion took place to the NW, near the Celestia monastery, where a powder store was built, followed by the Riparto, the Vasca and the Canale de le Galeazze (all 1539–64), designed for a new type of vessel, the *galeasse*. This expansion was the maximum extent of the Arsenale until after the fall of the

Republic in 1797. Among many other works during the sixteenth century, however, was the shed to house the ducal state barge, the Bucintoro, 1544–7, and the impressive wet docks, the Gaggiandre, 1568–73. In 1579–83, too, the extraordinary Corderia was rebuilt by Antonio da Ponte.

The Napoleonic conquest resulted in immediate decommissioning; every ship within the walls was sunk or otherwise destroyed. After 1806, though, the base was reactivated, and new building works undertaken, to build *vascelli* and frigates. The Celestia monastery was annexed, and the Porta Nuova was built. Following Unification in 1866, the two main basins were joined to form one large body of water, and in 1875–8 reclamations to the NE resulted in three new dry docks. The Arsenale was actively used in 1914–18, and had a limited role in 1939–45.

The Buildings

The watergate and the land gate

The buildings are described in groups, roughly corresponding to the Arsenale's chronological expansion. We begin at the main entrances at the Campo de l'Arsenale. The present impressive **watergates** were built in 1686–92, replacing earlier gates, successively rebuilt to provide access for larger ships. The towers contain bells that rang the working day for the *arsenalotti*, and were used to lower masts into place as the last stage of the fitting-out process. The adjacent **land gate** was built in 1458–60, under Doge Pasquale Malipiero, and is the first fully Renaissance structure in the city: a classical triumphal

arch, representing the power of the Venetian navy and the enlightened patronage of the Republic. The paired Greek marble columns are capped by recycled Byzantine capitals, above which are a rich trabeation and an attic containing an over-sized

The Arsenale: the land gate: detail of the upper part, with inscription of Doge Pasquale Malipiero and the winged Venetian lion. The crowning St Justina is by Girolamo Campagna, 1578

The Arsenale: the land gate, 1458–60, with later embellishments (1578 and 1682)

winged lion; the scallop in the pediment represents the maritime empire. The gate was elaborated after the victory over the Turks at Lepanto (1571), which took place on St Justina's day; hence the figure on top of the pediment (by Campagna, 1578) and the winged Victories in the spandrels. It was elaborated further in 1682 when the front terrace was added, with its array of mythological statuary. Finally, following the recapture of the Morea by Francesco Morosini in 1687, the large flanking lions were added in 1689, taken from

Athens as war booty. Within the vestibule inside the gate is the fine *Madona de l'Arsenale* by Jacopo Sansovino, 1533.

The Darsena Vecchia

The oldest part of the Arsenale, immediately inside the gates. The sheds on the W side of the basin are from 1456–8, and have Gothic arches; some are roofless, following a fire in 1920. On the east side is the **Comando Militare**, a large square block (*circa* 1880) housing the administration of the Arsenale. To the N, across the short linking canal, is the **Casa del Bucintoro**, 1544–7, built to house the ducal state barge. Its W façade is very simple, but the impressive E façade has rusticated stonework and Doric columns, in the manner of Sanmicheli. Above the central bay is a relief sculpture of Justice.

The zone south of the Darsena Grande (the central basin)

Several notable buildings, extending S as far as the massive Corderia. Flanking the east side of the Rio de l'Arsenale is the impressive **Officina Remi**, its W wall forming the enclosing wall of the naval base. Built in 1562 for the storage of oars, it has three large bays, with brick cross-walls and massive open timber trussed roofs. Today

The Arsenale: Casa del Bucintoro, 1544–7

it houses historic vessels, part of the Museo Storico Navale. Immediately E is the **Stradal Campagna**, a long 'street' that formed the nucleus of this area, dedicated to foundries and the production of arms. Towards its E end is the **Porta Artiglieria**, 1591, often attributed to Sanmicheli; another strongly modelled, rusticated work, with a central arch, its keystone representing Neptune, and flanked by Doric columns. The S edge of this zone is defined by the **Corderia**, one of the most extraordinary structures in the city, a massive shed 315 metres long, built by Antonio da Ponte from 1579 to replace a smaller, older ropeworks. It has forty-four bays, defined internally by stout circular brick columns; a tall, central 'nave' is flanked by aisles, above which is a clerestory. The aisles have tall single windows, one to each bay, and the whole is covered by an open timber trussed roof. The Corderia is used by the Biennale for exhibitions.

The **Cantieri de l'Arsenale Nuovo** are a long row of sheds along the S shore of the basin, built in 1456–8, but extensively modernised in 1821–4. At the E end they abut the **Sala d'Armi**, a large four-bay structure, again *circa* 1460, modernised in 1561–4 and again in 1821. The Sala contained bulk stores of weapons and was highly defended. It currently awaits restoration.

The Darsena Grande: east side

The **Artiglierie**: a long series of buildings in the SE corner, their eastern wall forming the enclosing wall of the Arsenale; built in 1561–4, and today also used for Biennale exhibitions. At their N end are the **Tese Sud del Isolotto,** the two surviving remains of the double row of sheds that formerly divided the great basin into two; most were demolished in 1876. Immediately N are the four surviving bays of the **Tese Nord**, of similar date. All have brick cross-walls supported on arches. To the N again is the isolated block of **Le Gaggiandre**, an impressive building housing two wet docks; built in 1568–73, damaged in the First World War, but restored. Each shed measures 51 metres long and 20 metres wide; the open timber roofs are supported on semicircular brick arches, carried by massive, plain, cylindrical, Istrian stone piers. Nearby, on the edge of the basin, is the imposing **hydraulic crane**, built by Armstrong Mitchell of Newcastle in 1883, the only survivor in the world of nine originally built to the same design. It had a capacity of 160 tonnes, and stands on a large base of Istrian stone, which housed the hydraulic pump. To the east of Le Gaggiandre is a large undeveloped area formerly

The Arsenale; remains of the wet docks, Le Gaggiandre, 1568–73

The Arsenale: the Armstrong Mitchell steam crane, 1883

occupied by Le Vergini nunnery, but annexed after 1806, when the dividing canal was reclaimed.

The Darsena Grande: north and west sides

At the NE corner is the monumental **Porta Nuova**, built in 1810 to define this new access into the naval base, shifting emphasis from the ancient SW gate. In Gothic Revival style, with an unusual tapering form; brick with Istrian stone detailing. To the E: two small contemporary octagonal towers. Along the N shore of the basin is a long row of sixteen sheds, the **Tese Novissime**, 1508–45, but altered in 1880, when the open ends were enclosed; recently restored, as are the adjacent contemporary **Tese San Cristoforo**, immediately W. At the very W end are the **Tese alle Nape**, with three more bays, all of similar design. In the NW corner, on the W side, are the four surviving bays of the **Tese Novissimette**, early sixteenth century, but partly destroyed.

The Canale delle Galeazze

The last stage of development of the historic dockyard (1568–9), for the construction of the new galleasses. On the E side is the imposing **Officina Squadratori**, rebuilt by Scalfarotto (1739), to replace earlier structures with a similar function: the storage, seasoning and squaring of timber for a ship's 'skeleton'. Nine of the original thirteen bays remain, all of brickwork, to an impressively simple design. The Officina is to become a teaching centre for the Istituto Militari Marittimi. Immediately N are the **Scali di Alaggio**, two slipways for beaching vessels. The northern section of the Canale delle Galeazze is the Vasca (basin); the three large sheds on the W side and two to the E all date from 1585.

5 FROM THE ARSENALE TO SAN FRANCESCO DE LA VIGNA

Return to the main land gate of the Arsenale.

Walking W back towards San Martino, on the right: two attractive small houses, **Palazzetto dell'Inferno** and **Palazzetto di Purgatorio**; both take their names from Dante's famous visit to the dockyards, to which he later referred in Canto XXI of the *Inferno*. They housed the Provveditori or general commissioners of the Arsenale. Palazzetto di Purgatorio is the older, a mixture of late Gothic and early

The Arsenale: Palazzetto dell'Inferno (left) and Palazzetto di Purgatorio (right)

Renaissance fenestration; 1419, but modernised in the early sixteenth century. The other *palazzetto* is purely Renaissance, with an asymmetrical four-bay façade.

From the church square, in front of Ponte Storto, is the fine fourteenth-century Gothic **Palazzo Venier** (CS 2452), with an asymmetrical but elegant façade; a trilobate three-light window to the upper hall.

From Campo San Martino, cross Ponte dei Penini, and follow the *fondamenta* around into Campo de le Gorne. These houses were all occupied by trade masters in the Arsenale; some retain their title carved above the door lintels. Take Calle del Bastion and Calle de le Muneghete into Campo Due Pozzi, a quiet corner with several medieval houses (but only one well). CS 2599 (NE side) is a small fourteenth-century house with a symmetrical façade, while CS 2610 (NE corner) is of a similar date, but asymmetrical. Next door is CS 2611, a larger house occupying most of this side of the square: probably late fourteenth century, and again asymmetrical, with the main axis to the left. Just off the W corner of the square, taking Calle del Mandolin, we reach **Palazzo Zeno Venier Pizzamano** (CS 2654–5), land entrance on Ponte dei Scudi; fifteenth-century Gothic, with an asymmetrical canal façade, lacking the left wing.

Back in Campo Due Pozzi, turn N along Calle Magno. To the left is the long, complex façade of **Palazzo Manolesso** (CS 2687), again fifteenth-century Gothic, with a five-light window to the upper hall. The water façade can be seen from Ponte de la Scoazzera (see below). At CS 2596 is the **Arco dell'Angelo**, a portal above which is a sculpted thirteenth-century figure of an angel, set into a later, fourteenth-century arch. Adjacent, at CS 2693, is **Palazzo Magno Bembo**, a substantial late fourteenth-century Gothic house. The internal courtyard has a good open stair, supported on arches. At the N end of Calle Magno, turn left along Calle Donà, towards Ponte de

la Scoazzera. On the right is **Palazzo Celsi Donà** (CS 2716), a large seventeenth-century house, with a broad symmetrical canal façade, later extended; the land gate gives onto a large courtyard. The Celsi have been recorded here since the eleventh century. Cross the bridge into Campo Santa Tèrnita. The church stood on the N side, by the canal, and was founded in the

The Arco de l'Anzolo: thirteenth-century sculpture in a fourteenth-century arch (CS 2693)

eleventh century; it was closed in 1806 and demolished in 1832. At cs 3060 is an attractive seventeenth-century *palazzetto*, immediately adjacent to **Palazzo Sagredo** (cs 2720).

Cross Ponte del Suffragio; continue right along the quay, then left into Campo de la Celestia. **Santa Maria de la Celestia** was founded in 1199 by the Celsi, but in 1810 the nunnery was closed and most of the buildings, including the church, demolished; only the cloister block survives, housing the city archives. Take Calle del Cimitero out of the NW corner of the square, and continue via Calle drio la Chiesa into the spacious Campo de la Confraternità; on the N side is San Francesco de la Vigna (see below). At the W end is the restrained **Palazzo de la Nunziatura** (cs 2785), a double palace, with two elements divided by a courtyard. It was built by Doge Andrea Gritti in 1525, but his successors sold it to the Republic, and in 1564 it was given to Pope Pius IV to become the seat of the apostolic nuncio (Rome's ambassador to the Republic). In 1800 it passed to the Franciscans of the adjacent friary, who built the high-level corridor, linking the palace to their adjacent accommodation.

At the E end of the square is the **Scuola de San Pasquale Baylon**, dedicated to a Spanish Franciscan saint; built in 1603, in a simple Renaissance manner. Behind the three-bay façade is a square plan, with two superimposed halls, the lower one with a Baroque altar and four free-standing Doric columns; the upper hall, reached by paired staircases, is extremely plain, its art works all dispersed.

San Francesco de la Vigna is one of the most important churches in Venice, named after the extensive vineyards that once flourished here. Within them was a tiny chapel, said to have been where St Mark was washed ashore in a storm, and where he heard an angel saying the famous words 'Pax tibi, Marce, Evangelista meus' (Peace to you, Mark, My Evangelist), prophesying the future site of Venice itself. (The chapel was demolished in 1810.)

Marco Ziani bequeathed vineyards to the Franciscans in 1253, soon after St Francis visited the lagoon. The basilica survived until the sixteenth century, by which time it was in poor condition, and a new design was prepared by Sansovino. The foundation stone was laid in 1534, although Sansovino's proposal was modified after consultation with Francesco Giorgi, one of the friars and a notable humanist scholar; the design is based on Platonic theories of harmony and proportion. It was consecrated in 1582. The church had many wealthy patrons, several of whom adopted the side chapels; the inner façade was devoted to the Grimani family.

The last element to be built was Palladio's façade, *circa* 1562. The adjacent elegant campanile (1571–81) is one of the tallest in the city, modelled on that of San Marco. At the Napoleonic suppression, the monastery became a barracks, but in 1866 the Franciscans returned, and remain today. In 1810 it also became a parish foundation, replacing the adjacent suppressed parishes of Santa Giustina, Sant'Antonin and Santa Ternità.

Palladio's monumental façade marks a stage in his development of the 'temple front', a transitional work that was more fully realised later at San Giorgio Maggiore (q.v.). The central giant order of four Corinthian columns supports a heavy pediment, while a smaller version of the same composition forms the entrance portal. The two outer bays represent the side chapels within, and are capped by half-pediments.

Sansovino's interior is refined and imposing, on a Latin-cross plan. The articulation is all in grey stone, Doric, with plain white plaster for the planar surfaces. The five-bay nave has a simple barrel-vaulted ceiling; its broad, column-free space was ideal for preaching to large congregations. No aisles; instead, two rows of deep side chapels. Beyond is the square crossing, which was to have been covered by a large cupola, never executed. The transepts have the same depth as the nave chapels, while beyond the crossing is the exceptionally deep chancel; the altar is located halfway down its length, with the choirstalls behind it, so that the choir could not be seen by the congregation, but could be heard easily. The plan was later adopted by Palladio at San Giorgio and the Redentore.

A number of notable chapels: nave, right side: first chapel: the Bragadin family; third chapel: the Contarini, 1659 (altarpiece by Palma il Giovane); fourth chapel: the Badoer (altarpiece by Veronese); fifth chapel: the Barbaro (monuments to Ermolao and Marcantonio Barbaro). The high altar is originally sixteenth century but was perhaps modernised by Longhena. In the chancel: monument to Doge Andrea Gritti (+1538). Within the choir: paintings by Palma il Giovane and Domenico Tintoretto. Left transept, left chapel: that of the Badoer-Giustinian, exceptionally beautifully decorated by Pietro Lombardo and his sons Tullio and Antonio. It was built following a bequest by Girolamo Badoer in 1478. The altar is richly carved with relief sculptures, and on the side walls are sixteen relief panels illustrating the life of Christ and portraits of Prophets and Evangelists.

Facing page: San Francesco de la Vigna: part of the west façade, by Andrea Palladio, *circa* 1562

The door in the transept end wall leads to the sacristy and the Cappella Santa; the latter has an altarpiece by Govanni Bellini. The sacristy, a square hall with a high, vaulted ceiling, is also by Sansovino, 1555. Back in the church: nave chapels, left side: second chapel: the Dandolo; third chapel: the Sagredo, with decoration by G. B. Tiepolo; fifth chapel: the Grimani, a noteworthy Roman Renaissance work with a coffered barrel-vaulted ceiling. Statues by Tiziano Aspetti, 1592.

The extensive medieval monastic buildings survive to the N and NW of the church; among the oldest in Venice, built in the fourteenth century around two smaller square cloisters, together with a third, much larger, partially enclosed cloister, with only two wings.

6 FROM SANTA GIUSTINA TO THE SCUOLA DEGLI SCHIAVONI

From the front of the church, take Calle San Francesco W, and turn left down Fondamenta Santa Giustina.

The former church of **Santa Giustina**: said to have been one of the twelve founded by St Magnus in the seventh century. Later, it became an Augustinian nunnery, with accommodation built around two cloisters N of the church. It was rebuilt several times prior to the definitive modernisation in 1514. The façade is by Longhena (1640), following a bequest by Giovanni Soranzo. The monastery was closed in 1810, and in 1844 the church interior was drastically altered for use as a military academy; the uppermost part of the façade was removed. In 1924 it was altered again to become part of the Liceo Scientifico G. B. Benedetti, which it remains. The interior is lost; the only element of interest is Longhena's mutilated façade, with its Corinthian giant order and heavy trabeation. On the upper order are three monuments to the Soranzo family, but the crowning statues are also gone.

Opposite the S side of the church is **Palazzo Gradenigo** (CS 2838 and 2854), reached by its own bridge; sixteenth century, extended in the eighteenth. The plan is traditional and tripartite; inside: stuccoes and fresco decoration by Costantino Cedini. Cross Ponte del Fontego; immediately left is **Palazzo Morosini da la Sbarra** (CS 2842–5), sixteenth century, recently restored. A little further on the right is **Palazzo Valier** (CS 2856), water façade to Rio de la Pietà. Built in 1712 by Domenico Rossi for the Da Riva family,

Palazzo Contarini de la Porta di Ferro: detail of the portal, with thirteenth-century arch, in which is set a winged angel

who bought the site from the Valier. The canal façade is rich and elegant; the plan is conventional, the *androne* terminating with a loggia onto the courtyard. Some eighteenth-century stucco decoration survives.

At the s end of the *calle*, turn left into Salizada Santa Giustina. On the left (CS 2926) is the land entrance to **Palazzo Contarini de la Porta di Ferro**, so called for the notable medieval ironwork to the land portal, which survived until it was stolen in 1839. The house was built *circa* 1400 for the Contarini, and in 1799 passed to the Tiepolo. The canal façade (N) is much altered, but the courtyard contains an attractive open Gothic staircase, *circa* 1420, attributed to Matteo Raverti, very similar to his staircase at the Ca' d'Oro, also for the Contarini. The unusual land gate incorporates a rich thirteenth-century Byzantine arch; above the lintel is an angel bearing a cartouche, formerly flanked by the Contarini arms. On the outer corner of the garden wall is a *Virgin and Child* by Giuseppe Torretti (1715).

At the end of the Salizada, turn right down Salizada San Francesco, and its continuation, Salizada de le Gate; at the end, turn right into the square. The name derives not from cats, but is a corruption of 'de le legate', i.e., the papal legates, who lived here before moving to Palazzo Gritti. At the NE end: two attractive small Gothic houses. Leave by the sw corner and turn right down Calle dei Furlani. At CS 3302: a large eighteenth-century block of apartments, built by the Zaguri family; four storeys above the ground-floor shops, a typical speculative development of the period. On the right, just before the end: a cul-de-sac leading to **San Giovanni dei Cavalieri di Malta,** founded in the eleventh century, together with an adjacent hospital, by the Knights Templar. When the order was abolished in 1312, the church passed to the Knights of Rhodes, and then to the Knights of St John of Malta. They were expelled in 1797, but in 1839 the order of the Knights of Jerusalem was re-established here, and remains today. A very simple early Renaissance façade; the interior has an aisle-less nave. Its high altar is an elaborate sixteenth-century work, with sculptures salvaged from the lost San Geminiano. Adjacent is the entrance to the hospital, built around an elegant cloister, comprehensively modernised in 1565. Extensive gardens to the E.

On the corner, adjacent to Ponte de la Comenda, is the **Scuola de San Giorgio degli Schiavoni** (CS 3253). Established in 1451 by 'Slavs' (Dalmatians), many of whom settled in this zone. It was dedicated to their patrons, St George, St Tryphon and St Jerome. In 1502 the Scuola was given a relic of St George, as a result of which its prestige increased greatly, and it commissioned a famous cycle of paintings by Vettor Carpaccio. The impressive stone façade was added in 1551, by Giovanni de Zan, a follower of Sansovino. Three bays and two orders; in the centre of the upper part is a relief of *St George and the Dragon* by Pietro da Salò (1552). Directly above: a relief of the *Virgin and Child (circa* 1350s), from the adjacent hospital.

In common with most *scuole*, there are two superimposed halls, linked by a staircase. The small lower hall has an almost domestic scale, with a richly decorated, gilded timber ceiling. Around the walls, at high level, are Carpaccio's paintings, relocated from the upper hall. They narrate the lives of the three patrons, beginning, to the left of the entrance, with George killing the dragon; next is the triumphant return of the saint. After the doorway to the stairs, to the left of the altar is St George baptising King Ajo and his queen (1508). The altarpiece is perhaps by Vettor's son Benedetto. To the right of the altar is St Trifone as a child, exorcising a demon from the emperor's daughter; there follow two episodes from the Gospels, and finally scenes from the life of St Jerome. First, Jerome leading the tamed lion to his monastery; then his funeral; and finally the famous St Augustine in his study, hearing Jerome's voice through the window. The cycle is full of fascinating incidental detail, with the scenes set against contemporary cities or landscapes, partly drawn

Scuola di San Giorgio degli Schiavoni: entrance
portal by Giovanni de Zan, 1551; sculpture in the
second order by Pietro da Salò, 1552

from observation, partly imaginary. The stair is lined with
unremarkable seventeenth- and eighteenth-century paintings, while
the upper hall itself was modernised in 1551, again with a decorated
timber ceiling (1605), and paintings by Andrea Vicentino.

7 SANT'ANTONIN AND THE GRECI

Take Fondamenta dei Furlani s to **Sant'Antonin,** another early
parish foundation, established by the Badoer in the seventh century.
Little is known of its history, but after a series of restorations it was
rebuilt in 1668, and re-consecrated in 1680; the campanile was
reconstructed in 1750. The plain exterior has a west portal and two
flanking doorways; the interior is richer, deriving from Longhena. A
square plan, with a deep chancel flanked by altars. That to the left is
of the Tiepolo family, with stucco decoration perhaps by Vittoria; the
paintings are by Palma il Giovane.

Palazzo Zorzi Liassidi; fifteenth-century Gothic, with later Baroque balconies

Cross the bridge in front of the church into Salizada dei Greci. At CS 3305–9 is a sixteenth-century apartment block. At the w end, turn N into Campielo de la Fraterna, and right into Calle Coppo. At CS 3336 is **Palazzo Coppo**, a sixteenth-century Renaissance house, with balconies decorated with stone lions. Turn N along Ramo de la Fraterna and then left into Calle Lion. Continue to the bridge at the w end, and cross onto Fondamenta San Lorenzo. On the E bank opposite are three palaces.

Palazzo Lion Treves Bonfili (CS 3393): a big eighteenth-century palace, with its large, austere, canal façade almost devoid of decoration. It has a luxuriant garden at the side. Next to Ponte Lion is **Palazzo Maruzzi Pellegrini** (CS 3394), late sixteenth century, again with a garden, this time at the rear. To its right is **Palazzo Zorzi Liassidi** (CS 3405), next to Ponte dei Greci. Fifteenth-century Gothic, with an eclectic façade, containing archaic trilobate windows as well as *gotico fiorito* elements. First recorded in 1436, in the early nineteenth century it passed to the Liassidi, of Cypriot origin. Today

San Giorgio dei Greci, by Sante Lombardo; begun 1539, consecrated 1561

it is a hotel; the attractive courtyard can be seen from Calle de la Madona, with the upper floors on *barbacani*.

The Greeks in Venice: the Collegio Greco Flangini and San Giorgio dei Greci

Greeks were resident in Venice from its origins, but their modern history begins in the fifteenth century, when their numbers increased considerably. They had no dedicated church, and the Orthodox rite was practised in various churches until a further wave of migration after 1453, when Constantinople fell to the Turks. Thereafter, they were granted a chapel at San Biagio. Finally, in 1526 the Greeks bought a site in the parish of Sant'Antonin; the present church was begun in 1539 by Sante Lombardo. Thereafter it formed the hub of the Greek community in Venice, and other community facilities were added.

San Giorgio dei Greci was consecrated in 1561, and completed ten years later, when the cupola was added; the campanile followed in 1587–92. The tall, richly elegant façade reflects the single volume of the church behind: two superimposed Corinthian orders, each of three bays, surmounted by a tall aedicule; the upper order is a refined composition, centred on a large *ocio*. Unusually, the church is free-standing; the two long side façades are clad in stone, with a central doorway.

Inside: a tall nave, with the women's *barco* above the west end; the east end is defined by the traditional Greek iconostasis, enriched with marble and painted decoration. The chancel is flanked by small side chapels; all three have semicircular eastern apses. The pulpit is by Giovanni Grapiglia, 1597.

The adjacent campanile has a notable inclination towards the canal; it is capped by a tall bell-chamber and a bulbous lead-clad cupola. Immediately N of the church are two buildings by Longhena, the **Scuola de San Niccolò** and the **Collegio Greco Flangini**. Longhena was appointed *proto* to the Greek community in 1678, and the composition is visually united by his stone entrance screen and gateway. The Scuola is set back from the canal, and has a narrow façade but a deep plan: Istrian stone cladding, strongly rusticated, with circular columns to the lower order, and three large pedimented windows, with balconies, to the *piano nobile*. The Collegio Greco Flangini (CS 3412) is a larger, more dominant element, approached axially from Rio de l'Osmarin. It resembles a strongly modelled Venetian *palazzo*, with five bays and three storeys. The fielded panels between the windows are characteristic of Longhena.

8   BRAGORA AND ENVIRONS

We now turn to the ancient island parish of Bragora; return down Calle de la Madona and Salizada dei Greci, as far as Ponte Sant'Antonin. Adjacent to the bridge on the right is the late sixteenth-century **Palazzo Salvioni** (CS 3463), once attributed to Sansovino, although also influenced by Scamozzi. The impressive canal façade has a large watergate and a Serliana. Continue E along the flank wall of Sant'Antonin. Divert left briefly, down the long, straight Calle de'Arco: at the far end, just before the bridge, are two palaces, one on each side. To the left: **Palazzo Patavin** (CS 3512), seventeenth century, with an attractive rear garden. To the right is **Palazzo Querini** (CS 3520), originally fourteenth-century Gothic, but modernised in the sixteenth century. Both houses have façades to Rio de San Martino.

Return to Salizada Sant'Antonin, and continue s. At the corner, turn right into the attractive, tree-planted Campo de la Bragora (probably from *bragola* = a marketplace). On the N side is **Palazzo Gritti Morosini Badoer** (CS 3608), a prominent Gothic house, late fourteenth century, with an imposing, asymmetrical façade. Two *piani nobili*; the principal feature is the five-light first-floor window, with decorative marble discs and a relief sculpture above the dentil framing. On the right, an unusual two-light window wraps around the corner, like those at the nearby Palazzo Priuli, but earlier. To the left is **Palazzetto Soderini** (CS 3610), with a plaque to the martyred Bandiera brothers, killed in the Risorgimento cause in 1844. Adjacent, left again (CS 3626): another fourteenth-century Gothic house with a *quadrifora* to the principal floor.

Before turning to the titular church: a brief excursion W to the adjacent islet. Take Calle de la Pietà out of the W side; cross Ponte de la Pietà. To the NW is the water façade of **Palazzo Bollani** (CS 3647), a substantial sixteenth-century house, reached via Calle drio la Pietà and Corte Bollani (right). The land façade has a small collection of relief sculptures. Taking Calle Bosello N, we reach the land entrance to **Palazzo Cappello Memmo** (CS 3698–702), with water façade to Rio dei Greci (visible from Ponte dei Greci). Late fifteenth-century Gothic, with two *piani nobili*, each with a *quadrifora*. Immediately adjacent, again with façade to Rio dei Greci, is **Palazzo Gritti** (CS 3702), early Lombard Renaissance. The canal façade is unusually long and asymmetrical, with polychrome marble paterae. It was originally frescoed by Giulio del Moro. Return s down Calle Bosello, and cross Ponte de la Pietà once again. To the right is Sotoportego and Corte del Papà, named after Pietro Barbo (Pope Paul II), who was born here. The house has ancient origins, with a Venetian-Byzantine watergate and two badly weathered lions to the arch imposts. Continue back into Campo de la Bragora.

The ancient foundation of **San Giovanni in Bragora** (SE corner) is one of twelve churches established in the early eighth century, and rebuilt in the ninth century to house relics of St John the Baptist. The Byzantine church survived until 1475, when it was rebuilt in the late Venetian Gothic style. The *campo* façade is simple but attractive, with a Gothic portal and complex parapets. The reconstruction reused the earlier nave columns, while the chancel, the last element to be rebuilt (*circa* 1490s), contains Renaissance elements. Modernisation in the 1730s resulted in the loss of the choirstalls, but restoration has revealed fifteenth-century frescoes on the nave walls. The nave is flanked by robust Gothic arches and is capped by a timber roof; the chancel has a cross-vault. Second-right nave chapel: decorated by Alvise Vivarini and others (late fifteenth century). Chancel: *Last Supper* by Paris Bordone; *Washing of the Feet* by Palma il Giovane; *Baptism of Christ* by Cima da Conegliano. Stucco vault decoration by Vittoria, 1593. Left flank column to chancel: *Christ Resurrected* by Alvise Vivarini.

Adjacent to the church façade (N) is the former **Scuola de San Giovanni Battista** (CS 3811B), 1716 (plaque), with a symmetrical façade and a stone portal with broken pediment.

Leave the square by Calle del Dose (SW corner), then turn left (Calle de la Malvasia Vechia) into Campielo del Piovan, a tranquil corner only a few metres from the busy Riva degli Schiavoni. On the W side (CS 3753 and adjacent nos): a short terrace of sixteenth-century houses; on the N side (CS 3790): a small fourteenth-century Gothic house. Leave the *campielo* by the NE corner, taking Calle del Forno into Crosera, a busy shopping street. Turning right, it opens into Campielo de la Pescaria. Take Calle Morosini into Calle Erizzo.

Palazzo Erizzo (CS 4002): an impressive Renaissance pile, with façade to Rio de San Martino. Asymmetrical, with an additional wing to the right (N), incorporating a second watergate. Said to have been modernised by Longhena in the 1640s for Francesco Erizzo (doge 1631–46). An attractive loggia to the rear courtyard; the interior conserves much seventeenth- to eighteenth-century decoration. Immediately s is **Palazzo Grandiben Negri** (CS 4009), originally Gothic but heavily restored. Returning down Calle Erizzo, take the narrow Calle del Cagnoleto onto the Riva degli Schiavoni.

9   THE RIVA DEGLI SCHIAVONI

One of the principal quays of the city. Forming the northern shore of the basin of San Marco, for centuries it was the main location for mooring commercial shipping, which was first required to unload cargoes at the Dogana da Mar, at the western end. Its deep water and spacious dimensions made the basin a perfect natural harbour. The Riva was widened considerably in the nineteenth century, so that the buildings no longer have a close relationship with the water.

At CS 4107–9 is **Palazzo Gabrieli**, today a hotel; late fourteenth-century Gothic, with a long, rather low, asymmetrical façade, and one principal *piano nobile*. The plan is a T, with the *cortile* (containing an open staircase) in one of the rear angles. A good *quadrifora* to the main upper hall, with irregular side lights. Continue W along the Riva.

The former **Convento de San Sepolcro** (CS 4142) occupies a substantial site just before Ponte del Sepolcro. Founded in 1409 as a pilgrims' hostel, it was modernised in 1570, when the fine portal to the façade (perhaps by Vittoria or Sansovino) was added. It was suppressed in 1808, and most buildings demolished; the present building houses a Presidio Militare, incorporating the portal. Next door, just before the bridge, is **Palazzo Navagero** (CS 4145–8), fifteenth-century Gothic, with later Baroque balcony, and a façade to the *rio* at the side. It was owned in the later fifteenth century by the humanist scholar Andrea Navagero. The Petrarch plaque is erroneous; in fact, he lived in Palazzo Molin da le Due Torri, demolished when Santo Sepolcro was enlarged in the sixteenth century.

Crossing Ponte del Sepolcro, we reach **Santa Maria de la Visitazione**, popularly known as the Pietà. It originated in the mid-fourteenth century as an orphanage for abandoned children; it was enlarged in 1388 and modernised again in 1493 and 1515. Seventeenth- to eighteenth-century expansion resulted in the foundation occupying all the land between Rio dei Greci and Rio de la Pietà. Like the other orphanages, it developed a famous reputation for music. In the early eighteenth century it was decided to rebuild; a competition was won by Massari, whose design was based on Palladio's Zitelle, with the church flanked by two large wings of residential accommodation. Work on the church began in 1744, and it was consecrated in 1760, but the residential blocks were never built. The heavy neo-Palladian façade was finally completed in 1906, approximately to Massari's design.

The plan is rectangular, and the interior is based on the practical and acoustic requirements for music, particularly choral performances. The nave is approached via a lobby, providing acoustic isolation. It has a vaulted ceiling, and the corners are radiused, again for acoustic reasons, while the choir galleries occupy the two sides of the nave, with further balconies on the inner face of the front wall. Antonio Vivaldi was choirmaster for many years, but died in 1743 before the church was complete, and never performed here.

Among the principal works of art: *Fortitude* and *Peace* by G. B. Tiepolo, above the main entrance; the altarpiece is the *Visitation* by

Giambattista Piazzetta; chancel ceiling: the *Cardinal Virtues*, again by Tiepolo, as is the ceiling fresco, the *Triumph of Faith*.

Continue w across Ponte de la Pietà. Halfway down the quay is the imposing bronze equestrian memorial to Victor Emmanuel II (Ettore Ferrari, 1887). Crossing Ponte del Vin, we reach **Palazzo Dandolo Gritti Bernardo**, the present Danieli Hotel (cs 4193–6). Built in the late fourteenth century by the Dandolo, it then passed to the Gritti. In 1822 it was bought by Giuseppe da Niel, who converted it into a hotel, one of the first of the modern era. It was transformed internally, and after 1945 was extended by two new side wings by Virgilio Vallot, linked by bridges; neither has architectural distinction. Although the ground floor is altered, the palace's façade is broad, impressive and symmetrical. The main feature is the large six-light *piano nobile* window, with quatrefoils modelled on those of the adjacent Doge's Palace. The interior is much altered, and centres on a spacious atrium, formed by Tranquillo Orsi in a lavish late nineteenth-century neo-medieval manner, with a good leavening of exotic orientalism. The richly decorated staircase also has 'Moorish' arches. The hotel has a long history of famous guests, including Gabriele d'Annunzio, Marcel Proust, Honoré de Balzac and George Sand.

Immediately w of the Danieli extension is the **Palazzo de le Prigioni**. For centuries the Republic's prisons were located within the Doge's Palace, but there was frequently insufficient capacity; in 1563 Gianantonio Rusconi proposed a new purpose-designed prison

The Palazzo de le Prigioni; front block by Antonio da Ponte, completed by Antonio Contin *circa* 1600

across the Rio di Palazzo. In 1566 construction began on the rear block, with a façade to Rio di Palazzo, N of the present Ponte dei Sospiri. By 1567 it was already decided to construct a second phase, a larger block further S; it was completed in 1574. Rusconi died *circa* 1589, and the third, final stage, including the wing facing the Riva, was designed by Antonio da Ponte. It was completed by Antonio Contin just after 1600. Contin also designed the Ponte dei Sospiri, linking the prisons with the Doge's Palace.

The stone front wing has a typically High Renaissance appearance: two orders and seven bays, the lower order rusticated and colonnaded, the upper with large rectangular pedimented windows. The principal *piano nobile* rooms housed the offices of the Signori di Notte, the night security police. The prison also contained cells for women, a chapel and an infirmary. The block is planned around a square central courtyard, with a second one towards the rear. It was perhaps the first purpose-designed state prison in Europe, its accommodation of a much higher standard than any built over the next 300 years. The prisons remained in use until 1919.

Other than the front block, the remainder is devoid of decoration, appropriately finished with massive roughly finished blocks of Istrian stone; heavy iron grilles to the windows. By contrast, the adjacent Ponte dei Sospiri (*circa* 1602) has an inappropriately frivolous early Baroque appearance, supported by a shallow three-centred arch and crowned by a radiused pediment, with pedestals and volutes.

10 SANTI FILIPPO E GIACOMO AND SAN ZANINOVO

Take Calle dei Albanesi inland next to the Prigioni, to the small, congested Campo Santi Filippo e Giacomo. Turn left into Rugheta Sant'Apollonia, then left again along the short quay. At CS 4310 is the former **Scuola dei Linaroli**, the guild of linen weavers; only the Renaissance portal survives. At the end is the entrance to the **Chiostro Sant'Apollonia**, the only surviving Romanesque cloister in Venice. It formed part of the conventual buildings of the adjacent de-consecrated church of Santi Filippo e Giacomo. The church was probably founded in the twelfth century, and the dedication extended to include St Apollonia, dedicatee of the adjacent Scuola. After the Napoleonic dissolution, the surviving monastic buildings became the official residence of the primate of San Marco. The

The thirteenth-century cloister of Sant'Apollonia

cloister is late twelfth or early thirteenth century; a rectangular plan, five broad bays across the ends, eleven narrower ones down the sides; simple semicircular brick arches of two different sizes, supported on large monolithic columns for the larger arches, narrow paired columns for the smaller ones. They stand on a brick plinth, and the cloister has traditional herringbone brick paving.

Returning to Ponte de la Canonica, on the E side of the canal is the richly decorated façade of **Palazzo Trevisan Cappello in Canonica** (CS 4328–30), one of the finest early Renaissance palaces in Venice. Sometimes attributed to Bon the Bergamasco, it was built for the Trevisan, *circa* 1490s or very early 1500s, but in 1577 was bought by Bartolomeo Cappello, father of Bianca (see p. 290). The impressive façade has four orders of nearly equal importance, and is tripartite and symmetrical, decorated with inset panels of marble and relief sculptures, and with elegant six-light windows to the upper halls. The plan is unusual, and is reflected in the lowest order of the façade, with three large portals; the right one is a *cavana*, while the middle and left watergates lead to two separate entrance halls and stairs, which in turn rise to two superimposed apartments. Land access is via the bridge over the canal, terminating in two doorways, again one to each apartment. The relief sculptures on the top floor were added by Cappello after 1577.

Palazzo Trevisan Cappello in Canonica: detail of
the façade, *circa* 1490s

Return to Campo Santi Filippo e Giacomo; take Calle drio la
Chiesa out of the NE corner, and turn left around the church into
Campo San Zaninovo.

San Zaninovo, formally San Giovanni in Oleo, was founded by
the Trevisan (see above) in 968. It was rebuilt in the twelfth century,
and again in the fifteenth; re-consecrated in 1463. In 1753 the church
was rebuilt again, as we see it today; the architect was the little-
known Matteo Lucchesi. It remained a parish foundation until 1808,
when it was subordinated to San Marco, then, in 1812, to San
Zaccaria. The design is based on Palladio's Redentore, but on a
much more modest scale. Its site is tightly circumscribed, and the
stone façade was never completed. The single nave has a square
chancel and a barrel-vaulted ceiling. Down the side walls Corinthian
pilasters support a continuous cornice; two altars on each side. The
church contains few art works and is generally closed.

On the W side of the square: **Palazzetti Querini** (CS 4386–8), a
matching pair, both sixteenth century. In the NW corner: a small
Gothic house, annexed to the rear of Palazzo Michiel (see below).
Take the *sotoportego* near the NW corner of the square, continuing
along the attractive quay; turn left down Calle del Rimedio. The

façades of several palaces on the E side of Rio de Palazzo can be seen from the bridge at the end. The furthest one, adjacent to Palazzo Trevisan, is the seventeenth-century **Palazzo Morosini** (CS 4391), reached by a private bridge. Next to it (towards us) is **Palazzo Foscarini** (CS 4392), also seventeenth century but modernised in the eighteenth; a narrow Palladian façade with three large single windows to the *piano nobile*. Next again is **Palazzo Michiel Baffo Molin Piacentini** (CS 4391A–4392A), originally Gothic, but modernised in the seventeenth century. Finally: the substantial but rather plain eighteenth-century **Palazzo Rota Campana** (CS 4409), today the Hotel Colombina. Still on the bridge, now facing N, immediately right is **Palazzo Soranzo** (CS 4415–9), known as the Casa de l'Angelo after the prominent fourteenth-century figure set into the canal façade. Originally thirteenth century, the house has later Gothic elements and other partial modernisations. The L-shaped plan centres on an internal courtyard, with the main façade to Rio de Palazzo, and a longer, secondary façade to Rio de l'Angelo (del Mondo Novo). The former has fourteenth-century Gothic windows and is said to have been frescoed by Tintoretto. The internal courtyard façade contains much original material, including two *quadrifore*. The upper floors are supported on *barbacani*, carried by marble columns; an open stair on the W wall.

Return E along Calle del Rimedio, then turn N along the *fondamenta* to Ponte Pasqualigo. Across the canal to the NW is the attractive, asymmetrical fifteenth-century Gothic **Palazzo Venier** (CS 4425 and 5270), with Baroque balconies. Immediately in front of us (E) is the heavy seventeenth-century Baroque **Palazzo Avogadro** (CS 4426), with façade to Campielo Querini; prominent stone balconies and a crowning cornice. At CS 4429, just W of Ponte Pasqualigo, is **Palazzo Pasqualigo**, with its façade to the N, facing Palazzo Venier; seventeenth century, with sculpted heads as keystones.

11 SAN PROVOLO AND SAN ZACCARIA

Return down the *fondamenta* to San Zaninovo, returning again around the back of the church and into Campo Santi Filippo e Giacomo; this time turn E, taking the short, busy Salizada San Provolo, towards San Zaccaria. On the left (CS 4512): a block of apartments built in 1735, after a fire. Directly opposite (CS 4622): another, larger block, rebuilt by the noble Michiel family in the same

San Zaccaria: upper part of the façade, by Mauro Codussi,
after 1483

period. Crossing Ponte San Provolo, we enter the small eponymous
square. The former church stood on the E side; it had been founded
in 809 by the Partecipazio family, and survived several
reconstructions until it was suppressed in 1805; by 1825 it had been
demolished. At cs 4711 (w side) is the massive, heavy, seventeenth-
century **Palazzo Priuli**.

Continue under the arch in the se corner; above is a fine relief
sculpture of the Virgin and Child (mid-fifteenth century) in the
manner of Bartolomeo Bon; we enter Campo San Zaccaria,
dominated by the imposing stone and marble façade of the church.
San Zaccaria is one of the most ancient foundations in Venice, and
one of its most notable churches. Said to have been founded by St
Magnus, in the ninth century a Benedictine convent was annexed to
the parish church; in the same period the body of St Zacharias
(father of John the Baptist) was given to the church by Pope Leo X.
Thereafter, it became a pilgrimage site, and grew extremely wealthy,
patronised by popes and emperors; several early doges were buried

San Zaccaria: interior, towards the faceted chancel;
Gothic arches above, Renaissance ones below; by
Antonio Gambello, after 1456

here. The monastery was partially reconstructed in the tenth century;
the crypt, below the chapel of San Tarasio, survives, one of the oldest
structures in Venice. Further reconstruction took place after a fire in
1105, but the definitive late Gothic rebuilding took place in the
1440s; much survives to the s of the present nave.

In 1456 the nunnery petitioned the pope and the Signoria for
funds for a further reconstruction. This is the present main church,
but its thirty-five-year construction programme embraced the
transition from Gothic to Renaissance, a rare fusion of two styles
within a single structure. The first architect was Antonio Gambello,
and the new church stands directly N of the older Gothic brick
structure, the N aisle of which was subsumed by the s aisle of the
new building. The older nave was subdivided into three elements:
the w end formed the nuns' parlour (where visitors were received);
in the centre was the nuns' choir or chapel of Sant'Atanasio; while
the chancel, with its faceted apse, became the chapel of San

Tarasio. It retains frescoes by Andrea del Castagno and Francesco da Faenza, 1442.

The imposing new façade was begun by Gambello, who died in 1481, with only the lower order (and perhaps the second) completed. In 1483 Codussi began to complete the church, and all the upper parts are his work: a massively imposing, confident composition, almost a triumphal arch, a mature development from his earlier façade for San Michele; the complex rhythm of the lower orders is climaxed by a mighty curved pediment crowning the central bay, with quadrants to the lower side bays.

The interior is as notable as the façade. The short nave has only three extremely spacious bays, defined by monolithic columns on tall, complex bases of extraordinary design. At the E end is the faceted chancel, beyond which is an ambulatory, with a series of radiating chapels, a quintessentially French arrangement. The only nearby precedent is Sant'Antonio at Padua, where the ambulatory was also used for processions. The chancel has two orders, all in stone, an openwork late Gothic screen above an early Renaissance colonnade, an arrangement as eclectic as it is successful; both orders are by Gambello, assisted by Giovanni Buora. Below the high altar: the tomb of St Zacharias. All the upper parts of the interior, including the nave ceiling and the cupola on pendentives, are by Codussi, in his characteristically refined, elegant manner.

Several notable works of art: right aisle, first altar: *Virgin and Child with Saints* by Palma il Giovane. The second altar is by Vittoria. Adjacent to the high altar is a series of paintings depicting scenes from the life of Christ, by Palma il Giovane. Central ambulatory chapel: organ by Callido, 1790. Left aisle: adjacent to the sacristy door: monument to Vittoria, 1566. Left aisle, second altar: *Virgin and Child Enthroned, with Saints*, an exceptionally fine work by Giovanni Bellini, 1506. Adjacent: two works by Aliense. Off the south side of the nave, within the nuns' choir, are the original choirstalls by the Cozzi workshop (1460s), and paintings by Tintoretto, Palma il Vecchio and Giandomenico Tiepolo. In the San Tarasio Chapel are three fine altarpieces by Ludovico da Forlì, 1443–4.

Back in the square, to the S of the earlier church is the thirteenth-century campanile, one of the oldest in Venice. The extensive monastic buildings stand S and E, extending to Rio dei Greci. Most are early sixteenth-century Renaissance, built around two cloisters, the smaller to the S; both simple and refined. Along the N side of the square is a colonnaded 'cloister', now filled in, and built (perhaps by Codussi) just before 1500, to link the church with the *campo* entrance. In the SW corner is the wilfully eclectic **Palazzina Kress** (CS 4686), a nineteenth-century Gothic confection by Ambrogio Narduzzi, incorporating a range of historicist devices.

12 PALAZZO QUERINI STAMPALIA AND RUGA GIUFFA

Return to Campo San Provolo and leave by the NE corner; continue below the *sotoportego* and cross Ponte dei Carmini. Follow Calle de Corte Rota (two bends) to its junction with Calle Corona and Ruga Giuffa. On the corner (CS 4745): a good small Gothic house, with the Lion family arms. Continue up Ruga Giuffa, taking Calle drio el Magazen to the left; walk along the picturesque quay, and take Calle Querini N. The garden of Palazzo Querini is on the right. Cross the bridge into Campielo Querini.

   Palazzo Querini Stampalia (CS 4778 and 5252): a sizeable early sixteenth-century palace, home of the eponymous Fondazione. The long main façade follows the curve of the canal, and is reached by two private bridges, one a refined minor work by Carlo Scarpa (1961–3). The house was built in two stages prior to 1522; the interior was modernised extensively in the eighteenth century. The Stampalia title derives from the Querini's lordship of the Aegean island of that name. In 1868 the last of the line, Giovanni, bequeathed his notable library and art collection to the foundation that flourishes today.

   The slightly earlier nucleus of the house is to the right (W) with the extension to the E; the former has a symmetrical tripartite façade, the latter with a long row of single-light windows.

   Inside, the lower *piano nobile* is occupied by the library, the upper by the art collection, containing works by Giovanni Bellini, Palma il Vecchio and G. B. Tiepolo, as well as important collections of Gabriele Bella and Pietro Longhi. There is also good eighteenth-century furniture.

   Scarpa's interventions of 1961–3 are outstanding: he remodelled the water-level storey, bringing the canal directly inside the building, with a miniature canal inside the *androne*. At the back is his delightful enclosed garden, with characteristically refined use of water, channelled through a series of spaces.

   Leave the *campielo* by the narrow gap in the NE corner, and enter the S end of Campo Santa Maria Formosa, one of the finest in the

Palazzo Querini Stampalia; part of the early
sixteenth-century façade; footbridge by
Carlo Scarpa, 1961–3

Palazzo Malipiero Trevisan: detail
of the façade, with stone bridge
and first-floor *quadrifora*

city, surrounded by notable houses. At the SE corner, adjacent to the
bridge, is **Palazzo Malipiero Trevisan** (CS 4852 and 5250), later
Diedo and Bembo. An important early Renaissance palace with a
fine, rich façade facing the square across the canal. An earlier Gothic
house was radically modernised in the early sixteenth century for the
Trevisan; the façade is broad but rather low, perhaps reflecting the
proportions of the earlier house. It has features in common with the
other Trevisan house 'in Canonica' (see above), both with rich relief
panels and paterae adorning the façades. They probably had a
common architect, perhaps Bon the Bergamasco. The plan and façade
are traditional and tripartite, and the three orders are defined by
broad string-courses, with inset paterae. The canal façade has unusual
features: one is the bridge access, flanked by two arched watergates;
another is the decorative balustrading to the *piani nobili*. The
aedicules in the outer bays perhaps contained statues.

Take the adjacent bridge, and continue down Ruga Giuffa. At the
first left corner (CS 4860) is the seventeenth-century **Palazzetto**

Grimani, with rusticated quoins. At the far end of this cul-de-sac is the impressive land gate to **Palazzo Grimani** (CS 4858), one of the largest and most notable – and least-known – Renaissance palaces in the city. This massive house fills an entire block at the junction of Rio de Santa Maria Formosa and Rio de San Severo; the water façade is best seen from Fondamenta San Severo, to the E. It was built by the wealthy, influential Grimani family, and has a long, complex history. The first palace was owned by Doge Antonio Grimani, who died in 1523; his son Domenico, patriarch of Aquileia and an avid antiquarian, inherited part of it, and the palace was enlarged and embellished in two stages, in 1537–40 and after 1558, when it became the sole property of Giovanni, grandson of Antonio. Giovanni extended the house over an adjacent orchard and added the rusticated stone watergate.

In its final form, the palace has a roughly square plan, centred on an imposing 'Roman' courtyard, perhaps by Giovanni himself. The house became the setting for Grimani's extensive collection of antiquities; some rooms were remodelled for their display. Giovanni also amassed a remarkable art collection, with works by Titian, Tintoretto and Veronese. The palace has two *piani nobili*, with one spacious apartment on each floor, each with its own water access. Many of the principal rooms retain rich sixteenth-century decoration, including paintings by Francesco Salviati and Giovanni da Udine. The outstanding sculpture hall is lined with niches for statues, and has a faceted cupola.

In 1586 Giovanni's antiquities were given to the Republic, and form the nucleus of the present Museo Archeologico Nazionale in the Piazza. The palace has been slowly restored over twenty years, and since winter 2008–9 has become an archaeological museum and study centre, based on the Grimani's original collections.

Continue down Ruga Giuffa. At the end of Calle de l'Arco, left, is **Palazzo Zorzi Bon** (CS 4907); water façade to Rio de San Severo. One of the earliest fully Gothic palaces in the city. Although dating is difficult, much of the canal façade is mid-fourteenth century. Broadly symmetrical, other than the two watergates; the heavy stone Renaissance balconies are considerably later. The narrow land façade to Calle de l'Arco has a fine two-light window to the first floor, again fourteenth century; in the aedicule is a Roman bust of an emperor.

Facing page: Palazzo Grimani: detail of the late sixteenth-century land gate, with the Grimani arms and three Roman busts

Palazzo Zorzi Bon: detail of the five-light window to the first floor; probably early fourteenth century

Palazzo Zorzi: the colonnade to the courtyard, by Mauro Codussi, probably *circa* 1480

Continue to the s end of Ruga Giuffa; turn left into Salizada Zorzi. On the left: the fine Renaissance land gate to **Palazzo Zorzi** (cs 4930). An unusual early Renaissance palace by Codussi, with a long façade to Rio de San Severo. The house was built for Marco Zorzi, whom Codussi knew from his patronage at San Michele; it was probably begun in the 1470s, but not complete until the 1490s. An earlier house constrained the plan, because the foundations and some walls were reused. The central *portego*, running e–w, has two bays of rooms to the n and three towards the s, six elements in all. The canal wing is very broad, but has comparatively shallow depth; at the rear is a large courtyard, beyond which was a garden (now a restaurant). The land gate gives onto an elegant colonnaded portico, at the end of which is the main staircase.

The canal façade is clad with stone and marble, and is nearly symmetrical. Its complex fenestration reflects the internal plan and the incorporation of existing cross-walls; the refined detailing is typically Codussian. The long, continuous main balcony is original, although those to the outer lights are Baroque additions.

Cross Ponte San Severo into the small, rather anonymous **Campo San Severo**. The church, founded in the ninth century, was demolished by the Austrians in the 1820s, and a prison for political prisoners was built on its site (CS 4999); it has a faux rusticated façade with heavily barred windows. At the S end of the square is the impressive **Palazzo Priuli** (CS 4979). An important Gothic palace, occupying the block between the square and Rio de l'Osmarin. It has been said that the house was built by Giovanni di Costantino Priuli, who died in 1456. Examination of the complex façades, however, shows two principal periods of construction, the first the later fourteenth century, and the second *circa* 1420. The principal façade is towards the canal, with a varied collection of windows; two *piani nobili*, the upper the more important. The windows of the lower one are fourteenth century, the upper ones perhaps later. Both outer angles have unusual two-light windows, wrapping around the

Palazzo Priuli: detail of canal façade, fourteenth to fifteenth century

corner, with a column at the angle; the pendant tracery to the sw window (*circa* 1418?) was used as a model for that at the Ca' d'Oro (early 1420s). The façade was once frescoed by Palma il Vecchio. The *campo* façade is asymmetrical, with an unusual portal consisting of two superimposed elements, an upper pointed arch set above a square-headed portal. Inside the small central courtyard is a good open staircase on stone arches.

From Campo San Severo, take the long *fondamenta* N; good views of Palazzi Zorzi, Zorzi Bon and Grimani to the left. Turn right along the Borgoloco. Down each side are two long terraces of housing; at CS 5091–101 (N side) a terrace of thirteen houses, 1539–40, with paired plans. Opposite, at CS 5075–101, is a row of ten identical houses, of similar date but restored by the adjacent nunnery in 1665. Continue to the E end. A short distance down Fondamenta San Lorenzo is **Palazzo Ziani** (CS 5053), a substantial seventeenth-century house, with a prominent Serliana. At the rear: remains of a large garden, and a small contemporary *casinò*. Cross Ponte San Lorenzo into the large, empty square. **San Lorenzo**: reputedly founded in the sixth or seventh century, the church was patronised by the Partecipazio clan, who produced several early doges. In the ninth century a Benedictine nunnery was established, which became extremely wealthy; in 1664 Grand Duke Cosimo of Tuscany claimed that it was the richest religious house in Venice. The church was rebuilt on several occasions, the last in the late sixteenth century, when the monastic buildings were also rebuilt; the church was completed by Simon Sorella in 1602, although the massive façade was never begun.

The plan and interior are both highly unusual and monumentally impressive. The interior has a single huge volume, approximately square on plan, all Corinthian, and divided in half transversely by a great three-bay screen. In the central bay is the richly monumental free-standing high altar, with one face onto each of the spaces. The two flanking bays are treated like giant windows, filled with decorative ironwork. The two halves of the church thus created were used by the public (w) and by the nuns, in the eastern half. There were two organs, one at each end of the nave.

In 1810 the nunnery was suppressed, and the art works dispersed. Shortly afterwards, some monastic buildings that stood between the church and the canal were demolished, doubling the size of the square. In 1842 the house passed to the Dominicans, but in 1865 was reacquired by the city council. The church was damaged in 1914–18,

San Lorenzo: the *campo* and the uncompleted church façade,
circa 1602; the monastic buildings (left) have been restored
for sheltered housing

but restored in the 1950s; it remains closed. The extensive monastic
buildings to the N, built around three cloisters, have been recently
restored for sheltered housing.

14 SANTA MARIA FORMOSA (1)

From the square in front of the church we re-cross the bridge, turn
right and take Calle Larga westwards, then Calle Cappello to the
right. Just before Ponte Cappello, on the left, is the seventeenth-
century **Palazzo Gabrieli** (CS 5152); next to it, visible from the
bridge, is **Palazzo Bembo** (CS 5153), fifteenth-century Gothic, with a
tripartite, symmetrical canal façade.

Return to the Calle Larga, and continue westwards; then take
Calle de la Madoneta (right). The *calle* reaches a short *fondamenta*. On
the right: **Palazzo Morosini Cavagnis** (CS 5171), with canal façades
on the corner of Rio de San Severo. The site was bought in 1712 by

Antonio Cavagnis, who demolished an earlier house to build the present one, probably by Domenico Rossi. Its form is traditional and tripartite, with a fine land gate leading to a small courtyard. In 1811 the interior was richly decorated by Carlo Bevilacqua. The palace was damaged by an Austrian bomb during the First World War.

Cross the bridge to reach the short quay adjacent to Calle Lunga Santa Maria Formosa, a busy local shopping street. Continue down the Calle Lunga back into Campo Santa Maria Formosa. On the east side, facing the three apses of the church, is the early **Palazzo Vitturi** (CS 5246), late thirteenth century, although considerably altered. The façade is tripartite and symmetrical, while the L-shaped plan has a small courtyard in the internal angle. Two *piani nobili*, the upper slightly more prominent. The first has a *trifora* to the main hall, the second a *quadrifora*, all similarly detailed, with inflected arched heads, and flanked by pairs of single windows. The heavy stone balconies are perhaps seventeenth century. **Chiesa de Santa Maria Formosa**: one of the ancient parishes said to have been founded by St Magnus in the seventh century; dedicated to the Virgin, who appeared to him in a vision as a buxom (*formosa*) woman. The present church, by Mauro Codussi, is an outstanding early Renaissance work. It was rebuilt several times prior to this definitive reconstruction after 1492, and was completed just after Codussi's death in 1504. The church was generously patronised by the Cappello, who paid for both façades.

The plan is an ingenious fusion of two forms: the Latin cross and the centralised Greek cross. The basic form is centralised, and the overall 'footprint' is nearly square, with a cupola over the crossing; the nave is slightly extended, but has only three bays, and the chancel has almost the same length, terminating with a semicircular apse, as do the two flanking chapels. The transepts are two bays long, almost the same length as the nave. Codussi thus contrived a carefully graduated hierarchy of spaces: first, the central crossing; then the nave; then the lower side aisles; finally, rows of deep lateral chapels flanking the aisles.

The architectural language is equally refined. All the structural elements – columns, capitals, corbels, pilasters – are of stone, while the non-structural, planar surfaces are of simple white plaster. The vocabulary is strongly influenced by Brunelleschi's work in Florence, and had no precedent in Venice at the time.

The church was the base for several trade guilds, with altars here. Nave chapels, east side, first altar: *Madonna de la Misericordia* by

Santa Maria Formosa: the canal façade, 1541, in the form of a memorial to Admiral Vincenzo Cappello

Bartolomeo Vivarini, 1473. Second chapel: *Pietà* by Palma il Giovane. Transept, right wall: *Last Supper* by Leandro Bassano. Chapel of the Scuola dei Bombardieri: altarpiece: *SS Barbara, Sebastian and Anthony Abbot*, a notable work by Palma il Vecchio. Right of the high altar: chapel of San Lorenzo Giustinian; statues by Campagna. High altar by Smeraldi, 1592. Left of the high altar: chapel of the Scuola dei Casselleri dedicated to the Madonna del Parto (altarpiece brought here in 1612).

There are two façades, the architect of neither of which is known. The principal (w) façade is a restrained classical work (1541), in the form of a monument to Admiral Vincenzo Cappello. The rather flat *campo* (transept) façade, attributed to Smeraldi, was added in 1604, as

Santa Maria Formosa: interior by Mauro Codussi,
1492–1504

a memorial to three other members of the Cappello clan. The prominent campanile, adjacent to the NW corner, was rebuilt in 1611 by Francesco Zucconi, but not completed until 1688. It is capped by a rich, complex, bell-chamber and a pinnacled roof; at the base, above the doorway, is a grotesque keystone, said to ward off demons. Between the campanile and the church: former **Scuola dei Fruttaroli** (1684), which combined with the **Scuola de la Purificazione** (1601); the two were unified as an oratory in 1833.

Also adjacent to the church's canal façade (S) is the former **Scuola dei Bombardieri** (CS 5266); a plain exterior. The Scuola occupied the two lower floors of the building, with its meeting hall on the first floor. Its altarpiece, *St Barbara*, the dedicatee, is now in the church.

15 LA FAVA AND SAN LIO

Cross Ponte de le Bande, and continue down Calle de le Bande. On the left, at CS 5273, is the impressive seventeenth-century **Palazzo Cabrini**, difficult to see in the narrow street. Continue down Calle al Ponte de la Guerra; on the left is the narrow Casseleria, where the medieval chest- and box-makers were based. Just before Ponte de la Guerra, right, a short *fondamenta* leads to **Palazzo Veggia Papafava Tasca** (CS 5402). The fine stone portal (*circa* 1540) was reassembled here from Palazzo Tasca at Portogruaro; a good stone watergate, too, although the palace itself is much altered and extended. Cross Ponte de la Guerra, continue down the Campo; turn right into Calle San Zulian, and right again into Piscina San Zulian. At CS 5492, just over the bridge, is the seventeenth-century **Palazzo Scalfarotto**, while to the left of it is **Palazzo Licini** (CS 5507), also late seventeenth century, modernised *circa* 1741. Take the *sotoportego* and Corte Licini, and continue through Calle drio la Fava to the small Campo de la Fava, dominated by the tall façade of the church.

Santa Maria de la Consolazione, popularly de la Fava, was founded to house a miracle-working image of the Virgin discovered nearby. In 1496 a small oratory was built, surviving until *circa* 1700; four years later the present church was begun. The popular name perhaps derives from a nearby shop selling beans (*fave*). The church is by Gaspari, who produced numerous alternative designs, before one was finally agreed by the friars of San Filippo Neri, who administered the shrine. Although much larger than the earlier oratory, space was highly constrained, and it is closely surrounded by other buildings. Work continued until 1715, but the façade was never completed.

The plan has a single nave, with three large bays, impressively tall and monumental, the finishes opulent but restrained. A giant order of Corinthian pilasters frames the flank walls, terminating in a massive continuous trabeation. There are three chapels down each side; the nave is lit by high-level thermal windows, and is covered with a simple plastered vault. The lateral altars were added in 1725, perhaps by Domenico Rossi. In 1750 the chancel was begun by Massari, who added a cupola above the altar, following Gaspari's intention. The nave statues are mostly by Giuseppe Torretto, while the altarpieces are by G. B. Tiepolo, Amigoni, Morleiter and Giambattista Piazzetta.

Back in the square, turn down Ramo de la Fava, along the flank of the church. At the end is the **Oratorio de San Filippo Neri**, a rectangular upper hall, approached by steep steps. The ceiling contains a large eighteenth-century fresco. Most of the other fittings are dispersed. Take Calle de la Fava; halfway down, at CS 5601, is **Palazzetto Gussoni**, with a small but rich façade to Rio de la Fava; visible from Ponte San Antonio, and from Corte Zocchi, off the E

Palazzetto Gussoni: detail of the canal façade, very early sixteenth century

side of Campo San Bartolomeo. The *palazzetto* is noted for this rich early sixteenth-century Renaissance façade, all of finely carved stone and marble; probably commissioned by Jacopo Gussoni, patron of the chapel in nearby San Lio (see below). The asymmetrical façade reflects the plan behind it, with the main hall to one side, lit by a tall *quadrifora*. The left side is built on corbels over a narrow alley, and has two tall single windows. All the main openings are framed by pilasters finished with refined relief carving in the Lombardo manner. The much plainer upper floor was added later. The plan is unusual; although the canal façade is narrow, the plan widens out and is built around a square central courtyard.

At the end of Calle de la Fava, enter the small, busy Campo San Lio. **San Lio (Leone)** was founded by the Badoer in the ninth century; originally dedicated to St Catherine, in 1054 it was changed to honour Pope Leo x, who had defended the Venetian church's independence. It was reconstructed several times; the present church was built in 1783. In 1810 it became subordinate to Santa Maria Formosa.

The *campo* façade is broad and plain; two orders and a stone pedimented portal. Inside: a single large spacious nave; there is little of architectural importance, other than the Gussoni Chapel, on the right side, *circa* 1480–90, and a survivor from the earlier fabric. It has been attributed to Pietro Lombardo, but is probably by one of the many other Lombard masters in the city in this period. The plan is square, and the chapel is approached by a rich, heavy classical, pedimented archway. Four radiused arches springing from the corner pilasters support a cupola on pendentives. The cupola is ribbed, differing from other early examples at San Giobbe and San Michele; *tondi* of the Evangelists are set into the pendentives. All the finishes are rich, with marble cladding to the walls and the semi-dome of the apse.

A few notable paintings: above the sixteenth-century high altar is *Christ Sustained by Angels* by Palma il Giovane; second altar, left side: *James the Apostle* by Titian, in poor condition; on the nave ceiling: *St Leo in Glory* by G. D. Tiepolo.

Back in the square: on the N side (CS 5658) a small early house from the thirteenth or fourteenth century. On the second floor: a good *quadrifora*, while on the top floor is a full-width three-bay *liagò*, or covered loggia.

Continue down Salizada San Lio, an important route, with several other early surviving buildings. On the SW side, at CS 5472 and adjacent numbers, a terrace of four fourteenth-century Gothic houses, with shops below. At CS 5691–705 (NE side), a high-level arch connects two blocks; the left one has a *bifora*, probably thirteenth century. A little further, on the same side, at CS 5662–72, is a second example, the arch spanning Calle del Volto; another two-light window of similar date.

A little further on the left is the well-known **Calle del Paradiso**, one of the best-preserved medieval streets in Venice, with two long parallel blocks, extending to Ponte del Paradiso. The terraces originally consisted of shops or workshops on the ground floor and a single storey of accommodation above, supported on continuous *barbacani*. Today, the section towards the Salizada is mainly sixteenth century, although a plaque on the Salizada wall bears the date 1407, when some of the houses were built. The section towards the bridge is earlier, with some thirteenth-century material, and some later medieval. At the E end, the blocks are united by the Foscari Mocenigo arch (early fifteenth century), bearing the arms of both families, joined by a marriage in 1491. The twenty-six houses in the

calle formed part of the marriage settlement. On both faces is a large relief, the *Madona de la Misericordia*, surmounted by a quatrefoil and a steeply pointed arch.

Abutting the NW side of the arch is **Palazzetto Foscari Mocenigo** (CS 5743–5); façade to the canal. Originally thirteenth century; the façade has a *trifora* and a single window from that period, as well as a later Gothic watergate and Renaissance elements.

The Arco del Paradiso, early fifteenth century, with the Foscari and Mocenigo arms

16 SANTA MARIA FORMOSA (2) AND SANTA MARINA

Cross Ponte del Paradiso, turning right along Fondamenta dei Preti; a short *ramo* (left) brings us back into Campo Santa Maria Formosa. The N end is occupied by the imposing **Palazzo Ruzzini Loredan Priuli** (CS 5866): the canal façade to Rio del Pestrin is probably mid-sixteenth century, but the palace's completion is generally attributed to Manopola (after 1580) for the Ruzzini; it was completed *circa* 1600. The palace has a broad but shallow plan, basically tripartite but with an additional wing on one side. The central axis runs from the *campo* façade to the canal at the rear; two spacious *piani nobili*, and two watergates. The canal façade (difficult to see) is typically sixteenth century, but that to the square is an impressive composition deriving from Scamozzi. It is articulated with string-courses and pilasters, with three superimposed orders: Doric, Ionic and Corinthian. The main upper halls have prominent stone balconies to the four *portego* windows, and the roofline is capped by an *abbaino*. The picturesque chimneys are not original.

The adjacent NE side of the square is lined with a good group of mostly Gothic palaces, beginning with **Palazzo Donà** (CS 6121–2), in the corner adjacent to Ponte del Borgoloco. Originally Gothic, as

Palazzo Donà in Campo Santa Maria Formosa;
Gothic, *circa* 1460

can be seen from surviving windows on the flank wall to the short
calle. This façade has two fine superimposed sixteenth-century
quadrifore, one Ionic, the other Corinthian, both with balconies. The
tabernacle on the wall once contained a miracle-working image of
the *Virgin* (1612), today in the nearby church. The water façade has a
Serliana and the family arms.

Continuing along this side of the square, the second **Palazzo
Donà** (cs 6123–4) is Gothic, with an almost symmetrical tripartite
façade, but an off-centre portal. The main storey has a good florid
quadrifora, mid-fifteenth century. Right again is a third **Palazzo Donà**
(cs 6125–6), with a narrow, asymmetrical plan and façade, probably
circa 1460. The portal is also offset to the right, but has an early
Renaissance shield, supported by *putti*, in the tympanum. The
fenestration is partly trilobate – rather archaic – and partly *gotico
fiorito*. Some windows (first and third floors) are framed in soft
yellow sandstone (very unusual), badly weathered. The deep plan has
a rear façade onto Corte del Pestrin.

Finally: the long, low **Palazzetto Venier** (cs 6127–30), extending
to the corner of the Calle Lunga. Gothic again, probably *circa* 1450–

70, with a broad, asymmetrical, tripartite plan and façade. The ground floor has always been occupied by commercial functions; the *piano nobile* is the second floor, with a *quadrifora* and the usual flanking windows, but irregularly spaced.

Return to the NE corner of the square, and cross the bridge into **Borgoloco Pompeo Molmenti**, named after a noted historian. The house at CS 5867 is early seventeenth century, with a tripartite façade of unusual proportions; massive *barbacani* support the upper floors. Continue NW, over the next bridge, and into **Campo Santa Marina**. On the S side: two sixteenth-century apartment blocks, united by a high-level arch, the usual device indicating common ownership.

The square lacks its church, founded in the eleventh century, and which survived until its demolition in 1820, following years of undignified use as a tavern. It contained two ducal monuments, to Michele Steno (+1413) and Niccolò Marcello (+1474), both reassembled at Santi Giovanni e Paolo (q.v.). The church stood on the site of the present hotel. At the W end of the square (CS 6043–4): an attractive sixteenth-century *palazzetto*, while on the NE side is **Palazzo Dolfin Bollani** (CS 6073–5), probably later thirteenth century; the *campo* façade is earlier than that to the canal, as indicated by the five-light window to the second floor, with stilted arches. Directly below are later, Gothic windows; the canal façade, too, is mostly Gothic, with superimposed *quadrifore*.

Leave the square by the NW corner, take the *sotoportego* and Calle Scaleta, as far as Ponte Marco Polo; on the right (NE) is the water façade of **Palazzo Bragadin Carabba** (CS 6039–48), facing the Malibran Theatre. Fifteenth-century Gothic, with superimposed *quadrifore* and the family arms. The house was modernised internally by Sanmicheli in the sixteenth century; he may also have designed the land gate (off Campo Santa Marina), in the form of a triumphal arch. Return to Campo Santa Marina, and re-trace the route back towards Santa Maria Formosa. On the left (CS 6107–8) is **Palazzo Marcello Pindemonte Papadopoli**, the water façade of which can be seen from Ponte del Cristo, just off the square. Originally Gothic, acquired in 1474 by Doge Niccolò Marcello. It was rebuilt by Longhena (*circa* 1640s), but in the eighteenth century was extended towards the street by the Pindemonte. The canal façade is robustly detailed, with rustication to the lower levels, and two *piani nobili*. Two huge stone *stemmi* were added by the Papadopoli after 1808. Land access is via the rear courtyard, with an attractive balcony/loggia to the upper floor. After it was bought by the Papadopoli, the interior was enriched in the Neo-classical style by Francesco Hayez, Giovanni Borsato and Carlo Bevilacqua. Next door is **Palazzetto Simonetti** (CS 6109); a Gothic land gate gives onto a courtyard with an open staircase. Back in the Borgoloco, to the left there are Gothic portals at CS 6108 and 6109, and Gothic houses at CS 6112 and 6113; those on the other side are mostly sixteenth to seventeenth century.

1 7   SANTA MARIA FORMOSA (3) AND SAN GIOVANNI LATERANO

Re-enter Campo Santa Maria Formosa and turn into the Calle Lunga. To the N is a series of long, straight *calli* leading to a group of houses with water façades to Rio del Pestrin and Rio de Santa Marina. Some may be seen from Calle del Verrocchio, off the corner of Campo Santi Giovanni e Paolo. They are described here as approached by land.

Palazzo Morosini dal Pestrin (CS 6140), access via Corte del Pestrin, off the Calle Lunga: an impressive seventeenth-century house, with a powerful Palladian water façade, including a rusticated watergate. Two *piani nobili*, both with *trifore* and balconies; pedimented first-floor windows. Land access via a small, attractive garden. **Palazzetto Cocco** (CS 6165): at the end of the long, narrow Calle Cocco. A small eighteenth-century house, with a robust late Baroque façade; the narrow façade masks a deep, elongated plan. **Palazzo Bondulmer Pisani** (CS 6213) is at the far end of Calle Cicogna, just before Ponte Minich; sixteenth-century Renaissance, with two superimposed *trifore*.

Take Calle Bragadin, the last on the left off the Calle Lunga; cross Ponte Conzafelzi at the end. On the left (CS 6317) is a Gothic house, modernised in the sixteenth century; today a hotel. Across the bridge, on the right a narrow walkway leads to a *sotoportego*, which in turn leads into **Corte Bottera** (CS 6267–81), a picturesque semi-private courtyard, the nucleus of which is the house of the Contarini dalla Zogia. The finely carved thirteenth-century portal has survived (opposite), although damaged; remains of an external stair down the E side. From the adjacent quay, looking E, we see the unusual end façade of **Palazzo Tetta** (CS 6378–9), where Rio de San Giovanni Laterano divides into two. The plan is trapezoidal, with two longer façades to the north and south. The house was originally Gothic, but modernised in the seventeenth century.

To reach Palazzo Tetta and San Giovanni Laterano, return over the bridge, back down Calle Bragadin into the Calle Lunga. Turn left, along the Fondamenta and over Ponte Tetta. Continue along Calle Tetta, and then right along Fondamenta San Giovanni Laterano. The former monastic house occupies most of the eastern part of the island. Take Calle San Giovanni, then Fondamenta Seconda to Campielo Cappello.

San Giovanni Laterano originated in a small oratory of unknown date. In 1504 an Augustinian nunnery was established here, aggregated to the Lateran canons in Rome. It nearly closed in the sixteenth century after a fire, but was revived and flourished. During the early seventeenth century the nunnery was rebuilt, with several floors of accommodation around a large central courtyard. The little church was also restored in 1763. The house was suppressed in 1806, and the accommodation used as a barracks, later a high school and a technical institute. The chapel was partially demolished in 1810. The main surviving structure is the imposing block between the two branches of the *rio*, bounded on the E by Campielo Cappello. The courtyard has a stone colonnade on all sides, with four storeys above, all of very simple appearance.

The group of houses known as **Palazzo Cappello** and **Palazzo Maggi Cappello** occupy the E side of the *campielo*, with canals on the other three sides. Two principal buildings, the southern one mainly Gothic, probably *circa* 1440s, with a land gate (now filled in) adjacent to the bridge. The long E canal façade (partly visible from Campo San Lorenzo) has three main elements: the tall S section is *gotico fiorito*, then a smaller Gothic section, and then the later northern part, the Renaissance element known as Palazzo Maggi Cappello; late sixteenth century, and attributed to the Contin.

18 BARBARIA DE LE TOLE AND THE OSPEDALETO

From the N end of the *campielo*, take Ponte Muazzo. To the right is the formidable pile known as the **Palazzi Muazzo** (CS 6451–5), built by the Giustiniani, early seventeenth century. The water façades take the form of two adjacent palaces, with two *piani nobili*. The complex is built to very high density around the central courtyard, the inland blocks having no fewer than eight storeys. Access to the courtyard is by Sotoportego Muazzo, with curious, archaic capitals. Immediately E of the water façades is that of **Palazzo Bragadin Bigaglia** (CS 6480), originally Gothic, with land access off Calle del Cafetier (see below). Two watergates and two *piani nobili*.

The next three palaces all have water façades to Rio de San Giovanni Laterano, and land access from Calle del Cafetier and Campo Santa Giustina. To reach Calle del Cafetier, take Calle Muazzo, then turn right into the busy Calle del Cafetier. Its E end opens into Campo Santa Giustina (de la Barbaria). At CS 6495 is **Palazzo Basadonna**, with an attractive Lombard Renaissance water façade (early sixteenth century); next is **Palazzo Zon Zatta** (CS 2836 and 6511), and **Palazzo Cima Zon** (CS 6512), with water façade towards Santa Giustina; originally fourteenth century, but much altered in the eighteenth.

Take the long, narrow Calle de le Capucine out of the NW corner of Campo de la Barbaria; at the far end are the Fondamente Nove. On the left is **Santa Maria del Pianto**, founded by order of the Senate in the 1640s as a Capuchin nunnery, in a remote, isolated location. Construction began in 1649; the compact monastic buildings stand directly S of the church, around a small colonnaded cloister. Once attributed to Longhena, the church is now ascribed to Francesco Contin; it was consecrated in 1687. The nunnery survived until the Napoleonic suppression in 1810.

The church has an unusual octagonal plan, with four longer and four shorter facets; one of the longer facets, facing north, forms the façade. There were originally seven altars, although only three remain. Each principal bay is defined internally by a large arch, flanked by Corinthian pilasters. The intended central octagonal cupola was never built, and the nave has a simple flat ceiling.

Return down Calle de le Capucine, and turn right (W) along Calle del Cafetier, which becomes Barbaria de le Tole. The second part of the name derives from the planks of wood (*tole* = *tavole*) from the timber yards that once occupied the land between the street and the lagoon to the N. Near the W end, right, is the extraordinary Baroque façade of the **Ospedaletto (Santa Maria dei Derelitti)**, founded in 1527 by the Republic to care for the old and infirm. In 1662 Bartolomeo Carnioni left a large sum in his will for its enlargement and modernisation, and so that it could accommodate poor young girls. Two years later Sardi was appointed to rebuild the church, but was dismissed two years later, following a dispute. He had begun the refectory and a new wing with an elegant oval staircase. Longhena completed the project, including the

The Ospedaleto: detail of the façade, by Baldassare
Longhena, 1670–72

dormitory and the extravagant street façade (1670–72). In the
eighteenth century the delightful Sala de la Musica was added by
Matteo Lucchesi; like the other charitable establishments, the
Ospedaleto had developed a famous reputation for music. It retained
its original function until 1807, when it became a convalescent home
for older people, as it remains today.

Longhena's exaggerated, deeply sculpted façade is a response to the
narrow street: it can be seen only from an acute angle. The lower
order is defined by raking buttresses, while the upper one has huge
stone caryatids supporting the upper cornice; in the centre is a bust
of the benefactor, Carnioni.

The church interior is almost all by Longhena; a single aisle-less
volume, with a flat painted ceiling. It contains paintings by Palma il
Giovane, G. B. Tiepolo and Gregorio Lazzarini. Lucchesi's Sala de la
Musica is an attractive small hall, decorated with *trompe l'œil*
columns and entablatures. At one end is a curved choir gallery; the
ceiling is frescoed by Guarana and Agostin Mengozzi Colonna
(1776).

Continue W down the short Salizada Santi Giovanni e Paolo, into the large, spacious square, its N side dominated by the vast mass of the eponymous church.

19 SANTI GIOVANNI E PAOLO, THE SCUOLA GRANDE DI SAN MARCO, THE OSPEDALE CIVILE AND SAN LAZZARO DEI MENDICANTI

The final part of the tour of Castello includes its most outstanding monument, the great monastic church of Santi Giovanni e Paolo. There is a close historical connection between the four buildings noted above, and we start with **San Lazzaro dei Mendicanti**, reached by crossing the square in front of the great church, and walking N along the Fondamenta dei Mendicanti, towards the Fondamente Nove. It was established by a group of wealthy Venetians at the end of the sixteenth century; construction took place in conjunction with that of the Fondamente Nove (see below,

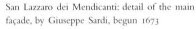

San Lazzaro dei Mendicanti: detail of the main façade, by Giuseppe Sardi, begun 1673

Campo Santi Giovanni e Paolo, from de' Barbari's engraving of 1500

pp. 173–4), and the friary was built on reclaimed land. The associated 'hospital' was to house the poor and indigent, as well as orphan girls, who were educated here. Many were taught music, and the house developed a reputation similar to that of the Ospedaleto and the Pietà. Scamozzi, the architect, took as his model Palladio's Zitelle, where the church is located centrally and flanked by two blocks of accommodation; the Mendicanti is considerably more ambitious, with both side wings planned around large courtyards.

Construction began in 1601 and took thirty years. The monumental Palladian church façade (begun 1673) was added later by Giuseppe Sardi, funded by the wealthy Jacopo Gallo. A giant Corinthian order, and a large triangular pediment; three statues enliven the skyline. The flanking accommodation has three storeys, with simple, severe façades.

The church plan has a single nave without aisles, and was designed for the dual use of services and musical recitals. It is approached by a transverse lobby, providing acoustic isolation. The impressive rectangular nave terminates with a square chancel; down the two sides are the choir galleries, reached directly from the two side wings. Nave side altars: right side, first altar: *Christ on the Cross* by Veronese; second altar: *Annunciation* by Giuseppe Porta; left side, first altar: *Adoration of St Helena*, by Guercino, his only work in Venice; second altar: *St Ursula* by Tintoretto.

We return to the square.

Santi Giovanni e Paolo: the west portal, by Bartolomeo Bon, 1458–62

Santi Giovanni e Paolo (San Zanipolo) is one of the city's greatest medieval churches, and repository of a superb collection of ducal monuments. It originated in 1234 when Doge Jacopo Tiepolo (supported by the Republic) donated a large, marshy tract of land to the Dominicans, then established in the city for about ten years, following St Dominic's visit in 1221. The first church was completed in the later thirteenth century. It rapidly became far too small, and reconstruction began on a much larger scale in the early fourteenth century; work began at the east end, and the apses were built by *circa* 1340. By 1368 the church was complete as far as the east end of the nave. The nave itself was built in 1390–1430, and was consecrated in the latter year; in 1458–62 Bartolomeo Bon's magnificent west portal was added. In 1448 the chapel of the Nome di Gesù was added to the s aisle, although its interior was remodelled in the Baroque manner in 1639. During the fifteenth century an ornate choir was added in the centre, but was destroyed in 1682. Further additions included Vittoria's Rosary Chapel, off the N transept (begun 1575); the chapel of San Domenico (south aisle, 1582); the sacristy (north aisle, by Scamozzi, 1605); and finally, the Valier Chapel, again off the south aisle (Tirali, 1705–8). The friary was suppressed in 1806, but four years later the church was given parish status, under the administration of the Dominicans, which it retains today.

The façade is a noble, imposing example of *gotico fiorito*, although never completed with stone cladding to the lower part, as intended. Bon's portal is a masterful, mature work, with Renaissance elements in the rich decoration. The main arch is Gothic, framed by Corinthian marble columns, but the entablature incorporates rich Renaissance relief work. Flanking the portal are ducal sarcophagi, including those of Jacopo Tiepolo (+1249) and his son Lorenzo (+1275). On the skyline are three Dominican saints, Thomas Aquinas, Dominic and Peter Martyr. The exterior of the Addolorata Chapel, projecting into the square, and the rich complex eastern apses exemplify the Venetian tradition of fine decorative brickwork. The latter are especially impressive, with the deep faceted central apse flanked on each side by pairs of tall, narrow, side chapels.

The plan and the interior: together with the Frari (q.v.) it is the largest church in Venice, with internal dimensions of 101 metres in length, 46 metres wide across the transepts and 32 metres in height to the nave vaulting. The plan is a Latin cross, with a five-bay nave, the chief function of which was a clear open space to preach to large congregations. The extremely large bays (15 × 13 m) are defined by huge, plain, cylindrical stone piers, with transverse timber tie beams above the capitals. Above the tall clerestory are simple brick-ribbed cross-vaults. At the square crossing, the cupola is supported on plain pendentives. The aisles are half the width of the nave, and considerably lower; the transepts each have a single very large rectangular bay. Beyond the crossing are the five deep eastern chapels; the larger central one, the chancel itself, has a square bay with a faceted eastern end, and seven exceptionally tall narrow lancet windows.

The interior: this summary proceeds anti-clockwise from inside the west doorway. Inner face of the west façade: Mocenigo family monuments. Monument to Doge Alvise Mocenigo I (+1577) by Grapiglia; right side: monument to Bartolomeo Bragadin (+1507) by Lorenzo Bregno; monument to Doge Giovanni Mocenigo (+1485) by

Santi Giovanni e Paolo: detail of the eastern apses

Santi Giovanni e Paolo: monument to Doge Pietro Mocenigo by Pietro Lombardo, 1481

Tullio Lombardo, a refined Renaissance work. Left of the entrance: monument to Doge Pietro Mocenigo (+1476) by Pietro Lombardo, 1481; an exceptionally fine, ambitious work, beautifully lit by raking light from one side.

Nave, right aisle, first bay: high-level monument to Doge Renier Zeno (+1268). First altar: the *Virgin and Saints* altarpiece, by a follower of Giovanni Bellini. Between first and second altars: monument to Marcantonio Bragadin (+1571). Second altar: famous polyptych of St Vincent Ferrer, by Giovanni Bellini (and assistants), 1464. Third bay: no altar; instead, the Addolorata Chapel, dedicated in 1563 to the Nome di Gesù, and in 1639 transformed again into the present Baroque appearance, and new dedication. Fourth bay: Valier family chapel, overwhelmed by the vast mausoleum that precedes it. The monument, a huge triumphal arch, is to Doge Bertuccio Valier (+1658) by Tirali, 1708. Fifth bay: no side altar, but the chapel of San Domenico (or the Blessed Sacrament) by Tirali (*circa* 1690–1716), with richly gilded vaulting by Francesco Bernardoni. In the ceiling: the fine *Glory of St Dominic* by Giambattista Piazzetta, 1727.

Right (s) transept: on the side wall: *Christ Bearing the Cross* by Alvise Vivarini, 1474; *Coronation of the Virgin* by Giovanni da Udine.

At high level: monument to Niccolò Orsini; two figures of the Virtues by Tullio Lombardo. The s wall is filled by a magnificent stained-glass window, mostly of fifteenth-century Murano glass, although restored and augmented. The six orders represent: top: *God the Father*; first row: the *Annunciation*; second row: *Virgin and Child with SS Paul, Peter and John the Baptist*; third row: quatrefoils of the *Four Evangelists*; fourth row: the *Doctors of the Early Church*; fifth row: *Dominican Saints*; sixth row: *Warrior Saints*. At low level on the end wall, right side: *St Anthony* altarpiece, by Lorenzo Lotto.

South transept chapels: first chapel (of the Crucifixion or of the Dead): altar and bronze figures all by Vittoria; right wall: monument to Edward Windsor (+1574), again by Vittoria. Second chapel (of the Magdalene): on the vault: frescoes of the Evangelists, perhaps by Palma il Giovane; right wall: monument to Vettor Pisani (+1370), victor of the War of Chioggia; the altarpiece is a good Lombard Renaissance work.

Chancel and high altar: right wall: monument to Doge Michele Morosini (+1382), a fine late Gothic work. On the same wall: monument to Doge Leonardo Loredan (+1521), erected in 1572 by Grapiglia; the naturalistic figure of the doge is by Campagna, the flanking figures by Danese Cattaneo. The high altar: a grandiose Baroque work, *circa* 1619, perhaps by Mattia Carnero. Chancel, left wall: monument to Doge Andrea Vendramin (+1478), an exceptional work by Tullio Lombardo, rich and imposing. It was originally in the Servi; transferred here in 1817 when the Servi was deconsecrated (and then demolished). On the same wall: monument to Doge Marco Corner (+1368), by Nino Pisano, relocated to make room for the Vendramin monument. Nearby are two pulpits, formerly part of the lost choir, *circa* 1513–21.

North transept chapels: first chapel (of the Holy Trinity): altarpiece by Leandro Bassano; on the walls: late Gothic monuments to Pietro Corner and Andrea Morosini. Above is the *Adoration of the Shepherds*, attributed to Veronese. Second chapel (of Pope Pius v, formerly Cavalli family): right wall: monument to Jacopo Cavalli (+1384) by Paolo dalle Masegne; left wall: monument to Doge Giovanni Delfin (+1361). North transept: on the end wall: bronze figure of Sebastiano Venier, victor of Lepanto (1571), by Antonio dal Zotto, 1907; below the clock: monument to Doge Antonio Venier (+1400); to the left of the portal: monuments to his wife Agnese and daughter Orsola.

Facing page: Santi Giovanni e Paolo: interior of the chancel: high altar (*circa* 1619) by Mattia Carnero

The doorway in the end wall leads to the large Rosary Chapel, by Vittoria, begun 1582. It was destroyed by fire on 16 August 1867; many works were lost, including paintings by Titian, Tintoretto, Palma il Giovane and Francesco Bassano. Restoration finally concluded only in 1959. The ceiling has three inset pictures by Veronese. On the walls are paintings by Giambattista Zelotti, Carlo Caliari (son of Veronese) and Bonifacio de' Pitati. In the sanctuary: further pictures by Veronese; altar by Campagna; the four statues behind the altar survived the fire, two by Campagna and two by Vittoria.

Back in the church: north aisle, fifth bay (adjacent to the transept): organ gallery, with famous eighteenth-century organ by Callido. Below: triptych by Bartolomeo Vivarini, 1473. Entrance to the sacristy: by Scamozzi, part of what was intended to be a monument to the two Palma and Titian; the latter is instead in the Frari.

Sacristy: by Scamozzi; ceiling of white and gold stucco, lunettes by Leandro da Bassano. On the right wall: *Resurrection* by Palma il Giovane.

North aisle, fourth bay: monument to Doge Pasquale Malipiero (+1462) by Pietro Lombardo, a notable work, perhaps his first major Venetian commission, still a mixture of Gothic and Renaissance elements. Next: a double doorway, formerly leading to the cloisters. Adjacent: figures of St Dominic and St Thomas Aquinas, attributed to Antonio Lombardo. Inside the first archway: monument to Doge Michele Steno (+1413), brought here from Santa Marina in 1811, badly damaged. Next: equestrian monument in gilded wood to the *condottiere* (mercenary captain) Pompeo Giustinian (+1616).

Third bay: adjacent is the monument to Doge Tommaso Mocenigo (+1423), very late Gothic with Renaissance hints, by Pietro Lamberti and Giovanni da Fiesole. Next again, between the third and second bays: monument to Doge Niccolò Marcello (+1474), a fine work by Pietro Lombardo, *circa* 1481–4, simpler but more powerful than his other two in this church. Adjacent: memorial slab to Doge Marin Zorzi (+1312), transferred from the nearby cloister.

Second bay: altar of St Peter Martyr; the altarpiece is a copy of a work by Titian. Next: monument to the Bandiera brothers and Domenico Moro (+1844), heroes of the Risorgimento. First bay: altar of Verde Scaligera (+1364), daughter of the Marquis of Ferrara; originally in the Servi; by Guglielmo de' Grigi, 1524; figure of St Jerome by Vittoria, 1576.

When the church was completed, there was little space to the north for **the conventual buildings**, which were built in stages as reclamation proceeded. None of the earliest survives; they were all replaced in the later seventeenth century by the present extensive complex by Longhena, begun *circa* 1660. The buildings are planned around three open spaces, two cloisters and a *cortile*, in a row from s to N; they are all linked by an extremely long corridor down the E side, and from which all the friars' cells were reached; at the s end the corridor connects directly to the church. Partway down the corridor, on the E side, is Longhena's fine monumental staircase (1664), derived from that at San Giorgio. The library is another notable work, again by Longhena, retaining its richly carved interior fittings. It was opened to the public in 1683. The friary survived until 1809; it then became a military hospital. Ten years later it became a civil hospital, and the buildings form part of the Ospedale Civile today.

We return to the square. On the N side is the extraordinary façade of the former **Scuola Grande de San Marco**. It was one of the three original *scuole grandi*, founded in 1260, and originally based at Santa Croce. Like the others, it was a voluntary lay confraternity, which all classes of society could join, engaging in devotions, processions and charitable activities, principally to their members and their families. Although the *scuole grandi* had equal status, the fact that this one was dedicated to the Republic's own patron gave it a particular prominence.

In 1437 the Scuola transferred to Santi Giovanni e Paolo, leasing the present site from the monastery. The first Scuola was built with great speed, but in 1485 it was destroyed by fire. The Republic granted funds for its reconstruction, and the present building was completed between *circa* 1487 and the mid-1490s. Its plan and accommodation follow the pattern characteristic of the *scuole grandi*: a large ground-floor hall, the *androne*, directly above which stands the *sala capitolare*, the assembly hall for Masses and other gatherings of the membership. On the right side is a much smaller wing, which on the first floor contains the *albergo*, the room where the governing board met, and where valuable relics were kept.

The architect was Pietro Lombardo, assisted by Giovanni Buora; they began the lower hall and the façade, but after eighteen months Lombardo was dismissed and replaced by Mauro Codussi, who completed the upper façade and the upper hall from November 1490 to 1495; he also built the fine double-branch staircase.

The Scuola's most remarkable feature is the rich, complex façade, entirely clad with marble and enriched with statuary. It consists of

Scuola Grande di San Marco: detail of the upper left façade, begun by Pietro Lombardo, *circa* 1487, completed by Mauro Codussi, 1490–95

Scuola Grande di San Marco: upper right façade by Mauro Codussi, 1490–95

two elements: the larger, to the left, is the façade to the *androne* and the chapter hall; the three-bay section to the right is the façade of the smaller *albergo* wing. The western part has three bays, the larger central one containing the tall, deeply moulded portal, in which is a lunette relief salvaged from the earlier structure; above, the figure of Charity (Bartolomeo Bon, *circa* 1437) also survived the 1485 fire. The flanking false-relief panels of lions are early works by Tullio Lombardo. The western façade terminates with a crescendo of gables; at high level: a bold winged lion on corbels.

The eastern façade is more restrained, with a fine secondary portal, flanked again by two illusionistic panels representing the healing of Anianus, scenes from the life of St Mark, again by Tullio Lombardo; above is a fine lion *tondo*.

Today the *androne* is the land entrance hall to the city hospital; inside: a double row of columns on tall decorative plinths, with timber beams supporting the chapter hall floor. Down the right side is the staircase, with a fine portal at each end, giving access to two long flights that meet in the middle at the top landing. The upper hall is imposing, although bereft of the original magnificent cycle of paintings that once lined the walls; some are in the Accademia, the rest at the Brera, Milan. The high altar at the north end is by Sansovino (1533). The gilded, coffered ceiling was made by Vettor da Feltre, begun 1519. The *albergo* also has its original blue and gold ceiling, *circa* 1504. Its walls were also lined with a painting cycle, for many years also in the Accademia, but now returned; they include pictures by Mansueti, Domenico Tintoretto and Palma il Vecchio.

The more modern buildings of the Ospedale Civile lie NE of the conventual buildings. Most are fairly undistinguished, although the new emergency department and ward block by Luciano Semerani and Gigetta Tamaro (2000) is of interest. Two elements, influenced by Aldo Rossi, and built in phases: the first a square block with a central atrium, the other a long rectangle, with a row of barrel-vaulted roofs.

Back in the square: on the SW corner is **Palazzo Dandolo** (CS 6824), a substantial seventeenth-century house; just off the south side of the square is the picturesque Corte Bressana (CS 6784). **The Colleoni monument**: in the centre of the square is the splendid bronze equestrian statue of the great *condottiere* Bartolomeo Colleoni; he left funds in his will for his own monument, with the notorious condition that it be erected 'at San Marco'. Since the Republic forbade any personalised monuments in the Piazza di San Marco, it

was decided to relocate it here, at the Scuola Grande di San Marco instead. The commanding figure sits astride 'an ordinary street horse', as it was described at the time; it is mostly by the Florentine sculptor Verrocchio, but completed by Leopardi after his death in 1488; the tall, richly finished marble plinth is also by Leopardi.

The monument to the *condottiere* Bartolomeo Colleoni, begun by Andrea del Verrocchio, 1481–8, completed by Alessandro Leopardi

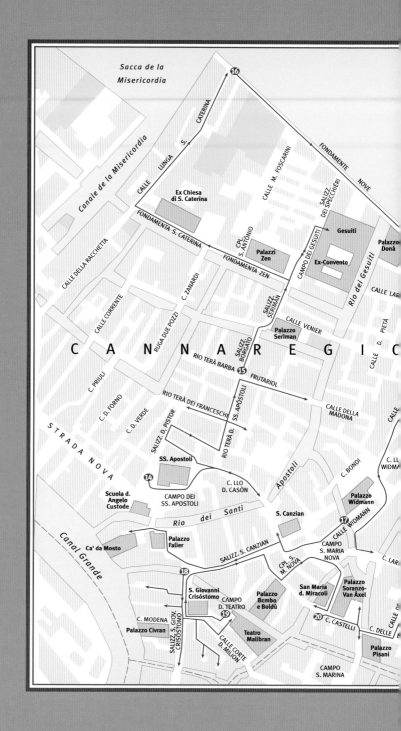

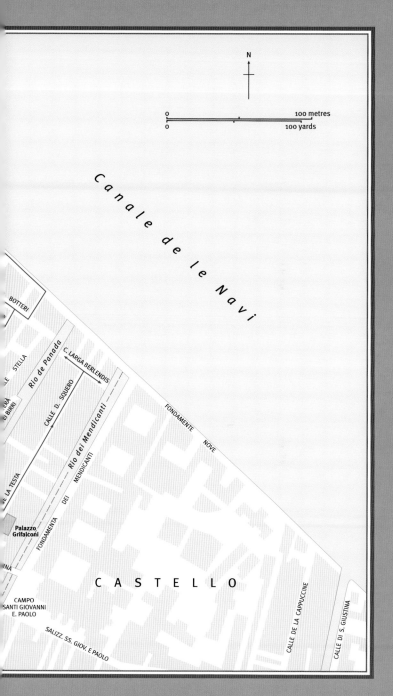

BOTTERI

STELLA

Rio de Panada

C. LARGA BERLENDIS

CALLE D. SQUERO

Rio dei Mendicanti

DEI MENDICANTI

FONDAMENTE NOVE

EL BIRRI

E LA TESTA

FONDAMENTA

Palazzo
Grifalconi

CASTELLO

CALLE DE LA CAPPUCCINE

CALLE DI S. GIUSTINA

CAMPO
SANTI GIOVANNI
E. PAOLO

SALIZZ. SS. GIOV. E PAOLO

Canale de le Navi

N

0   100 metres
0   100 yards

Cannaregio East

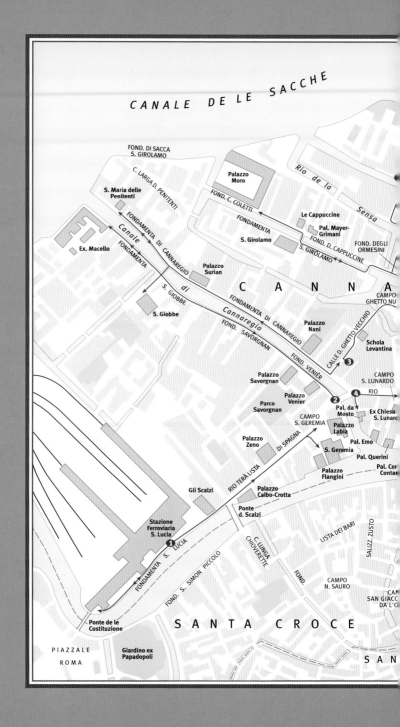

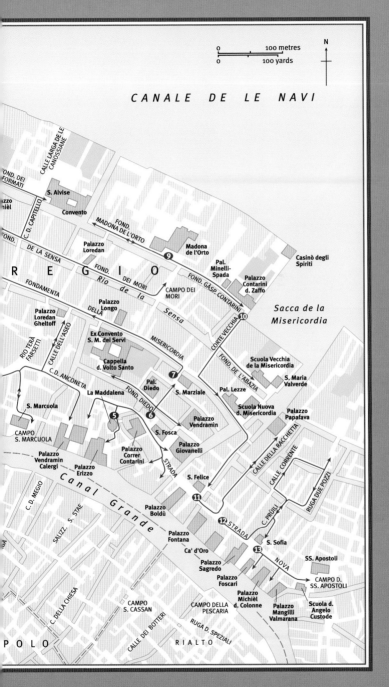

CANALE DE LE NAVI

N

0   100 metres
0   100 yards

Sacca de la
Misericordia

Casinò degli
Spiriti

CALLE LARGA DE LE
CANOSSIANE

FOND. DEI
FORMATI

S. Alvise

Convento

Palazzo
chièl

C. D. CAPITELLO

FOND.

DE LA SENSA

FOND.
MADONA DE L'ORTO

Palazzo
Loredan

Madona
de l'Orto

Pal. Minelli-
Spada

Palazzo
Contarini
d. Zaffo

R E G I O

FOND. DEI MORI

Rio de la

Sensa

FOND. GASP. CONTARINI

CAMPO DEI
MORI

FONDAMENTA

Palazzo
Loredan
Gheltoff

Palazzo
Longo

FOND. DELLA

MISERICORDIA

CORTE VECCHIA

Scuola Vecchia
de la Misericordia

S. Maria
Valverde

RIO TERÀ
FARSETTI

CALLE DELL'ASEO

Ex Convento
S. M. dei Servi

FOND. DE L'ABAZIA

C.D. ANCONETA

Cappella
d. Volto Santo

Pal.
Diedo

7

Pal. Lezze

S. Marciale

S. Marcuola

La Maddalena

FOND. DIEDO

6

Palazzo
Vendramin

Scuola Nuova
d. Misericordia

Palazzo
Papafava

5

S. Fosca

CAMPO
S. MARCUOLA

Palazzo
Vendramin
Calergi

Palazzo
Erizzo

Palazzo
Correr
Contarini

STRADA

Palazzo
Giovanelli

CALLE DELLA RACCHETTA

CALLE CORRENTE

C. D. MEGIO

Canal Grande

SALIZZ. S. STAE

S. Felice

11

RUGA DUE POZZI

C. PRÜLI

Palazzo
Boldù

12 STRADA

13

S. Sofia

SS. Apostoli

Palazzo
Fontana

Ca' d'Oro

Palazzo
Sagredo

NOVA

CAMPO D.
SS. APOSTOLI

C. DELLA CHIESA

CAMPO
S. CASSAN

CAMPO DELLA
PESCARIA

Palazzo
Foscari

Palazzo
Michièl
d. Colonne

Palazzo
Mangilli
Valmarana

Scuola d.
Angelo
Custode

P O L O

CALLE DEI BOTTERI

RUGA D. SPEZIALI

R I A L T O

Cannaregio West

Sestiere of Cannaregio

This extensive *sestiere* covers most of the northern part of Venice. Its name probably derives from the reeds (*canne*) that were widespread in this marshy, marginal area. It is defined to the south by the Grand Canal, to the north and west by the lagoon; to the east, it abuts Castello. Cannaregio's development is best understood in terms of its relationship with the city's commercial centre, Rialto, and with the Grand Canal. The small nucleus of Santi Apostoli was one of the first island parishes to be settled; the castle-palace of Doge Angelo Partecipazio (811–27) was located here, and was the seat of government before the definitive Doge's Palace on its present site was begun.

Further settlements followed, most forming a chain of island parishes along the north bank of the Grand Canal: San Marcuola, also *circa* 810–11, San Geremia (813), Santa Sofia (866) and Santa Fosca (873). They were followed by a second wave a century or more later, including San Felice (960), La Madalena and San Lunardo (both in 1025), and San Marziale in 1133. For some time lay settlement was largely confined to this chain along the north bank of the canal. In the same era, though, monastic houses were founded further north, first Santa Maria in Valverde (939), followed by the Madona de l'Orto (1192), and later again, the important nunnery of the Servi (1316) and Sant'Alvise (1388). With these exceptions, however, the northern zone remained marginal marshland.

Facing page: Santa Maria dei Miracoli: flank façade to the canal

Although less important than the Grand Canal, the Cannaregio Canal linked the emerging city with the mainland shore; also vital was the short route northwards via the Rio de Noal (Noale), which led towards Murano and the formerly numerous settlements of the northern lagoon, including Burano and Torcello. As the *sestiere* became more highly urbanised, two distinct elements could be identified: first the island parishes, with their characteristically organic forms, and secondly the districts further north, which developed in a much more rational manner in the thirteenth and fourteenth centuries, based on the courses of three parallel canals, the Rio de San Girolamo, the Rio de la Sensa and the Rio de la Madona de l'Orto. This development was modelled on the Cannaregio Canal, and the three newer canals all have continuous quays along their northern sides. This is the only ancient part of Venice that was developed in this rational manner. As it became built up in the fourteenth and fifteenth centuries, the houses were all erected along the three quays, with gardens and orchards behind them. The zone became favoured by the nobility in the Renaissance because there was space to lay out gardens, by now impossible in the densely developed city centre. These northern districts remain a quiet backwater today, their houses varying widely in style and scale, but with a homogeneity resulting from the regular plan of the district.

1 FROM THE FERROVIA TO PALAZZO LABIA

The railway causeway linking Venice to the Terraferma was inaugurated on 11 January 1846; it transformed this zone from a quiet, peripheral district into a major transport hub. To construct the station, the monastery of Corpus Domini was demolished, as was the church of Santa Lucia (which gave its name to the new station), and several noble palaces.

The first station was a utilitarian structure, but in 1854–66 a larger one was built, requiring further demolitions. A design competition for its replacement was launched in 1934, but the project was then 'frozen', and revived in 1952; the present terminus is by Paolo Perilli and the Ferrovie dello Stato (State Railways), and was opened in 1955. It has been widely criticised; although the design itself has merit, its simple, low horizontal form does not relate well to the context, and the large formless space in front lacks character. The station stands on a plinth, and is faced with Istrian stone, with

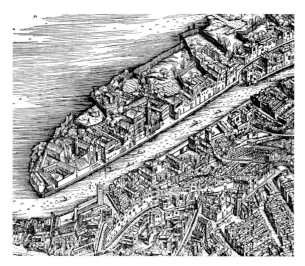

Detail of the former peninsula of Santa Lucia, from de' Barbari's engraving of 1500

Verona *broccatello* detailing. The main concourse lies parallel to the façade, with a flat, coffered roof above a clerestory; the ancillary functions are located at the left and right ends. There is no train shed behind. Despite its shortcomings, the station provides a memorable experience for the visitor arriving by train, with the Grand Canal literally at one's feet.

To the sw is the huge bulk of the **Regional Railway Offices**, built in two phases, the first, late nineteenth century, monumentally Neo-classical, while the second phase, built in the 1930s, is in a heavy international modern style. Neither relate to the context with grace or sensitivity.

At the sw corner of the railway offices is Santiago Calatrava's new **Ponte de la Costituzione**, across the Grand Canal, 2007–8, linking the station with Piazzale Roma. The first since the Accademia and Scalzi bridges were rebuilt in the 1930s: a single, sweeping, shallow-arched span of steel, with a ribbed supporting substructure, and refined stone and glass detailing.

To the e of the station is the **Ponte degli Scalzi**. The first bridge (1852) was of iron, by the British engineering company Neville; it was replaced in 1932 by the present attractive Neo-classical stone structure by Eugenio Miozzi. **Santa Maria de Nazaret (I Scalzi)**

The Scalzi church: Baroque façade by Giuseppe Sardi,
completed 1680

stands at the foot of the bridge, taking its name from the Carmelite
or 'barefoot' (*scalzi*) friars, who arrived from Rome in 1633 and
settled here in 1647. In 1649 Longhena began the monastic
buildings, later demolished to build the station. The church was built
in 1656–89, again by Longhena. It was funded by the nobleman
Girolamo Cavazza, and consecrated in 1705; the dedication arose
from a venerated image brought from an island in the lagoon, the
Lazzaretto Vecchio. The rich Baroque façade is by Sardi, Longhena's
pupil, completed in 1680 and also funded by Cavazza. The
monastery was suppressed in 1810 but the order returned in 1840
and remains there today.

The complex but well-ordered façade is one of the most
important of its era in the city: two superimposed orders, the lower
with five bays, the upper with three, all defined by paired Corinthian

columns. The upper order is flanked by rich volutes, while the façade is crowned by a triangular pediment with a radiused one set inside it. Several large figures enrich the skyline, some by Bernardo Falcone, with others set into niches.

The plan has a nave without aisles, flanked by deep lateral chapels, three on each side. There are no transepts; behind the high altar is a deep choir. The remarkably rich interior has extensive polychrome and inlaid marble, although its slightly fragmented appearance is probably the result of Longhena not retaining control of the later stages of decoration. The flamboyant high altar is by Giuseppe Pozzo, one of the friars. One of the original principal features is lost: the nave ceiling was decorated with a large fresco by Giambattista Tiepolo (1743), destroyed by a bomb in 1915. The side chapels contain monuments to noble clans, including the Giovanelli, Ruzzini and Mora (right side); on the left side that of Ludovico Manin, last doge of the Republic. All the chapels are decorated by Pozzo, Falcone and Giovanni Marchiori. **The Lista di Spagna** is a busy thoroughfare, today entirely devoted to tourism; a few buildings of interest. At CN 122 (and adjacent numbers) is a group of houses of various dates, today a hotel, collectively known as **Palazzo Calbo Crotta**; the earliest parts are fourteenth century. A little further, at CN 134, is the small fifteenth-century **Palazzetto Lezze**; at CN 168 is the imposing **Palazzo Zeno Manin Sceriman**. In the seventeenth century it was the Spanish embassy. The present structure, with its long, eleven-bay façade, dates from a modernisation in 1759–71. The architect is unknown (perhaps Tirali), but it has a noble, severe appearance, with three portals; the lower order is rusticated. The palace is one of a handful from this period that eschewed the usual multi-light central window in favour of a regular pattern of single windows. In the eighteenth century it was owned by Ludovico Manin, the last doge.

Continuing E, at CN 233 is a Gothic portal, the remains of **Palazzo Morosini de la Tressa**. Formerly the French embassy, the house was destroyed after the fall of the Republic. At the end of the Lista on the right is Campielo Flangini; **Palazzo Flangini** (CN 252) has a rich Baroque Grand Canal façade, probably by Sardi. The Flangini were Cypriot nobles who joined the Venetian aristocracy in 1664. They failed to acquire an adjacent plot, so the house is asymmetrical, lacking one wing; it was completed *circa* 1682. The impressive façade has rustication to the two lower floors, and a prominent portal; both *piani nobili* have continuous balconies. The rich sculptures may be by

San Geremia from the Grand Canal; on the right the
chapel of Santa Lucia, 1863

Falcone, who worked at the nearby Scalzi church. The interior is
well preserved, with an *androne* framed by four free-standing columns,
and a fine staircase; original stucco decoration to the *piani nobili*.

The Lista now opens into the spacious Campo San Geremia,
formerly famous for public spectacles such as bull-running. On the
south side: **San Geremia**, probably founded in the eleventh century,
but the earliest records date from 1116. The present grandiose
reconstruction was designed by a priest, Carlo Corbellini (begun
1753), but took decades to complete. The plan revives the Greek
cross, with four equal arms, each terminating with a semicircular apse
and a half-cupola; a large central cupola covers the crossing. The
three similar façades were completed only in 1871, the result of a
legacy from Baron Pasquale Revoltella. The *campo* façade has a heavy
Baroque character, and was modified for those to the E and S. Above
giant Corinthian columns and pilasters is a tall clerestory. The interior
is cold but imposing, with the cupola supported by four massive
piers. Projecting from the south side is a chapel, extended in 1863,

Palazzo Labia: detail of the principal façade to the Cannaregio Canal; probably by Andrea Cominelli and Giorgio Massari, *circa* 1720–50

and dedicated to Santa Lucia, whose remains were brought here following demolition of the nearby church.

Palazzo Labia (CN 275 and 334): a notable Baroque palace, whose looming mass fills the E side of the square. It has two principal façades, this one and that to the Cannaregio Canal, with a short third façade towards the Grand Canal. The palace has a complex history; it was built by the Labia, a wealthy Catalan family, ennobled in Venice in 1646. The site was probably chosen for its proximity to the Spanish embassy, but was constrained by the thirteenth-century campanile of the adjacent church. The palace was built in stages, the first completed *circa* 1663, perhaps by Tremignon. The impressive *campo* façade is comparatively restrained, and was originally symmetrical and tripartite. The second stage (*circa* 1730–40) is perhaps by Andrea Cominelli, although there are attributions to Massari; the two canal façades are both in the manner of Longhena, with bold, rich decoration, rustication, prominent keystones and much use of the carved eagle, the family symbol. The palace was extended towards the N, almost doubling its size and resulting in its present asymmetry. These last stages included the famous ballroom. After the Labia sold the palace, its ownership changed many times; in 1964 it was acquired by RAI (the state TV and radio organisation), which instigated a long programme of restoration.

The core remains the usual Venetian axial hall, three bays wide, extending from the *campo* façade to that facing the Cannaregio Canal; an imposing staircase to the *piano nobile*. The interior is noted for a cycle of frescoes by Giambattista Tiepolo, begun in 1750. It was his most important non-religious commission in Venice, and he worked closely with Girolamo Mengozzi Colonna, who provided the fictive context for Tiepolo's narrative frescoes, including *trompe l'œil* columns, doorways and balconies. The principal paintings are the cycle in the ballroom, depicting scenes from the life of Cleopatra; the main work is the *Banquet*, inspired by Veronese. Other rooms were also decorated by Tiepolo; only two survive, one of which is the Hall of Mirrors.

2 THE CANNAREGIO CANAL

Nearby is the busy **Ponte de le Guglie**, or Ponte de Cannaregio, one of only two bridges across this important waterway. It was originally of timber, but was rebuilt in stone in 1580 and restored in 1777, when the obelisks (*guglie*) were added. Just s of the bridge are the **Palazzetti Zatta** (CN 328–30), two fourteenth-century Gothic houses.

We proceed NW along the quay that runs the full length of the canal. Despite its importance for transit, the district was not highly developed until the eighteenth century, when the nobility began to appreciate the tranquillity and the space available for gardens. At CN 336 is **Palazzetto Surian**, a picturesque small fourteenth-century Gothic house. At CN 342–3 is the imposing **Palazzo Priuli Venier Manfrin**, by Tirali, 1734–7, one of his most mature works. The broad, restrained façade gives it an unusually 'modern' appearance, with three orders of almost equal importance. In the centre of the *portego* are seven individual lights, another departure from the usual multi-light window. The plan reflects the broad façade, with a square central hall. Its interior was decorated by Giuseppe Zais and Giambattista Mingardi, in a rich late Baroque manner, in sharp contrast to the reticent exterior.

The Cannaregio Canal from the Ponte de le Guglie

A little further, at CN 349, is the imposing **Palazzo Savorgnan**, together with Palazzo Surian, the largest on the canal, designed by Giuseppe Sardi towards the end of the seventeenth century. After his death in 1699, work continued under Domenico Rossi, his nephew, and was completed by Gaspari, architect of Palazzo Zenobio, with which it has features in common. In 1765 it was further enlarged, but was seriously damaged by fire in 1788; further alterations took place after 1826.

The impressive stone façade is in the manner of Longhena. Its rusticated ground floor is surmounted by two spacious *piani nobili* and an attic. The fenestration follows the traditional pattern, with a large Serliana to the two central halls and two prominent family *scudi* on the upper *piano nobile*. The interior is much altered, and many original features are lost; the grandiose staircase remains, reached by a fine portal from the ground-floor *androne*. Decoration included works by Schiavone, Palma il Giovane and Marco Ricci, all dispersed. The palace was renowned for its extensive gardens, enlarged in 1752 and decorated with statuary and exotic species; they were contiguous with those of the Spanish embassy. The gardens were remodelled in 1802 and in the 1830s, in the Romantic English manner; they survive as a public park.

Further along the quay, on Calle Rielo (CN 418–39) is a long terrace of sixteenth-century houses, built for rent by the Muti family. The repetitive plan has nine 'modules', each with three apartments.

At CN 462 is **Palazzo Bonfadini Vivante**, 1648–61; a simple façade centred on a Serliana. In the late eighteenth century the interior was decorated by Carlo Bevilacqua and Giuseppe Borsato, with rich Neo-classical stucco, much of which survives.

At CN 468 is **Palazzo Testa**, an attractive fifteenth-century Gothic house, enlarged and altered in the sixteenth and nineteenth centuries. The square portal is of red Verona marble; the upper hall has an elegant *gotico fiorito* four-light window.

Behind Palazzo Testa is a large site, formerly the SAFFA industrial complex, today occupied by housing by Vittorio Gregotti, 1984–94. The high-density scheme only partially successfully reinterprets the characteristic Venetian urban grain of *calli* and *campieli*, incorporating such traditional features as roof terraces and *cortili*, together with new forms of fenestration.

Further along the *fondamenta*, at CN 534–5, are the **Palazzetti Cendon**, a pair of Gothic houses, stylistically fourteenth century, although an inscription bears the date 1437. Both façades are asymmetrical. The Cendon patronised San Giobbe, nearby.

Continue past the narrow Rio de la Crea, and at the foot of the Ponte dei Tre Archi (see below), turn left into Campo San Giobbe. **San Giobbe** originated in a hospital for the poor, established in 1378, attached to which was an oratory. In the 1390s Franciscans established a house here, and the oratory was incorporated into a larger, new church. It was late Gothic, begun *circa* 1450, perhaps by Antonio Gambello. The church was patronised by Cristoforo Moro (doge 1462–71), who, on his death, left 10,000 ducats for the construction of the chancel, an important early Renaissance work by the Lombardo workshop. Moro was a close friend of Bernardino of Siena, who preached here, and was later canonised. The monastic buildings stood to the SW; only one wing of the cloister survived the Napoleonic suppression.

The church has a plain façade, much altered, but the elegant portal (generally given to Pietro Lombardo) has refined early Renaissance decoration; within the lunette is a relief of St Job with St Francis. The interior: a single nave, covered by a cross-vaulted ceiling; its east end is dominated by the rich, rather heavy chancel arch, flanked by two smaller arches. Beyond is the presbytery, crowned by a cupola on pendentives, probably the earliest

Renaissance example in the city. Set into the pendentives are the *Evangelists*, by Lombardo himself; the work is strongly influenced by Brunelleschi, notably his Pazzi Chapel in Florence. The free-standing altar is flanked by two small chapels, those of the Corner and Marin families. Behind the chancel is a long choir.

Several chapels of note: down the left side those of the Testa, Martini and Grimani. The Martini is a remarkable Tuscan work, its vault decorated with glazed terracotta by the della Robbia workshop in Florence, the only example in Venice. The Grimani Chapel, by contrast, is in Lombard Renaissance style. Although many art works have been relocated, the church contains paintings by Antonio Vivarini, Bordone, Zanchi and Querena, and sculptures by Lorenzo Bregno and the Lombardo.

Returning to the *fondamenta*, in front is the **Ponte dei Tre Archi**, originally of timber, but first built in stone in 1503. The present structure is by Tirali, 1688. Continuing NW along Fondamenta San Giobbe, at CN 652–7 are the **Palazzetti Amadi**, early fifteenth-century Gothic, but altered.

The final tract of quay is occupied by the impressively restrained brick and stone Neo-classical former **Macello** (slaughterhouses), by Giambattista Meduna and Giuseppe Salvadori, 1841–3. The front block, with a three-storey entrance pavilion, is flanked by lower side wings; behind is a central 'street' flanked on both sides by a series of long, narrow rectangular pavilions. The complex was converted in the 1990s to house departments of Ca' Foscari university; the sensitive restoration left the original structure largely intact. In 1965 Le Corbusier made a famous proposal to rebuild the city's hospital on this site.

Return to Ponte dei Tre Archi, cross the bridge and turn left up the Fondamenta di Cannaregio; at the far end is a housing project, **Sacca San Girolamo**, by Francesco Bortoluzzi, 1987–90, on a prominent site facing the lagoon. It is planned around an axial central *calle*, and, like the Gregotti scheme, reinterprets the city's vernacular style, with prominent chimneys and Istrian stone detailing. Here the historic influences are clearer, with tall, elegant windows and traditional shutters.

Returning SE along the quay, adjacent is the former **Santa Maria dei Penitenti**. Founded at Santa Marina in 1703, for penitent women, it transferred here in 1705. Funding was provided by Elizabetta Rossi and Marina da Lezze; the present buildings are by Massari. The site is a long rectangle, with a short canal frontage;

Massari adopted the plan first used by Palladio at Le Zitelle, with the church in the centre, flanked by two symmetrical wings of accommodation. The church has a compact, square plan, with a harmonious interior, all by Massari; its façade was never completed. The residential accommodation is ranged around two rectangular cloisters, one behind the other. The complex, empty for many years, is to be converted for sheltered housing.

Further down the quay, at CN 923, is **Palazzo Roma**, sixteenth century, badly altered. This quay is dominated by the impressive **Palazzo Surian Bellotto** (CN 967–75), by Giuseppe Sardi for the Surian, a clan of Armenian origin; it was probably complete *circa* 1663, but was later extended to the right, and remodelled internally after 1685 by the Bellotto, ennobled in that year. Above the rusticated ground floor are two superimposed *piani nobili*, one of which has a complex 'double' Serliana. The original house is regular and symmetrical, but has a broad, colonnaded, double-width atrium, with paired columns, reflected in the double portal to the quay. In the eighteenth century the palace housed the French embassy, but thereafter declined, and was divided into apartments. One of the two grandiose staircases was also lost; the other survives. The once famous garden is also gone.

Continuing back towards Ponte de le Guglie, we reach the fine **Palazzo Nani** (CN 1105), early sixteenth century, but with later additions to the right side. Its basic plan and façade are traditional, tripartite and symmetrical. The house remained in Nani ownership for centuries. During the ownership of Antonio Nani (1562–1619) the interior was elaborately decorated by Vittoria; much remains, as does the handsome staircase portal. Like many palaces in this zone, it had a garden, fragments of which survive.

Just beyond Palazzo Nani, a *sotoportego* adjacent to CN 1248a gives access to the famous Venetian Ghetto.

3 THE GHETO

There are records of Jews in Venice from 1152; they settled on the Giudecca and at Mestre, on the Terraferma. In the fourteenth century they were accused of usury and banished to Mestre, but were later allowed to return, and in 1386 were granted a burial ground on the Lido, which survives. Many Jews fled to the city during the crisis of the League of Cambrai in 1509, and as a result of this pressure of numbers in 1516 the Senate decided to establish a legally defined zone for them in the city. This was the Gheto or Ghetto, the first in the world. Although there were major restrictions on their activities, including a curfew and a veto on owning property, Jews thereafter lived in Venice with considerably more stability and security than elsewhere; they also established several synagogues, among the oldest in Europe.

The site was called a Gheto since it had been formerly used for foundries for casting metal (*gettare* = to cast), activities then transferred to the Arsenale. There were two adjacent pieces of land, the so-called Gheto Vecio and Gheto Novo, the former a rectangular plot of land next to the Cannaregio Canal, the latter an adjacent pentagonal island, surrounded by narrow canals.

Jews were recognised as a legally defined foreign community, collectively known as the Università degli Ebrei, and consisting of three distinct groups. One was the Ebrei Tedeschi, Germanic or Ashkenazi Jews, many of whom were, in fact, Italian; the second were the Ponentine or 'western' Jews, Sephardic Jews from Spain, Portugal and the Middle East. The third was a small group of Levantine Jews, technically subjects of the Ottoman Empire.

The Gheto Vechio and its Synagogues

The Gheto Vechio (Gheto Vecio) consists of a rectangular plot surrounded by tall apartment blocks and bisected by a *calle*, which opens in the centre into the small Campielo de le Scuole. On opposite sides of this *campielo* are two synagogues, known in Venetian as *schole*, the Schola Levantina and the Schola Spagnola. The **Schola Levantina** (CN 1228) was founded in 1538, but modernised by Longhena in the seventeenth century; today it retains this Baroque character. The exterior shows his typical detailing, including raised wall panelling and oval attic windows. There are two entrances, one giving access to the little Schola Luzzato (see below). The synagogue is reached by a staircase, which rises first to the main hall on the *piano nobile*, then continues up to the women's gallery or *matroneo*. The interior is lavishly decorated, with particular attention focused on the pulpit (*bimah*), reached by two curved flights of steps; behind is a polygonal apse. At the other side of the hall, the ark (*aron*), containing the scriptures, is equally richly decorated, with Corinthian detailing and a pediment on marble columns. All the rich woodwork is by Andrea Brustolon, the finest woodcarver in the city.

The Gheto Vechio: portal to the Schola Levantina, generally attributed to Baldassare Longhena, *circa* 1680

The **Schola Luzzatto** is a rare survivor of a number of small *midrash*, centres for study and learning. Its interior was reassembled on the ground floor of the Schola Levantina in the mid-nineteenth century, after the original building was demolished by Napoleon; a simple, modest Renaissance hall, with limited decoration.

The **Schola Spagnola** (CN 1144) is the largest of the surviving synagogues; it was established in 1555 by Spanish Jews, who became a large, wealthy community. Originally followers of the Ashkenazy rite, by the early nineteenth century the synagogue had turned to the Sephardic rite. It was perhaps rebuilt in 1584, but the present structure is again by Longhena, who modernised the interior in 1635–57, and perhaps rebuilt the basic fabric as well.

The exterior is relatively restrained, although both this and the Levantina have a much stronger presence than those in the Gheto Novo (see below), representing the increased wealth and self-confidence of the Jews in Venice by the seventeenth century. The entrance leads first into an atrium, at the end of which are two stairs, one to the main hall, the other to the *matroneo*. The interior is grand, rich and imposing, with the entrance in the middle of one long side, and the *aron* and *bimah* at the two ends. The hall is generously lit by tall, single windows, alternating with arches supported by columns. The *aron* has a similar design to Longhena's Vendramin monument at San Pietro in Castello, *circa* 1633, with four black striated marble columns supporting two superimposed pediments, one curved and one triangular. The *bimah* is framed by Corinthian marble columns supporting a square trabeation; at the rear is a blue cupola set above a polygonal apse. The rich, heavy ceiling is reminiscent of those at Ca' Pesaro, while the *matroneo* has an elegant elliptical plan, with a Baroque balustrade.

The Gheto Novo and its Synagogues

To reach the centre of the Gheto, continue to the NE end of Calle del Gheto Vechio and cross the bridge into the large pentagonal *campo*; it was formerly enclosed on all sides by towering tenements, of up to seven or eight storeys, but those to the N and NW were demolished in the early nineteenth century, leaving only those on the SE and SW sides. The Jews remained tenants, and the land was

The Gheto Novo: tenements on the east side of the campo

owned by the Scuola Grande di San Rocco. Although few Jews reside here today, the square remains the symbolic heart of the historic community, with a distinctive atmosphere. Within the fabric of these tenements are three synagogues. The **Schola Tedesca** is on the SE side; founded in 1528, it is one of the oldest in Europe. Externally, its location can be identified only by a row of five identical windows; it was located on the upper floor chiefly for liturgical reasons, so that there was no structure above, only the sky. It was rebuilt in 1732, and little of the earliest fabric has survived. The plan of the hall is trapezoidal, and within it is skilfully set the elliptical plan of the women's gallery. Although small, it is richly decorated; the original wall panelling and benches have survived the later restorations. An octagonal lantern brings light down from above, while the *bimah*, originally in the centre, below the roof light, is now at one end, opposite the ark. This last is a complex structure, originally made in 1528, but remodelled in 1666.

The **Schola Canton** is a little later than the Tedesca, founded in 1532; it stands in the s angle of the island (*canton* is Venetian for a corner), and was built for the Ashkenazy rite. Again it occupies the uppermost storey of the apartment block and again is identifiable externally only by five windows overlooking the canal. The synagogue was rebuilt in 1553, and remodelled several times later, the present internal decoration being largely early eighteenth century. The layout follows the usual pattern, and the rich Baroque *aron*, containing the *torah*, was made in the late eighteenth century. The *bimah* is earlier (1672), made in the manner of Bernini, with twisted columns.

The final surviving synagogue is the **Schola Italiana**, built into the sw block of apartments. It was founded in 1575, and again has a row of five windows. The Italian Jews were few in number, a fact reflected in the hall's modest size, modernised in 1739. The internal plan follows the typical arrangement, although the hall itself is almost square. The *bimah* is raised well above the floor level, and above is an octagonal lantern. Both *bimah* and *aron* are Corinthian, decorated in dark gilded wood, in a later Renaissance style.

Located within the eastern block of apartments, at CN 2902B, is the small **Museo dell'arte ebraica**, with an important collection of codices, religious artefacts and fabrics.

The third section of the Gheto is the **Gheto Novissimo**, reached by passing under the *sotoportego* in the centre of the eastern apartment block and crossing the timber bridge. It was established as a result of the appalling losses from the plague of 1630, when one-third of the city's population died. The ensuing economic crisis led the Senate to permit twenty Jewish families to settle here in a new annexe of the Gheto. The Novissimo consists of three apartment blocks, CN 1444–5, 1448–52 and 1468–9, between the Calle del Gheto Novissimo and Rio de San Girolamo; the blocks are separated by a T-shaped arrangement of *calli*. Each block has a different layout, that to the north, facing the canal, being the most imposing. Its plan is that of two tripartite palaces abutted together, and originally containing four very large apartments. The façade is typical of the mid-seventeenth century, and the development represents a high-density adaptation of well-established Venetian typologies.

4 SAN LUNARDO AND SAN MARCUOLA

The next itinerary starts from the Ponte de le Guglie.

There are a few buildings of note on the east side of the Cannaregio Canal, near the bridge. At CN 1291 is **Palazzetto da Pozzo**, a small fifteenth-century Gothic house, and at CN 1295 is the sixteenth-century **Palazzo Superchio**. On the corner of Rio Terà San Lunardo (CN 1298): another fifteenth-century Gothic house with a highly irregular plan and façades.

On the S side of the bridge, opposite Palazzo Labia, is a group of palaces, which turn the corner as the Cannaregio Canal meets the Grand Canal. At CN 1535 is **Palazzo da Mosto** or **Balbi dai Colori**, a substantial seventeenth-century house, once owned by the explorer Alvise da Mosto. Adjacent (CN 1554) is the eighteenth-century **Palazzo Manzoni**, while beyond is the eighteenth-century **Palazzo Emo** (CN 1558), the façade of which follows the curve of the canal. Finally, **Palazzo Querini** (CN 1574), which faces the Grand Canal, and whose long, plain, twelve-bay façade conceals a much earlier *fondaco*; inside are Byzantine and medieval traces. The house was remodelled after a fire in 1815.

From the bridge, proceed E along the broad Rio Terà San Lunardo, reclaimed in 1818, with a busy street market. Further E, it opens into Campo San Lunardo.

San Lunardo (Leonardo), on the S side, is a parish foundation, whose oldest record dates from 1089. It was reconstructed more than once, but in 1595 the campanile collapsed, damaging the church; it was rebuilt in a Rococo manner in 1794 by Bernardino Maccaruzzi.

The façade has two orders, capped by a pediment, with a large central portal; a similar portal to the N side. The parish was suppressed in 1805, and the church adapted for a succession of other uses; today it houses the local civic centre.

Continuing E along the Rio Terà, a succession of *calli* off the right (S) side lead to a group of palaces with their façades onto the Grand Canal. The most prominent is **Palazzo Correr Contarini Zorzi** (CN 1633), an imposing seventeenth-century structure, reached from Calle de la Pagia. The canal façade is broad but asymmetrical, with two watergates giving access to the two *piani nobili*.

Returning to the Rio Terà, at CN 1744, on the corner of Rio Terà del Cristo, is an attractive Renaissance *palazzetto*, with finely carved stonework, and a second façade at the side. Continue down Rio Terà del Cristo to the **Scuola del Cristo**, CN 1750; built 1635–44, one of few that survived the Napoleonic suppression in 1810. The Scuola had responsibility for organising the burial of people drowned at sea or in the lagoon. The impressive façade is articulated by giant Corinthian pilasters, surmounted by a heavy, rich cornice. It shows Longhena's influence, although is probably by Francesco Contin. The ground floor was decorated in 1701 with a cycle of paintings by Gianantonio Pellegrini, now in the Museo Diocesano. Upper-hall paintings are attributed to Pietro Ricci.

Directly opposite the Scuola is Campielo Memmo; land access to **Palazzo Memmo Martinengo Mandelli** (CN 1756), with Grand Canal façade. Rebuilt in the eighteenth century; an asymmetrical canal façade, with a narrow quay. The lower storeys are clad with rusticated stonework, while the *piano nobile* has four single-light windows. Adjacent is **Palazzo Gritti Dandolo** (CN 1758), rebuilt in the seventeenth century on the site of an earlier Gothic house.

Walking E along the wide Rio Terà drio la Chiesa, we reach Campo de la Chiesa, which leads around the end of San Marcuola into its square, open on the S side towards the Grand Canal.

San Marcuola (an ingenious corruption of Santi Ermagora e Fortunato): established in the ninth or tenth century, but reconstructed in the twelfth; it was re consecrated in 1332, but by the mid-seventeenth century it had become unstable. In 1663 the chancel was rebuilt, shortly after which Gaspari began reconstructing the rest of the church. Work proceeded slowly, and Gaspari died in 1730, the church well short of completion. It was finally completed by Massari in 1736, although the canal façade was never built, other than the stone portal.

The nave has a square plan, as has the chancel, which is defined by four free-standing columns supporting an oval cupola; beyond is a small radiused apse. The chancel is flanked by two small sacristies. The nave has a barrel-vaulted roof, with eight altars, arranged in pairs down the sides; above the entrance portal are two pulpits. At the w end is the Oratorio del Cristo, added by Massari in 1735, in the form of a rectangular hall with an altar at one end. Within the church, most of the sculpted figures are by Morleiter; left of the chancel is the *Last Supper*, an early Tintoretto. Other paintings are by Francesco Migliori, Padovanino and Niccolò Bambini.

On the e side of the square: two small houses, **Casa Gatti Casazza** (CN 1760) and **Palazzetto Zorzi** (CN 1762). Both originally fourteenth-century Gothic, but the first was refaced in the eighteenth century, although it retains Gothic windows to the square. The second is an attractive small medieval house, with superimposed *trifore*.

Return to Rio Terà San Lunardo, which continues e as Calle del Pistor, thence into Campielo de l'Anconeta. Briefly diverting, take the long, narrow Calle de l'Aseo out of the n side; at the far end, on the left corner is **Palazzo Loredan Gheltoff** (CN 1864). Façade towards the n, to Rio de San Girolamo. A substantial late Gothic house, *circa* 1450–60, built by the Loredan, later passing to the Gheltoff, merchants from Antwerp. Its l-shaped plan encloses a courtyard; a broad, asymmetrical canal façade. The main hall is lit by a fine six-light window, with a further *quadrifora* to the top floor, all *gotico fiorito*.

Returning to Campielo de l'Anconeta, on the north side is the cheerful Gothic Revival façade of the former **Teatro Italia** (CN 1943), later a cinema, currently closed. The ground floor has fine wrought-iron screens set into the arches, while the upper floor has tracery modelled on the Ca' d'Oro. A large winged lion on the parapet completes the historic allusions.

Continuing e, crossing the bridge, turn right down Calle Larga Vendramin. At the s end is the land gate to **Palazzo Loredan Vendramin Calergi** (CN 2040), one of the most magnificent Renaissance palaces in the city, and Codussi's masterpiece. It was commissioned in 1481 by Andrea Loredan, an early patron of Codussi at San Michele, although it was begun only in 1502; Codussi died two years later, and the palace was probably completed *circa* 1508 by his son Domenico. Loredan himself died in 1513.

The later history of the palace is complex; for a time it was owned by the duke of Mantua, then Vettor Calergi, and then

The Gothic Revival Teatro Italia, Campielo de l'Anconeta

Vincenzo Grimani. The 'white wing' (E side) was added in the early seventeenth century by Scamozzi for Grimani, although following the murder of a member of the Querini Stampalia by three Grimani brothers, it was torn down; it was rebuilt in the 1660s. In 1740 the palace passed to the Vendramin, then to the duchesse de Berry. Richard Wagner lived here until his death in 1883. In 1946 Conte Volpi ceded the palace to the city, and it has housed the winter casino ever since.

The palace is remarkable for the magnificent 'Roman' canal façade, one of the most imposing in the city, and a maturation of Codussi's earlier façades at Palazzo Zorzi and Palazzo Lando Corner Spinelli; it is best seen from the Fondamenta del Megio, opposite.

The plan is basically traditional, although the entrance hall is widened out towards the canal to form a spacious loggia, giving a T-shaped plan. The pattern of bays on the façade is 1–3–1; this rhythm is repeated on the upper floors. This façade is a great stone screen, richly decorated, and with three equal orders articulated by Corinthian columns; the two-light windows with an *ocio* above are characteristic of Codussi. The façade terminates with a massive cornice.

The sumptuous interior contains lavish decoration added by successive owners. The ground-floor *androne* was once frescoed by Giorgione, tragically destroyed in 1766; it now bears the French arms, and a noble classical portal to the staircase. Among other notable features are a fireplace by Vittoria and later decorations by Niccolò Bambini.

Immediately to the E is a group of palaces with Grand Canal façades, and land access from the tangle of *calli* behind the Madalena church. The first is **Palazzo Molin Erizzo Barzizza** (CN 2138), reached from Corte Erizzo; fifteenth-century Gothic, with an asymmetrical canal façade, lacking the left wing. The central window has tracery modelled on the Doge's Palace. The interior was richly decorated with stucco in the seventeenth century. Immediately to the W is **Palazzo Marcello** (CN 2139), rebuilt in the seventeenth century on the site of an earlier house; two superimposed *piani nobili* and hence two watergates. In 1686 the composer Benedetto Marcello was born here. From Corte Erizzo we return northwards to the attractive Campo de la Madalena, the W and S sides of which are bounded by smaller vernacular houses.

5   LA MADALENA AND SANTA FOSCA

La Madalena was first recorded in 1155, and rebuilt *circa* 1220 by the Baffo or Balbo. In 1398 the adjacent Rio de la Madalena was reclaimed, one of the earliest recorded. The church survived until 1760, when it was demolished for the present structure, a notable Neo-classical work by Tommaso Temanza, an important theorist and writer, but who built little.

A centralised plan, the dominant external form being a large drum, surmounted by a shallow, copper-clad cupola. To the N is the impressive main portal, with giant paired Ionic columns supporting a heavy pediment. Within the pediment: an eye set in an equilateral triangle, representing the Omniscient Father and the Trinity. External decoration is refined and minimal. The interior, though, is more complex, and the plan is hexagonal, six facets divided by paired columns, between which are niches containing statues. Four facets contain side altars, with the entrance portal and the chancel arch on the other two sides. The rectangular chancel has apsidal ends to left and right. In 1810 the church's parochial functions ceased, and it was closed for many years; it later reopened as an oratory. Among the few art works is a *Last Supper* by Giandomenico Tiepolo.

Following the quay to the E of the church, a maze of *calli* leads to a further group of palaces with Grand Canal façades. **Palazzo**

Campo Santa Fosca, with the church façade (left); Emilio Marsili's statue of Paolo Sarpi (1892) and the two Palazzi Contarini Correr

Soranzo Piovene (CN 2176) is reached from Calle del Forno and then Ramo Piovene; a sixteenth-century house with an elegant, slightly asymmetrical façade, sometimes attributed to Sante Lombardo. It contains an impressive *androne* and staircase. Adjacent is the seventeenth-century **Palazzo Emo** (CN 2177), with a rear garden; its two unusual angled façades follow the course of the Grand Canal. The main feature is the large double Serliana. Just across Calle del Tragheto is the land entrance to **Palazzo Molin Querini Gaspari** (CN 2179), again with a curved façade; also seventeenth century and again with a prominent Serliana.

Return to the Madalena, and cross Ponte San Antonio into Campo Santa Fosca.

The rectangular *campo* is dominated by the heavy stone church façade; in the centre is Emilio Marsili's monument to Paolo Sarpi (1892); Sarpi was a notable theologian and adviser to the Republic, who recorded the deliberations at the Council of Trent, and represented the Republic during the papal interdict of 1606. Occupying the sw side of the square: two contiguous palaces: **Palazzi Contarini Correr** (CN 2214 and 2217): built by the Contarini, in the late seventeenth century they passed to the Correr, who modernised both extensively. No. 2217 is the earlier Gothic palace, the façade of which remains intact, except for later balconies: mid-fifteenth-century *gotico fiorito*, with a multi-light window to the first-floor hall. The *campo* façade of the later house (no. 2214) is clad with stone, and detailed in a similar manner to Tirali's nearby Palazzo Diedo. The unusual *piano nobile* windows are all individual lights, with no central *polifora*. The plan is conventional; the interior was originally decorated by the Tiepolo but the works were destroyed in the war of 1939–45. Both houses have secondary façades to the canal at the rear. **Santa Fosca**, like most of the island parishes along this bank of the Grand Canal, is an ancient foundation, established in the ninth century, when the body of the titular saint was brought to Torcello, and a church (which still stands) was built there to house her remains. The first written document is from 1297, and the early basilica survived until the campanile collapsed in 1410; it was rebuilt in the late Gothic style, as we see today. The church deteriorated by the seventeenth century, and was rebuilt in 1679; the architect is unknown.

It has a single nave, with side altars, and a square chancel flanked by two small chapels. Fifty years after its reconstruction, the church was badly damaged by fire; the Donà family paid for the present heavy Palladian façade (1733–41), sometimes attributed to Domenico Rossi; its giant order of Corinthian pilasters supports an equally heavy pediment. There are few notable art works; in the chancel is the *Holy Family* by Domenico Tintoretto.

The Salizada and Campo Santa Fosca are continued SE by the first section of the Strada Nova, an important element in the mid-nineteenth-century urban clearances, intended to facilitate movement between Rialto and the new railway station. On the right, off Campielo dei Fiori: a group of palaces facing the Grand Canal, with land access from the *campielo* or the adjacent Fondamenta and Corte Barbaro. First, two adjacent houses, both once owned by the Barbaro and Barbarigo, at CN 2252 and 2255. **Palazzetto Barbaro** is reached from Corte Barbaro, and has a narrow canal façade, lacking one side wing. The larger, late sixteenth-century **Palazzo Barbaro Barbarigo** also has an asymmetrical façade, but less restricted: two *piani nobili* and an off-centre portal. The façade was originally frescoed by Camillo Ballini, a follower of Palma il Giovane; a few traces, rare survivors, can be seen. Adjacent is the early seventeenth-century **Palazzo Zulian** (CN 2253), again with a Grand Canal façade, and land access from Corte Bragadin. A regular tripartite plan and façade; the ground floor is clad with stone and the two superimposed *piani*

Palazzo Gussoni Grimani de la Vida: Grand Canal façade, begun *circa* 1548; sometimes attributed to Michele Sanmicheli

nobili each have a Serliana. In the late eighteenth century the house was owned by Girolamo Zulian, an early patron of Canova. Adjacent again is **Palazzo Ruoda** (CN 2256), again seventeenth century, built on the foundations of an earlier Gothic house. The upper *piano nobile* has a prominent Serliana. The modest but interesting **Palazzetto Bragadin** (CN 2268) is nearby, with land access from Corte Zulian. The house has two elements, a taller west wing and a much lower east wing, originally sixteenth century, but altered later.

Returning to Campielo dei Fiori, take the short Calle de Noal (right), and right again into Calle Minio.

Palazzo Gussoni Grimani de la Vida (CN 2277): a fine palace on a prominent site on the corner of the Grand Canal and the busy Rio de Noal. Begun *circa* 1548; the elegant, symmetrical canal façade has been attributed to Sanmicheli. It was originally frescoed by Tintoretto; traces survived into the nineteenth century. They were modelled on Michelangelo's Medici tombs in Florence. The courtyard façade was frescoed by Giambattista Zelotti. The house was commissioned by Marco Gussoni, brother-in-law of Zorzi Corner, Sanmicheli's patron at San Maurizio. Inside: an impressive *androne* with rich columns, and an attractive courtyard.

Returning to Calle de Noal, turn back into the Strada Nova, w of Ponte Pasqualigo. On the N side is the garden attached to **Palazzetto**

Palazzo Donà Giovanelli, *circa* 1460; *gotico fiorito*,
modernised by Giambattista Meduna in 1847–8

Pasqualigo Giovanelli (CN 2290), itself attached to the imposing
Palazzo Donà Giovanelli (CN 2291–2). Façade to Rio de Noal; land
access from Campielo de la Chiesa, to the w. The canal façade is best
seen from Fondamenta de la Stua, just over the bridge. One of the
most striking late Gothic palaces, although much altered. It was built
circa 1460, in the late *gotico fiorito* style, although the original owner is
not known. In the sixteenth century it was owned by the Republic,
which leased it to the duke of Urbino, Francesco Maria della Rovere;
notable banquets were held here. It was later owned by Giovanni
Battista Donà and then the Giovanelli, ennobled in 1668.

In the mid-nineteenth century Andrea Giovanelli established the
Congress of Italian Scientists (Convegno degli Scienziati Italiani)
here, and in 1847–8 began extensive alterations under Giambattista
Meduna. They included replacement of the staircase by a new neo-
Gothic stair with an octagonal plan, and transformations to the
androne, which has a double width, with a colonnade down the
centre, and a large arch onto the garden. The plan of the *portego*
above follows the same form. All is in a rich neo-Gothic manner.

The broad tripartite canal façade remains noble and imposing, with a spacious lower storey, a tall mezzanine and a *piano nobile*. Particularly notable is the central multi-light window, derived from the Doge's Palace; the unusual corner windows were modelled on those at Palazzo Priuli on Rio de l'Osmarin.

We now retrace our steps westwards, into Rio Terà de la Madalena; there are two substantial palaces on the north side.

Palazzo Donà da le Rose (CN 2343): modernised in the late seventeenth or early eighteenth century, with one façade to the Rio Terà, the other to Rio dei Servi, to the N. Sometimes attributed to Domenico Rossi, occasionally to Longhena. The broad, powerful s façade has eight single windows to the *piano nobile*, linked by a continuous balcony. The spacious *androne* originally had four free-standing columns, but the interior is much altered and most of the original decoration lost. **Palazzetto Contin** (CN 2346) abuts the Donà on the w side, again with N and s façades; fifteenth-century Gothic, with a large six-light window to the first floor hall, and eight single windows, all *fiorito* in style.

A little further w again, **Palazzo Tornielli** (CN 2370) is reached from the narrow Calle Tornielli, with its main façade to the N. Originally fourteenth-century Gothic, it was modernised in the later sixteenth century, when the Tornielli, originally from Novara and recently ennobled, bought the house from the Donà. The L-shaped Gothic plan was retained, as was the courtyard façade, but the stair was rebuilt, as was the interior and the main façade. This last is impressive, with two superimposed *piani nobili*, each with a large Serliana, and a similar arrangement to the watergate.

Our next excursion takes us further north; return to Campo Santa Fosca, and take the bridge out of the back left corner; continue NW along Fondamenta Diedo. Cross the bridge and continue w.

6 THE FORMER CONVENT OF THE SERVI (SERVITES) AND ENVIRONS

The Servite nunnery was one of the most important and extensive in the city, occupying almost all the island bounded by Rio de la Misericordia, Rio de Santa Fosca, Rio dei Servi and Rio Grimani. Its destruction, following the Napoleonic dissolution, was one of the greatest losses of post-Republican Venice.

Rio de San Felice with the Lucchesi Chapel, fifteenth-century
Gothic; survivor of the former Servi nunnery

The Servites came to Venice in 1316; the church was begun in
1330, but construction and embellishment continued for decades, and
it was consecrated only in 1491; the style was late Venetian Gothic,
and the church had an exceptionally long nave and choir, with a w
façade onto a small square. Most of the conventual buildings stood
to the N, adjacent to Rio de la Misericordia.

In 1769 a serious fire destroyed its conventual buildings and library,
and the nunnery never fully recovered. It was suppressed in 1805,
and the church was demolished after 1812; by 1821 nearly all had
gone, except the Lucchesi Chapel on the s side, and one imposing
lateral portal. Almost all the art works were dispersed or destroyed;
the monument to Doge Andrea Vendramin was reassembled at Santi
Giovanni e Paolo.

The surviving **Lucchesi Chapel** is a tall, brick, Gothic structure,
formerly connected to the south flank of the church, and built for
the migrant population from Lucca who settled in this district after
1309, forming a confraternity in 1360. Nearby is the tall south lateral
portal, an impressive work with two deep concentric arches. The
general lineaments of the conventual buildings can still be traced, as
can the eastern cloister, with its well-head.

Returning E along Fondamenta Canal, just before Ponte Diedo is
the site of the once-famous sixteenth-century **Palazzo Grimani** (CN

2381), demolished in the late eighteenth century; all that remains are three portals. Crossing Ponte Diedo, we reach **Palazzo Diedo** (CN 2386), an impressive pile (*circa* 1710–20), generally attributed to Tirali; a development from his earlier Palazzo Grassi in Chioggia, larger and more refined. The plan is traditional and tripartite, but with one unusual feature: the main *androne* also has a cross-axis, divided from the *androne* by arches, and with a doorway at each end. The imposing stone-clad façade has two *piani nobili*; in the centre, three individual windows denote the *portego*, rather than the usual multi-light group. The Neo-classical architect Antonio Diedo was born here in 1772.

Continuing SE along the quay, at CN 2396 is **Palazzo Costa**, with a simple eighteenth-century façade; at CN 2400 is the unusual **Palazzo Vendramin**, now a hotel. The early Renaissance façade is probably very late fifteenth century, with refined but eclectic detailing. Its large portal has fine relief carving to the pilasters, and is surrounded by five small *oci*. The principal *piano nobile* has an elegant four-light window. The rear façade to Rio del Trapolin is less elegant; each window on the principal floor is surmounted by a circular light in *gotico fiorito*. In the sixteenth century the palace belonged to Gabriele Vendramin, patron of Titian and a notable art collector.

Return NW along the quay and take Calle Zancani northwards; cross the bridge into Campo San Marziale. Along the quay at CN 2446 is **Casa Moro**, a house of Venetian-Byzantine origin, but with later Gothic windows.

7 FROM SAN MARZIALE TO SAN GIROLAMO

San Marziale was founded in the ninth century; the church was rebuilt in 1133. The site is restricted, and its N side rises directly from Rio de la Misericordia, with its façade to the small *campielo* to the w. The twelfth-century basilica survived until the late seventeenth century; it was then completely reconstructed (1693–1721). The tall, plain, box-like exterior conceals a much richer interior: a single nave, with a vaulted ceiling, decorated with three canvases by Sebastiano Ricci in gilded frames (1700–05). Down the flank walls: a series of Baroque altars, each one different, very ornate, with marble sculptures. The second right altar has an altarpiece by Tintoretto, *SS Martial, Peter and Paul*, 1548. The chancel was also originally decorated by Tintoretto, who lived nearby; its vault is again decorated by Ricci. The high altar is also a rich Baroque work. In the sacristy is Titian's *Archangel Raphael and Tobias*, *circa* 1543, in poor condition.

From the *campielo* in front of the church, cross the bridge to Fondamenta de la Misericordia. Continue NW; at CN 2527–8 is an attractive fifteenth-century Gothic house, with two portals and superimposed *quadrifore*. On the SW side of the canal is the high enclosing brick wall of the former Servi convent; on the NE angle, a fifteenth-century *Virgin and Child*, sometimes attributed to Bartolomeo Bon. At CN 2536 is **Palazzo Michiel**, an imposing early sixteenth-century house with superimposed *quadrifore*. In 1580 Francesco Sansovino claimed it as one of the best new palaces in the city. At CN 2591 is **Palazzo Longo**, *gotico fiorito*, with columns of red Verona marble to the main three-light window. Through the *sotoportego* adjacent to CN 2611 is Corte de la Raffineria, named after a sugar refinery that flourished here in the eighteenth century. A monumental stone doorway survives, with rusticated pilasters and a bold pediment, in the manner of Sanmicheli. At CN 2625, on the corner of Rio dei Lustraferi, is **Palazzo Caotorta**, an attractive seventeenth-century façade, with two *piani nobili*. Asymmetrical, with a Serliana to the main upper hall.

Cross Ponte dei Lustraferi, and continue along Fondamenta dei Ormesini.

Palazzo da Lezze (CN 2651) is sixteenth century, again with an asymmetrical plan and façade, lacking the left wing. The da Lezze

owned several houses in this district. Just before we reach Ponte dei Ormesini, on the right are the **Case Caliari (Alberegno)** (CN 2756–65 and 2766–79), a large complex of apartments, built in the mid-sixteenth century and early seventeenth. It consists of two long blocks running N–S, with the narrow Calle Caliari down

Corte de la Raffineria: rusticated portal of the eighteenth-century former sugar refinery

the centre and Calle de la Malvasia to the w. As is usually the case, the blocks are joined by high-level arches. The buildings are typical speculative developments for rent, notable for their early date: the earlier block is first recorded in 1565. It was developed by the Barozzi, later passing to the Dolfin and the Calergi, who built the final blocks at the s end in 1605. The plans are logical and repetitive, and the external detailing simple and standardised, although the s blocks have a little more ornamentation.

Just to the w are the **Case Labia** (CN 2832–57), a group of seventeenth-century rental houses. Continue w to Ponte San Girolamo; the church and former conventual buildings are across the canal.

San Girolamo occupies a large site bounded by canals on three sides. It was founded by Augustinians, whose nunnery outside the walls of Treviso was destroyed in the wars of 1346–8 with the king of Hungary. They fled to Venice and built accommodation here, including a small oratory. In 1456 it was damaged by fire, but rebuilt. The conventual buildings occupied the E and s site, with the church along the quay to the N. The nunnery survived until another disastrous fire in 1705, after which the church was rebuilt by Domenico Rossi and decorated by Francesco Zugno. It was re-consecrated in 1751 but suppressed in 1806, when the art works were dispersed. The church was used for profane purposes until 1930, when it was reacquired by a religious order and restored; it reopened in 1952. The tall exterior has a w façade articulated with Corinthian pilasters and surmounted by a bold trabeation; above is a large thermal window, capped by a pediment. The single nave is also lit by high-level thermal windows.

Continue w along Fondamenta San Girolamo. At CN 2967 is **Palazzo Marini**, probably seventeenth century; a conventional plan and symmetrical façade. Return back along the quay, and cross Ponte de le Capuzine to the N side. Further w, the quay becomes Fondamenta Coletti. At CN 2982–3000 is the unusual **Palazzo Moro**: not a palace at all, but an ambitious housing project designed by Jacopo Sansovino for the nobleman Leonardo Moro. As projected, the '*palazzo*' was to be a large quadrangular structure, with prominent four-storey *palazzetti* on each of the outer corners, all linked by lower blocks of accommodation, and with a large garden in the centre. Construction began *circa* 1544, and the s block, including the two corner houses, was complete *circa* 1550, when Moro probably moved into one of them. The lower terraces consist

Palazzo Moro, by Sansovino for Leonardo Moro, begun *circa* 1544

of three-storey ranges of artisans' housing, with workshops on the ground floor. There were eight in each wing, with a gatehouse in the centre to reach the garden. The basic fabric of this s range survives, much altered. Moro then bought more land to the rear, and began the two side wings, but the N wing was finally completed only *circa* 1560 – it is shown complete in Paolo Furlan's view of *circa* 1566. Much of these later stages is lost or badly altered.

Return E along the quay to the **Cappella de le Capuzine (Cappuccine)**. The formal title is Santa Maria Madre del Redentore. A Capuchin nunnery was established here in 1612; the church was consecrated in 1623, and faced the canal, with the conventual buildings behind it. The nunnery was suppressed in 1818, but the nuns returned a few years later and remained until 1911. The church is now a chapel subordinate to San Girolamo; a modest brick structure, with a pedimented Corinthian façade. Adjacent is the impressive **Palazzo Mayer Grimani** (CN 3023–4), once highly regarded, and recently restored. Early seventeenth century; the architect is unknown, although it shows the influence of Sanmicheli. The façade has a paired entrance portal, while the tall flanking side windows have an unusual arrangement, with a small square light above the main window. The house had an extensive garden, now lost.

For the next itinerary we walk further N, towards the margins of the city.

Continue down Fondamenta de le Capuzine, and cross Ponte de le Torete; take Calle Turlona (left), and at the end cross Ponte Turlona. Turn left along Fondamenta de la Sensa, and then N again along Calle dei Riformati. The bridge at the end takes us to Fondamenta dei Riformati.

8 THE RIFORMATI AND SANT'ALVISE; RIO DE LA SENSA

San Bonaventura (I Riformati) (CN 3144): the title refers to the reformed Franciscans, originally at San Francesco del Deserto in the northern lagoon. After several moves, they settled here in 1620; the church, consecrated three years later, was dedicated to St Bonaventure (1218–74), minister general of the order, canonised in 1482. Its extensive monastic buildings were built on land reclaimed from the lagoon. The monastery was suppressed in 1805 and the conventual buildings demolished. In 1859 the site was bought by Contessa Paolina Malipiero Giustinian Recanati, who established a Carmelite nunnery here. This was later replaced by the present Umberto I children's hospital, with extensive gardens. The nineteenth-century chapel has a simple Renaissance façade to the quay.

Continuing SE along the quay, we reach Campo Sant'Alvise. On the N side, at CN 3204–5, is the former **Scuola di Sant'Alvise**, founded in 1402, modernised in 1608, but suppressed in 1806. A modest structure: three bays and two storeys, with a large central portal and three windows to the first-floor meeting hall.

Sant'Alvise was founded by the noblewoman Antonia Venier in 1388, after receiving a vision of the saint (Alvise is the Venetian form of Luigi or Louis). Venier established an Augustinian house and took orders herself. Much of the land was reclaimed, and the monastic buildings were built E of the church. The nunnery was enlarged in 1411 and the church itself rebuilt in 1430. It survived until the 1810 suppression, and became a children's nursery. Today, it is occupied by the Suore de la Carità, who transferred here from Santa Lucia, after that house was closed and then demolished.

The church is a substantial, simple brick structure, in typical late Gothic style, with a small entrance portal (1450s) and the titular saint set into a Gothic arch.

The interior was much altered in the seventeenth century, when altars were added down the side walls; the Gothic chancel survives.

After 1674 the nave ceiling was decorated with a vast fresco by Pietro Antonio Torri and Pietro Ricchi. The s end of the nave retains the fifteenth-century nuns' choir or *barco*, supported by columns and carved timber *barbacani*, one of the oldest in the city. Several notable paintings, including three good works by G.B. Tiepolo, others by Palma il Vecchio and Lazzaro Bastiani.

The fifteenth-century campanile survives, as do most of the monastic buildings, ranged around a small *cortile* and two cloisters; the n cloister dates from the original construction in 1388.

Cross the bridge in front of the church and continue down Calle del Capitelo. At the s end, turn right (w) along Fondamenta de la Sensa.

Fondamenta de la Sensa: **Palazzo and Casinò Michiel** (CN 3218), an imposing early Renaissance work, sometimes attributed to Giovanni Buora. Probably begun *circa* 1503, with similarities to Palazzo Contarini dal Zaffo at San Vio. Perhaps altered later, since some elements (e.g., the ground-floor rustication) appear to be from later in the century. In the late sixteenth century it was the French embassy; King Henri III stayed here in 1574.

The tripartite, almost symmetrical façade has Corinthian stone pilasters down the quoins, and a prominent cornice. Traditional fenestration, with a *trifora* lighting the tall *piano nobile*; the façade was

originally frescoed by Andrea Schiavone. Although the interior is now a condominium, the *portego* ceiling has survived, as has its fine portal, with a rich Corinthian entablature. The *casinò* also survives, facing Rio de Sant'Alvise at the n end of the garden; a simple refined façade, five bays and two storeys.

Continue e along the Fondamenta; at CN 3240 is the sixteenth-century **Palazzo Cassetti**; an Ionic *quadrifora* to the main upper hall. Cross Ponte

Sant'Alvise: detail of fifteenth-century portal

Campo dei Mori, with one of the three 'Moors', probably late thirteenth century

Rosso and continue E. At CN 3318 is the seventeenth-century **Palazzo Loredan**, with a large Baroque balcony.

Further along the quay are the two **Palazzi Arrigoni Caragiani** (CN 3335 and 3336), the latter name a corruption of Ca' Reggiani. Both fifteenth-century Gothic, one with a contemporary portal, the other with an early Renaissance one. The houses were built as a pair, although the façades were altered later. Their plans are almost identical but mirrored; the two small courtyards abut each other in the centre. The stairs in both houses rise on the outer flank walls, with access from the long, narrow *androne*. Both also have long rear gardens.

A little further E, just before the narrow Rio Braso, is **Palazzetto Braso** (CN 3355), behind its courtyard wall; originally fourteenth century, with two three-light windows with trilobate heads. Crossing Ponte Braso, we reach **Campo dei Mori**, an attractive secluded corner. It has a triangular plan, and is noted for the four carved figures of 'Moors' set into the walls on the E side, and along the nearby quay The three on the square are known as Sandi, Afani and

Palazzo Mastelli del Cammello; on the right the
sculpted camel from which the house takes its name

Sior Antonio Rioba, and wear Middle Eastern dress. They are
popularly identified as members of the Mastelli family, whose house
is nearby, and are probably late thirteenth or early fourteenth
century; Istrian stone, with Greek marble turbans.

A short way SE along Fondamenta dei Mori is the **Casa del
Tintoretto** (CN 3399), a tall, narrow, fifteenth-century Gothic house;
Tintoretto lived here from 1574 until his death in 1594. On the left
corner of the façade is the fourth 'Moor', another Middle Eastern
figure with an over-sized turban, on a complex Renaissance pedestal.

Walk towards the narrow N end of the square. On the right (CN
3381) is the land gate to **Palazzo Mastelli del Cammello**: main
façade to the N, visible from Fondamenta Morosini, adjacent to the
bridge. Its nickname derives from the relief sculpture of a man
leading a camel, on the lower right façade. This remarkably eclectic
façade is mainly fifteenth-century Gothic, but with Renaissance
elements. The watergate is Renaissance, but is flanked by Gothic
trilobate windows, suggesting an original construction in the
fourteenth century. On the E corner: another unusual detail, a short,

fat stone column; the main hall is lit by a four-light window with high-level quatrefoils. The outermost corner windows derive from Palazzo Priuli, datable to *circa* 1420.

9 RIO DE LA MADONA DE L'ORTO

We visit the church shortly; from its square, continue NW along Fondamenta de la Madona. At the end is **Palazzo Benzi (Benci) Zecchini** (CN 3458); main façade to the S, and another to the short Rio dei Zecchini (W). Its history is long and complex; originally fourteenth-century Gothic, it was acquired by the Girardi Zecchini in 1581, who already owned the adjacent Gothic house. They began to modernise it, but in 1621 it was subdivided among various branches of the clan, and work was never completed. In 1649 the materials on site were sold to Longhena to build Ca' Pesaro. Today the house forms part of a hospital run by a religious order, the Fatebenefratelli.

The S façade is traditional Gothic, but the long W flank evinces the partial modernisation *circa* 1600, with complex, random fenestration. Behind the house is a large courtyard, bounded on its S side by the N face of the palace, a grandiose classical stone composition; at the N end of the courtyard there were two small pavilions or *casini*, one of which survives, with a prominent rusticated portal.

The adjacent house at CN 3459 also forms part of the complex, and is originally fourteenth century; a three-light window survives on the first floor.

Returning towards the church, on the left is **Corte Cavallo**, the name derived from the fact that Alessandro Leopardi's workshop was here, where the horse for the famous Colleoni monument was made. At CN 3499 is **Palazzo Rizzo Patarol**, probably late sixteenth century; a tripartite, conventional façade with rusticated ground floor, and capped by a pedimented *abbaino*. In the early eighteenth century Lorenzo Patarol developed a famous garden here, filled with exotic species. It was modernised in the 1830s by Giovanni Corner; much survives, extending almost to the lagoon edge.

Further down the quay is the former **Scuola dei Mercanti** (CN 3519), two façades, one to the quay and a longer side façade to the square. Built 1570–72, probably to an initial design by Palladio, who reused the foundations of an earlier structure. The merchants' confraternity moved here from the Frari in 1560; they survived until the Napoleonic suppression in 1806.

The façades are simple but impressive; that to the quay has a central portal surmounted by a relief of St Christopher and the infant Jesus. The *campo* façade has just three broad bays, with the Virgin and Child and saints above the portal. Internally, the accommodation resembles that of the *scuole grandi*, with two large rectangular superimposed halls, the *sala capitolare* and the *androne*, linked by a staircase in the NW corner. The Scuola amassed a fine collection of pictures, including works by Tintoretto, Palma il Giovane and Veronese, all dispersed on its closure.

La Madona de l'Orto: the square retains the traditional paving in herringbone brickwork, with strips of Istrian stone. The splendid Gothic church façade is one of the finest in the city; its interior is also well preserved.

The church was founded *circa* 1350, by a monastic order, the Umiliati, and was first dedicated to St Christopher; the dedication was changed after a miracle-working image of the Virgin was found in the adjacent orchard. The original church, probably completed *circa* 1370, shortly thereafter suffered serious structural damage at the N (chancel) end, and partial reconstruction began in 1399; the original nave was retained, and survives. Following the expulsion of the Umiliati in 1460, a succession of different orders was based here, until finally, in 1876, it was restored and reopened as a parish church.

The beautiful façade has several notable features, including the large flanking windows, with their complex tracery, and the high-level raking arcades with two rows of niches containing figures of the twelve Apostles, perhaps by the dalle Masegne. The façade is capped by a rich array of aedicules with tall pyramidal roofs; its fine portal is by Bartolomeo Bon, begun in 1460, but assembled only in 1483, after his death. It shows early hints of the Renaissance in its design. The crowning figure, *St Christopher* (by Bon himself) is flanked by the *Virgin Mary* and the *Angel Gabriel*, perhaps by Rizzo. Above the portal is a typical Venetian Gothic *ocio*.

Interior: a six-bay nave, with two colonnades of Greek marble, supporting pointed arches. Timber tie beams strengthen the upper walls, and the nave is flanked by lower aisles; an exposed timber coffered roof. Down the left aisle are side chapels; that nearest to the chancel is the Contarini Chapel, with paintings by Tintoretto and Danese Cattaneo, and busts by Vittoria. The next is the Morosini Chapel, built by Bartolomeo Bon in the 1450s, with pictures by

La Madona de l'Orto: detail of the portal, by
Bartolomeo Bon, 1460–83

Domenico Tintoretto; and then the Vendramin Chapel, with
paintings by Palma il Vecchio and Titian. The chapel nearest the
entrance is the Valier; on the Lombard Renaissance altar: *Virgin and
Child* by Giovanni Bellini, *circa* 1480.

In the polygonal chancel are two huge canvases by Tintoretto, the
Last Judgement and the *Worship of the Golden Calf*, *circa* 1562, as well as
smaller works depicting the Virtues; further paintings by him in the
right flanking chapel, where he is buried, together with his family.

Immediately E of the church is the attractive monastic cloister,
with colonnades supporting simple brick arches. To the NW is the tall
brick campanile, the upper part showing a mixture of late Gothic
and early Renaissance, capped by an unusual tile-clad 'onion dome',
circa 1503.

From the square, continue SE along Fondamenta Gaspare
Contarini. At CN 3536 is **Palazzo Minelli Spada**, an imposing
construction with features characteristic of Longhena, although
perhaps by his follower Sardi. Built *circa* 1650, when the Minelli
were admitted into the nobility, in a period in which this zone had

Facing page: La Madona de l'Orto: detail of façade window

The Casinò degli Spiriti, the early sixteenth-century summer villa attached to Palazzo Contarini dal Zaffo

become prized for its space for ample gardens. The broad stone façade is impressive but asymmetrical, with an additional left wing; the lowest order is rusticated and the whole is richly detailed with cornices and balconies; above rise two obelisks.

Immediately adjacent to the E is **Palazzo Contarini dal Zaffo** (CN 3539–41), built by Gasparo Contarini, an outstanding intellectual and diplomat, created a cardinal in 1535. The house (1530–40) remained in Contarini hands until 1898.

A long, simple façade, with a large family *stemma*. The interior preserves frescoes by Guarana and Giandomenico Tiepolo, the latter depicting Giorgio Contarini, first duke of Jaffa, in the Holy Land, from which the affix 'dal Zaffo' derives.

Behind the palace is an extensive garden, flanking the Sacca de la Misericordia. At its NE corner is a simple, isolated Renaissance villa, the **Casinò degli Spiriti**. The villa and gardens were a famous centre of intellectual life in the sixteenth century, when the Contarini's guests included Aretino and Titian. The *casinò* has magnificent views over the lagoon towards the Terraferma and the mountains; its name derives from the refined cultural spirits of those who gathered there.

At the end of the quay, cross Ponte de la Sacca, and continue down Corte Vecchia. At the end, turn left along Fondamenta de l'Abazia. The quay passes below the colonnades of the Scuola Vecchia de la Misericordia; across the canal (s) is the restored *casinò* attached to Palazzo da Lezze. We enter Campo de l'Abazia, a quiet, attractive corner, once the burial ground of the adjacent church; canals on two sides, with the former monastic church of Santa Maria in Valverde to the NE, and the Scuola Vecchia to the NW. Across the wide canal to the E is the fine Gothic Palazzo Pesaro Papafava (see below).

Scuola Vecchia de la Misericordia (CN 3549): one of the oldest of the *scuole grandi*, the Venetian lay confraternities, founded in 1303. Construction began *circa* 1327, after the adjacent abbey had donated land, but the Scuola was enlarged in 1362–90. It was altered again in 1441, when the present *campo* façade was constructed; the colonnade was built in 1503. In 1498 the governing board decided that the Scuola was still too small; despite acute financial difficulties, they embarked on construction of the vast new Scuola Grande to the S, just across the bridge (see below).

This original building remained in use until 1532, then became the silk-workers' guildhall. Its condition deteriorated seriously, and

The Scuola Vecchia de la Misericordia (left), mostly fifteenth-century Gothic; right: Baroque façade of Santa Maria in Valverde by Clemente Moli, 1651

the Scuola was suppressed in 1806. Recently it was used as a workshop for restoring art works.

The accommodation follows that common to all the *scuole grandi*, with a lower hall, the *androne*, and an upper one (*sala capitolare*) and a small *albergo* for meetings of the governing *banca*. The ground floor is much altered, but the upper hall remains largely intact. A small wing off the N side contains the *albergo*.

The *campo* façade is late Venetian Gothic, with pendant-traceried windows, and a complex moulded parapet. Two of the three aedicules survive, but the richly sculpted tympanum, by Bartolomeo Bon, which formerly stood over the square entrance portal, was removed in 1612, and is in the Victoria and Albert Museum, London.

Former monastic house of Santa Maria in Valverde: a monastery was founded here as early as 936; adjacent was a small 'hospital' for pilgrims to the Holy Land. Much of this marshy zone was reclaimed in the succeeding centuries, and the site was bounded by water on the N and E sides. The church was rebuilt in the thirteenth century; in 1651 it was given the present Baroque façade by Clemente Moli, a follower of Bernini. After the Napoleonic dissolution it deteriorated rapidly, and was partly ruined before a long programme of restoration after 1828. It was closed again in 1868, however; in more recent times it was acquired by the Servites, who left in 1969, when it was closed once more.

The façade was funded by Gaspare Moro, a local benefactor; his bust is over the portal. The interior of the Gothic church remains, but much altered. The campanile is in better condition; it was built in the thirteenth century, a simple, sturdy brick tower.

Return NW along the Fondamenta de l'Abazia. At CN 3554 is the late sixteenth-century **Palazzo Rubini**, in the style of Sansovino, modernised at the end of the seventeenth century, perhaps by Tirali or Gaspari. The unusual plan has a cross-axis as well as the usual central axis, thus creating a cruciform space; the ends of the cross-axis terminate with doorways onto the gardens. The façade is imposing and symmetrical; the carved stone goats on the adjacent quay are intended to ward off evil spirits. Just beyond are the remains of **Corte Nova** (CN 3560), originally fifteenth-century almshouses, now lost. The elaborate Gothic portal has a relief panel, the *Madona de la Misericordia* (late fourteenth century), and elements from elsewhere, added in the fifteenth century.

Cross Ponte de Corte Vechia, continue through Campielo and Calle Trevisan, onto Fondamenta de la Misericordia, and turn left

Palazzo da Lezze, by Baldassare Longhena, 1645–70

(SE). At CN 3584 is the sixteenth-century **Palazzo Trevisan**, and at CN 3586 **Palazzo Maggia**, of similar date, with Corinthian and Ionic colonnettes to the upper-floor windows. We now reach **Palazzo da Lezze Antonelli** (CN 3597–8), a noble, impressive monument, one of the most prominent Baroque palaces in the city. It was designed by Longhena, *proto* to the da Lezze family, and built in 1645–70. The palace was comprehensively sacked at the fall of the Republic, and in the early nineteenth century passed to the Antonelli, who established a printing house here; further internal damage ensued. Today it is divided into apartments, although the imposing exterior survives. The broad, symmetrical, stone-clad façade contains fifty-nine windows and has thirty balconies. Above the rusticated ground floor are two tall *piani nobili* and an attic. The paired windows are divided by Corinthian pilasters, with mask keystones.

As the façade indicates, the unusual plan is extremely broad: the central *androne* has three sets of ancillary rooms on each side – seven principal bays in all. The grandiose staircase rises to the left of the

Foreground: the mid-seventeenth-century *casinò* of
Palazzo da Lezze; beyond: the Scuola Grande de la
Misericordia, by Jacopo Sansovino, begun 1535

hall. Most of the rich internal decorations (including frescoes by
Giandomenico Tiepolo and paintings by Titian and Veronese) are
long dispersed. The palace had a fine garden to the N, terminating at
its *casinò* on Rio de la Sensa.

At the SE end of Palazzo da Lezze, we reach Campo de la
Misericordia, dominated by the vast bare brick façade of the **Scuola
Grande de la Misericordia**, this immense structure was intended to
replace the smaller, older building to the NE. The Scuola's history of
financial instability and maladministration, however, was further
evinced by the lengthy saga of the Scuola Nuova.

Models were first requested in 1507, and Leopardi's design chosen,
only to be replaced by that of Giovanni Fontana; the aged Pietro
Lombardo was appointed to supervise the work, but it was then
abandoned for twenty years. In 1530 it was resurrected; the earlier
design was now considered anachronistic, and four new ones were
sought. Sansovino's was chosen, and in 1532 he was named *proto*. The

project, however, was grossly over-ambitious for the Scuola's limited resources. Although the foundation stone was laid in 1535, five years later little had been achieved; relations between Sansovino and the Scuola deteriorated, and in 1544 they rejected his design for a vaulted roof. A further hiatus followed in 1556–61; by the late 1560s the Scuola was heavily indebted; and in 1570 Sansovino died. In the same period, a design for the façade was produced, often attributed to Palladio; as we see, it was never executed.

By 1576 the first floor was installed, and, after a final effort, by 1582 the great hall was roofed, although it still lacked a staircase. Smeraldi's design was approved in 1587, and two years later the Scuola's relics were brought here and a solemn Mass celebrated. No building works took place thereafter. The Scuola was suppressed in 1806, and suffered occupation first by the military, and more recently as a sports centre; it has been unused for many years.

The imposing brick exterior has two tall, superimposed orders, the façade terminating with a large pediment. The portal is flanked by niches for statues, while the upper floor has three large single windows. Bands of toothed brickwork indicate where substantial stone cornices would have been located. The long side façade has seven bays, defined by paired pilasters, and each with a single window.

The plan resembles those of the other *scuole grandi*, with two large superimposed halls; a smaller wing to the NW contains the *albergo* and the staircase. The unusual three-aisled lower hall is divided longitudinally by two rows of Corinthian stone columns, set in pairs on tall plinths. They support heavy continuous stone architraves, which in turn carry the *sala capitolare* floor. The upper hall conserves extensive fresco decoration, in poor condition.

From the square, looking E across the Rio de Noal, a garden marks the site of the former **Palazzo Tiepolo**, a large Gothic palace, modernised in the sixteenth century by Sansovino, but demolished in 1800. Take the bridge at the SE corner, and continue down the Ramo onto Fondamenta San Felice. At the corner of the quay is Ponte Chiodo, the only surviving example in the city of a bridge with no parapets (*bande*); the other survivor is at Torcello. A little way down the quay, at CN 3609, is the fifteenth-century **Palazzo Salamon**, successively altered and modernised, with a mixture of Gothic and Renaissance windows. The quay now becomes Fondamenta de la Chiesa; at the end, it opens into Campo San Felice.

San Felice is an early parish foundation from *circa* 960. The first records (1177) show that it already had parochial status, and in 1267 (or 1276) it was re-consecrated, following reconstruction. It survived until the early sixteenth century, by which time it was in poor condition; it was rebuilt in 1531–56, to a design closely derived from Codussi. His influence is seen in the façades and the centralised Greek-cross plan. Thereafter, the church survived unaltered until the Napoleonic closures; in 1810 it reopened as a parish church, as it remains.

The principal canal façade has three bays, Ionic pilasters and a stone portal. The other (sw) façade masks the south transept, and is simpler but broader, again with a central portal.

The interior has the cool, refined vocabulary characteristic of Codussi and his followers, with the structural articulation all in Istrian stone, and plain white plaster to the planar surfaces. The shallow cupola over the crossing is supported by four large arches. Among the art works are sculptures by Giulio del Moro, and an altarpiece by Tintoretto.

The square was enlarged by demolitions in the late 1860s (see below); as a result, it lacks the enclosed, well-defined character of the usual Venetian parish square. Three *calli* off the sw side give access to a group of *palazzi* with their façades onto the Grand Canal.

Calle del Becher leads to **Palazzetto da Lezze** (CN 3681), an attractive smaller fifteenth-century Gothic house, set back from the canal by a small terrace garden. Next to it, and reached by Calle Boldù, is **Palazzo Boldù Ghisi** (CN 3685–6), with a tall, asymmetrical Renaissance façade onto the Grand Canal. Above the rusticated ground floor are two *piani nobili*, the lower one lit by a Serliana. The house passed from the Boldù to the Ghisi and then the Contarini, who joined it to their palace next door at CN 3696. The house conserves frescoes by Guarana. The adjacent **Palazzo Contarini Pisani** (CN 3696) has a substantial, rather plain façade, raised above a tall colonnade, with a quay beneath.

From the square, cross Ponte Novo into the **Strada Nova**. The decision to cut the Strada Nova was made by the city council in August 1867, to open the tortuous route between Santi Apostoli and Santa Fosca. The section from Santa Fosca to San Felice was cut in 1868, while this section, a broad, straight street from Ponte Novo to Santi Apostoli, 250 metres long, was completed in 1872. Following extensive demolitions, it was lined with undistinguished new shops.

Palazzo Pesaro Papafava: late *gotico fiorito, circa* 1450–60

Although highly animated, it remains alien to the characteristic organic topography of the city.

From the N side, enter Corte dei Pali; turn out of the back left corner, and then right into Calle Larga Priuli. Just before Ponte Priuli, on the left, is **Palazzo Priuli Scarpon** (CN 3709–10, 3732). Originally a large seventeenth-century house built by Antonio Priuli (doge 1618–23), largely destroyed by fire in 1739 and rebuilt. Among the surviving original elements are two watergates. The plan was retained, with the main hall in the form of a T, with water access from both adjacent canals. Cross Ponte Priuli, and continue N down the long, straight Calle de la Racheta, named after an early form of tennis. At CN 3764 is the late Gothic **Palazzo Pesaro Papafava**, water façade to the W, facing Rio de Noal. Fine *gotico fiorito, circa* 1450–60, with a regular, symmetrical plan and façades. The *calle* façade (difficult to appreciate) has a good five-light window to the *piano nobile*. That to the canal (seen from the Misericordia) is symmetrical, with a central watergate; the principal storey has a richly detailed four-light window, flanked by tall pairs of single lights. The second floor is similar but more simply detailed. The plan is traditional, with a contemporary well-head inside the ground floor. The stair, rising on the south side, was rebuilt, probably in the seventeenth century, with robust stone balustrading. The first-floor hall has frescoes of a similar date.

At the N end of the *calle* is **Palazzetto da Lezze Molin** (CN 3770), a Gothic *palazzetto* on the corner of Rio de Santa Caterina. Return to the Strada Nova via Calle de la Racheta; down the E side: *scudi* of several noble clans, including the Trevisan (CN 3781) and Pisani (CN 3784).

12 THE STRADA NOVA (1) AND THE CA' D'ORO

From the SW side of the Strada Nova, several short *calli* lead to palaces with their façades to the Grand Canal. The first is Calle Fontana, leading to **Palazzo Fontana** (CN 3828–30).

An impressive early seventeenth-century palace built by the Fontana, merchants originally from Piacenza. In the 1690s it was rented to the Rezzonico; Carlo Rezzonico, the future Pope Clement XIII, was born here in 1693. It remained in Fontana ownership until 1810. The façade is traditional, symmetrical and tripartite, although the house was extended towards the SE. The deep plan has a long central hall and many smaller side rooms, used for storing traded goods. Two staircases, one on each side of the *androne*, each give access to one of the two *piani nobili*. The rear façade is unusually richly detailed.

Almost next door is **Palazzo Giusti** (CN 3843), reached from Calle dei Pali, off the Strada Nova. The house is by Visentini; its Grand Canal façade (dated 1766) has unusual features, notably on the ground floor, where four portals alternate with three niches for statues, all separated by stone pilasters. The two upper floors have continuous balconies across the width of the façade, which is capped by an *abbaino*.

Some of the accommodation now forms part of the gallery space for the Franchetti Foundation at the Ca' d'Oro next door (see below). Before we visit this famous house: a brief detour, crossing the Strada Nova, and taking Ramo Ca' d'Oro into Calle Zotti. At CN 3904–10: a rare surviving terrace of small Gothic houses, probably late fourteenth century. Beyond the southernmost house is a row of five identical cottages, each with a small rear courtyard; workshops

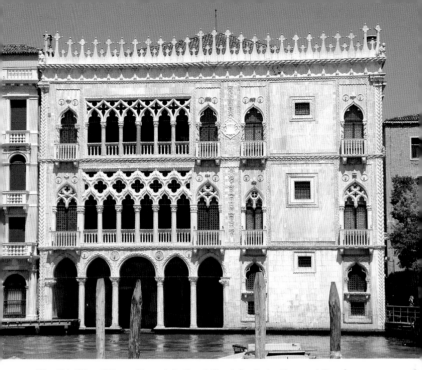

The Ca' d'Oro (Palazzo Contarini); Grand Canal façade, by Zane and Bartolomeo Bon and Matteo Raverti, 1422–*circa* 1430

on the ground floor and a two-storey apartment above, with alternating paired windows and single lights.

Returning to the Strada Nova, we now take the Calle Ca' d'Oro opposite, to the land gate of the **Ca' d'Oro (Palazzo Contarini)** (CN 3933), the most famous medieval palace in the city. The Ca' d'Oro has been noted for centuries as the apogee of the rich late Gothic style, famed for its exquisitely decorated façade, best seen from the Riva de l'Ogio, near the Rialto fish market.

It was begun by Marin Contarini in 1421 and completed in the mid-1430s, built on the foundations of an earlier Venetian-Byzantine house, which had belonged to the Zeno, his wife's family. Many decorative relief carvings from the old palace were carefully reused in the new one. The asymmetrical plan and façade also result from the reuse of the original foundations.

Contarini, supported by his father Antonio (procurator of San Marco), appointed Zane and Bartolomeo Bon as his principal masters, together with a second team from Milan, under Matteo Raverti, who made some notable individual features: the two splendid superimposed *logge* on the canal façade, the ostentatious land

The Ca' d'Oro: detail of the first-floor loggia, by Matteo Raverti, 1425–6

gate and the refined staircase in the courtyard. Almost everything else is the work of the Bon, including the crenellation, the pendant-traceried windows, the waterfront loggia and the fine well-head.

Contarini died in 1441, a few years after the palace's completion, and the house later underwent a series of ownerships. By the nineteenth century it was in poor condition, but in 1894 it was bought by Baron Franchetti, who effected further alterations but also restored what remained to its former splendour. The ground-floor *androne* was drastically altered, but the staircase was restored, as was the crenellation and the *riva*. These works took place in 1905–10; in 1916 Franchetti gave the palace to the state; six years later, on his death, his art collection also passed to the nation, and remains here today. In 1972–3 the interior was sensitively remodelled by Carlo Scarpa.

The plan is traditional, although asymmetrical, built around three sides of the courtyard. The central axis runs down one side of the courtyard, and there is the usual row of smaller rooms down the other side of the *portego*, towards the NW. This bipartite arrangement is reflected in the famous façade. There are three storeys, a generous ground floor (with a partial mezzanine) and two *piani nobili* of nearly equal importance. The first is reached by the open stair in the courtyard, while the second is reached by an internal timber staircase, of roughly contemporary date, salvaged from Palazzetto Agnello at Santa Maria Mater Domini.

The Ca' d'Oro: the courtyard; well-head by Bartolomeo
Bon (1427): staircase by Matteo Raverti

The courtyard is reached by the richly detailed land gate,
surmounted by the Contarini arms; in the centre is Bartolomeo
Bon's well-head of Verona *broccatello* (1427); Raverti's staircase (1425–
6) rises on two sides, supported by arches. The ground-floor *androne*,
remodelled by Franchetti, has a row of stone columns down the
centre, supporting timber *barbacani*. At the s end is an open stone
screen, made by the Bon, dividing it from the quay outside.

The plans of the two upper floors are almost identical, the main
hall terminating in a broad waterfront loggia, and with a large single
room in the other corner. There are three smaller rooms down the
side of the *portego*.

The façade was originally sumptuously decorated with gold leaf
and ultramarine. Although the gilding is long gone, the entire façade
is clad with stone and marble, richly carved and decorated. The
right-hand wing, seen from the quay opposite, is essentially solid,
with tall single windows (with Bon's refined pendant tracery) set
into the corners of the rooms behind. The left wing, by contrast,

The Ca' d'Oro: interior of the upper loggia, by
Matteo Raverti, 1426–7

is almost entirely open, with Bon's five-bay waterfront loggia
surmounted by Raverti's two refined upper *logge*, each with different
tracery. The lower one derives from the Doge's Palace, but the other
had not been seen in the city before. At both levels they are flanked
by further pairs of pendant-traceried windows. Finally, the entire
ensemble is crowned by Bon's exotic crenellation, again originally
painted and gilded.

Just across the *calle* is the early fifteenth-century **Palazzo Giustinian
Pesaro Ravà** (CN 3935), an attractive asymmetrical Gothic house built
around a small garden, with an L-shaped plan. The tall, narrow Grand
Canal façade is also asymmetrical, lacking the right wing; two *piani
nobili*, each with a four-light window to the main hall.

Returning to the Strada Nova, walk E as far as Calle Priuli on the
left; follow the *calle* (it changes direction twice) as far as Ponte Priuli.
On the left: the sixteenth-century **Palazzo Priuli Stazio** (CN 4013),
with façade towards the N, and an attractive rear garden. The design
shows the influence of Sanmicheli, with superimposed Serliane to
the façade. The interior has a fine staircase, perhaps by Scamozzi,
who worked for the Priuli elsewhere.

Crossing the bridge, around Campielo degli Albanesi is a development of sixteenth-century housing, consisting of two terraces and a block of four (CN 4014–24, 4025–6, 4041–2 and 4044–53). All the façades are in a simple Renaissance style typical of such speculative rental developments. Nearby, at CN 4054 (Fondamenta Priuli) is **Palazzo Perducci**, also late sixteenth century. Take Calle Corrente N, and cross the bridge to Fondamenta Sant'Andrea. At CN 4118 is **Palazzo Albrizzi**: a restrained, elegant, sixteenth-century façade; the rich interior contains eighteenth-century stucco decoration by Guarana. Adjacent to the bridge (CN 4130) is a house, originally thirteenth century, with a *trifora* to the first floor and a *quadrifora* to the second, both of the early cusped type. From the E end of Fondamenta Sant'Andrea, take Calle Zanardi N to Ponte Santa Caterina. Adjacent to the bridge, at CN 4132, is **Palazzo Zanardi**, built in the sixteenth century for the Rizzo, who owned several houses in this area. It was sold to the Zanardi in 1661, who had been ennobled in 1653 *per soldi* (by payment).

Retrace the route back down Calle Zanardi, and cross Ponte Sant'Andrea; continue down the broad Ruga Due Pozzi. At the end on the right is the attractive **Palazzetto Benedetti** (CN 4173–6), a good medium-sized Gothic *palazzetto*, very late fourteenth century or early fifteenth, with a *sotoportego* along the canal façade; a four-bay colonnade with timber *barbacani*. The symmetrical, well-proportioned façade has a *quadrifora* to the central hall on both upper floors. The side façade to the Ruga, by contrast, is long and randomly fenestrated.

Crossing Ponte Priuli again, this time turning left at the end of Campielo Priuli, into Calle del Cristo, down the side of the church of Santa Sofia. At CN 4228: a fine thirteenth-century Greek marble *formella* depicting two peacocks. Continue into the Strada Nova. On the N side (CN 4186–90): the **Scuola dei Pittori** (painters), with two relief panels of St Luke, the guild's patron, dated 1572.

13   SANTA SOFIA AND THE STRADA NOVA (2)

The broad Campo Santa Sofia, contiguous with the Strada Nova, opens directly in front of the church, extending to the Grand Canal. On the NW side is **Palazzo Morosini Sagredo** (CN 4199); main façade onto the Grand Canal, best seen from the market opposite. Originally thirteenth century, the palace has experienced numerous

Palazzo Sagredo: façade to the Grand Canal

alterations and modernisations over the centuries, some recorded on its façade. Its core is a Venetian-Byzantine palace once owned by the Morosini; in the early eighteenth century they sold it to Gherardo Sagredo, who began modernising it. The Grand Canal façade is long and asymmetrical, extended towards the right in the late fourteenth century. The chief evidence of the original house is the six-light window to the first-floor hall, flanked by similar single lights; the second-floor *portego* is lit by a *quadrifora*, modernised in the late Gothic era by the addition of four stone quatrefoils.

The radical eighteenth-century modernisation of the interior was completed by Tirali and Temanza in 1738; although the planned new façade was never executed, the *campo* flank was refaced by Tirali, who also inserted a grand new staircase (1734); much of the contemporary decorative stucco by Abbondio Stazio has survived. The house remained in Sagredo ownership until 1871, when the branch became extinct; today it is a hotel.

Santa Sofia: the modest church does not have a presence onto its own square, and remains hidden behind a row of shops, only the portal indicating its location. An early foundation, established in 866. The first reconstruction took place in 1225; further alterations followed in the early fifteenth century and again *circa* 1508. Finally, in 1698 it was modernised by Gaspari to achieve its present appearance. The church was closed in 1810, but reopened in 1836, subordinate to San Felice.

Palazzo Michiel da le Colonne: Grand Canal façade,
modernised by Antonio Gaspari, 1697

The basic plan survives, with a nave flanked by side aisles, all of
four bays, with stone colonnades; a small cupola. There is little of
note artistically, although four sculpted stone figures (*St Luke*, *St
Andrew*, *St Cosmas*, *St Damian*) are attributed to Rizzo's shop. The
adjacent campanile is part of the original thirteenth-century shaft,
once considerably taller.

On the SE side of the square is **Palazzetto Foscari** (CN 4201), an
attractive smallish Gothic house, *circa* 1450, now a hotel. The Grand
Canal façade is asymmetrical, with the watergate to the right and
the *portego* window to the left. Continue SE down the Strada Nova
towards Santi Apostoli. The next *palazzi* are reached by land from
the SE side, with façades to the Grand Canal; all best seen from the
Rialto market.

Palazzo Michiel da le Colonne (CN 4314): an imposing palace,
originally owned by the Grimani, who sold it to the Zen in the late
seventeenth century; in 1697 it was modernised by Gaspari. The
original Byzantine structure was retained, but the most prominent
feature was now the tall colonnade by which the palace is known.
Among several later owners was the duke of Mantua. The façade is

dignified and imposing, the full-width colonnade supporting three upper storeys. The basic arrangement is tripartite and symmetrical, with Serliane to the two upper halls.

Almost next door is the smaller **Palazzo Bianchi Michiel del Brusà** (CN 4391), extending back to the Strada Nova. First built in the fifteenth century, it suffered a serious fire in 1774, from which it takes its name (*brusà* = burned). Some Gothic material remains in the façade, probably 1440s, although the ground floor (paired watergates) and the top floor reflect the post-fire modernisations. The interior retains rich decoration, including frescoes by Guarana.

The last of this group is **Palazzo Mangilli Valmarana** (CN 4392), on the corner of Rio dei Santi Apostoli, with a garden on the Strada Nova. An earlier house dated from the fourteenth century, but in 1740 it was bought by Joseph Smith, British consul to the Republic. It was then rebuilt in 1751 by Visentini. Smith was both an art connoisseur and a wealthy businessman, who patronised Visentini, but also effectively became the agent of Canaletto, acquiring many paintings, most of which were later sold to the British royal family.

After Smith's death in 1770, the palace was modernised in 1784 by Selva for its new owner, Giuseppe Mangilli, adding the two top floors and decorating the interior in a rich Neo-classical manner. Its later owner, Benedetto Valmarana, housed a notable art collection here. The lower façade is a strongly modelled Neo-classical composition, with paired Corinthian columns to the main storey and a prominent pedimented central window with a stone balcony; the later upper floors are much more restrained.

14 SANTI APOSTOLI AND ENVIRONS

At the SE end of the Strada Nova, we enter the busy Campo dei Santi Apostoli, meeting point for several routes. This district was one of the earliest parts of the archipelago to be settled. On the S side, adjacent to the canal, is the tall, imposing former **Scuola de l'Angelo Custode** (CN 4448), today the German Lutheran church; designed by Tirali, begun in 1713. The plan has the usual form for a Venetian *scuola*, with two rectangular superimposed halls, linked by a staircase. Its island site resulted in four visible elevations, all treated in a similarly sober, monumental, Neo-classical manner. The *campo* façade has three broad bays, with a central pedimented portal, while on the upper floor the central aedicule is flanked by two large

Santi Apostoli: the campanile (1672); upper part by
Andrea Tirali, 1710

pedimented rectangular windows. In 1806, following suppression of
the *scuole*, it was converted for German Protestant services.

Santi Apostoli occupies the NE side of the square, one of twelve
foundations said to have been established by St Magnus in 643.
Rebuilt and modernised several times over the centuries; the medieval
brick basilica survived until the fifteenth century, when various
additions, including the Corner Chapel (see below), were made. The
last rebuilding took place in 1549–75; much survives, although
partially remodelled *circa* 1748. The campanile was rebuilt in 1672; its
exuberant and elegant bell-chamber was added by Tirali in 1710.

The exterior is very plain, but the interior has a spacious
rectangular five-bay nave, without aisles; a series of altars down each
flank wall. Articulation consists of a giant order of Corinthian
pilasters in dark grey stone, with large clerestory windows. The flat

ceiling has paintings set into it; the square chancel is surmounted by a cupola on pendentives, and flanked by smaller side chapels, with barrel-vaulted ceilings. Chancel left wall: the *Fall of Manna* by Veronese. The unusual high altar, by Francesco Lazzari, takes the form of a circular Neo-classical *tempietto*, flanked by statues by Torretto. Right chancel chapel: early fourteenth-century frescoes.

The most notable feature is the Corner Chapel, attached to the right nave wall, one of the earliest Renaissance works in Venice. It was begun by the immensely wealthy Zorzi (Giorgio) Corner in 1483; the architect is unknown, although there have been attributions to Codussi. The chapel has a square plan, approached by a triumphal arch, and surmounted by a cupola on pendentives. The whole is richly detailed, with Corinthian columns in each corner supporting a heavy cornice. The monument to Marco Corner (+1511), on the right wall, is attributed to Tullio Lombardo. The altarpiece is the *Communion of St Lucy* by Giambattista Tiepolo.

Back in the square, follow the s flank of the church eastwards, where the narrow *calle* opens into Campielo drio la Chiesa; take Calle del Manganer, and turn right, then left, into **Campielo de la Cason.** The term means a prison, and dates from the medieval era, when each *sestiere* had its own gaol. The site is said to be that of the palace-castle of the Partecipazio clan, which produced several early doges; it remained the ducal seat until the first Doge's Palace at San Marco was completed in the ninth century.

Take Calle de la Malvasia out of the far side; just before Ponte San Canzian, on the left, is the seventeenth-century **Palazzo Corner** (CN 4501–2), with the Sotoportego del Tragheto along the canal façade. The name refers to the ferries to Murano that used to leave from here. Next to Palazzo Corner is **Palazzo Morosini** (CN 4503), also known as Ca' Strozzi, because it was occupied in the sixteenth century by the wealthy Florentine banking family.

Return to Campielo drio la Chiesa; this time take Calle Manzini out of the N side, and then left, down Calle dei Preti, into Salizada del Pistor. At CN 4555: an interesting *palazzetto*, late thirteenth or early fourteenth century, with a broad, symmetrical façade, and a second-floor *trifora*. Continuing N, turn right into Calle Larga dei Proverbi, where there is a fourteenth-century house with a good portal (CN 4564), and at CN 4582 a house with a four-light window from the thirteenth century. At the E end, turn left up Rio Terà Santi Apostoli, as far as Rio Terà dei Franceschi, on the left. CN 4595 and 4597 are small fourteenth-century Gothic houses.

Returning to Rio Terà Santi Apostoli, on the E side is Ramo Valmarana, leading to the tiny eponymous *campielo*. Here stood **Palazzo Morosini Valmarana** (CN 4636), with a large and notable garden. It was built by the Morosini, and had two elements, a palace and a large *casinò*, with the garden between the two. The palace was reputedly designed by Palladio and was frescoed by Veronese; it was extended in the seventeenth century by Longhena. By the eighteenth century it was rented to many different people, and its condition had deteriorated; in 1829 it was demolished. Only a few fragments of doorways remain today.

Return to Rio Terà Santi Apostoli and continue N to Rio Terà Barba Frutariol. At CN 4714 is a relief of the arms of the Simbeni family (1485), by Antonio Rizzo. At CN 4720 is a small fourteenth-century house, and at CN 4726 a rare survivor from the thirteenth century. Walking E down the Rio Terà, just before Ponte Giustinian, left, is **Palazzo Giustinian Jager** (CN 4760), an impressive sixteenth-century palace, considerably altered later. It was built by the Giustinian but later underwent several changes of ownership; by the 1950s it was semi-derelict, but was restored and today houses a school. The plan and façades are symmetrical and tripartite, but with an extra wing on the N side. The impressive canal façade evinces the influence of Sanmicheli: two superimposed *piani nobili*, both detailed in a similar manner.

The interior was remodelled after 1788 for the Jager, probably by Maccaruzzi. A sumptuous staircase was installed, and the *portego* was frescoed by Guarana and Pierantonio Novelli. Most of the interior survives, and was restored in the 1970s.

15   THE GESUITI AND SANTA CATERINA

Return W along the Rio Terà, and take Salizada del Spezier off the N side. Cross Ponte dei Sartori at the far end, then left along the Fondamenta. At CN 4838 is the former **Scuola dei Sartori** (tailors), with a relief panel (1511) showing the Virgin and patron saints. Return to the bridge. At the corner of Salizada Sceriman is the imposing **Palazzo Contarini Sceriman** (CN 4831), a notable late *gotico fiorito* palace, *circa* 1466, built for the Dolce family; it passed to the Contarini, then the Gozzi; in 1725 it was auctioned to the Sceriman, a family of Persian origin. The *salizada* façade is impressive and symmetrical, with a fine portal and a *quadrifora* to the main upper hall. The long canal façade has three elements, the first the original three-bay Gothic section nearest the bridge; then a lower, modernised section, with a prominent watergate and a large Serliana. At the rear: a taller third element, again Gothic; all three have Baroque balconies. The garden at the E end is the site of the lost Palazzo Venier.

Immediately NE is a housing development, begun in 1495 by the Scuola Grande de la Carità; two long terraces, with Calle dei Volti down the centre, and a water façade to the N, onto Rio de Santa Caterina. They were funded by the will of Tommaso Cavazza, who left his palace at Santa Marina to be sold, and the money invested in these almshouses. The end façades of the four-storey blocks onto the *salizada* are united by a high-level arch. The development has typically simple detailing, with arched windows to the two main floors.

Cross Ponte dei Gesuiti into the long, spacious square of the same name; the eponymous church dominates its N end. **Chiesa e monastero dei Gesuiti (Santa Maria Assunta)**: one of the most important Baroque churches in Venice, with a richly decorated interior. The first monastic house was established here by the Crociferi *circa* 1150; the site was then on the edge of the lagoon. It was rebuilt after a fire in 1214. By the sixteenth century the Crociferi had become notorious for their licentious behaviour and in 1464 they were reformed. Another fire in 1514 caused further damage, but sixteenth-century reclamations provided more land for monastic buildings. Between 1644 and 1655 all the Crociferi houses were suppressed by Pope Innocent X, and in 1657 the Jesuits were admitted into the city. In 1715 they began a radical modernisation, including Domenico Rossi's new church.

Its design followed Jesuit principles, based on the model of Vignola's 'mother church' in Rome, and was completed by 1728. The Jesuits themselves, however, were suppressed in 1773, and the monastery was converted first into a school, later a barracks. In 1844 it was returned to the Jesuits, who remain there today, occupying the conventual buildings to the N.

The church plan is a long Latin cross, with a single nave flanked by deep interconnecting chapels, three down each side. The rich, massive façade is attributed to the obscure Giambattista Fattoretto, but the original concept was probably that of Rossi. The lower order is of large Corinthian pilasters, surmounted by a bold cornice; above are pedestals with statues of the Apostles. The portal is surmounted by a curved Baroque pediment, again with marble figures. The outer bays of the façade correspond to the depth of the lateral chapels

Gesuiti: lower order of the façade, probably by
Domenico Rossi, but perhaps executed by
Giambattista Fattoretto (1715–30)

inside; the upper order is thus narrower and also simpler. Corinthian
pilasters divide it into three bays, with a large central window. The
whole is capped by a pediment, crowned by a sculpted group, the
Assumption by Torretto.

The interior is characterised by lavish polychrome decoration to
almost every surface, from the geometric marble patterned floor to
the green and white *intarsio* to the pilasters and the gilded stucco
ceilings; the last are by Abbondio Stazio, with inset paintings by
Francesco Fontebasso. The huge, complex high altar is by Giuseppe
Pozzo, inspired by Bernini at St Peter's, Rome; an impressive
baldacchino, with twisted *verde antico* marble columns.

A number of notable works of art include paintings by Palma il
Giovane, Campagna, Morleiter, Titian and Tintoretto; the sacristy
contains a cycle, also by Palma il Giovane.

Palazzi Zen, begun *circa* 1510, completed 1550s

The sixteenth- to seventeenth-century conventual buildings
to the s have a severely plain *campo* façade, behind which the
accommodation is built around three internal courtyards. They have
been empty for many years, and are to be converted for housing.

On the w side of the square were once several *scuole piccole*. At
CN 4905 is the **Oratorio dei Crociferi**, founded in the thirteenth
century, but rebuilt in 1556, with some surviving Gothic details. The
s façade is symmetrical, with a relief of the Virgin and Child above
the portal. The interior contains paintings by Palma il Giovane.
Among the other *scuole* based here, that of the Varoteri (leather-
workers) was relocated to Santa Margherita (1725). Those of the
silk-workers and barrel-makers also stood here, as well as that of
the Sartori (see above).

From the Ponte dei Gesuiti, take Fondamenta Zen w; at the
corner of the square is the end façade of the unusual **Palazzi Zen**
(CN 4922–5), a long row of three contiguous palaces, begun by
Francesco Zen in the very early sixteenth century; the façades have
an eclectic mixture of late Gothic and early Renaissance motifs.

Zen may have collaborated with Serlio, who was a close friend. The palace was completed only in the 1550s; it was a radical modernisation of earlier structures, unified by this complex façade, with an overall length of twenty-three bays. The basic rhythm is provided by four robust stone balconies, below each of which is an entrance portal. On the *piano nobile*, simple Renaissance arched windows alternate with odd late Gothic windows and blind Gothic arches, a unique arrangement. The façades were originally frescoed by Tintoretto and Schiavone, while the interiors were later decorated by G. B. Tiepolo and Amigoni, with paintings by Strozzi and Rosalba Carriera.

Continue w along Fondamenta Santa Caterina. Towards the end, on the right is the **Chiesa e convento de Santa Caterina**, foundation date unknown, but the first occupants were probably Augustinian friars. They were suppressed in 1274 and the house was acquired by Giovanni Bianco, a merchant, who donated it to Bortolotta Giustinian, who in turn established an Augustinian nunnery. It was rebuilt in the mid-fifteenth century; much survives, although damaged in the First World War, and by fire in 1977. The nunnery remained until 1807, when it was amalgamated with Sant'Alvise. It later became a high school, but is currently closed.

The church's long axis is along the quay; there is no main façade. The nave is flanked by aisles, and is approached by two doorways from the quay. The campanile, originally Romanesque, was replaced by the present simple brick construction in the eighteenth century.

The interior retains its Gothic appearance, the nave having an open timber 'ship's-keel' roof; at one end is the *barco* or nuns' choir gallery. Most of the paintings are now dispersed. The monastic buildings to the N largely survive, some modernised in the eighteenth century; the large refectory dominates the w side of the cloister.

Continue to the w end of the quay, and then take Calle Lunga to the right, terminating at the Fondamente Nove.

16   THE FONDAMENTE NOVE (1) AND BIRRI

The Fondamente Nove ('new quays') were a major reclamation project of the late sixteenth century, intended to increase substantially the 'buildable' extent of the city. The decision was made by the Senate in 1546, but work began only in 1590, following a further decision of the Collegio two years earlier. The original plan was to develop according to a rational rectangular grid of streets, but, as we can see, it was not strictly followed, although the street pattern is a little more regular than the usual Venetian organic layout.

From the w end: a fine view of the Sacca de la Misericordia and the Casinò degli Spiriti; good views also towards San Michele and Murano (NE). Walking SE along the Fondamenta, we pass the entrance to the Campo dei Gesuiti, continuing to Ponte Donà. The bridge also dates from the 1590s. At the far side is the simple but impressive **Palazzo Donà da le Rose** (CN 5038). Begun by Doge Leonardo Donà in 1610; it has two external façades, one to the Fondamenta, the other to Rio dei Gesuiti. The Donà da le Rose take their name from a golden rose given to them in 1470 by Pope Sixtus V. Donà himself was closely involved with the reclamations, and was one of the earliest 'settlers' in this new zone. The palace was incomplete when he died in 1612, but was completed by his brother Niccolò; it is still owned by his descendants.

The palace shows the influence of Serlio, and has been attributed to Manopola and the Contin. The plan has a long *androne* parallel to the canal, and joined to the canal façade by a hallway, the two spaces forming a T-shape. The main façade is that to the w, broad, simple and sober, with two superimposed Serliane as its principal features. The fenestration reflects the internal plan, with two rooms on each side of the central *portego*.

The interior has been almost perfectly preserved as it was originally built, with rich decoration, notably to the sumptuous main staircase. It contains a portrait of the Emperor Ferdinand II by Titian, and portraits of the Donà clan by Tintoretto.

Continue E along the Fondamente; take Calle Ruzzini (right), and turn into Calle Larga dei Boteri. Near the w end is the studio built for Titian in 1527 (today a marble workshop, CN 5112). At the time, the 'new quays' had not yet been reclaimed, and it faced the open lagoon. At the eastern end of Calle Larga is **Palazzo Corniani Algarotti in Birri** (CN 5356), façade to Rio de la Panada. Built by the Stella in the sixteenth century, in 1722 it passed to the Algarotti, who began a major modernisation. The interior was decorated by Pierantonio Novelli and Giambattista Crosato; the architect may have been Temanza, a friend of Francesco Algarotti. It then passed to the Corniani, who amassed a notable collection of prints, paintings and minerals, which was opened to the public after 1797.

The plan is the usual tripartite type, with the *androne* and the courtyard together forming a T-shaped plan. The land façade to the *calle* is typical of the mid- to late sixteenth century. The district s of the Fondamente Nove is known as **Birri**, perhaps from *bierum*, a water-mill. Formerly remote and isolated, today it lies on the route from the city centre to the *vaporetto* stops on the Fondamente Nove, and is better frequented. The E part is characterised by long, parallel *calli*, while the w section has a more complex network of *calli* and *campieli*.

From Calle Larga dei Boteri, take the long, straight Calle del Fumo, and continue s through Campielo del Pestrin, Calle del Pestrin, Campielo Stella and Campielo Widmann. Then take Rio Terà dei Biri southwards, to the *fondamenta*. Turn left under the *sotoportego*, and left again into Calle Larga Giacinto Gallina. At CN 5396, by Ponte de la Panada, is **Palazzo Loredan**: a Gothic canal façade and a seventeenth-century street façade. Adjacent (CN 5400) is **Palazzo Cappellis**, probably late fourteenth-century Gothic, with a symmetrical, tripartite façade. The windows follow the usual pattern, with good *quadrifore* to the upper floors. Return to the w end of the Calle Larga, and turn right along Fondamenta Widmann. At the end, at CN 5403, is **Palazzo Widmann Rezzonico Foscari**, a notable early work by Longhena, built for Ambrogio Sarotti, but acquired by Giovanni Widmann, a noble from Carinthia, in the 1620s. It was complete before 1630; after his death, Giovanni's family continued to enrich the interior, although the house later passed to the Rezzonico and the Foscari. The plan and façade are regular, with two internal stairs, each serving one of the *piani nobili*. The impressive canal façade has rustication to the lower levels, and a broken pediment to the main portal. The *piani nobili* have Longhena's typical raised panelling between the windows.

Immediately SE is a smaller house (CN 5409), with a *sotoportego*. The side façade is enlivened with a collection of Byzantine paterae.

17 FROM SAN CANZIAN TO CA' DA MOSTO

Cross Ponte Widmann, continue down the Calle Larga into Campo Santa Maria Nova, and continue down Calle del Spezier, turning right into Campielo Crovato. On the NW side is **San Canzian (San Canciano)**, an ancient parish foundation, dedicated to three early Christian martyrs, Canzio, Canziano and Canzianilla, killed at Aquileia in AD 304. Probably founded in the late ninth century; a major restoration in the 1300s, and re-consecration in 1351. The church survived until the mid-sixteenth century, when it was rebuilt as we see it today; the architect is unknown. The simple Neo-classical façade was added by Gaspari in 1705–6.

The interior: a central nave and two side aisles. The general 'vocabulary' is grey stone, with plain plastered wall surfaces. The four nave bays are supported by a Corinthian colonnade, with a shallow vaulted ceiling. Flanking the large chancel arch are two small stone pulpits. Above the square chancel is an octagonal drum supporting a cupola on pendentives; four roundels (the Evangelists?) are set into them.

The chancel is flanked by two small chapels; the right one is that of the Widmann, whose palace is nearby. Like the palace, it is probably by Longhena. The left chapel is dedicated to St Filippo Neri.

From CampiElo Crovato, take the busy Salizada San Canzian sw. On the right: a group of late Gothic houses. At CN 5547 and 5549–50 is **Palazzo Contarini**; above the land gate at CN 5547 is a saint holding the model of a church. The former courtyard adjacent to the *salizada* is now lost, but the Gothic crenellation survives. Adjacent are the two **Case Gherardi** (CN 5552 and 5553), both with façades to Rio dei Santi Apostoli. One has a courtyard (Corte Gherardi) accessible from the *salizada*, with an attractive open Gothic staircase.

To reach the next group of ancient palaces, continue down the Salizada into Campielo Flaminio Corner. Take the short Calle Dolfin into Campielo Riccardo Selvatico, and Calle Dolfin again until you reach the *sotoportego* along Rio dei Santi Apostoli. Continue left to the end of the *sotoportego*; directly in front is a courtyard with a large open staircase, Corte del Leon Bianco. This is the rear façade of the well-known **Ca' da Mosto** (CN 5631), an important early Venetian-Byzantine *palazzo*, today semi-derelict. Early thirteenth century, perhaps built by the da Mosto, whose most notable member was the explorer Alvise (b. 1432), who sailed around west Africa and 'discovered' the Cape Verde islands. It later became a famous hotel, the Leon Bianco, hosting many illustrious guests, including the Emperor Franz Josef in 1769 and 1775.

Its main interest today is the Grand Canal façade, seen from the market opposite; although altered, the lowermost order retains three arches of the original colonnade, with rich relief decoration. The *piano nobile* has a very fine central six-light window, flanked by single lights, and with relief panels above and between the arches. A refined

Ca' da Mosto: Grand Canal façade; the two lower
orders are early thirteenth century

string-course defines the top of this level; the upper floors were
added later. In the centre of the second floor is a Serliana, probably
seventeenth century.

Returning from the Corte del Leon Bianco to the *sotoportego*, this
colonnade forms part of **Palazzo Falier** (CN 5643), another early
survivor, partly from the 1170s. The house is well known (or
notorious) as having been the home of Doge Marin Falier, who
attempted a plot against the elected government of the Republic,
was discovered, tried, found guilty of treason and decapitated in the
Piazzetta on 7 April 1355.

The façade rises above the colonnade, facing Campo Santi
Apostoli; the colonnade itself is mostly original, as are the two upper
orders of the façade. Both *piani nobili* are of equal importance; the
lower one has a four-light window (with traces of a fifth), while the
upper has a second *quadrifora*, offset to one side; all the windows
have stilted arches. Several contemporary relief sculptures are set into
the façade. The plan is traditional and tripartite, but with a narrow
central hall.

Return towards the small, congested Campielo Selvatico; off to the right is the narrow Calle de la Posta de Fiorenza, at the end of which is the land entrance to the **Palazzetti Dolfin** (CN 5655), two small fifteenth-century Gothic houses, with Grand Canal façades. Next to them is **Palazzetto Bolani Erizzo** (CN 5662), again with canal façade, also best seen from the markets on the far side. For many years (1529–51) it was the home of Pietro Aretino, the writer and chronicler of Venetian life. In a letter to Domenico Bollani (1537), Aretino describes and praises the view from his window over the Grand Canal and the markets.

18 SAN GIOVANNI GRISOSTOMO AND THE 'HOUSE OF MARCO POLO'

From the Campielo, cross Ponte San Giovanni Grisostomo (Ponte de' Zogatoi). Before the church, take Calle de la Stua to the right. At the far end of the long *sotoportego* is **Campielo del Remer**. The picturesque courtyard is open to the Grand Canal; good view of the markets and Rialto bridge. It is surrounded by a complex of buildings, of which the oldest is the thirteenth-century Palazzetto Lion. The chief surviving elements are the portal at the top of the open staircase and the adjacent flanking windows. The staircase is heavily restored and contains little (if any) original material.

Return to the busy Campo San Giovanni Grisostomo. Off the right side, Calle Sernagiotto leads to **Palazzo Sernagiotto** (CN 5722), an imposing structure, again with its façade towards the markets. It was rebuilt in 1847 by Giovanni Battista Benvenuti, with a prominent waterfront colonnade, and a tall symmetrical façade. Back in the square: **San Giovanni Grisostomo**, according to tradition, was founded in 1080 by the Cattaneo family. In 1475 it was badly damaged by fire, and by 1488 reconstruction was necessary. In 1495 the old church was demolished and the present one begun by Codussi; it was probably nearly complete at his death in 1504 and was completed by his son Domenico, although consecrated only in 1525.

The main *salizada* façade derives from San Michele, although with simpler detailing. The tall central bay is capped by a curved pediment, with lower flanking quadrants to the side aisles; a good stone portal. The s flank elevation is equally restrained, and has a second fine portal, again Corinthian.

Campielo del Remer: detail of thirteenth-
century window to Palazzetto Lion

The site was extremely constricted and resources modest; Codussi's
compact plan responds to these conditions: a centralised Greek cross,
almost square overall, with the large, square central bay forming the
nave. It is surmounted by a shallow cupola on pendentives. The
narrow side aisles have barrel-vaulted ceilings, while the small square
bays in each corner are also surmounted by pendentive domes, but
at a lower level. The plan of the chancel is rectangular, but with
radiused corners.

All the internal detailing is characteristic of Codussi, simple and
well defined, with grey stone for the structure and plain white
plaster for the planar surfaces. Most of the light derives from four
large high-level *oci* and clerestory lights to the chancel. Two chapels
were designed by Codussi as an integrated part of the whole; that to
the N transept is of the Bernabò family (1498–1502), with a rich
refined altarpiece by Tullio Lombardo (1506); the Diletti Chapel was
competed in 1509 after Codussi's death. Its altarpiece is the last
known work of Giovanni Bellini (1516).

The prominent campanile formerly stood across the street, but
was rebuilt after the street was widened in 1532; it was completed
in 1590, capped with a rather heavy bell-chamber.

Continue s down the *salizada* towards the Fondaco dei Tedeschi. On the right is Calle Civran, leading to the land entrance of **Palazzo Civran** (CN 5745 and 5751); generally attributed to Massari, probably *circa* 1710. It is best seen from the Erbaria. The tall, imposing Neo-classical façade has rustication to the two lowermost orders, and two spacious *piani nobili* above. The large, tall windows are capped by pediments. Despite the façade, the plan is asymmetrical, with a broad central axis but only one side wing. Inside: a fine rich staircase, with a square plan, although most of the interior is altered and the decorations lost.

Next to Palazzo Civran is the small, attractive Gothic **Palazzetto Perducci** (CN 5768), late fourteenth or early fifteenth century, with land access from Calle de l'Aseo. Two principal storeys above an off-centre watergate, with paired central lights. The last house off the right side of the *salizada* is **Palazzo Ruzzini** (CN 5783–5), flanking Rio del Fontego, by the Ponte de l'Olio. It was rebuilt in the late nineteenth century on the site of the ancient Fondaco dei Persiani, which had stood here since the middle ages, but was demolished in 1830.

On the other side of the *salizada* is the Coin department store (CN 5787); the original fabric is Gothic, as can be seen on the water façade adjacent to the bridge. It has been transformed internally, however, with an atrium rising the full height of the building.

Return back down the *salizada*, turning right just before the church, into Calle Cagnoleto, then Calle Morosini. On the right is Corte Amadi, with the late medieval **Palazzetti Amadi** (CN 5810). Water façades onto Rio del Fontego, *circa* 1430–40, visible from Ponte de l'Olio. The courtyard façades also contain Gothic windows. Returning to Calle Morosini, turn right and under the *sotoportego* into Corte Morosini. Above the entrance lintel is a fine fourteenth-century arch with decorative relief work. The attractive courtyard has traditional brick paving. **Palazzo Morosini** (CN 5825) occupies the N, E and S sides, the W side being shared by Palazzetto Amadi. In the NE corner is an open staircase. The Morosini house is dated to 1369 (plaque on façade); this courtyard façade is earlier than that to the canal.

Return towards San Giovanni Grisostomo, but this time turn right under a *sotoportego* into Corte Prima del Milion. Take Calle del Milion out of the far side, under another *sotoportego* into Corte Seconda del Milion. The **'House of Marco Polo'** (CN 5845 and

Facing page: San Giovanni Grisostomo: upper façade by Mauro Codussi, 1495–1504; campanile rebuilt in 1590

Corte Seconda del Milion, with twelfth-century arch,
said to be part of the house of Marco Polo

5947): a complex of houses built around Corte Seconda del Milion,
with early Venetian-Byzantine work, as well as fourteenth- and
fifteenth-century elements. Most of the *corte* façade is fourteenth
century; the houses originally had only two storeys but were later
extended upwards, probably in the fourteenth century. The oldest
feature is the archway in the N corner, often claimed to be part of
the House of Marco Polo; fine relief carving to the intrados and
extrados, probably early twelfth century.

Polo was born in 1254, and was 17 when he accompanied his
uncle Matteo on the first of his famous journeys. The name 'il
milione' derives from the nickname given to Marco after his return
to Italy following his travels in the Far East between 1277 and
1295. He recounted his chronicles to Rusticiano da Pisa while they
were prisoners of the Genoese; Polo was freed in 1299 and
returned to Venice, where he died, probably in 1324. His house later
passed to the Trevisan, and in 1678 was bought by Giovanni Carlo
Grimani; much was probably demolished to build the Teatro
Malibran (see below).

Go through the 'Marco Polo' arch and turn left into the little Corte del Teatro. **Teatro Malibran** (CN 5870) was originally built by Giovanni Carlo Grimani in 1678; the oldest surviving theatre in Venice, given its present name in 1834 in honour of the singer Maria Malibran.

When first built, it was also the largest in the city, and in 1678 the first opera was performed here. After 1747 it concentrated on drama, and was reconstructed after 1834 by the Gallo family, to a design by Giuseppe Salvadori. Further major modernisations followed again in 1882–6 and in 1920. It was used for many years as a cinema before its most recent restoration in 1999–2002, and its reopening as a lyric theatre. An attractive, though restrained façade to the little square in front.

19 SANTA MARIA NOVA AND SANTA MARIA DEI MIRACOLI

From the front of the theatre, take the short Calle del Teatro back to San Giovanni Grisostomo. Turn N again, to the Ponte San Giovanni; from the bridge, the canal façades of the Corner, Boldù and Malipiero houses can be seen. Turn right back into Salizada San Canzian. Calle Boldù on the right leads into Campielo Santa Maria Nova. At the s end is the Gothic **Palazzo Bembo Boldù** (CN 5999–6000), with a fifteenth-century façade towards the square, but a sixteenth-century Renaissance façade to the canal. The land façade is rich but narrow, with two four-light *gotico fiorito* windows. Turn E along Calle dei Miracoli; Calle Maggioni on the right leads to **Palazzetto Maggioni** (CN 6006), with a Gothic canal façade. Just before the bridge on the right is **Palazzo Malipiero** (CN 6007–8), with two water façades and six Gothic windows. Return to Campielo Santa Maria Nova, and continue NE into Campo Santa Maria Nova. The attractive little square achieved its present appearance after demolition of the eponymous church, which occupied its E end. It was an ancient parish foundation, established in 971; the church survived until 1808, when it was closed and used as a warehouse. In 1839 the campanile was demolished, and in 1852 the church followed. The E end of the square is dominated by the richly clad exterior of the famous **Santa Maria dei Miracoli**; always described as one of the 'jewels' of the early Venetian Renaissance; the church is a tour de force of ingenious planning and rich, refined decoration. It was designed and largely executed by Pietro Lombardo in 1481–9, with his sons Tullio and Antonio.

It was a new foundation, established following the discovery of a miracle-working image of the Virgin in the courtyard of a nearby house belonging to the Amadi family (see below). The church was funded by numerous private donations, much from the Amadi themselves. A group of houses was demolished for its site, which remained highly restricted, with a canal down one side and pedestrian routes on the other three. In 1481 construction began, and an adjacent nunnery was begun across the street for Franciscan 'Poor Clares', who were to administer the shrine.

Lombardo rose to the challenge of the confined site by designing a tall, narrow, box-like church, with a single nave and no side aisles, covered by a barrel-vaulted roof. The external appearance is of a richly decorated object, free-standing on all sides (very unusual in Venice), and entirely clad with rich marble panelling; the sumptuous detailing was unprecedented at the time. Although the interior has a single volume, the exterior has two superimposed orders of blind arcading; the lower order has acanthus capitals, while the upper is of Doric derivation. The 'vocabulary' of all the external elements is detailed in fine limestone, with panelling of several types of marble. All three doorways have surrounds enriched with relief decoration.

The main façade dominates its tiny square. Its portal has a curved lunette with the *Virgin and Child* (by Pirgotele) set into it; five bays, the wider central bay containing the portal. Above the spandrels of the upper order are sculpted figures of the Prophets, which continue around the church perimeter; the order terminates with a rich frieze. Above is a great semicircular gable, with an unusual array of windows, a large *ocio* surrounded by smaller discs, three *oci* and two porphyry *tondi*. The flank is detailed in a similar way to the façade, with two fine doorways, and fourteen bays, eleven representing the nave and three the chancel.

The internal plan directly reflects the box-like exterior, and is strongly directional. Above the w end of the nave is the nuns' choir, originally reached by a bridge from the adjacent convent. The nave walls are clad with marble in the same manner as the exterior, and it is roofed by a richly carved timber barrel-vaulted, coffered ceiling, with paintings set into it. The axial space focuses on the chancel, raised 2.5 metres above the nave and approached by a long flight of steps, thus allowing a clear view for the congregation of the venerated image on the altar. Flanking the front wall of the chancel

Santa Maria dei Miracoli: detail of the
main façade, by Pietro Lombardo,
1481–9

Santa Maria dei Miracoli: flank façade
to the canal

Santa Maria dei Miracoli: upper part of the main façade, by Pietro Lombardo,
1481–9

are two little doorways giving access to the sacristy, tucked underneath the chancel, an ingenious solution to the cramped site. The chancel has a square plan and is roofed with a shallow cupola on pendentives, which in turn sit on a drum, pierced to provide more light; the four *tondi* of the Evangelists in the pendentives are also by Pietro Lombardo.

The richest decoration is concentrated in the chancel, beginning with the complex carved balustrade at the top of the steps. At each end are two small projecting marble pulpits, while on the balustrade are little figures of St Francis, St Clare and the Annunciation, probably (like much of the chancel) by Tullio Lombardo.

The high altar dates from 1887, but is surrounded by superbly carved parapets, again from the Lombardo shop. The rear section of the chancel, in which the altar is set, is framed by a large arch with richly detailed pilasters, a refinement from Lombardo's earlier work at San Giobbe.

20   FROM PALAZZO SORANZO VAN AXEL TO THE FONDAMENTE NOVE (2)

Leaving the church through the main doorway, we enter Calle Castelli. In the corner, at CN 6076, is **Palazzo Amadi**, built by the family that funded the church. A *gotico fiorito* portal gives access to the attractive Corte de le Muneghe, where the miraculous image was found; upper floors supported on *barbacani*. Adjacent is **Palazzo Castelli** (CN 6091), late sixteenth or early seventeenth century. It was modernised in the eighteenth century, perhaps by Tirali. Next again is **Palazzo Zacco** (CN 6097), again with a water façade to Rio de Santa Marina, visible from Ponte del Cristo. The attractively asymmetrical canal façade is Gothic, late fourteenth or early fifteenth century, and follows the curve of the canal. At the end of Calle Castelli, we reach Fondamenta Sanudo; turn left along the quay, terminating at the land gate of the notable **Palazzo Soranzo Sanudo Van Axel** (CN 6071, 6099), one of the most interesting late medieval palaces in the city. An earlier Venetian-Byzantine house was bought by Niccolò Soranzo in 1473, who then rebuilt it; it thus (unusually) can be precisely dated, and the style is very late *gotico fiorito*. It passed to the Van Axel, Flemish merchants, in 1652, and remained in their ownership until 1920.

The plan is complex and ingenious, with two separate internal courtyards, reached from separate street entrances, one on Calle de

Palazzo Soranzo Sanudo Van Axel: doorway to the quay, 1473–8, with original medieval door

la Chiesa, the other on the quay; the latter conserves its original magnificent medieval timber door, the only one in the city. Each courtyard has an open staircase to one of the two *piani nobili*. The plan of the principal upper halls takes the form of an L, with one wing terminating at each of the two principal water façades.

The latter are difficult to see; one is visible from Ponte de la Panada, the other from Ponte de le Erbe. The former retains traces of the earlier Byzantine house; the latter is more impressive. The interior conserves several fine late medieval fireplaces and exposed decorated timber ceilings to the principal rooms.

From Fondamenta Soranzo, turn s towards Ponte del Cristo. Across the canal is the imposing **Palazzo Pisani** (CN 6103–4), again with two canal façades, the other around the corner, onto Rio di Santa Marina. Fifteenth-century Gothic, but altered considerably in the sixteenth century. Both façades contain a mixture of medieval and Renaissance elements, that to Rio de la Panada having more random fenestration. The plan is c-shaped, with a small internal

Palazzo Soranzo Sanudo Van Axel: staircase in the small courtyard, after 1473

Palazzo Soranzo Sanudo Van Axel: medieval fireplace in one of the upper rooms

courtyard. The interior contains attractive eighteenth-century stucco decoration.

Our final section of the Cannaregio walk takes us back towards the Fondamente Nove for the last time. Cross Ponte de le Erbe and continue down Calle de le Erbe, then turn left into Calle de la Testa, a long, straight *calle* that runs N, continuing as Calle del Squero. Just before the Fondamente Nove is the cross-axis of Calle Berlendis. At its W end is the seventeenth-century **Palazzo Mosca Semenzi** (CN 6270), with façade to Rio de la Panada. At the opposite end, facing Rio dei Medicanti, is the double **Palazzo Berlendis** and **Palazzo Merati** (CN 6293 and 6296). The houses were built in 1601, by Stefano Protasio, one for each of his two daughters, Maddalena and Cornelia. One was sold to the Berlendis in 1679. The impressive canal façades are almost identical (they can be seen from the *fondamenta* opposite), with Serliane to the principal floor. In 1690 the other house was sold to the Merati, who spent huge sums on elaborate internal decoration, perhaps by Abbondio Stazio.

Returning down Calle del Squero and Calle de la Testa, at CN 6359 is **Palazzo Grifalconi Loredan**, late fourteenth-century Gothic. The rear façade towards the canal is separated from it by an attractive garden, visible from Fondamenta del Mendicanti. A little further down Calle de la Testa is **Palazzo Cappello** (CN 6391), originally Gothic, but modernised in the early Renaissance, as can be seen from the water façade.

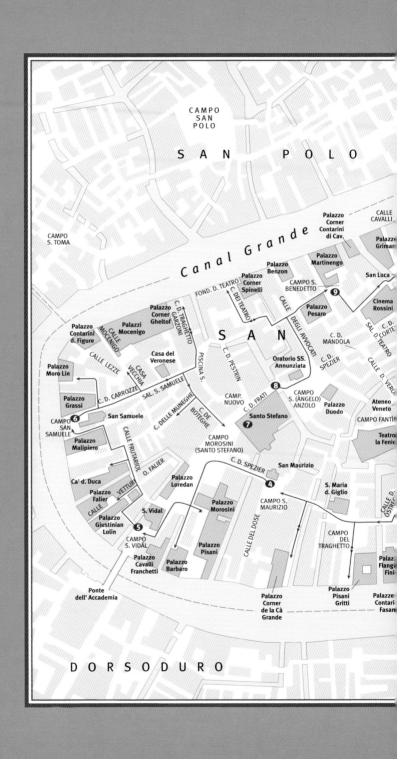

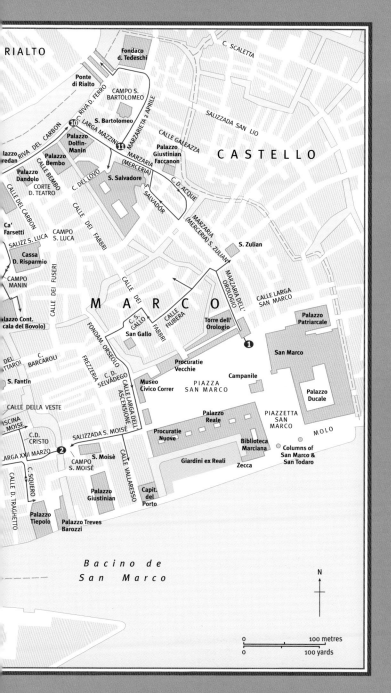

RIALTO

Fondaco
d. Tedeschi

C. SCALETTA

Ponte
di Rialto

CAMPO S.
BARTOLOMEO

SALIZADA SAN LIO

RIVA D. FERRO

S. Bartolomeo

CALLE LARGA MAZZINI

azzo
redan

RIVA DEL CARBON

Palazzo
Dolfin-
Manin

CALLE BEMBO

Palazzo
Bembo

MARZARIETA 2 APRILE

CALLE GALEAZZA

Palazzo
Giustinian
Faccanon

MARZARIA
(MERCERIA)

CASTELLO

Palazzo
Dandolo

C. DEL LOVO

S. Salvadore

CORTE
D. TEATRO

CALLE DEL CARBON

Ca'
Farsetti

SALIZZ S. LUCA

CAMPO
S. LUCA

S. SALVADOR

CALLE DEI FABBRI

C. D. ACQUE

MARZARIA
(MERCERIA) S. ZULIAN

S. Zulian

Cassa
D. Risparmio

CAMPO
MANIN

CALLE DEI FUSERI

MARZARIA DELL'
OROLOGIO

CALLE LARGA
SAN MARCO

Palazzo
Cont.
cala del Bovolo)

M A R C O

C. S.
GALLO

CALLE
FABBRI

CALLE
RIVERA

Torre dell'
Orologio

Palazzo
Patriarcale

DEL
ATTARO!

C.
BARCAROLI

FONDAM. ORSEOLO

San Gallo

①

San Marco

S. Fantin

FREZZERIA

Procuratie
Vecchie

Palazzo
Ducale

CALLE DELLA VESTE

C. D.
SELVADEGO

CALLE LARGA DELL'
ASCENSIONE

Museo
Civico Correr

Campanile

PIAZZA
SAN MARCO

PISCINA
MOISE

C.D.
CRISTO

SALIZZADA S. MOISE

②

LARGA XXII MARZO

CAMPO
S. MOISE

S. Moisè

Palazzo
Reale

Procuratie
Nuove

PIAZZETTA
SAN
MARCO

MOLO

C. SQUERO

CALLE VALLARESSO

Biblioteca
Marciana

Columns of
San Marco &
San Todaro

CALLE D. TRAGHETTO

Palazzo
Tiepolo

Palazzo
Giustinian

Giardini ex Reali

Zecca

Palazzo Treves
Barozzi

Capit.
del
Porto

B a c i n o   d e
S a n   M a r c o

N

San Marco

0   100 metres
0   100 yards

Sestiere of San Marco

The *sestiere* is the heart of the city, dominated by the world-renowned Republican monuments around Piazza San Marco. It is defined on three sides (N, W and S) by the southern bend of the Grand Canal; to the east it has a short boundary with Cannaregio and a longer one with Castello.

The monumental heart is atypical of the district as a whole, most of which is densely developed, and centred on the characteristic *campi* of several notable churches: San Moisè, Santa Maria del Giglio and San Maurizio towards the S; San Samuele to the W; and San Luca, San Beneto and San Bartolomeo to the N. Towards the SW, this typical island-parish configuration is interrupted by the large *campo* of Santo Stefano, with its eponymous church and monastic buildings. Other than this chain of island parishes, following the winding course of the Canalazzo, the other major feature is the N–S axis, linking the Piazza with the bridge and markets of Rialto. These links include the group of streets collectively known as the Marzaria (Merceria), and the parallel axes of the Frezzeria and Calle dei Fabbri. The banks of the Grand Canal are lined with palaces from all eras, from the earliest Venetian-Byzantine survivors (Ca' Farsetti) to the Gothic (Ca' Giustinian), the early Renaissance (Palazzo Corner Spinelli) and the High Renaissance (Ca' Corner).

Facing page: The Porta della Carta

THE PIAZZA AND PIAZZETTA

The choice of the large firm islet of San Marco for the fortified palace of the *dux* (doge) was chiefly defensive: it commanded the large Basin of San Marco and the route towards the sea, as well as the entrance to the future Grand Canal. The first castle-palace was built at the water's edge, with the narrow Rio di Palazzo to the E. To the W was an inlet or *cavana*, later reclaimed to form the Piazzetta; to the N, another narrow canal divided the palace from the islet further N, where the little church of San Todaro was built. The palace was thus surrounded by a natural moat on all sides. When San Todaro was replaced by the first San Marco, the church faced a *piazza*, but one that was less than half the length of the present one, bounded at its W end by another canal, Rio Batario; on its far bank was a church dedicated to San Geminiano. San Marco itself was largely rebuilt in the later eleventh century, and the basic fabric has survived today, much elaborated over the centuries.

The definitive transformation of the zone came during the dogeship of Sebastiano Ziani (1172–8). The *cavana* was reclaimed, creating the new Piazzetta, and to emphasise its role as the point of arrival in the city, Ziani erected the two great monolithic columns of San Todaro and San Marco, which stand on the Molo. He also reclaimed the narrow canal at the W end of the Piazza, and demolished San Geminiano. The orchard behind the church was acquired from the nunnery of San Zaccaria, and the Piazza thereby doubled in length to its present 160 metres; San Geminiano was then rebuilt at its far end, directly facing San Marco.

By 1200, therefore, the definition of the Piazza was well advanced; the surrounding buildings were Venetian-Byzantine in style, most

Piazza San Marco and environs in 1500, from de' Barbari's engraving

San Marco: the Molo from San Giorgio, with (left to right): the Zecca; Biblioteca Marciana; the campanile and the Doge's Palace

with only two storeys. On the N side was the old Procuracy building, facing the Ospizio Orseolo, a hostel for pilgrims, on the s side. Ziani's Doge's Palace, too, had a single storey above a colonnaded ground floor.

The next transformation came in the fourteenth century, with the beginning of the definitive reconstruction of the Doge's Palace (1340), and at the end of the century, the elaboration of the façades of San Marco. By 1420 the basilica had essentially been completed as we see it today, while the rebuilding of the Doge's Palace continued after completion of the Molo wing, with that to the Piazzetta and finally the Porta della Carta (*circa* 1443). In the 1490s the Torre de l'Orologio was built, adding a new element in the square, in a new Renaissance style. The old Procuracy was next to be replaced; in 1512 an earthquake and a fire resulted in the decision to reconstruct it completely, this time on three floors.

The last great programme of urban renewal was begun by Sansovino, but took decades to conclude; it resulted in the present configuration of both Piazza and Piazzetta. First, he designed the rich little loggia at the foot of the bell-tower; then the new government mint, on a site just around the corner from the Piazzetta. And thirdly, he began the new Library of San Marco, which ultimately occupied the W side of the Piazzetta. This last had the most important urban significance, since Sansovino decided to terminate the north end of the new Library several metres short of its abutment with the campanile; this not only freed the campanile's base and gave the Library a north façade, but also widened the Piazza at this end, enhancing the setting of the church. Sansovino's plan to continue the design of the Marciana Library down the S side of the Piazza was not realised in his lifetime; but the imposing Procuratie Nuove was finally completed by Longhena in the 1640s. The Piazza's brick paving was replaced by Tirali in 1723 by the stone that we see today.

The Piazza remained thus until after the fall of the Republic; Napoleon's interventions, though, were radical. The Procuratie Nuove became his viceroy's palace, and the W end of the Piazza was transformed by demolishing San Geminiano and constructing the new Ala Napoleonica, with its monumental staircase and ballroom, both serving the new function of the 'Palazzo Reale'. To this end, too, the Republic's ancient granaries were also demolished (to improve the view from the 'Palazzo Reale'), and the Giardinetti Reali were laid out. The last new building is the Neo-classical Palazzo Patriarcale, on the E side of the Piazzetta dei Leoncini, completed in 1850 by Lorenzo Santi.

Their Historic Functions

Although directly linked, the two spaces fulfilled distinct functions as they developed over the centuries, with the soaring campanile forming the 'hinge' between the two. The larger Piazza was associated with the shrine of St Mark, and was thus primarily a religious space. All the surrounding land was owned by the Republic, and was administered by the procurators of San Marco, who received large revenues from pilgrims' donations and from the commercial activities under the colonnades, as they still do today.

As the square of the Republic's patron, the Piazza was the setting for countless religious festivals and processions, principally the patron's day (25 April), and the feasts of Corpus Domini and Ascension Day (La Sensa); the last was celebrated every year from 1177, when the doge sailed in the state barge, the Bucintoro, to the Porto di Lido, and symbolically 'married' the sea. After 1180 a fair was held in the Piazza, famous all over Europe.

Numerous other ceremonies ranged from ducal coronations to the celebration of naval victories; the ducal *andate* (processions) to the

Symbols of the Republic: the winged lion on
the Molo and the campanile of San Marco

city's churches all originated here, among them the famous festival of
the Redentore (third Sunday in July) and the Madona de la Salute
(21 November).

By contrast, the Piazzetta was associated with the Republic's
government, particularly the execution of justice. The colonnade
down the east side, the Liston, was the nobles' traditional meeting
place, while the dispensation of justice often resulted in the reading
of a death sentence from the loggia of the Doge's Palace, and the
stringing up of malefactors between Ziani's two columns.

THE BASILICA OF SAN MARCO

History of the Fabric

In 813 the seat of lagoon government was transferred to Venice from
Malamocco; fifteen years later, the body of the Evangelist was
brought here from Alexandria, hidden (as tradition relates) in a barrel
of pork, to escape detection by the Muslim authorities. Venice's first
patron, St Theodore (Todaro), was joined, then largely superseded, by
this far more notable patron. Part of the first chapel to house his
remains may survive today in the immensely thick walls of the

church's treasury. The chapel was consecrated in 832; recent excavations suggest that it had a Greek-cross plan, similar to that of its successor. It was damaged by fire in 976, but repaired and re-consecrated only two years later, under Doge Pietro Orseolo.

The third, definitive reconstruction began *circa* 1063 under Doge Domenico Contarini; it took thirty years, and this basic fabric survives today, almost entirely clad in later marbles and mosaics. The new church again has a Greek-cross plan, with four equal arms, and was roofed with shallow brick cupolas, a daring form of construction in such a context, where settlement was a perennial danger. The tall outer cupolas, clad with lead, were added in the thirteenth century to give the church a more dominant presence. This new construction included the absorption of the chapel of San Todaro on the N side, and a new atrium or narthex was added across the W façade. The next stage, in the thirteenth century, consisted of the extension of this narthex along the N flank, the construction of the baptistery on the S side, and the raising of the outer cupolas. In the same period the façade received its five splendid portals, with their rich marble columns and capitals.

In the following century, the reign of Doge Andrea Dandolo (1343–54) saw the construction of the chapel of Sant'Isidoro and the installation of the rood screen across the chancel. Towards the end of the century, the upper façades were further elaborated with aedicules, statuary and wave decoration; this was completed in the early fifteenth century and in the same period the Mascoli Chapel was built, next to the N transept; it was decorated in 1430–50. Later, in 1486, the large sacristy was built by Giorgio Spavento; shortly afterwards, the Zen Chapel was formed out of the S corner bay of the west narthex. Its interior was decorated in 1504–21. In 1529 Sansovino was appointed *proto* and spent many years restoring the fabric. The final interventions took place in the sixteenth century, when the chapel of the Nicopeia Madonna was formed in the N transept. The endless cycle of restoration has continued to this day, under such notable *proti* as Longhena, Sardi and Tirali.

The Exterior

West façade

The principal façade, dominating the Piazza, is one of the essential images of the city; it has five bays and two superimposed orders. The lower order terminates in a terrace across the width of the façade; its

San Marco: the portal of Sant'Alipio, with original mosaic of *circa* 1260–70 showing the basilica

dominant features are the five great arches, with their numerous columns of rare marble. Four of the five doorways are closed by bronze doors; the fifth, the Zen Chapel, has a window instead. The central doors are the oldest, probably contemporary with the construction of the church, while the other three, to the same design, date from 1300.

From N to S, the doorways are as follows: Porta di Sant'Alipio; within the lunette is the only surviving original mosaic, *circa* 1270–80, showing the body of St Mark being taken into the basilica. In the background is an invaluable contemporary image of the church. The arch is decorated with Byzantine vines and figures; in the lunette: five small pierced stone screens. Second portal: the arch is decorated with late thirteenth-century relief sculptures. In the lunette: mosaic by Leopoldo dal Pozzo, 1728; directly below it is a Gothic *trifora* with a traceried head and bronze shutters, 1300.

The central portal is much larger and more richly decorated than the rest. Its outermost arch rises above the parapet, and has complex relief decoration. The inner portal has three concentric arches, showing a stylistic progression from the inner one (early 1200s) to the outer (early 1300s). Innermost arch: on the soffit are vines and animals; on the outer face: hunting scenes and representations of the Virtues. Middle arch: on the soffit are the months of the year, with seasonal activities; on the outer face: the Beatitudes and the Virtues. Outermost arch: on the soffit a notable series of sculptures of trades and crafts; on the outer face: the Prophets, set between vines, with Christ Blessing in the centre.

The fourth portal: in the lunette: a mosaic, the *Arrival of the Body of St Mark, circa* 1660, after Pietro Vecchia. The decorations repeat those to the second portal. Fifth portal: in the lunette, another mosaic after Vecchia. Set into the inner arch is a richly decorated Moorish inflected arch, in which are set pierced stone screens. The doorway, adapted to form a window to the Zen Chapel, has a figure of Christ blessing, from the earlier Orseolo church. Above and between the five portals are rectangular relief sculptures, late thirteenth century.

Above the portals is the terrace, from which the doge watched spectacles in the Piazza below. The five bays of the upper order were decorated in the early fifteenth century, when the four-centred outer arches were added to the earlier semicircular ones, and the wave decoration was added to the extrados. The Gothic elaborations are ascribed to the dalle Masegne, followed by Matteo Raverti. On the four outer arches: figures by G. B. Albanese (1618), *St Constantine*, *St Demetrius*, *St George* and *St Theodore*. In the large central arch, the original elaborate screen is replaced by a large plain window. Around it are scenes from the Old Testament and the *Prophets*; in the soffit are *Patriarchs* and *Evangelists*, set into niches. Directly above the inner arch is the gilded Venetian winged lion, a replacement (1826) for that destroyed by Napoleon. On the pinnacle of the outer arch is *Mark the Evangelist* by Niccolò Lamberti; on its extrados: six gilded angels, again attributed to Lamberti. The six tabernacles rising between the crowning arches are late fourteenth century or early fifteenth; they contain the *Evangelists*, and the *Annunciation*, attributed to Pietro, son of Niccolò Lamberti. In the lunettes of the four outer arches are mosaics by Alvise and Girolamo Gaetano (1617–18), replacing the thirteenth-century originals: the *Deposition* and the *Descent into Hell* (left) and the *Resurrection* and the *Ascension* (right). In the centre of the terrace are copies of the four famous gilded bronze horses: see below.

Facing page: San Marco: detail of the great central portal, early thirteenth century

San Marco: south façade from the Piazzetta

South façade

Although shorter than that to the Piazza, it is equally richly decorated, since it was the first part of the church visible to the visitor approaching by water. Two main bays, as well as the third open bay at the sw corner; these principal bays were also once open. Again two orders, with the upper terrace continuing around this façade. The first main (left) arch was the 'sea-gate' (Porta da Mar), filled in when the Zen Chapel was formed, *circa* 1504; it has particularly fine marble capitals, as does the smaller, open arch at the left corner. The right-hand bay is smaller, with a rectangular doorway and bronze doors contemporary with those on the main façade; they formerly gave access to the baptistery. Above is a Gothic *trifora*, similar to that on the Piazza façade.

The upper order reflects that below. Both bays are filled in with a colonnade of small Byzantine arches, five in the left bay and four in the right; above are fine Byzantine panels and pierced screens. The

San Marco, north façade: detail of the Porta dei Fiori

façade is crowned by a continuation of the statuary and pinnacles on the w façade; the figures at the pinnacles of the arches are *Justice* and *Fortitude*, those in the kiosks are *St Anthony Abbot* (left) and *St Paul the Hermit*, both again from the Lamberti workshop.

Adjacent to the south façade are three notable sculpted works. At the sw corner is a short porphyry column (from Acre, 1256), used as a proclamation stone by the Republic. Set into the se corner of the basilica is the red granite group known as the *Tetrarchs*, representing the emperor-colleagues of Diocletian; carved in Egypt in the fourth century AD. On the adjacent flank wall of the church is a fine, random collection of decorative relief panels. Adjacent are the richly carved Pilastri Acritani, the two columns from Acre; also taken in 1256, after the Venetian victory over the Genoese, and generally believed to be fifth-century Syrian work.

North façade

The longer N façade (restored 2005–8) has four principal bays, three of equal size, and one, containing the Porta dei Fiori, larger and the most richly decorated. Beyond these four bays, the N transept projects into the Piazzetta dei Leoncini. The arches of the two right-hand bays are filled in but the third has a Gothic window similar to those on the other two façades. All are decorated with relief carvings from the earlier churches of Partecipazio and Orseolo. The fourth arch, the Porta dei Fiori, gives access to the eastern end of the N atrium; its lower, inner arch has a rich Moorish profile. In the centre is a relief of the Nativity, while the outermost arch is decorated with thirteenth-century figures of the Prophets. Next to the Porta, at right angles to it, is a fifth arch, corresponding to the Mascoli Chapel inside. Above the stilted arch are three relief panels, Christ flanked by two Evangelists, the other two flanking the Porta dei Fiori.

Turning the outer corner of the Mascoli Chapel, set into the lower arch is the sarcophagus of Daniele Manin (by Luigi Borro), who led the unsuccessful uprising against the Austrians in 1848.

The upper order of the N façade again has four bays; the Gothic decoration to the upper parts is largely by the Lamberti; within kiosks are the four western doctors of the early Church: *Gregory*, *Ambrose*, *Augustine* and *Jerome*. On the uppermost pinnacles are Virtues: *Charity*, *Faith*, *Temperance* and *Prudence*.

The Plan of the Church

The atrium precedes the church itself, its five bays corresponding to the five great portals; structurally, it is independent of the church, and it continues with a further three bays along the N side. On the S side, the equivalent bays are occupied by the baptistery.

The church plan is a Greek cross, with four nearly equal arms, each roughly square on plan and vaulted, as is the central bay, with a shallow brick cupola on pendentives. The easternmost arm, containing the chancel, terminates with a semicircular apse. Flanking the nave are side aisles, which extend across the W end and continue into the transepts. The central eastern apse is flanked by two smaller radiused apse chapels, that of San Pietro (N) and San Clemente (S).

The plan's origin has been debated for centuries, although it derives from many diffused early examples in the Eastern Empire, particularly the lost sixth-century church of the Twelve Apostles in Constantinople. The centralised form was also widely used for reliquary chapels, with early examples in Trieste, Rimini and at Santa Fosca, Torcello, in the Venetian lagoon itself.

The Atrium and its Mosaics

The atrium is richly decorated, both by the columns, capitals and arches of its structure, and by the glittering mosaics that cover its vaults. The floor, too, is covered with complex marble mosaics in the form of wheels. Flanking the central doorway are the earliest surviving mosaics in the church: the *Virgin* and *Saints*, set in niches on each side; they date from *circa* 1071–84, earlier than the atrium itself. The bronze doors (1112–38) are copies of the adjacent San Clemente doors. Flanking the main portal are stairs rising to the former women's galleries and the front terrace. The right portal is dedicated to St Clement, the left to St Peter, corresponding to the dedications of the eastern apses; the bronze doors to the former are Byzantine (*circa* 976), while the latter are twelfth century.

In the atrium: tombs to three early doges: Vitale Falier (+1096), who consecrated the new church in 1094, Marino Morosini (+1253) and Bartolomeo Gradenigo (+1342). The mosaics were begun in the early 1200s and continued for much of the century; they represent many stories from the Old Testament and are summarised here beginning at the south end, adjacent to the Zen Chapel:

First cupola: the *Creation*, twenty-five scenes from the Creation story, set in concentric circles; in the pendentives are cherubim with six wings. In the three lunettes: *Cain and Abel*.

First vaulted arch: *The Flood*, fifteen scenes from the story of Noah.

Central bay: the vault is interrupted by a large opening (the 'pozzo'), surrounded by sixteenth-century mosaics by the Zuccato.

The *Noah* sequence continues on the next arch, with the *Fall of Noah* and the *Tower of Babel*.

The next cupola: that of *Abraham*, with nineteen scenes from his life, continued in the three lunettes, with the *Birth of Isaac*. In the pendentives: four Prophets: *Isaiah, Ezekiel, Jeremiah* and *Daniel*. On the next transverse arch: *Justice, St Alipius* and *St Simeon*.

The next three cupolas depict the life of Joseph, with forty scenes over the three domes. The first contains twelve scenes, with four more Prophets in the pendentives (*Samuel, Nathan, Habbakuk* and *Elijah*). On the arch between the first and second cupolas: *St Cristopher with Christ* and *Charity*. Next cupola: nine scenes from the life of Joseph; in the pendentives: *Pharaoh's Dream*. On the arch between the second and third *Joseph* cupolas: *St Agnes, St Catherine, St Silvester, St Geminiano*. Third cupola: a further eight scenes from the life of Joseph, continued into the lunettes. In the pendentives: four *Apostles*.

In the final cupola are scenes from the life of Moses, again continued into the lunettes. In the pendentives: *Zacharias, Malachi, David* and *Solomon*. Above the apse doorway: the *Virgin Enthroned* between *St John the Baptist* and *St Mark*.

The Zen Chapel occupies the s bay of the atrium, formed after the death of Cardinal Giambattista Zen in 1501; he left a large legacy to the Republic, and the work took place in 1504–21. The Lombard Renaissance altar, on the s wall, has a bronze *baldacchino* by Pietro Campanato, with a rich architrave and pediment. The *baldacchino* soffit is a relief of the *Holy Spirit* and *God the Father* by Antonio Lombardo. The fine altarpiece, the *Virgin and Child*, is also by Lombardo, flanked by *St Peter* and *St John the Evangelist* by Paolo Savin. The cardinal's bronze sarcophagus is perhaps based on a lost work by Antonio Rizzo.

The vault mosaics (*circa* 1280s–1290s) are contiguous with those in the atrium; in the N hemisphere: the Virgin flanked by angels; the central vault has scenes from the life of St Mark.

The Interior

The underlying fabric is brick throughout; the marble veneers to the main structure were added over many decades, perhaps begun under Doge Vitale Michiel (1156–72), as was the mosaic cladding to the upper levels. The high-level women's galleries formerly extended over the aisles, but were reduced after a fire in 1145 to the present narrow walkways. The nave columns and capitals come from several sources and are of various dates; the oldest are recycled classical pieces, others are early Christian, still others were made to match in the eleventh century. The nave floor is covered by an extraordinary surface of tessellated marble mosaic, mostly of complex geometrical forms. It was laid in the late thirteenth century, but restored many times.

Right aisle: on the first column is a porphyry holy water stoup, with Roman elements. Left of the baptistery door is a twelfth-century relief of the *Virgin and Child*.

The baptistery: three bays, south of the south aisle. It achieved its present appearance under Doge Andrea Dandolo in the 1350s; it was originally approached directly from the outside. The first small rectangular bay is an antechamber, in the second bay is the font, while the third bay has an altar. s wall: monument to Doge Dandolo (+1354), a fine Gothic work. The font is by Sansovino, *circa* 1545; he is also buried here, behind the altar. The baptistery has fine mosaics: two cycles, the *Life of John the Baptist* (on the walls), and the *Childhood and Life of Christ* (vaults and spandrels), all mid-fourteenth century.

Right transept: the treasury doorway has a rich, complex Moorish profile, similar to the Porta dei Fiori. At high level is a splendid fifteenth-century Gothic rose window. On transept E wall: the Sacrament Chapel (formerly of San Lunardo); rich marble altar by Tommaso Contin, 1617. On the left pier, a lamp marks the location where the body of St Mark was miraculously rediscovered in the 1094 reconstruction. Attached to the pier is the little early Renaissance altar of St James (late fifteenth century, Lombardo workshop).

The treasury: reached by a door in the transept S wall. It consists of three small linked spaces, housing the remains of an extraordinary collection begun by Enrico Dandolo after the Fourth Crusade in 1204. After the Napoleonic conquest (1797) this priceless collection was irrevocably damaged, many pieces being melted down or broken up; 300 items survive. Of the three rooms, one (the sanctuary) contains 110 reliquaries, while the main room, the treasury proper, has some fine pieces on display: icons, chalices, crucifixes, lamps and more reliquaries.

Chapel of San Clemente: several steps above the nave floor. Across the front: iconostasis by Jacobello and Pier Paolo dalle Masegne, 1397. Across the top: *Virgin and Child, with SS Christina, Chiara, Catherine and Agnes*. In the hemispherical E vault: thirteenth-century mosaic of St Clement. On the chancel side wall: late Gothic tabernacle, again by the dalle Masegne.

At the nave crossing: in front of the right corner pier is the large Epistle pulpit, assembled in the early 1300s from pieces from elsewhere; a polygonal plan, supported by nine marble columns. From this pulpit the doge was presented to the nobility during the coronation rite.

The chancel: raised above the nave level, with the crypt beneath it. Across the front is the fine iconostasis, again by the dalle Masegne, made of Verona *broccatello*. Above the trabeation: the central *Crucifixion*, bronze and silver, is by Jacopo Bennato; flanking figures of the Virgin and Apostles (1394), all by the dalle Masegne. The ducal throne was formerly located just beyond the iconostasis on the right side. On the chancel flank walls: *cantorie* (choirstalls), with bronze relief panels by Jacopo Sansovino (1537–44). In the centre is the free-standing high altar, below which is the tomb of the Evangelist.

Above the altar: a *baldacchino* of *verde antico* marble, supported by four richly carved alabaster columns. On the top in the centre is *Christ*, probably by Tullio Lombardo. The origin of the columns remains debatable, with proposed dates ranging from the seventh century to the thirteenth.

The **Pala d'Oro** (golden altarpiece): its nucleus is said to have been commissioned by Doge Ordelaffo Falier in Constantinople in 1102; it was further embellished with jewels after the sack of Constantinople in 1204, when the upper panel was added. It was completed *circa* 1209, but was reordered in 1345 by Doge Andrea Dandolo, when further elaborate Gothic decoration was added.

The screen measures 3.44 by 1.40 metres; its appearance is truly dazzling, and is said to contain 1,927 gemstones, including 526 pearls, 320 emeralds, 255 sapphires and 183 amethysts. The surfaces are almost entirely clad with gold, ultramarine and other enamelled colours. Its nucleus consists of several rows of gilded, enamelled panels, reading from top to bottom: top row: six feast days of the Byzantine Church; second row: small square panels of the life of Christ; next row: angels in niches (six on each side); third row: the *Twelve Apostles* (two rows of six); fourth row: *Prophets* (two rows of six). In the centre of all these rows: *Christ the Pantocrator*, with four roundels containing the *Evangelists*. At the base in the centre is the Virgin in prayer, flanked by the Empress Irene of Byzantium and Doge Falier.

The chancel apse: in the centre the small altar of the Sacrament, flanked by St Francis and St Bernardino by Lorenzo Bregno (early sixteenth century). The choirstalls were brought here in 1810 from Sant'Andrea de la Certosa. The adjacent sacristy is a rectangular hall by Giorgio Spavento (1486–91); its contemporary ceiling mosaics are heavily restored. The sacristy contains wooden cabinets (Antonio and Paolo Mola, 1496–1506), decorated with notable intarsia work, with *trompe l'œil* scenes of the city. The chapel of San Todaro (N of the sacristy): again by Spavento (1486), built as an oratory; it has a simple early Renaissance courtyard façade. Back in the church:

The crypt: directly below the chancel and the flanking chapels. Rows of stone columns with simple cushion capitals, supporting brick cross-vaults. The structure probably dates from the eleventh-century construction of the church. At the E end, the body of St Mark was kept from 1094 until the 1834 restoration, when it was moved up into the church.

Chapel of San Pietro, N of the chancel. Adjacent is the other pulpit, fourteenth century, of complex form, again with a polygonal plan. There is a circular upper level, roofed by a small Moorish cupola. The Gospel was read from the upper one, the Epistle from the lower. The chapel again has an iconostasis by the dalle Masegne, capped by the Virgin flanked by saints.

North transept: on the nearby pier is the little altar of St Paul, matching that of St James on the other side; Lombard Renaissance, also funded by Doge Cristoforo Moro. In the E transept chapel: the *Nicopaea Madonna*, on an altar by Tommaso Contin. The icon is a famous miracle-working image, probably brought to Venice from Constantinople after the Fourth Crusade (1204).

Chapel of Sant'Isidoro, off the N end of the N transept: built in the 1350s to house the saint's remains, brought here in 1125. Patronised by Doge Andrea Dandolo and completed *circa* 1355. The sarcophagus is typical late Venetian Gothic; the chapel is richly decorated with mosaics, some showing the life of the saint.

Mascoli Chapel, off the W side of the N transept: established by Doge Francesco Foscari, 1430; the name derives from a confraternity called the Mascoli, which met here. A rich, late Gothic marble altar, with figures perhaps by Bartolomeo Bon. The barrel vault has fine mosaics by Michele Giambono, showing the life of the Virgin.

The Mosaics within the Body of the Church

The original programme began under Doge Domenico Selvo (1071–84), followed by a second phase in the late 1100s, continuing over much of the next century. The programme follows a carefully considered 'master plan', centred on the three cupolas down the main axis. The theme conveys the fundamental Christian message of salvation, and the sequence followed here is: central axis, right side, then the left side.

Central axis, first arch: that of the Apocalypse: *Vision of St John the Evangelist* by Francesco Zuccato (1570–89). Above and behind this arch is the Arco del Paradiso, best seen form the upper gallery; *Last Judgement* based on a cartoon by Tintoretto.

The Pentecost cupola, the first of the five: probably the earliest, first half of the thirteenth century. The dove of the Holy Spirit descends as tongues of fire to the Apostles; around the base: figures representing the nations of the world. W great arch: the *Passion of Christ*, in five sections.

Central cupola (of the Ascension): in the centre: *Christ in Glory*, with four angels; lower down: the *Virgin Praying*, and the *Twelve*

Apostles. Around the base: *Virtues* and *Beatitudes*. E great arch: the *Life of Christ*, after Tintoretto.

E cupola, above the high altar: Christ's religion as foretold by the Prophets; in the centre: *Christ the Pantocrator*; lower down: the *Virgin* and *Prophets*. Eastern apse: *Christ Enthroned*, remade in 1506 following the original. Around the walls: four Venetian patrons: *St Nicholas, St Peter, St Mark, St Hermagoras*, late eleventh or early twelfth century.

Right (S) nave aisle: scenes from the life of Christ and the Apostles. S great arch: four scenes from the life of Christ. S cupola: that of *St Leonard*: four Venetian patrons: *St Nicholas, St Clement, St Blaise, St Leonard*. Arch over the S transept aisle: *Acts of the Virgin*. On the end wall at high level: *Presentation of the Virgin*; below: *Finding the Body of St Mark*. On the great arch above the rose window: *St Anthony, St Bernardino, St Vincent* and *St Paul*, 1458. Arch over the altar of the Sacrament: *Parables and Miracles of Christ*.

Left (N) nave aisle: the upper-order mosaics were remade in the sixteenth century: scenes of the life of Christ and the Apostles. N great arch: sixteenth century again: *Miracles of Christ*; N cupola: *St John the Evangelist* or of the *Virgin*: the *Fathers of the Church* and the *Acts of St John the Evangelist*. Arch over the N transept aisle: *Acts of the Virgin*; the *Infancy of Jesus*. Great arch over the Sant'Isidoro Chapel: *Miracles of Christ*. Great arch over the *Nicopea Madonna*: episodes and miracles in the life of Christ.

Marciana Museum

Reached by long, steep stairs adjacent to the main portal. It occupies several rooms above the atrium, once used by the mosaic masters as workshops. Principal works displayed include: organ doors, painted by Gentile Bellini; Flemish tapestries; Persian carpets; fragments of early mosaics; vestments; and graduals; sixteenth-century ducal throne; altarpiece by Paolo Veneziano, dated 1345.

In the large NW corner room: the four magnificent horses of gilded bronze, brought here by Doge Enrico Dandolo after the Fourth Crusade (1204). They stood over the great central portal for 600 years until they were taken to Paris by Napoleon, but returned in 1815. After centuries of speculation, they are generally accepted as Greco-Roman works, but have been dated from the fourth century BC to the fourth century AD. They probably once decorated a triumphal arch in Constantinople, and are the only surviving *quadriga* from the classical era.

THE DOGE'S PALACE (PALAZZO DUCALE)

History of the Fabric and the External Façades

When the seat of government was transferred to Rivo Alto from Malamocco in 810, a central hall for assemblies was begun almost immediately. We know almost nothing of this earliest structure, which was probably fortified, and more castle-like than a palace. It was destroyed by fire in 976, after a popular uprising against the perceived tyranny of Doge Pietro Candiano IV, who was assassinated. Although rebuilt, it was damaged again by fire in 1105, but had been restored by the time of the state visit of Emperor Henry V in 1116. Before Sebastiano Ziani's reclamations, these early structures were all surrounded by water, and were roughly square on plan, with a tower at each corner. The surviving treasury of San Marco may be the base of one of these early corner towers. The palace was largely rebuilt by Ziani, and resembled contemporary surviving Venetian-Byzantine palaces such as the Fondaco dei Turchi and Ca' Loredan. It was built on two storeys, with ground-floor colonnades, and although it retained corner towers (*toresele*), these were no longer defensive. The three wings ranged around a central courtyard, with San Marco on the fourth side. The E wing contained the ducal apartments, the Molo wing the hall of the Maggior Consiglio, and the W wing the magistracy and halls for the dispensation of justice; this layout was broadly retained in the Gothic reconstructions. The *serrata* or 'locking' of the Maggior Consiglio in 1297 closed membership to newcomers, but it also tripled the size of the noble electorate, resulting in the need for a much larger assembly hall.

Reconstruction begun in 1340 lasted for a century. The Molo wing was completed by the 1350s, with the new great hall on the upper floor, and two levels of subsidiary accommodation below it; the hall had an open timber roof, similar to those in other city assembly halls, such as the Palazzo della Ragione in Padua. The 'architect' of the new palace has been debated for centuries, and the names of Filippo Calendario and Pietro Baseggio are often cited, although their roles and responsibilities remain far from clear. Following a hiatus of almost a decade following the Black Death (1348), Guariento's vast frescoes of *Paradise* and the *Coronation of the Virgin* were completed *circa* 1367. The final touch was the central balcony overlooking the Molo, by the dalle Masegne, 1404.

The Molo wing has seventeen bays, thirteen representing the length of the hall of the Maggior Consiglio, and four representing

The Doge's Palace: the Molo façade, begun 1340

the Liagò, the south-east corner, where part of the earlier fabric was incorporated into the new wing; as a result, two large upper windows are at a different level from the rest. The upper loggia has two bays to each of the bays below, thirty-four in all. The lower colonnade is simply detailed, except for the richly carved capitals (now replaced by replicas). Although the upper loggia is more richly detailed, it lacks the splendid capitals of the lower order; instead, above and between the arches is a row of quatrefoils set inside circles, a form of tracery imitated in many late Gothic private palaces. The massive top storey is lit by six large windows, three on each side of the central balcony; all had stone tracery, but that in the Maggior Consiglio was lost in a fire in 1577 and never replaced. The whole upper part is clad with small rectangular pieces of stone, chiefly white Istrian stone and a decorative chevron pattern of pink Verona *broccatello*.

The façade corners were given special attention; on the SE corner, next to the Ponte de Paglia, at high level is the *Archangel Raphael*

The Doge's Palace, Molo façade, south-east corner: detail of the *Drunkenness of Noah*, *circa* 1420s

with Tobias; below is the *Drunkenness of Noah*. On the corresponding sw corner is the *Archangel Michael* at high level, and the *Fall* (Adam, Eve and the serpent) on the lower order. Considerable speculation still surrounds their authorship.

The Molo wing façade returned into the Piazzetta with the first six bays of the lower colonnade; its original extent is marked by a larger ground-floor column. In 1422 it was decided to replace the crumbling 'palace of Justice' of Doge Ziani (then more than 200 years old), which stood between this new Molo wing and San Marco, by a second new wing, continuing the design of the first. It was probably completed by the late 1430s, although internal decoration continued for some time thereafter.

The exterior repeats the Molo façade almost exactly, although it is slightly longer. The ground-floor capitals also repeat many of the earlier themes. The upper floor, chiefly occupied by the large Sala dello Scrutinio, has an impressive central window, completed in 1536, and is thus Renaissance rather than Gothic. The nw corner terminates with another fine sculpted group: at the upper level the *Archangel Gabriel*, and below the *Judgement of Solomon*, attributed variously to Bon, Jacopo della Quercia and Pietro Lamberti.

Between this nw corner and San Marco is the Porta della Carta, the final flourish in this reconstruction programme; a tour de force of richly elaborate Venetian Gothic. It was begun in 1438 by Bartolomeo Bon and his father Zane, and completed *circa* 1443. The Porta was to be the formal state entrance, the point of arrival for illustrious visitors. Its iconography revolves around the theme of Venice as the Republic of St Mark and of Justice. The Porta is made of various types of marble, and was originally extensively painted and gilded. Its principal sponsor was Doge Francesco Foscari, whose figure (in replica) kneels in front of the winged lion in the central sculpture. In the side niches are Temperance, Fortitude, Prudence and

The Doge's Palace: central part of the Piazzetta façade, begun 1422

The Doge's Palace: detail of the upper loggia and the Justice roundel on the Piazzetta façade, probably *circa* 1430

Charity; again many different attributions have been made, including Lamberti, Antonio Bregno and Bon. Above the square main portal is a complex traceried window, derived from Bon's earlier work at the Ca' d'Oro; directly above is a *tondo* of St Mark; the outer flanks of the upper arch are decorated with *putti* and wave decoration, while at the very top is the figure of Justice, carved by Bon himself.

Entering the Porta della Carta, it is directly continued by the Foscari colonnade, a six-bay portico culminating in the rich form of the Foscari Arch. The colonnade was probably begun by Bon (who died *circa* 1464), but was continued by Antonio Bregno and Antonio Rizzo. The style is very late Gothic, essentially transitional, since it was not completed until the 1470s. The arch itself is best seen from the central courtyard; it is a fussy, complex work, with a semicircular arch to the lower order, flanked by niches originally housing Rizzo's famous figures, *Adam* and *Eve* (today kept inside). On top is a miscellany of sculptures forming a picturesque group on the skyline.

The Doge's Palace: detail of the Porta della Carta, by Bartolomeo Bon, 1438–*circa* 1443

In 1483 fire destroyed the northern part of the old Ziani E wing, which contained the ducal apartments, and faced the Foscari Arch, with its back (E) wall onto the Rio de Palazzo. Reconstruction began under Rizzo, although we have little detail of progress. His Scala dei Giganti formed a crucial element in this new wing, since it terminated the axial vista down the Foscari colonnade. It was probably completed by *circa* 1494, and was to form the central feature of the new ducal coronation rite. Henceforth, the doge was to be presented to the nobility from the large landing at the top of the Scala; it was therefore richly decorated in marble, much of it overtly triumphal and Roman in derivation, a result of the patronage of Doge Agostin Barbarigo; in 1566 the two giant figures of Mars and Neptune were added by Sansovino to enhance the setting further.

Construction of the remainder of the monumental E wing took many years; after Rizzo fled the city, facing charges of fraud in 1498, work continued under the aged Pietro Lombardo, from 1499 to 1511, when he retired. The wing was structurally complete by *circa* 1503 but internal decoration continued; it was to contain the halls of all the highest institutions of Venetian government, other than the Maggior Consiglio, as well as the ducal apartments. The courtyard façade is most impressive, with rich relief carving to all four orders. The two stages of its construction can be seen at a distinct break on the roofline; the northern section is by Rizzo and Lombardo, the southern was begun by Lombardo and completed by Scarpagnino and Spavento. To the N of the Scala dei Giganti is the small Cortiletto dei Senatori, again by Spavento and Scarpagnino, a refined work again all clad with marble, with two superimposed orders. On top is a small roof garden, once the private domain of the doge.

The Doge's Palace suffered two further serious fires within a short time; the first, on 11 May 1574, destroyed the interiors of the halls of the Collegio and Senate in the rebuilt E wing; the second, on 20 December 1577, destroyed the interior of the Maggior Consiglio. Many paintings were also lost, including great cycles by the Bellini, Vivarini, Carpaccio, Titian and Veronese.

Five architects were approached for recommendations for reconstruction: Palladio, Rusconi, Guglielmo de' Grandi, Paolo da Ponte and Andrea da Valle. Despite Palladio's radical proposals, both wings were rebuilt inside their retained shells. Reconstruction was supervised by Antonio da Ponte, with contributions from Palladio and others; essentially, the results are the interiors of both wings as we see them today (see below).

The last stage in the palace's construction was the s face of the Foscari wing, added by Bartolomeo Manopola in 1603–14. The façade is a rich Mannerist work of five bays and two orders, crowned by a large aedicule containing a clock, by Pietro Cittadella.

The Doge's Palace remained the seat of Republican government until the Napoleonic invasion of May 1797. Considerable damage was inflicted because many images of doges and the winged lion were defaced or destroyed. In 1848–9 the short-lived libertarian government of Daniele Manin was based here; in 1874, after Unification, a major programme of structural restoration was begun. In this period, too, the Biblioteca Marciana was transferred from here to the Zecca, and the archaeological collection into the

Facing page: The Doge's Palace: east façade to the courtyard, begun by Antonio Rizzo (1485), completed by Pietro, Antonio and Tullio Lombardo (1489–*circa* 1510)

adjacent rooms of the Museo Civico Correr. Both outer façades were restored in 1876–87, when many of the capitals were replaced with copies. Further major restorations took place in the first years of the 2000s.

The Interior

The principal staterooms and apartments

The following description is based on the itinerary usually followed by visitors, and provides a logical, roughly chronological sequence; but this is varied from time to time.

The **Museo dell'Opera** was established here in 1996. It occupies several ground-floor rooms in the s and w wings, once occupied by stables and the offices of the Signori di Notte, the palace guard. The first three rooms contain many original capitals from the 1340s Molo wing, while the rooms towards the Piazzetta contain twenty-nine capitals from the upper *logge*, as well as pieces of tracery and the architrave of the Porta della Carta (signed by Bon) and the surviving head of Doge Francesco Foscari from the same location.

Internal itinerary: the route takes the Scala dei Censori up to the first-floor loggia. The **Avogaria** (advocates' offices) extend n towards the Scala d'Oro; in the first room, the Sala dei Notai, is the *Resurrection* by Domenico Tintoretto. Other works include the *Virgin with Three Avogadori* by Leandro Bassano and *St Mark with Three Avogadori* by Domenico Tintoretto. **Sala dei Censori**: at high level above the frieze: paintings by Antonio Palma and Domenico Tintoretto. Adjacent to the entrance is Domenico Tintoretto's *Annunciation*. Also the arms of the 266 *censori* who held office from 1517 to 1629; their function was to manage electoral procedures. The **Sala dello Scrigno** contained the safe in which was kept the Libro d'Oro, the book registering the names of the Venetian nobility, and the Libro d'Argento, the names of the 'original citizenry'. The **Saletta della Milizia da Mar**, the three navy commissioners, contains paintings by G. D. Tiepolo and Sebastiano Ricci. A passage leads to the **Cancelleria Ducale**, the ducal chancellery, and from here we turn out onto the loggia, and then left to the **Scala d'Oro**. This extraordinarily rich work was built in 1538, but remodelled by Sansovino *circa* 1555. It was the formal state approach to the halls of the Senate and Collegio on the top floor. The rich gilded stucco decoration is by Vittoria, with marble figures by Tiziano Aspetti and inset pictures by Battista Franco. Rising from the first to the second

The Doge's Palace: the Scala d'Oro, begun in 1554 by Jacopo Sansovino, completed by Scarpagnino, 1558; decoration by Alessandro Vittoria

floor, we reach the **Ducal apartments**; these occupy the northern end of the E wing at this level. The apartments are planned like those of a Venetian private palace, with a long central hall and smaller rooms on either side; they were rebuilt in the same location as they had been before the 1483 fire. The **Sala dei Scarlatti** takes its name from the scarlet magistrates' robes. The richly carved, decorated ceiling, chiefly in blue and gold, is by Pietro and Biagio da Faenza, *circa* 1505. The fine fireplace is by the Lombardo shop, probably Tullio and Antonio; the relief of the Virgin and Child over the doorway is attributed to Pietro Lombardo. The **Sala dell Scudo** forms a cross-axis, with one end facing the courtyard and the other the Rio di Palazzo. The shield and arms of the incumbent doge were kept here, and the hall formed an antechamber to the ducal apartments. The maps that dominate the room were painted by Giambattista Ramusio in 1540, but largely remade in 1762.

The **Sala Grimani** is the first room of the inner apartments, named after Doge Marin Grimani (1595–1605). The ceiling is from the Rizzo–Lombardo reconstruction, *circa* 1490s. The fine fireplace is another work from the Lombardo shop, bearing the arms of Agostin Barbarigo (1486–1501). The rich stucco decoration was added by Doge Pasquale Cicogna *circa* 1585–95. Among the various paintings is the famous emblematic winged lion by Carpaccio, 1516.

The **Sala Erizzo** is the next room, with another elegant fireplace, and again with later stucco decoration, with the arms of Francesco Erizzo (1631–46). The rich ceiling forms part of the original Rizzo–Lombardo rebuilding, *circa* 1490s. A short corridor gives access to the little **Sala degli Stucchi**, with the arms of Lorenzo Priuli (1556–9) over the fireplace. The stucco decoration dates from Doge Marino Grimani (1595–1605). A passageway (now lost) once gave direct access to the ducal banqueting hall, later incorporated into the nearby Palazzo Patriarcale.

The **Sala dei Filosofi** forms the central axis or *portego* of the apartments, its name derived from the twelve portraits of philosophers, by Veronese and Tintoretto, that once decorated the walls. They were later transferred to the Biblioteca Marciana. On one wall is a fresco, *St Christopher* by Titian. On the E side of the Sala are three rooms forming the doge's private apartments; the second has a richly painted open timber ceiling; the second and third have fine Lombardo fireplaces. Returning via the Sala dello Scudo and the Sala dei Scudieri, we reach the Scala d'Oro again, and now continue up to the top floor. Here we reach the halls of the highest institutions of the Republic, all sumptuously decorated.

At the top of the stair is the **square antechamber**, forming a lobby to the Sala delle Quattro Porte. It was decorated in 1559–67, originally with allegories by Tintoretto, later transferred to the Ante-Collegio. The ceiling is richly decorated and gilded; in the centre is Tintoretto's painting of Doge Girolamo Priuli receiving the scales and sword of Justice.

The **Sala delle Quattro Porte** is an impressive hall, which housed the Collegio before the 1574 fire; when rebuilt, it became the antechamber to the Senate and the Collegio. It was built by da Ponte, following designs by Palladio and Rusconi. The rich stuccoed ceiling is in the Roman manner, while the frescoes are by Jacopo Tintoretto, 1578–81, but extensively restored. In the centre of the ceiling is *Jove Leading Venice to Dominion over the Adriatic*; the smaller outer pictures show cities of the Terraferma empire: Vicenza, Treviso, Padua and Brescia. The decorations were completed in 1606; the final works included the magnificent doorways of rare marble, probably designed by Palladio; the wall decorations are by Titian, Marco Vecellio (his nephew) and others. Formerly on the wall, but now on an easel, is the famous *Neptune Offering Venice the Riches of the Seas*, an outstanding work by G. B. Tiepolo (1756), his only painting in the palace. The NW doorway leads to the **Ante-Collegio**, a small but sumptuously decorated hall, redecorated after the 1574 fire, with marble and stucco decoration designed by Palladio and Rusconi. Set into Palladio's ceiling, made by Marco del Moro, are paintings by Veronese and Tintoretto. In the central octagon is *Venice Conferring Rewards and Honours* by Veronese. The four paintings, originally executed by Tintoretto for the square antechamber (see above), were relocated here in 1713. On the W wall is a fine Palladian fireplace, later elaborated with telemons by Scamozzi.

The **Sala del Collegio** is the most richly decorated stateroom, although by no means the largest. The Venetian 'cabinet' met here, and illustrious foreign visitors were received by the doge and his council. The design is by Palladio and Rusconi, supervised by Antonio da Ponte. The exceptionally rich coffered gilded ceiling and the ducal throne are by Francesco Bello and Andrea Faentin, 1577. The great glory of the ceiling, other than its structure, is the superb series of paintings by Veronese. The three large central ones are *Mars and Neptune*, *Faith* and *Venice Triumphant, with Peace and Justice*. The eight smaller paintings down the sides depict allegories of the Virtues. On the walls are several notable pictures: behind the tribune is Veronese's *Victory of Lepanto*; directly opposite, on the entrance wall: *Doge Andrea Gritti* by Tintoretto. On the long wall facing the windows: three paintings by Tintoretto. On the window wall is a fine fireplace, perhaps by Campagna.

The **Sala del Senato**, like all the other staterooms, was remade after the 1574 fire, under da Ponte's direction; it is the third largest hall in the palace, and has a magnificent carved gilded ceiling by Cristoforo Sorte, *circa* 1581. The wall and ceiling paintings were largely made during the reign of Pasquale Cicogna, 1585–95. In the ceiling are five large paintings: in the centre is the *Exaltation and Triumph of Venice*, designed but not executed by Tintoretto; the other four paintings are by Tommaso Dolabella, Marco Vecellio, Andrea Vicentino and Aliense. The N end of the hall is occupied by the tribune; in the centre: the *Dead Christ Supported by Angels* by Tintoretto; the two flanking paintings are both by G. D. Tiepolo. On the long side wall next to the Collegio: three pictures by Palma il Giovane and one by Tintoretto. On the S end wall: *Doges Lorenzo and Girolamo Priuli with Patrons*, both by Palma il Giovane. On the canal-side wall: *Lorenzo Giustinian*, first patriarch of Venice, by Marco Vecellio; and *Ptolemy* by Palma il Giovane.

In the NE corner of the hall a doorway leads to the **ante-chapel**, decorated with eighteenth-century stucco; the ceiling paintings, by

Jacopo Guarana, depict the Virtues. The **chapel** was converted by Scamozzi in 1593 for the use of the doge and Senate; it was restored in 1766 by Girolamo Mengozzi Colonna, with allegorical images again by Guarana. On the altar is a marble *Virgin and Child* by Sansovino.

We now return to the Sala delle Quattro Porte, passing the Scala d'Oro, and entering the **Sala del Consiglio dei Dieci**. The Dieci (Ten) were established in the aftermath of the Tiepolo conspiracy of 1310, and their purpose was to uphold state security. The hall has a square plan, with the curved seventeen-seat tribune on the w side. The ceiling decoration is by Veronese and assistants, *circa* 1553–4, probably his earliest work in Venice. The themes are said to have originated with Daniele Barbaro, the notable humanist scholar, and illustrate allegories of the functions of the Ten. On the walls: paintings by Francesco Bassano (N) and Marco Vecellio (s). Continue into the **Sala della Bussola**, which served as an antechamber for the Sala dei Dieci; next to the doorway is a *bocca de leone*, lion's mouth, where secret denunciations were placed for investigation by the Ten. A simple wooden ceiling, with monochrome paintings of scenes from Roman history, from the shop of Veronese. The marble fireplace is by Sansovino, with caryatids by Danese Cattaneo and Pietro da Salò. We continue into the **Sala dei Capi dei Dieci**, the three heads of the Ten, chosen on a rotating basis to schedule trials and hearings. The ceiling is again from the shop of Veronese, with the central octagon by Zelotti. The four rectangular panels illustrate allegories of the Ten's activities. The fireplace is again by Sansovino, Cattaneo and Pietro. On the walls: three paintings by Francesco Bassano. A doorway in the s wall leads to the **Sala dei Inquisitori**, a small room formerly housing the three state inquisitors. All the original fittings are gone; directly above is the torture chamber, from which a passage leads to the Ponte dei Sospiri and thence to the prisons.

Ducal armouries: a suite of rooms in the se corner of the palace. They are reached by a stair up from the Sala dei Inquisitori. The nucleus of the collection was founded in 1532, and contained not only arms for immediate deployment but also a superb collection of historic and decorative pieces. Many were dispersed after 1797, but a good collection survives in three principal halls. The first, **Sala del Gattamelata,** is named after the Republic's *condottiere*, and contains the white armour of Henri iv, king of France, donated to the Republic in 1603. There is a fine collection of pikes, halberds, lances, etc., as well as pistols and carbines. On the ceiling: the Turkish flag captured at Lepanto in 1571. At the w end a doorway leads to prisons, known as the Torresella; the walls are covered with historic graffiti. The **Sala Morosini** has a collection of arms surrounding the bust of Francesco Morosini, hero of the Peloponnese wars; the displays include swords, broadswords, helmets, crossbows, pistols and quivers of arrows. There are also two suits of heavy jousting armour. The third hall, the **Hall of rare arms**, has some very fine and rare pieces, including broadswords, pikes, arquebuses, shields, rapiers and pistols. Also portrait busts of Marcantonio Bragadin and Sebastiano Venier, heroes of Lepanto, by Tiziano Aspetti. We return to the vestibule, and descend the Scala dei Censori to the second floor, the level of the Maggior Consiglio. Turning left, we enter the **Liagò**, the long, high-ceilinged hall that served as a lobby for the Maggior Consilgio itself. The ceiling is richly decorated. Rizzo's famous *Adam* and *Eve* are usually on display here. To the left are two parallel halls, the first is the **Sala della Quarantia Civil Vecchia**, the forty nobles who formed a civil appeal court; there was a matching forty for criminal cases. After the fifteenth century the Quarantia was subdivided into two, the Vecchia dealing with the city and Dogado, the Nuova dealing with the Terraferma empire. Immediately adjacent is the **Sala del Armamento (del Guariento)**, originally housing an arms supply, but taking its later name from the remains of Guariento's frescoes, formerly in the Maggior Consiglio, but now located here. They were painted in 1365–7 but badly damaged in the 1577 fire.

From the Liagò we enter the vast **Sala del Maggior Consiglio**, one of the most imposing sights in the city. This great hall measures 54 metres in length, 25 metres in width and 12 metres in height. Every adult male noble in the Republic was required to attend and vote at its sessions, which debated all major aspects of the Republic's politics, and voted for all the other highest organs of state. At its peak the hall contained around 2,500 voting members. On rare occasions the great hall was used for other purposes; for example, the state visit of Henri III of France in 1574, when a great banquet was held here, only three years before the hall was destroyed by fire.

The Sala is dominated by the gilded Baroque timber ceiling by Cristoforo Sorte. Its inset sections contain thirty-five paintings, the three most important being *Venice as a Queen* by Tintoretto; *Venice Supreme, Crowned by Victory* by Palma il Giovane; and the *Apotheosis of Venice*, a fine work by Veronese. The other principal paintings are by Veronese, Francesco Bassano and Tintoretto and his shop.

Around the walls at high level is a frieze containing imaginary portraits of the first seventy-six doges, mostly by Domenico Tintoretto; on the w end wall is a gap where the portrait of Marin Falier should be sited; Falier was executed for treason in 1355. Around the walls is a large series of narrative paintings, depicting episodes from the Republic's history; they are by various artists including Veronese's studio, Leandro and Francesco Bassano, Domenico Tintoretto, Palma il Giovane, Giulio del Moro and Andrea Vicentino. The E wall, behind the ducal dais, is covered by Tintoretto's huge *Paradise*, said to be the largest canvas in the world; he was assisted by Domenico and by Palma, but the vast scale seems to have daunted even him, and it is by no means his most imposing work.

From the NW side of the Sala a door leads to the **Sala della Quarantia Civil Nuova,** formerly housing the forty magistrates established in 1492 to deal with civil cases in the Terraferma empire. On the walls are seventeenth-century allegorical paintings. The hall leads in turn to the impressive **Sala del Scrutinio,** the largest in the palace after that of the Maggior Consiglio, occupying most of the Piazzetta wing. In 1532 it was designated for counting ballots from the adjacent hall of the Maggior Consiglio, and for meetings of the commissions to elect a new doge. The interior was badly damaged in the 1577 fire, and notable pictures were lost. It was restored by Antonio da Ponte, and redecorated from 1587. The theme is the overseas empire, most of the pictures being by followers of Tintoretto and Veronese, including Andrea Vicentino and Aliense. The rich, elaborate ceiling resembles that of the Maggior Consiglio, and is again by Cristoforo Sorte, *circa* 1585. The inset paintings depict naval victories. The high-level frieze continues the series of ducal portraits from the Maggior Consiglio, with a further forty-two doges, culminating with the last, Ludovico Manin (1787–97). On the s end wall is another huge canvas, the *Last Judgement* by Palma il Giovane, which, like the Tintoretto *Paradise*, seems inadequate for the huge scale required. At the other end is a triumphal arch by Andrea Tirali, installed in 1694 to commemorate the re-taking of the Morea by Francesco Morosini. All the wall paintings down the two long sides, by Andrea Vicentino, Sante Peranda and others, depict naval victories.

BUILDINGS ON AND AROUND THE PIAZZA

The Campanile

The massive bell-tower is another of the iconic images of the city. According to tradition, it was first built in AD 888, but was altered or restored several times; the first open bell-chamber was added in the 1170s. In 1489 it was badly damaged by lightning and a consequent fire; further damage followed after an earthquake in 1511, after which the upper part was rebuilt, probably by Bon the Bergamasco. At this stage a new attic storey was added, as well as a tall pyramidal roof. In 1515 the gilded angel was hauled to its place on the peak. Numerous further lightning strikes followed, until in 1776 a lightning rod was added, perhaps the first in Europe.

On 14 July 1902, however, after several ill-advised structural alterations, the tower collapsed into a pile of rubble, taking Sansovino's Loggetta with it; all the bells except one were broken, but the adjacent basilica was undamaged. That same evening, it was decided to rebuild it precisely as it was ('com'era e dov'era'), but with a more substantial structure. It was inaugurated on St Mark's Day, 1912.

The tower has a square plan, with sides of around 12 metres, tapering slightly upwards. The height of the brick shaft is approximately 49.5 metres (160 ft), and the superstructure is the same height again, the apex being 98.6 metres from the pavement. Above the shaft is the tall colonnaded bell-chamber; above again is a square attic, from which rises the copper-clad pyramidal roof, surmounted by the 5-metre gilded angel; its original purpose was a beacon for shipping. Structurally, the tower has an inner brick shaft and an outer one, with a ramped staircase rising between the two; there is also a high-speed lift in the centre.

The Loggetta

The richly decorated Loggetta, in the form of a Roman triumphal arch, was designed by Sansovino to replace an older one, which functioned as a meeting place for noblemen. It was begun in 1537, and completed *circa* 1540, although the applied sculpture was added a little later. In 1569 it was used as a guardhouse, and after 1734 it housed the state lottery. It was altered several times; in the sixteenth century the two side windows were converted into doorways, and the terrace was added in front. In 1735–7 the bronze gate was added,

The Loggetta: detail of the attic; by Jacopo Sansovino, mostly 1538–40

and the attic was extended across the full width of the façade. After its destruction in 1902 it was` painstakingly reassembled, using as much original material as could be salvaged.

The main three-bay façade has paired free-standing Corinthian columns, with niches for statues set between them; the rich materials include Carrara marble, Verona *broccatello*, *verde antico* and Istrian limestone. The columns are of rare eastern marble. The four niche figures, by Sansovino, are *Pallas*, *Apollo*, *Mercury* and *Peace*, while the three large attic relief panels are *Venice as Justice* (centre), flanked by *Jupiter, King of Crete* (left) and *Venus, Queen of Cyprus* (right), two of Venice's principal overseas possessions; the last two by Danese Cattaneo.

Torre de l'Orologio

The construction of the clock tower was one of the most important works of civic improvement in early Renaissance Venice. The clock itself was begun in 1493, to replace an old one formerly on the façade of San Marco, and was made by Gian Paolo Rainieri and his son, Gian Carlo, in Reggio Emilia. Two years later it was decided to house it in a new tower, to be built where the Merceria, the principal commercial axis linking the Piazza with Rialto, enters the Piazza itself: a crucial location in the urban structure of the city. Part

The Torre de l'Orologio, 1493–9: detail of the second
and third orders, with the clock face and the Virgin
and Child

of the old Procuracy building was demolished to provide its site. On
1 February 1499 the tower and clock were inaugurated by Doge
Agostin Barbarigo. The architect is unknown, although it has often
been ascribed to Codussi.

In 1506 the two side wings were constructed; in 1755 columns
were added at the base to reinforce its stability, and the set-back
upper terraces were added by Massari.

The tower has five elements; the first is the large archway, above
which is the Rainieri inscription. The next order, containing the
clock, is a triumph of mechanical complexity and sophistication.
There are three concentric rings: the innermost one is a blue disc
with gold stars and the moon; the next contains the signs of the
zodiac; while the outer ring has the twenty-four hours in Roman
numerals. The hour is indicated by a gold sun at the end of a hand.
The next order contains the most complex symbolism; the dominant
element is the large semicircular balcony, above which is a niche
containing the Virgin and Child. There are small doorways on each

side, on the faces of which are the hours and minutes. During Ascension Week, the doors open and the figure of Gabriel appears, blowing a trumpet, followed by the Three Magi, who genuflect, before disappearing into the other doorway. Ascension Day was one of the most important events of the Venetian calendar, when the doge symbolically married the sea, and a great trade fair was held in the Piazza.

The next order has more obvious symbolism: a large winged Venetian lion, originally accompanied by a kneeling figure of Doge Barbarigo, destroyed by Napoleon. The final element is the bronze group on the top, the 'Moors' (in fact, figures of an old man and a youth, signifying the passage of time), originally gilded, who ring the hours with hammers on the bell. They were made by master founders in the Arsenale.

The Torre has a much simpler N façade, on the Meceria, with a large circular clock face, again with twenty-four hours in Roman numerals, and a gilded sun in the centre.

Procuratie Vecchie

The exceptionally long range of the Procuratie occupy the N side of the Piazza from the NW corner to the Torre de l'Orologio. The original Procuracy was a long Venetian-Byzantine building, with a single storey of apartments above a ground-floor colonnade. It was built in the 1170s, but by the end of the fifteenth century was in poor condition. The eastern end was demolished *circa* 1492 to build the Torre de l'Orologio, and the building was damaged by fire in 1512. It was rebuilt completely, but with three storeys instead of two, the building thus having a much stronger presence on the Piazza, and with more spacious procurators' apartments on the upper floors. The architect is not known; Codussi may have furnished initial designs, although he died ten years before reconstruction began. The work was perhaps supervised by Bartolomeo Bon the Bergamasco, or Pietro Bon, *proto* of the procurators. The design is closely modelled on its predecessor, with a continuous fifty-bay ground-floor colonnade; the arched windows to the two upper floors are half the width, giving 100 bays to the upper orders. The detailing is repetitive, but rich and refined, crowned by a fanciful crenellation.

This hypnotically repetitive screen masks the intricate internal planning, which incorporates a central 'spine' service *calle* down the length of the building, as well as *sotoporteghi* and high-level bridges.

The Procuratie Vecchie, begun 1514, perhaps to an original design by Mauro Codussi, executed under Bon the Bergamasco and completed by Jacopo Sansovino, *circa* 1532; detail of the upper orders

The ground floor has always been occupied by commercial functions, and today contains two famous coffee shops, among the oldest in Venice. At no. 120 is the Caffè Quadri, founded 1775, and refurbished in 1858, as we see it today. At no. 123 is the Caffè Lavena, established in 1750 by Carlo Lavena, and still in the family's ownership. It has a fine early nineteenth-century interior, with original mirrors, panelling and a large Murano chandelier. Both cafés have had numerous famous patrons, including Wagner, Byron, Proust, Balzac and Liszt. At no. 101 is the former Olivetti showroom, remodelled by Carlo Scarpa in 1957–8, with refined and ingenious detailing.

Procuratie Nuove

The massive Procuratie Nuove occupy the s side of the Piazza, from its abutment with the Biblioteca Marciana to the sw corner, where it meets the Ala Napoleonica. Sansovino's original proposal was to continue the design of the Library, removing the miscellany of existing buildings that stood here, thereby unifying the Piazza's appearance.

In 1582, after Sansovino's death, a competition was held, won by Scamozzi, but his new Procuracy was to have three storeys rather

The Procuratie Nuove, begun 1582 by Scamozzi;
completed after 1640 by Baldassare Longhena

than Sansovino's two. Construction took place in stages, from E to
w. By 1600 the first block was complete and occupied, but the
second stage had different internal planning, and Scamozzi was
succeeded first by Francesco de Bernardin, and then, in 1640, by
Longhena, who completed the last bays in the sw corner, as well as
seven new bays across the w end (later demolished by Napoleon).

The Piazza façade is grandiose and impressive, but its abutment to
Sansovino's Library is awkward, and Scamozzi's original 'gap' was
filled in; his first ten bays are more richly detailed than the
remainder. The three orders are Doric, Ionic and Corinthian, with a
continuous ground-storey colonnade; the first two orders follow
Sansovino closely, but the third is different, with rectangular
pedimented windows and a rather weak cornice.

The plan is complex, with a series of square internal courtyards;
the eight procurators' apartments had their principal rooms onto the
Piazza; at the rear was ancillary, domestic accommodation. Each
apartment had access from the Piazza, and water access from the *rio*
at the back.

After the Napoleonic occupation, the building became Napoleon's viceroy's palace (1805–15); in that period, the ancient granaries were demolished and the plain s façade (never intended to be seen) was exposed to the new Giardinetti Reali, set out on their site. After Venice's secession to Austria, the Procuratie became the governor's residence. For a short time in 1848–9, Daniele Manin's liberation government was based here, before falling to Austria again. After Unification, it was briefly used by the king, Victor Emmanuel II, but after 1918 it was ceded to the state.

Most of the first and second floors are today occupied by the Museo Civico Correr and the Pinacoteca Correr, the museum established from the extraordinary collection amassed by Teodoro Correr, who died in 1830.

Within the ground floor, at nos 56–9, is the famous café, Florian, established in 1720 and one of the oldest in Venice; its decoration is by Ludovico Cadorin, 1858.

Ala Napoleonica (Napoleonic Wing)

Construction was a direct consequence of the fall of the Republic in 1797; Napoleon's Italian viceroy, Eugène de Beauharnais, having established the Procuratie as his palace, decided to extend it by building a new Neo-classical wing to contain a ballroom and a great ceremonial staircase. To do so, the whole w end of the Piazza was demolished, including seven bays of the Procuratie Nuove, part of the Procuratie Vecchie and Sansovino's San Geminiano. The architect was Giuseppe Maria Soli; work began in 1810. The wing has two storeys and a tall, plain attic. At ground level, there are two colonnaded areas, a bank of shops and the block containing the entrance and ceremonial staircase. The front colonnade links the two original Procuracy buildings, thus providing a continuous covered walkway. The façade has fifteen bays, the lower Doric, the upper Ionic, based on the Procuratie Nuove; the attic was intended to be adorned with a giant statue of Napoleon, never installed.

The Neo-classical interior is imposing and richly detailed. The great stair has two lower flights, meeting at a half-landing and rising in a single central flight; a large square vestibule then leads to the ballroom, an elegant, refined hall with a semicircle of columns at each end, and a richly coffered shallow vaulted ceiling. The interior is all by Lorenzo Santi, the city's director of public works, with decoration by Giuseppe Borsato, Carlo Bevilacqua and others.

BUILDINGS ON AND AROUND THE PIAZZETTA

The Zecca (Mint)

The Venetian mint was administered under the Consiglio dei Dieci. By the 1530s the economy was expanding rapidly, and the mint was unable to meet the demand for new coinage. In 1535 it was decided to rebuild on the same site, but on a larger scale and using fireproof construction, to minimise danger from the furnaces. Sansovino submitted a successful proposal, and the work was complete by 1547. Masonry vaults were used throughout, with no timber floors. The site was very restricted, and work proceeded in phases so that production of coin could continue. Sansovino's design is elegant and rational: the front block facing the Molo housed the gold and silver foundries (gold upstairs, for greater security), while the larger N block is built around a courtyard, surrounded by workshops for the manufacture of coinage, again silver below, gold above. The courtyard is five bays wide and ten bays long. In 1558 a third floor was added, partly because the first-floor furnaces, facing S and with a roof directly above, suffered from intolerable summer overheating. This extension, perhaps also by Sansovino, was complete by 1566. The mint remained operational until 1866; after 1905 it became part of the Biblioteca Marciana, as it remains today, the central courtyard (now roofed) forming the main reading room, with surrounding book stacks.

The Zecca has only one formal façade, facing the Bacino; it is heavy and severe, faced with rusticated stonework, and with nine bays. The first floor is a tour de force of visual strength, with massive rusticated Doric columns and windows with heavy stone lintels; it is capped by a massive cornice, the original termination of the façade before the more conventional Ionic second floor was added. The internal courtyard façades are more restrained, with a rusticated ground floor; the two upper levels are respectively Doric and Ionic.

Biblioteca Nazionale Marciana

The Library of St Mark occupies the W side of the Piazzetta, with a rich twenty-one-bay stone façade; it is often claimed to be Sansovino's masterpiece. The tardy decision to build it was taken in 1537, the *raison d'être* being a magnificent collection of Greek and Latin manuscripts left to the Republic in 1467 by Cardinal Bessarion, patriarch of Constantinople. The instigators were the humanist scholars Vettor Grimani and Pietro Bembo, the latter the librarian of

The Zecca (left) and the south end of the Biblioteca Marciana; the former by Jacopo Sansovino, 1535–47; third storey added in 1558

The Zecca: detail of first-floor rustication

the collection. Sansovino had been appointed *proto* of the procurators in 1529, but it was necessary to build the new library in stages, because the site was occupied by inns and shops that yielded high revenues; Sansovino relocated them as the work progressed. Construction began at the N end, near the campanile. Sansovino's ingenious design for turning the corner was followed by disaster, since on 19 December 1545 the first bay collapsed without warning; he had chosen a shallow masonry vault for the reading room, rather than the traditional Venetian flat timber ceiling and roof trusses, a dangerous decision in a city with such difficult subsoil. After a night in prison, he was released by his patrons, supported by Titian, but had to pay 1,000 ducats for the remedial work, and to abandon the vault in favour of a timber ceiling. The final design resembles a vault but is all non-structural timber.

Work continued through the 1540s; by 1550 the first seven bays were complete; progress thereafter was rapid, and by 1556 sixteen bays had been built. In 1553 work began on the impressive marble portal to the reading room; three years later the reading room ceiling was begun. Finally, in 1564, almost a century after the bequest, Bessarion's collection was installed. In 1559 decoration of the vestibule began; this was intended to house a school of humanist study, with a ceiling decorated by Titian. In 1591 the vestibule was remodelled to display classical sculpture from the Grimani collection; it was redecorated, although Titian's ceiling survives.

Sansovino died in 1570; in 1588–91 the library was extended southwards, the last five bays added by Scamozzi. It remained here until 1812, when it was requisitioned by Napoleon and transferred to the Doge's Palace; it returned in 1905, now also occupying the former Zecca.

The Library's form is long and narrow, with the reading room occupying the seven N bays, followed by a three-bay vestibule, and a further four for the staircase. The remaining seven were originally occupied by procurators' offices; the two short N and S façades each have only three bays. The whole is richly detailed, with the ground floor occupied by a deep colonnade, behind which were shops for rent, as they remain today. The lower Doric order has prominent lion-head keystones, the arch spandrels filled with classical reliefs. Above is a deep classical frieze, with triglyphs and metopes, crowned by a bold cornice. The upper order is Ionic, with a continuous stone balustrade; above the arches is another rich, elaborate frieze, into which are set small oval windows. Above the crowning cornice is another continuous balustrade, while the roofline is enlivened by corner obelisks and statues of classical gods, some by Cattaneo and Vittoria.

The main entrance is flanked by giant stone caryatids, one by Vittoria, the other a copy. The grandiose staircase rises in two long, straight, flights, with a barrel-vaulted ceiling in the Roman manner, richly carved and gilded, again by Vittoria. At the top is the square vestibule, with ceiling decoration by Cristoforo Rosa; in the centre is Titian's *Wisdom*.

The main reading room, 26.4 metres long, has a shallow vaulted gilded ceiling, with three rows of coffers, each containing seven panels. Seven artists were commissioned, each painting a row of three panels: from the entrance portal, they are: Giovanni Fratina, Giuseppe Salviati, Battista Franco, Giulio Licinio, Giambattista Zelotti, Paolo Veronese and Schiavone. Sansovino's original wall decoration was augmented in the late seventeenth century with paintings in niches,

The Biblioteca Nazionale Marciana: detail of the façade. Begun by Jacopo Sansovino, 1537; the last bays completed by Vincenzo Scamozzi, 1588–91

some by Tintoretto. Later again, these were transferred to the Sala dei Filosofi in the Doge's Palace, and new bookcases were added to house the Bessarion collection. In 1929 the paintings were returned here once again. Flanking the doorway are two *Philosophers* by Veronese, and on the courtyard wall two more by Veronese and four by Tintoretto.

Piazzetta dei Leoncini

The little square N of the basilica takes its name from the two diminutive lions of Verona *broccatello*, by Giovanni Bonazza, 1722. On the N side is the former **chiesa di San Basso** (SM 315), established in 1076; after various restorations, it was rebuilt *circa* 1675–8. Traditionally ascribed to Benoni, it is now accepted as the work of Longhena. It was closed in 1809, and became a workshop for restoration of the basilica. It was restored in 1951 and today houses exhibitions and conferences.

The entrance is on the narrow Calle San Basso, but the principal façade is that to the Piazzetta. It is of stone with three bays, and prominent Corinthian columns. Above is a heavy entablature; the upper order was never built. The interior has an aisle-less nave, with Corinthian pilasters supporting another heavy entablature; the ceiling is flat. There were originally five altars, but the interior fittings are dispersed.

The E end of the Piazzetta is dominated by the restrained Neo-classical façade of the **Palazzo Patriarcale** (Lorenzo Santi, 1837–50). The palace was formed after the transfer of the patriarchate from San Pietro in Castello to San Marco; Santi's principal work was this new front block, behind which are several disparate pre-existing structures. These include the former banqueting hall of the Signoria (Manopola, 1618–23), now subsumed within the palace. It has eighteenth-century decoration by Guarana and Niccolò Bambini. Santi's five-bay façade has a giant order of fluted Corinthian pilasters; decoration is largely confined to relief panels between the attic windows.

1   FROM SAN ZULIAN TO SAN MOISÈ

Take the Merceria under the Torre de l'Orologio, and continue to the small, congested, Campo San Zulian.

San Zulian (Giuliano) was reputedly established in 829, the year the body of St Mark was brought to the city. It was rebuilt in 1105 and again after 1553; this latter reconstruction survives. It was funded by Tommaso Rangone, a wealthy physician and philologist. Work was initially limited to a new façade to the pre-existing church, but after the façade had been nearly completed (1555), the church itself was reconstructed. Both church and façade are by Sansovino, although he died before its re-consecration. The ceiling was completed in 1585, the chancel in the 1590s. It remained a parish foundation until 1810, when it was subordinated to San Marco. The ancient campanile was demolished in 1775.

The site is very restricted, and the façade dominates the tiny square; a commemorative screen, with two orders capped by a pediment, rather like a triumphal arch, and with Rangone (also by Sansovino, 1554) prominent in the centre above the doorway; this was the first time in Venice that a patron was directly represented on a church façade.

San Zulian: detail of the façade, by Jacopo Sansovino,
1553–5

The interior: a simple cubical volume, with small eastern
projections for the chancel and side chapels. Most of the little light
comes from high-level windows, and the chancel is approached by a
large arch, flanked by Corinthian pilasters. The rich gilded coffered
ceiling was funded by Girolamo Vignola; in the centre: *St Julian in
Glory* by Palma il Giovane. The church contains several other
paintings by Palma, as well as Veronese's *Dead Christ* (first right altar).
In the small chapel of the Sacrament is stucco decoration by Vittoria
(*circa* 1583) and paintings by Veronese and Palma.

Take the short Marzaria directly opposite the church, cross Ponte
dei Ferali into Calle Fiubera, taking the next right, Calle degli
Armeni. At the end, on the right, is **Santa Croce degli Armeni**.
The Armenian community had been based here since 1253, and
flourished, particularly in the fifteenth century. In 1496 a small
chapel was built, reconstructed on a larger scale in 1682; decoration
was complete by 1704. The chapel remains administered by the
Mechitarist friars of San Lazzaro degli Armeni. It is embedded
within surrounding housing, only the small cupola and campanile
identifiable externally. The interior has a centralised plan, surmounted
by the cupola on pendentives. The decoration is rich and refined,

more classical than Baroque, despite the date. The architect is not known; attributions have been made to Sardi and Longhena.

Turn left along the picturesque Rio Terà de le Colonne; then left (Calle dei Fabbri) and right into Calle San Gallo, continuing into the square. On the sw side is the tiny **Oratorio de San Gallo**, 1581, built in conjunction with the relocated Ospizio Orseolo. It was restored in 1703, and was directly patronised by the doge. The Ospizio was demolished in 1872 and replaced by a hotel. The little oratory façade has three bays, with Corinthian pilasters, and a stone arched portal. Inside: three marble altars.

Take Calle Tron out of the w side of the square; on the left is the **Banco Nazionale del Lavoro**, 1900, by Enrico Pellanda, an impressive stone-clad Neo-classical pile; opposite is the **Banco di Napoli**, similarly opulent and monumental, 1915, by E. Grisostolo. Cross Ponte Tron, turning left down the quay to the Bacino Orseolo. Continue down Calle del Selvadego into Bocca de Piazza and Calle Larga. On the N corner is the much-restored **Palazzo Selvadego** (SM 1238), originally late thirteenth century or early fourteenth; for 500 years it was an inn or hotel. It has a boldly overhanging Tuscan roof, and a *liagò* or covered loggia across the top floor. From Calle Larga, take Calle seconda, and then turn left down the long Calle Vallaresso. On the quay at the end (left), next to Harry's Bar, is the **Capitaneria del Porto** (SM 1324), a notable early Renaissance building (1492) to house offices for the flour magistrates; the huge granaries of the Republic stood nearby, on the site of the present Giardinetti. A five-bay façade, originally with an open ground-floor colonnade; the tripartite upper floor resembles contemporary palaces, with simple, refined detailing. Just over the adjacent bridge is Lorenzo Santi's **Coffee House**, *circa* 1838, an attractive Neo-classical confection in the form of a small pavilion, all of Istrian stone.

From the *vaporetto* stop, towards the right (w), is the good late Gothic façade of **Palazzo Giustinian** (SM 1364), today the Biennale headquarters. It was rebuilt in the 1460s and 1470s, although partially modernised again in the seventeenth century. The Gothic windows remain, and the façade is symmetrical and tripartite; a central *quadrifora* flanked by pairs of single lights. On the far side is a smaller contemporary annexe.

Return to Calle seconda, turn left into Salizada San Moisè, and continue into the square.

San Moisè is an early parish foundation (797), originally dedicated to San Vittore. It was rebuilt in the ninth century by Moisè Venier,

San Moisè: central part of the façade, by Alessandro
Tremignon, begun 1668

who altered the dedication to reflect his own name. The medieval
structure survived until 1632, when it was rebuilt. The architect of
the church itself is unknown, although the remarkable Baroque
façade is by Alessandro Tremignon, begun in 1668. The tripartite
composition has two orders, a tall lower one, with fluted Corinthian
columns on tall plinths, and a much lower upper one, in the centre
of which is a thermal window. The luxuriantly complex decoration
was generously funded by the Fini family, who lived nearby;
Vincenzo Fini's memorial is in the centre of the façade.

The simple interior has a large rectangular nave and a plain groin-
vaulted ceiling. Around the perimeter: a giant order of flat
Corinthian pilasters, surmounted by a deep entablature. The
rectangular chancel is flanked by square side chapels; its principal
feature is the extraordinary stone altarpiece by Tremignon and
Enrico Meyring, depicting Moses receiving the Commandments on
Mount Sinai.

Cross the bridge in front of the church and continue down Calle Larga XXII Marzo, cut through in 1880 and named after the date when the Austrians were expelled from the city in 1848. Take Calle del Cristo on the right, then Piscina San Moisè. On the opposite bank of Rio dei Barcaroli are the Gothic **Palazzetto Sanudo** (SM 1626) and the unusual **Palazzo Cocco Molin** (SM 1659), with a long early Renaissance façade.

Return W down the Piscina and turn right, over Ponte de le Veste; continue into Campo San Fantin, a small irregularly shaped square, surrounded by notable buildings. On the N side is the rich stone façade of the **Scuola de San Fantin (Ateneo Veneto)** (SM 1897).

Founded in 1458, when two confraternities joined together. The original small structure survived until 1580, when the present much more impressive replacement was begun; the architect is now known to have been Vittoria. The Scuola was suppressed by Napoleon in 1806, but in 1810 the Società veneziana di medicina was established here, later merging with other learned societies to become the Ateneo Veneto.

The two-order façade has three broad bays, surmounted by a large aedicule; the basically classical screen incorporates Baroque elements. The lower order is Ionic, with paired columns, the upper Corinthian; both have broken pediments.

Inside, the ground-floor hall has a cycle of paintings by Leonardo Corona (*circa* 1606), showing scenes from the *Passion*; also an *Assumption* by Veronese and a portrait bust of Tommaso Rangone by Vittoria. The heavy wooden coffered ceiling is decorated by Palma il Giovane. The main upper hall is today the library reading room, and its original paintings are dispersed. The decoration is from the Veronese school; the ceiling is mostly from the workshop of Palma il Giovane, *circa* 1600.

The church of **San Fantin** projects into the square, which wraps around its plain stone W end. An early parish foundation, rebuilt *circa* 1200 by the Pisani, modernised in the early fifteenth century, and finally completely rebuilt after 1507. It is usually ascribed to Scarpagnino, but may have been continued after his death (1549) by Sansovino; it was completed in 1564. The exterior is simple, particularly the W bay, with doorways on three faces. The interior is monumental and imposing, with an unusual structure: two large square bays form the nave, separated by a smaller half-sized bay. A further square bay defines the chancel, surmounted by a small cupola

Scuola di San Fantin (Ateneo Veneto): detail of upper façade, by Alessandro Vittoria, 1592–1600, and Tommaso Contin, 1600–04

on pendentives; in the corners: four fluted Corinthian columns, set into niches. The chancel terminates with a semicircular apse, lit by five single windows. The articulation is restrained and refined, almost Neo-classical, with unusual composite Ionic/Corinthian capitals. Among the works of art are paintings by Palma il Giovane and a monument to Vinciguerra Dandolo (+1518) by Tullio Lombardo.

Gran Teatro la Fenice: the restrained Neo-classical façade of this famous theatre occupies the w side of the square; one of the finest opera houses in Italy, with a complex, eventful history. The first Fenice was founded by a group of Venetian nobles, and designed by Gianantonio Selva, following a competition; it was completed with remarkable speed in 1790–92. In 1807 a short-lived imperial box was added for Napoleon; extensive alterations were carried out by Giuseppe Borsato in 1828. The theatre was destroyed by fire on 13 December 1836, but was rebuilt, again with great rapidity, by Tommaso and Giambattista Meduna, who modified some aspects of Selva's design. Further modernisation took place in 1854, resulting in the rich neo-Baroque interior with which we are familiar today. On 29 January 1996 the theatre was once more destroyed by fire, only the perimeter walls and the façade surviving. The complex saga of reconstruction concluded in 2004, with the historic interiors faithfully replaced 'as they were and where they were' (*com'era e dov'era*). The principal architect was Aldo Rossi.

The *campo* façade is tripartite, symmetrical and restrained, with a dominant Corinthian portico above a tall flight of steps. The only other façade of consequence is the watergate at the rear, with a five-bay rusticated colonnade for patrons to disembark by boat.

Selva's plan was ingenious, since the site, though large, has a very difficult shape. There are five component elements: the first, the front wing, contains the foyer, the grand stair and the Sala Apollinea on the first floor. This element was returned to its original appearance in the Rossi restoration. The complex ceremonial stair leads up to a suite of rooms, the chief of which is the Sala Apollinea, richly decorated, used for receptions and temporary exhibitions.

The second element is the horseshoe-shaped auditorium, where similar fidelity to the original has been followed. Its form has been carefully re-created, with 314 seats on the floor level and 690 in five superimposed tiers of richly decorated galleries. The plan is very compact; the distances from the stage are thus very short, with excellent acoustics.

The third is the stage and fly-tower, now incorporating complex computerised stage machinery and equipment. The orchestra pit can also be raised and lowered. The fourth is the N wing, containing changing and rehearsal space, where major modernisation was possible, and a large scene dock added. The fifth is the S wing, where Rossi also made major changes, including the insertion of a new hall, the Sala Rossi, for rehearsals and chamber performances. It incorporates wooden copies of part of Palladio's Basilica in Vicenza.

Since its first construction, the Fenice has played a pivotal role in the cultural, social and political life of the city. In 1848, under Manin's revolution against the Austrians, the Napoleonic imperial box was torn out; later performances (including premieres) of several of Verdi's operas were regarded as sympathetic to the Risorgimento cause. In recognition of this cause, from 1851 to 1866 (the last fifteen years of foreign occupation) there were no performances here by the Fenice company. Numerous other world premieres have taken place here, including works by Rossini, Wagner and Stravinsky.

3 FROM CALLE LARGA XXII MARZO TO SAN MAURIZIO

Returning to Calle Larga XXII Marzo, a series of parallel *calli* off the s side leads to a group of palaces facing the Grand Canal; the façades can be seen from the Salute quay on the other bank. **Palazzo Barozzi Emo Treves Bonfili** (SM 2156) is reached by Calle del Squero and Calle Barozzi. The original house, an important thirteenth-century Venetian-Byzantine building, was rebuilt in the early seventeenth century. The imposing long principal façade is to Rio di San Moisè, with a short-end façade towards the Grand Canal. The plan is unusual, with a long row of rooms down the side canal and the *portego* forming a cross-axis in the centre. It has been attributed to Manopola. Almost next door, on the w side of Corte Barozzi, is **Palazzo Badoer Tiepolo** (SM 2161), again seventeenth century, with an asymmetrical Grand Canal façade.

The next two houses are reached by Calle del Pestrin, again off the s side of the Calle Larga. **Palazzo Venier Contarini** (SM 2307) is a fine, smallish, fifteenth-century Gothic house, with a well-proportioned canal façade, tripartite and symmetrical, with traditional fenestration. Immediately w is the considerably smaller **Palazzetto Contarini Fasan** (SM 2318), the so-called house of Desdemona.

Gotico fiorito, *circa* 1450, with an exquisitely detailed canal façade of great richness and refinement, especially the finely carved balconies on the first and second floors. Their wheel motif is unique, perhaps deriving from northern European sources. The *palazzetto* is only one bay wide, with no watergate, a *trifora* to the *piano nobile* and two tall lights to the second floor.

Immediately w again, reached from Fondamenta de le Ostreghe and Calle Minotto, is the

Palazzetto Contarini Fasan: the refined carving of the façade; *gotico fiorito*, *circa* 1450

impressive **Palazzo Manolesso Ferro** (SM 2322), originally fifteenth-century Gothic. The Grand Canal façade has a mixture of Gothic and Renaissance elements: the mezzanine has 'Codussian' windows, while the *piano nobile* remains Gothic. w again, also off Fondamenta de le Ostreghe, is the imposing double **Palazzo Flangini Ferro Fini** (SM 2340), from *circa* 1688, generally attributed to Tremignon. It was converted into a hotel in the nineteenth century, when many interior features were lost. The house is 'double' in that there are two main axes, each with a *trifora* and a watergate to the canal.

From the quay, cross Ponte de le Ostreghe towards Santa Maria del Giglio. On the right is **Palazzo Zobenigo** (SM 2434, 2516), originally thirteenth century, but heavily restored and altered; a few original windows with stilted arches. Continue into the square, and walk left as far as the Grand Canal *tragheto* stand. On the corner is the land entrance of **Palazzo Pisani Gritti** (SM 2466), today the Gritti Palace Hotel. Early fifteenth-century Gothic, with an exceptionally broad canal façade, said to have been frescoed by Giorgione in the early sixteenth century. There were originally two *piani nobili*; the third was added in the nineteenth century. The short *campo* façade was modernised in the late sixteenth or early seventeenth century.

Just w of Campielo del Tragheto, at SM 2469, is **Palazzo Venier Contarini**, a small seventeenth-century house; immediately w again is **Palazzo Marin Contarini** (SM 2488), fifteenth-century Gothic, with an asymmetrical plan and façade.

Santa Maria Zobenigo (del Giglio) dominates the N end of the square. Founded by the Zobenigo family *circa* 900, it was destroyed by fire more than once. It was completely rebuilt in the late seventeenth century; the church is perhaps by Benoni, but the rich Baroque façade is by Sardi, the result of a legacy (30,000 ducats) from Antonio Barbaro in 1679. The façade was completed by 1683, an exuberant monument to the wealth and power of the Barbaro clan. It was roundly condemned by Ruskin for its triumphalist iconography and almost total lack of religious imagery.

The façade is well composed, with two orders surmounted by a radiused pediment. Both orders are defined by paired Ionic columns, the lower having five bays, the upper with three. The arched entrance is flanked by figures of Antonio's four brothers, while on the plinths are relief models of (mostly Venetian) cities: Zara, Candia, Padua, Rome, Corfù and Spalato (Split). Barbaro himself has pride of place on the upper order, flanked by figures of Honour and Virtue.

Santa Maria del Giglio: upper part of the façade by
Sardi, 1683

On the uppermost parapet are trumpeting angels; most of the
sculpted figures are by Giusto le Court.

The interior is spatially simple, with a rectangular five-bay nave
(three large bays and two smaller intermediate bays) flanked on both
sides by shallow rectangular chapels. At the end is a square chancel.
The right nave chapels are those of the Barbaro, Barbarigo and
Duodo, the last with an altarpiece by Palma il Giovane. The Molin
Chapel, also off the right side, consists of two chambers; the chapel
contains a cycle by Giovanni Antonio Pellegrini and Rubens's *Virgin
and Child*, his only work in Venice.

Below the organ in the chancel are two *Evangelists* by Tintoretto;
the organ is decorated by Zanchi. In the three left nave chapels are
altarpieces by Tintoretto, Morleiter and Zanchi.

In the square nearby: the remains of the campanile, largely
demolished in 1775.

At the W end of the church, cross Ponte de la Feltrina, into the
tiny eponymous *campielo*. The N side is occupied by the elegant,
slightly curved Gothic façade of **Palazzo Malipiero de la Feltrina**

Palazzo Malipiero de la Feltrina: detail of the
façade: fifteenth-century Gothic

(SM 2513), late fifteenth century; the *piano nobile* has an attractive
quadrifora. Taking the next bridge, Ponte Zaguri, on the adjacent quay
is the impressive Gothic **Palazzo Pasqualini Zaguri** (SM 2631), with
its second façade on Campo San Maurizio; originally fourteenth
century, but extensively modernised *circa* 1425. Both façades are
tripartite and symmetrical, and, other than the mezzanines, largely
unaltered. The main *piano nobile*, with its *quadrifore*, is surmounted by
a second generous upper floor.

Before entering Campo San Maurizio, take Fondamenta Corner
(left) along Rio di San Maurizio. The quay terminates at the land
entrance to **Palazzo Corner de la Ca' Grande** (SM 2662), built in
the mid-sixteenth century by Sansovino; one of the most impressive
Renaissance palaces in Venice. The previous house on the site had
been developed by the immensely wealthy Zorzi (Giorgio) Corner
in the early sixteenth century, but in 1532, five years after his death,
it was destroyed by fire. By 1537 Sansovino had been appointed to
design the replacement. Progress was slow, however, the result of
financial difficulties and complex inheritance arrangements, and did

Palazzo Corner de la Ca' Grande: façade to the Grand Canal; by Jacopo Sansovino, 1545–*circa* 1570

not begin until after 1545. It was probably complete *circa* 1570, the year of Sansovino's death. It remained in Corner ownership until after the fall of the Republic; today it is occupied by the Prefettura.

Sansovino's noble, powerful façade (best seen from the terrace of the Guggenheim) is all of stone, with three orders, respectively Doric for the massive rusticated base, Ionic and Corinthian for the two *piani nobili*; a low attic. The façade is treated as a great screen, with little of the traditional Venetian central emphasis. It is more Roman than Venetian, with a large three-bay entrance loggia, flanked by paired single lights; the two *piani nobili* each have seven bays, with inset arched windows and rich detailing closely reminiscent of the Marciana Library.

San Maurizio: façade by Antonio Diedo and Gianantonio
Selva; completed 1806

The plan is formal and axial, with the canal loggia leading directly
into a spacious *androne*, at the end of which is a square courtyard,
with restrained, monumental detailing. On one side of the courtyard
is the land gate to the *fondamenta*. The single grand staircase rises
from the *androne*. The most imposing room is the Council Hall, the
original *portego*, with a rich ceiling fresco by Giuseppe Vizzotto-
Alberti (1890s). Most of the many other art works are from the
Italian state collections. Return to Ponte Zaguri and turn left into
Campo San Maurizio.

San Maurizio was founded in the ninth century by the Candiani
(Sanudo) family; rebuilt two or three times, the present Neo-classical
church was completed in 1806 by Diedo and Selva. The stone *campo*
façade is severely disciplined, with three broad bays and a central
Ionic portal. At high level: two relief panels by Bartolomeo Ferrari
and Luigi Zandomeneghi. In the pediment: a relief of the life of the
soldier-martyr.

The plan is a Greek cross, broadly modelled on Sansovino's lost
San Geminiano; the central cupola is surrounded by four smaller
bays, each with a blind cupola. The interior is refined and restrained,
all Corinthian, reminiscent of Codussi. The high-altar tabernacle is
also by Selva, as are the other altars.

On the w side of the square: a row of palaces. At the NW corner
is **Palazzo Bellavite Soranzo Terzi Baffo** (SM 2760), mid-sixteenth

century, and occasionally attributed to Sansovino. The impressive façade, with superimposed Serliane, was originally frescoed by Veronese, *circa* 1555, shortly after his arrival in Venice. The plan and façades are traditional, tripartite and symmetrical. Next to it is **Palazzo Molin** (SM 2758), originally Gothic, and a kind of double palace, with two elements, one tripartite and symmetrical, the other (N) asymmetrical. The fenestration is *gotico fiorito*; three Gothic watergates at the rear. A little further down Calle del Dose is **Palazzo da Ponte** (SM 2745), built by Doge Niccolò da Ponte (1578–85). Unusually, he continued living here after his election, since the fires of 1574 and 1577 had destroyed much of the Doge's Palace. The land façade is impressive (although difficult to see), with superimposed Serliane. The interior was richly decorated and contained a fine library, but much was lost in a fire in 1801.

4 SANTO STEFANO (1): PALAZZO PISANI, PALAZZO LOREDAN AND SAN VIDAL

Back in the square, leave by the NW corner; on the right, just before the bridge, is the attractive little **Scuola degli Albanesi** (SM 2762), established by the expatriate Albanian community in 1497–1502. The façade is decorated with reliefs by Giovanni Zorzi, *circa* 1531, showing the sieges of Scutari. In 1504 Carpaccio was commissioned to paint a cycle of paintings of the story of the Virgin, now dispersed; one is in the Correr and two are at the Ca' d'Oro. The Scuola was closed in 1780.

At Ponte San Maurizio, looking left, is the long canal façade of **Palazzo Morosini Gattemburg** (SM 2803); land façade to Campo Santo Stefano. The square is one of the largest in Venice, with a complex, elongated plan; the eponymous church at the NE corner. Palazzo Morosini has two elements, both originally sixteenth century; the larger faces the canal, while the smaller block faces the square. In 1690 it was owned by Francesco Morosini (doge 1688–94), victor of the battles for the Morea in 1687. Gaspari remodelled the house extensively for Morosini, when sumptuous interiors were installed, with stucco decoration and sculptures. In the 1790s it was remodelled again, by Selva, who removed some of the more opulent interiors. The restrained *campo* façade contrasts with the adjacent powerful entrance gate, a triumphal arch representing Morosini's military victories.

Detail of a *palazzetto* in the *gotico fiorito* style in Campo
Santo Stefano; the upper order is early sixteenth century

In the SE corner of the square, a broad opening leads into
Campielo Pisani, dominated by the vast façade of **Palazzo Pisani**
(SM 2810), one of the most grandiose Baroque palaces in Venice. The
history of this great house is complex and far from fully known. It
may have been begun *circa* 1614, but the Pisani acquired adjacent
properties in 1688 and 1716, and it was enlarged in stages. The first
architect is also unknown (perhaps Manopola); enlargements after
1728 are by Frigimelica, the family *proto*, who also designed their
great villa at Stra, near Padua. Frigimelica added the second *piano
nobile*, containing the library, a ballroom and new staircases; the palace
was also extended southwards. In 1751 it was extended again, with
another narrow wing terminating at the Grand Canal. During the
intervening decades, the interior was lavishly decorated by leading
Baroque masters, including Guarana, Ricci, Pittoni, Amigoni and G.
D. Tiepolo. After 1880 it was acquired by the state, and became the
Benedetto Marcello Conservatory of Music, as it remains today.

The plan is as complex as its history; the original nucleus is
traditionally planned but broad and shallow, with three banks of
rooms on each side of the central hall. The s extension doubled the
palace's size, and was joined to the original nucleus by a four-storey
link, with elegant superimposed open galleries. The massive *campo*
façade has rustication to the lower order, and a great portal flanked

Facing page: Palazzo Pisani at Santo Stefano: courtyard and main entrance;
begun *circa* 1614, perhaps by Manopola, extended by Frigimelica after 1728

by mythical statues; the *portego* balcony is carried by giant modillions, with superimposed Serliane to the two upper halls. The canal façade is extremely difficult to see, but is less richly detailed.

Internally, the Sala d'Oro is used for concerts, as is the ballroom. The former has a gilded stuccoed ceiling by Giuseppe Ferrari (1776). The chapels also contain fine stucco work, some from *circa* 1720.

Return towards the main square, and turn left along the quay to Rio de l'Orso; at the end is the land gate to **Palazzo Barbaro** (SM 2840); the water façade can be seen from the Ponte de l'Accademia. An interesting late Gothic house, incorporating early Renaissance elements. It was built *circa* 1425 by Zane and Bartolomeo Bon. The canal façade is symmetrical and tripartite, with superimposed *quadrifore*; the central watergate is later. The palace immediately to the E is a second Barbaro house, added by Gaspari in the 1690s, to house a ballroom; a narrow canal façade, with six storeys. The opulent ballroom is richly decorated, with stucco frames to pictures by Giambattista Piazzetta and Sebastiano Ricci; the library also has a rich shallow-vaulted ceiling.

Return to the S end of Campo Santo Stefano. Opposite, on the W side, is the extremely long façade of **Palazzo Loredan** (SM 2945), seat of the Istituto Veneto. The original house was Gothic, acquired by Leonardo Loredan in 1536; he then commissioned Scamozzi virtually to rebuild it. It is also unusual in having only two storeys above a basement; its shallow but elongated plan was later (1618) extended even further towards the NE. The *campo* façade has a prominent eight-light window to the first-floor hall; much of this façade was originally frescoed by Giuseppe Salviati and Giallo Fiorentino. The entrance leads into a square colonnaded atrium, on each side of which are three rooms, and from which a double-branch stair rises to the *piano nobile*. The 1618 wing has a short NE façade, all stone, often attributed to Palladio, although probably by Grapiglia; five bays and two orders, Ionic and Corinthian. The interior is well conserved, with stucco decoration by Abbondio Stazio (*circa* 1760); on the *piano nobile* an enfilade of rooms contains the Istituto's fine library. At the NE end is the former ballroom, with a monumental marble doorway by Grapiglia, and a richly decorated timber ceiling.

We now turn SW, towards the Ponte de l'Accademia; on the right: the heavy Palladian stone façade of the former church of **San Vidal (Vitale).** Founded in 1084 by Doge Vitale Falier, it was rebuilt after 1105; the campanile has survived, although the church was rebuilt by Gaspari. It was completed rapidly, 1696–1700, but his elaborate

Palazzo Loredan, Campo Santo Stefano: the stone-clad
north-east façade, *circa* 1618, probably by Gian
Girolamo Grapiglia

façade, intended to be a monument to Francesco Morosini, was too
expensive; instead, a simpler neo-Palladian design by Tirali was
eventually built in 1734–7. It is based on San Francesco de la Vigna,
with paired Corinthian columns supporting a heavy pediment. The
two lower side wings have half-pediments supported by square
Corinthian pilasters.

The plan is a simple rectangle, a five-bay nave covered with a
vaulted ceiling, and a square E end abutting Rio de San Vidal. The
altarpieces include works by Giambattista Piazzetta, Giovanni Antonio
Pellegrini and Sebastiano Ricci. The church is deconsecrated and
used for concerts and exhibitions.

Opposite is the attractive garden of **Palazzo Cavalli Franchetti**
(SM 2847). Built *circa* 1460 in *gotico fiorito* style, but altered
considerably, and extended, by Camillo Boito *circa* 1886, when it was
owned by Baron Franchetti. The Grand Canal façade (best seen from
the bridge) retains its Gothic proportions, with a large central
watergate and two *piani nobili*, each with a *pentafora*, but each with

Palazzo Cavalli Franchetti; detail of Grand Canal façade; fifteenth-century Gothic, modernised by Camillo Boito, *circa* 1886

Palazzo Cavalli Franchetti: detail of the staircase, by Boito, *circa* 1886

different tracery. The lower one is modelled on the Doge's Palace, the upper based on the upper loggia of the Ca' d'Oro. The façade was 'regularised' by Boito, who also added the grand neo-Gothic staircase on the NW side and the long narrow N wing. The sumptuous internal decoration is also by Boito, with extensive polychrome marble. The palace is owned by the Istituto Veneto, and used for exhibitions and conferences.

5 FROM SAN VIDAL TO SAN SAMUELE AND PALAZZO GRASSI

From Campo San Vidal, take Ponte and Ramo Giustinian into Calle Giustinian. In front is **Palazzo Giustinian Lolin** (SM 2873); Grand Canal façade visible from the Accademia bridge. Built for Giovanni Lolin, *circa* 1621, it is now attributed to the young Longhena, influenced by Scamozzi. Today it houses the Fondazione Musicale Ugo e Olga Levi. The plan and façade are rigorously symmetrical and tripartite; the elegant canal façade is clad with stone, with a rusticated lower order and two *piani nobili*, Ionic and Corinthian. Both have a type of Serliana to the main halls. The interior is well conserved, with an attractive rear courtyard; much original internal decoration survives.

Take Calle Giustinian NE as far as Calle del Frutarol, and turn left. At the far end of Calle Vitturi, with its façade to the Grand Canal, is the attractive **Palazzetto Falier** (SM 2914), a modest fifteenth-century Gothic house, with a small courtyard garden in the centre and two projecting side wings. Return to Calle del Frutarol, and turn left under a long *sotoportego*, over the bridge and under the second *sotoportego*; at Calle del Teatro, turn left into Corte del Duca Sforza. At the far end is the fragment of the famously elusive **Ca' del Duca** (SM 3051–2), façade to the Grand Canal. This extraordinarily ambitious proposal was begun *circa* 1457 by Bartolomeo Bon for the Corner clan, and was to have been the largest private palace in the city; three years later the site was acquired by the Republic and given to Galeazzo Maria Sforza, duke of Milan. Little further progress was made, and by 1465 the project was abandoned. All that survives is a corner column and two sections of a massive, rusticated base along the Grand Canal frontage.

Return to Calle del Teatro, and turn left along Calle Malipiero towards San Samuele. On the corner of the square (left): the long, complex flank façade of **Palazzo Malipiero Cappello** (SM 3198–201). Its origins are Venetian-Byzantine, but it was enlarged and extended in the early fifteenth century and again in the early sixteenth. The side façade contains a few Gothic elements, but is mainly sixteenth century. The Grand Canal façade was modernised *circa* 1620, probably by Francesco Contin; it is broad and nearly symmetrical. The interior was richly decorated in the 1660s, while towards the end of the nineteenth century the large side garden was laid out. The plan is as complex as the flank façade suggests, with two land gates and two watergates giving access to two superimposed apartments.

On the E side of the square is **San Samuele**, said to have been founded *circa* 1000 by the Boldù; it was rebuilt after 1107, and the campanile survives, one of the oldest in the city. The church was modernised in the Gothic era, but partly rebuilt again in 1685, to the same tripartite plan. The simple *campo* façade, with its large 'thermal' window, dates from this modernisation. The entrance is at the side, in Calle de le Carrozze. Inside, the high altar has a *Crucifixion*

Palazzo Grassi: flank façade to Campo San Samuele; by
Giorgio Massari, begun 1748, completed *circa* 1770

attributed to Paolo or Domenico Veneziano; on the adjacent altar is
a notable fourteenth-century icon, brought from the Morea in 1541.

The N side of the attractive square is dominated by the imposing
flank wall of **Palazzo Grassi** (SM 3231). The last great palace to be
built in Venice, it was designed in a restrained Neo-classical style by
Massari, begun in 1748; it was still not complete in 1766, when
Massari died. In recent times it was owned by the FIAT Foundation;
more recently, it has passed to François Pinault, who had the interior
remodelled by Tadao Ando; it continues to be used for large-scale art
exhibitions.

The broad plan narrows towards the rear; Massari adopted the
classical axial 'Roman' layout, with a spacious quay giving onto a
square colonnaded hall and then the large, square central courtyard.
On the far side of the courtyard, on axis, is the grandiose staircase.
Land access is from a portal on the square. The imposing Grand
Canal façade has three orders, symmetrical and tripartite, with flat
rustication to the lower order, and a three-bay loggia. The first *piano*

nobile is Ionic, the upper Corinthian. On the upper orders, five single windows define the location of the central hall.

The interior is impressive, if rather cold and restrained; the Doric courtyard now has a glass pyramidal roof. A lighter element is the grand triple-branch staircase, with attractive *trompe l'œil* decoration by Morleiter; on the ceiling is the *Glory of the Grassi Family*, by Fabio Canal. Several rooms also have richly decorated ceilings.

6 FROM THE MOCENIGO PALACES TO SANTO STEFANO

At the back of Palazzo Grassi, Calle Grassi leads to Calle Moro Lin, and the land entrance to **Palazzo Moro Lin** (SM 3242), with a long, unusual, Grand Canal façade, best seen from Ca' Foscari on the other bank. Built *circa* 1670, on the site of two Gothic houses, which probably constrained the plan; the uppermost storey was added *circa* 1703. The rusticated water storey has a seven-bay colonnade, surmounted by two *piani nobili* and an attic. There is almost no central emphasis on the façade, which has thirteen bays of single windows at both upper levels, the lower Doric, the upper Ionic. The plan is more traditional, with a central axial hall flanked by side rooms. The interior was richly decorated, and retains a *portego* ceiling by Bevilacqua, 1806.

Return to Calle de le Carrozze, and turn left; at the corner of Salizada Malipiero (SM 3216) is the former **Scuola dei Mureri**, the fifteenth-century guildhall of the builders' *arte*; at high level a plaque showing the tools of the trade. At SM 3338 (left): the former home of Veronese, who died here in 1588; an attractive Renaissance *palazzetto* with refined detailing. To the left of Salizada San Samuele, Calle Mocenigo leads to the land gate of **Palazzo Contarini da le Figure** (SM 3327); Grand Canal façade best seen from the San Tomà *vaporetto* stop, as are the Mocenigo houses (below). A notable early Renaissance palace, with an elegant stone façade, rebuilt 1504–46 on the site of an earlier Gothic house; the designation derives from the two caryatids above the watergate. Attributions vary widely, and include Codussi (although he died in 1504) and Scarpagnino. Andrea Palladio, a friend of the owner, Jacopo Contarini, lived here for several years after 1570. The water façade has three orders and three bays divided by Corinthian pilasters, with a large arched watergate and refined relief decoration. Its most prominent feature is the central pedimented *quadrifora*, perhaps derived from Sangallo's Medici villa at Poggio a Caiano in Tuscany. The plan is conventional and tripartite, with an imposing staircase towards the rear.

To the NW of the Salizada, bounded on one side by Calle Mocenigo and on the other by Calle Corner, is a long row of four Mocenigo palaces, all with façades to the Grand Canal. The two larger palaces at each end form 'bookends' to the two smaller, contiguous houses in the centre. The first (SM 3328) is known as **Palazzo Mocenigo Casa Vecchia**, since it is Gothic in origin, although rebuilt in the seventeenth century. The canal façade is almost symmetrical, and is attributed to Benoni, the architect of the Dogana da Mar; it was completed *circa* 1625. The two *piani nobili* have a large group of five central windows, with a long stone balcony. Next to it, towards the NE, are the two smaller *palazzi*, *circa* 1570s, an identical matching pair. The water façades were once frescoed by Benedetto Caliari, Veronese's brother; they retain a row of relief panels above the *piano nobile* windows. The fourth palace, at the NE end, **Palazzo Mocenigo Casa Nuova,** is the largest and most monumental, with a rich all-stone water façade. It was again originally Gothic, but rebuilt in the 1570s; it was the residence of Alvise Mocenigo I, doge 1570–77. The façade shows the influence of the de' Grigi and Vittoria, with three superimposed Serliane, the first incorporating the watergate, the others the two *piani nobili*. On the first floor are two ostentatious family arms. The plan, like the façade, is basically tripartite and traditional. Its interior was richly decorated, with one ceiling frescoed by G. B. Tiepolo, another by Ricci. In 1788 the palace was linked to the adjacent two, thus providing no fewer than forty rooms for festivities and banquets. The palaces retain some of their original gardens.

Adjacent to the last of these four is **Palazzo Corner Gheltoff** (SM 3378), comprehensively modernised at the end of the sixteenth century; a restrained symmetrical canal façade.

From the NE end of Salizada San Samuele, take the short *ramo* into the broad Piscina San Samuele. At the left end, Calle del Tragheto takes us to the land gate of **Palazzo Garzoni** (SM 3417), a well-proportioned late Gothic house, *circa* 1470, partly modernised in the Renaissance. Take the Piscina SE, then turn right into Calle de le Boteghe. Just off the *calle* (right) is Calle de le Muneghe, the SE side of which is occupied by the former church and nunnery of **Santi Rocco and Margherita** (SM 2975–6). Founded in 1488 by the patriarch, Maffeo Girardi, with the church at the NE corner and the simple conventual buildings ranged around a large rectangular cloister. In 1820, after its suppression, it was reopened as a school by Pietro Ciliota.

Take Calle de le Boteghe into the N end of Campo Santo Stefano. Opposite the church façade is the former **Scuola di Santo Stefano dei Laneri** (SM 3464), the wool-workers' guildhall. Founded in 1437 and enlarged in 1506, it retains a small Gothic relief on the façade.

7 SANTO STEFANO (2): THE CHURCH AND MONASTERY

Santo Stefano is one of the most important medieval churches in Venice, founded by Augustinians *circa* 1264. The present church was begun in 1294 and completed *circa* 1325; it was modernised in the early fifteenth century, and extended eastwards, the chancel bridging the adjacent canal. In 1810 the monastery was suppressed, and the church was given parish status. Recently, the extensive conventual buildings have been occupied by the finance ministry.

The brick façade is of the characteristic Venetian Gothic type, with pinnacles on the buttresses and a rich, complex *gotico fiorito* portal, *circa* 1430s, sometimes attributed to Bartolomeo Bon. The internal plan is tripartite, with a tall, spacious, six-bay nave and lower side aisles; the nave colonnades survive from the earlier church, and

support painted, gilded capitals, in turn supporting two rows of pointed arches. The principal feature is the rich, complex 'ship's-keel' roof, all of exposed timber, the finest surviving example in the city. Down the two flank walls is a series of rich Baroque altars. Towards the chancel were the choirstalls, again richly carved, and set behind a marble screen. The latter was dismantled in the sixteenth century; fragments

Santo Stefano: detail of the Gothic west portal, *circa* 1430, sometimes attributed to Bartolomeo Bon

survive. At the E end is the deep chancel, with a radiused east end, flanked by two similar, smaller, side chapels. A number of notable works of art: in the sacristy, off the right aisle, are three paintings by Tintoretto, and others by Bordone, Peranda and Bartolomeo Vivarini. In the little cloister, off the SE side of the sacristy: a small collection of sculptures and other pieces, some formerly in the church. They include pieces from the choirscreen by Pietro and Tullio Lombardo. In the right chancel chapel: altar from the lost church of Sant'Angelo. The high altar is from 1613, perhaps by Campagna. Behind are the fine late fifteenth-century carved timber choirstalls, made by Marco Cozzi. At the fifth left altar is the monument to the composer Giovanni Gabrieli.

The extensive conventual buildings stand to the NE of the church, built around two large cloisters and a smaller *cortile*. The first stage, adjacent to the Ponte dei Frati, was begun by Scarpagnino in 1530, following a serious fire. Earlier Gothic work survives on one side of the first cloister, and the portal on the bridge; Scarpagnino's design is simple and repetitive. The friary was extended in 1665, when the second cloister was built across Rio del Santissimo, and an extra storey was added to the first stage.

The detached campanile, one of the tallest in Venice, was begun in the late fifteenth century, completed *circa* 1520; it has a notable inclination, and is best seen from Campo San Maurizio.

8 FROM SANT'ANZOLO TO PALAZZO PESARO FORTUNY

From Ponte dei Frati, enter the spacious **Campo Sant'Anzolo (Angelo)**, on which are several palaces. The church, which stood adjacent to the canal, was demolished in 1837. On the N side, at SM 3817, is the little **Oratorio dell'Annunziata**, founded in the tenth century, but rebuilt in the fourteenth, and modernised in 1530, when the façade was added. At the NE corner is the splendid late Gothic **Palazzo Duodo** (SM 3584), *circa* 1460; a well-balanced, symmetrical façade with a large central portal and a smaller secondary one. A single *piano nobile* is centred on a six-light window, with the usual pairs of flanking lights. The adjacent house to the right is of similar date, but is asymmetrical.

At the NW corner of the square is **Palazzo Gritti Morosini** (SM 3832), also fifteenth-century Gothic, and regularly tripartite, although

Palazzo Gritti Morosini in Campo Sant'Anzolo; fifteenth-century
Gothic

the portal is offset to the left. A *quadrifora* lights the ground-floor
hall, with similar lights to the two upper floors. Immediately
adjacent, to the left, is **Palazzo Trevisan Pisani Somachi** (SM 3831), a
substantial house, *circa* 1650, with a broad façade and plan, but
comparatively shallow depth, restricted by a canal at the rear.

Take Calle dei Avvocati out of the NW corner of the square, turn
left on Ramo Michiel, cross the bridge and follow the quay into
Corte de l'Albero. The massive neo-Byzantine apartment block is by
Vittorio Fantucci, 1909–13. On the E side (SM 3870) is **Palazzo
Sandi**, by Domenico Rossi, *circa* 1721; a restrained façade, but richly
decorated internally by G. B. Tiepolo, Bambini and Cedini. At the
vaporetto stop, on the right facing the Grand Canal, is **Palazzo Lando
Corner Spinelli** (SM 3877), a notable early work by Codussi, *circa*
1480. It was built for the Lando, but sold to the Corner in 1542. Its
design marks a stage in Codussi's development of the palace façade:
three equal orders, the lower one with flat rustication, the first time
it had been used on a completed Venetian *palazzo*. The two upper
floors have a window that was to become a Codussi 'trademark': two
single lights beneath a semicircular arch, and with a small *ocio* at the
head. The central *portego* has two such elements, the side rooms have
one each, a pattern repeated on the upper floor. The inventive side
balconies have an unusual three-lobed plan, and the façade is framed
by tall stone pilasters.

The palace was modernised internally by Sanmicheli for the Corner in the 1540s, and Vasari painted a series of pictures for the *portego* ceiling, later dispersed. The ground-floor *androne* has a robust mid-sixteenth-century appearance, with powerfully modelled doorways.

Return to Calle dei Avvocati, and take the short Calle Pesaro to Ponte Michiel. On the left is the garden of **Palazzo Benzon** (SM 3927), with façade to the Grand Canal; a substantial sixteenth-century palace, with a broad, simple and comparatively low canal façade. In the eighteenth century it was the seat of a celebrated literary salon, whose members included Byron and Canova. On the right is the canal façade of the immense **Palazzo Pesaro Fortuny degli Orfei**, the largest medieval house in Venice. Continue down Calle Pesaro into the little Campo San Beneto; the land façade of Palazzo Pesaro occupies the w side. It was built by the Pesaro, perhaps as late as the 1480s, since, although *gotico fiorito*, there are Renaissance elements in the detailing; the Pesaro arms over the land gate. The suffix refers to concerts that were held here since the 1500s; later, in 1786, the Accademia degli Orfei was established here. In the early twentieth century it was bought by Mariano Fortuny, a Spaniard, who developed techniques in lighting, textiles and photography; since 1956 the palace has contained a museum of his effects and collections. It is built around two courtyards, in the larger of which the original external stair rises to the first *piano nobile*. The *campo* façade is imposing, but irregularly fenestrated, with one wing wider than the other; richly detailed balconies and corbels. The two

superimposed halls both have seven-light windows. The palace's size can be appreciated inside the upper hall, 45 metres long, with a series of rooms off one side and the two courtyards on the other. The canal façade (very difficult to appreciate) has a fine watergate and six-light windows to the two halls.

Palazzo Pesaro Fortuny degli Orfei: detail of the *campo* façade, with the Pesaro arms, perhaps *circa* 1480

From the little square, Calle del Tragheto passes the long flank of **Palazzo Pisani Martinengo Volpi** (SM 3947), with a short *campo* façade next to the church. The main façade is to the Grand Canal. It was built *circa* 1521 by the Florentine Talenti family, and the canal façade was frescoed by Pordenone; it was partly modernised in the eighteenth century. **San Beneto (Benedetto)** occupies the N side of the square. It was founded in 1005 by the Falier and others, but in 1540 the campanile collapsed, seriously damaging the church. It was rebuilt in 1619, with different orientation and a new, plain stone façade consisting of four giant Corinthian pilasters supporting a large pediment; the architect is unknown. The interior is equally restrained, but contains paintings by Bernardo Strozzi, Guarana and G. B. Tiepolo.

In the N corner, Corte Tron leads to the land entrance to **Palazzo Tron** (SM 3949), originally Gothic, *circa* 1440, with a Grand Canal façade, but altered later. The façade can be seen from Calle del Tragheto at San Polo. Immediately to the NE is the tiny **Palazzetto Tron**, a miniature piece of nineteenth-century Gothic, with overwrought detailing. Adjacent again is **Palazzo Corner Contarini dei Cavalli** (SM 3978), again with Grand Canal façade; originally Gothic, *circa* 1445, but the ground floor and mezzanine were modernised in the seventeenth century. The *piano nobile* has a fine six-light window, with tracery modelled on the Doge's Palace. The name derives from two small reliefs of horses on the canal façade. Next again, but with a façade onto Rio de San Luca, is the second **Palazzo Corner Contarini** (SM 3980), later Mocenigo and Giovanelli. Rebuilt in 1566, on the site of an earlier Gothic house; further modernised in the seventeenth century, when a grand staircase was added and the façade frescoed. The canal façade (perhaps by Sante Lombardo) is heavy but impressive and richly detailed. The three orders are defined by Corinthian pilasters; a large Serliana to the hall.

9   FROM SAN LUCA TO THE RIVA DEL CARBON

From Campo San Beneto take Salizada del Teatro, then Calle Sant'Andrea on the left, into Corte de le Muneghe. The **Cinema Rossini** stands on the site of a theatre, first built in 1756, and the most important in Venice until the Fenice was opened. Just across the iron bridge is the façade of **San Luca**, a parish foundation established in the eleventh century by the Dandolo and Pizzamano. In the mid-sixteenth century the church was rebuilt, completed in 1581. A simple Renaissance appearance, although the canal façade was rebuilt in 1827, following its partial collapse. The nave is rectangular, with no aisles, but with deep apsidal chapels. The trabeation down the side walls terminates with a triumphal arch at the chancel. The principal work of art is the high altarpiece, the *Virgin Appearing in Glory to St Luke* by Veronese. Immediately s of the church is **Palazzo Magno** (SM 4038–9), mostly fourteenth-century Gothic, with its façade to the canal. The thirteenth-century land entrance (corner of Campielo San Luca) is most unusual, with a steeply pointed outer arch, below which is set a lower round brick arch. Just N of the canal façade of San Luca is the massively imposing land entrance to **Palazzo Grimani (Corte d'Appello)** (SM 4041). One of the finest and most important Renaissance palaces in Venice, designed by Sanmicheli and built for the Grimani from 1556. Sanmicheli, however, died only three years later, by which time only the ground floor and perhaps part of the first were complete. For two years Girolamo Grimani directed the works himself, but in 1561 Giangiacomo de' Grigi was employed to supervise its completion. De' Grigi himself died in 1572, and it was finally completed by Gianantonio Rusconi in 1575. It remained in Grimani ownership until after the fall of the Republic; in 1881 it became the city's appeal court, as it has remained to this day, until its intended transfer to Piazzale Roma.

The plan is unusual, with an irregular site, much wider at the Grand Canal front than at the rear. Sanmicheli created an ingenious series of spaces from the canal entrance, beginning with a square colonnaded atrium, then the long off-centre *androne*, terminating in a courtyard. The plan may be influenced by Palladio; a very similar one was to be illustrated in *I quattro libri dell'architettura* (1570), and Palladio was in Venice in 1556.

The majestic façade (seen from San Silvestro) has three orders, the lowermost (incorporating the mezzanine) being the tallest; the overall composition is based on a repeated motif of the triumphal arch. The lowest order is defined by fluted Corinthian pilasters, with the great portal flanked by two lesser doorways; it terminates with a continuous stone balcony. The two upper orders are almost identical: five bays defined by paired fluted Corinthian columns. Three arched bays alternate with smaller square bays; the three central bays denote the upper hall, flanked by two smaller rooms; behind this hall is the

Palazzo Grimani at San Luca: Grand Canal façade by Michele Sanmicheli, begun 1556; completed by Gianantonio Rusconi, *circa* 1575

portego. The upper orders terminate with a deep trabeation and a massively impressive cornice. The courtyard façade repeats the Roman motifs of the canal façade, but in a less monumental manner. The asymmetry of the plan is reflected in the location of the Serliana to the rear façade, which is almost at the corner, rather than in the centre.

From Campielo de la Chiesa, behind San Luca, take the *ramo* in the E corner, and continue S into Campo Manin.

Palazzo Contarini dal Bovolo: the helical stair and
superimposed *logge*; *circa* 1490

The square approximates to the former Campo San Paternian, an
ancient parish foundation that survived until 1871. Shortly afterwards,
the prominent bronze statue to Daniele Manin (Luigi Borro, 1875)
was added in the centre of the enlarged square.

The NE side is occupied by the **Cassa di Risparmio di Venezia**
(SM 4216), by Angelo Scattolin and Pier Luigi Nervi, 1964. The
dynamic concrete internal structure is impressive, but the *campo*
façade remains controversial. Although the materials and detailing are
of high quality, the façade makes few concessions to the Venetian
tradition, and is uncompromisingly modern.

From the s side of the square, Calle de la Vida leads to Corte
Contarini del Bovolo, with the unique helical stair of **Palazzo
Contarini del Bovolo** (SM 4299) on one side. It is attached to a
substantial late Gothic palace; although in poor condition, the water
façade to Rio de San Luca is imposing. The famous *bovolo* (the
Venetian word for a snail, in recognition of its 'spiral' plan) was built
in the 1490s, and has two elements. The first is the stair itself,
contained within a tall brick drum and lit by raking groups of

Istrian stone window openings; at the top is an open belvedere capped by a cupola. The second element (right) consists of five superimposed *logge*, of varying heights. Although attractive, the whole is designed in a rather awkward transitional Gothic / Renaissance style. Today the palace is owned by IRE (the Istituto di Ricovero ed Educazione). In the little courtyard is a collection of well-heads.

Return to Campo Manin and Campielo de la Chiesa. Take Calle Cavalli to the Riva del Carbon at the far end. The next group of palaces all face the Grand Canal along this quay; their façades can be seen from the Riva del Vin opposite. At the left end, a narrow quay gives access to **Palazzo Corner Valmarana** (SM 4093), with a rich Renaissance façade, originally sixteenth century, largely rebuilt in the nineteenth. The façade is enlivened by paterae and relief panels. Next to it (SM 4089) is **Palazzo Corner Cavalli Martinengo Ravà**, with a slightly asymmetrical façade, probably sixteenth century; the detailing is simple but refined. Turning back towards the Rialto Bridge, we come to two important early Venetian-Byzantine *palazzi*, both today occupied by the city council. The first is **Ca' Farsetti Dandolo** (SM 4136); built *circa* 1200–06 by the Dandolo, in the mid-fourteenth century it was owned by Doge Andrea Dandolo, a humanist and friend of Petrarch. It was severely damaged by fire in 1524. In 1670 it was bought by Anton Francesco Farsetti, who extensively altered the interior, adding a large rear extension, with a second *portego*. In the centre, he built an imposing Baroque staircase. In 1826 it was acquired by the municipality, and in 1874 was extensively restored.

The quay façade, virtually rebuilt in 1874, retains the appearance of a substantial *palazzo-fontego* of the thirteenth century, although the second floor was added in 1892. The spacious ground-floor loggia has five central bays, while the end bays each have two smaller windows, an echo of the Venetian-Byzantine corner towers or *torreselle*. The first floor has a broad seven-bay central hall; again the corners are defined by narrower four-bay fenestration. All the arches are stilted, those to the first floor with slender paired colonnettes.

The plan, although altered by Farsetti, retains the original T-shape towards the quay, with the transverse loggia leading to a fairly short *androne*. Tirali's central staircase is light but monumental, with three branches. The upper *portego* retains its seventeenth-century appearance, with stucco decoration and inset paintings by Zanchi, Guarana and Tarsia. The hall is presently used as the council chamber; a fine eighteenth-century ceiling by Diziani.

Ca' Corner Loredan (left) and Ca' Farsetti (right); both *circa* 1200; the two upper floors of both houses were added later

Ca' Corner Loredan (SM 4137) stands immediately E of Ca' Farsetti. It is of similar date, although the original patron remains unknown. In 1364 it was bought by Federico Corner, one of the wealthiest men in the Republic. From *circa* 1404 to 1740 it was also owned by the Corner Piscopia, but then passed to the Loredan, after which it became a hotel. In 1864 it was acquired by the *comune*, and today houses administrative offices. Elena Corner (b. 1646), who lived here, became the first woman in the world to be awarded a doctoral degree, at Padua in 1678.

The house originally had only two storeys; the second floor and attic were added in the sixteenth century. In the mid-seventeenth century new stairs were built and the *androne* and *portego* were modernised; much of this work survives today. Like its neighbour, it was extended considerably at the rear, doubling its length, and with a long and narrow central courtyard.

The lower order of the quay façade has a spacious central five-bay colonnade, with paired lights on the outer corners; all have tall stilted arches. Some of the columns and capitals are original; the rest are copies. The first floor has a broad, full-width thirteen-bay colonnade, although the two outer corners are subtly emphasised by paired colonnettes, so the rhythm is really 3–7–3. The plan, similar to Ca' Farsetti, has a T-shape formed by the transverse loggia and central hall, with square rooms in the outer corners.

Palazzo Bembo on the Riva del Carbon; a 'double *palazzo*' from *circa* 1460

Again, like Ca' Farsetti, the interior has a grandiose staircase, added in the seventeenth century, linked by a triumphal arch to the *androne*. The first-floor hall contains paintings by Benedetto Caliari and Bonifacio de' Pitati.

A little further along the Riva del Carbon, at SM 4168–72, is the late fourteenth-century Gothic **Palazzetto Dandolo**; a small, narrow house immediately adjacent to a larger one of similar date; richly decorated, with a frieze, paterae and the arms of the Dandolo and Gradenigo. At the E end of the Riva is the unusual **Palazzo Bembo** (SM 4785, 4790–95), a substantial late Gothic house, *circa* 1460; a type of 'double *palazzo*', with two parallel central axes, flanked by the usual pair of outer wings. On the *piano nobile*, each of the two adjacent halls has a five-light window, with a similar pattern to the more modest second floor. Each half of the palace was occupied by a different branch of the Bembo clan, and each had its own quayside portal and staircase. At the level of the *portego* floor, a long Byzantine frieze is set into the façade. In 1479 the future cardinal and humanist scholar Pietro Bembo was born here.

Crossing Ponte Manin, we enter the colonnade forming the ground-floor quay to **Palazzo Dolfin Manin** (SM 4796–9), a substantial Renaissance palace designed by Sansovino for Zuanne Dolfin, begun in 1536. In the early eighteenth century the house passed to the Manin, who modernised the interior. It was further

Palazzo Dolfin Manin, by Jacopo Sansovino, begun 1536

modernised in the Neo-classical manner by Selva after 1787, when the palace was the property of Ludovico, last doge of the Republic.

The stone quay façade is largely unchanged, the colonnade providing additional space on the upper floors, while maintaining the public right of way. The six arched bays represent long narrow warehouses inside. The upper floors were originally occupied by two branches of the family; they are symmetrical and tripartite, with a *quadrifora* in the centre. The three orders of the façade are framed by classical pilasters, respectively Doric, Ionic and Corinthian. The plan is an irregular trapezoid, with a central courtyard.

10 SAN SALVADOR AND THE SCUOLA GRANDE DE SAN TODARO

Turn right down Calle Larga Mazzini and enter Campo San Salvador, a modest square with two monumental façades The first (sw side) is that of the **Scuola Grande de San Todaro** (sm 4811), originally a *scuola piccola*, but 'promoted' in 1552. The confraternity had its origins in the adjacent church (see below), but their first hall was built in 1530. The present building is a reconstruction from *circa* 1580; the architect is not known, although the internal stair is by Tommaso Contin. The façade was added by Sardi in 1655, following a donation of 30,000 ducats in the will of a wealthy merchant, Giacomo Gallo or Galli.

The site has an irregular plan, but the Scuola has the usual accommodation of two superimposed halls, with a small side wing containing the *albergo*. It was suppressed in 1810 and is currently used for concerts and exhibitions. Sardi's impressive stone façade has two similar superimposed orders, with three bays divided by paired columns on tall bases. On the skyline are four angels; in the centre is *St Theodore* by Bernardo Falcone. The grandiose stair is to the right of the *androne*, and has three flights, a similar arrangement to that at San Rocco.

San Salvador (Salvatore): the monumentally imposing façade occupies the SE side of the square. One of the most important Renaissance churches in Venice, it was founded in the seventh century, originally as a parish church. It was later occupied by Augustinian monks, then regular canons of the congregation of San Salvatore, Bologna. After many rebuildings and alterations, the church achieved its present impressive form in 1506–34, following a design by Spavento. He died shortly after work began, though, and it was continued by Tullio Lombardo until his own death in 1532, by which date the basic fabric was complete. In 1530 Sansovino was appointed *proto*; his main contribution was the new monastic buildings, completed *circa* 1564. In 1569 the nave roof was altered by Scamozzi, and lanterns were inserted above the cupolas to improve the light. The final stage was the façade, completed by Sardi in 1663, and funded (at a cost of 60,000 ducats) from the same bequest as that to the adjacent Scuola. In 1810 the monastery was suppressed by Napoleon; at present it is occupied by Telecom Italia. The church was restored and reopened in 1866–79.

The *campo* façade is imposing, almost Neo-classical in its restraint, but with Baroque touches, such as the festoons; two orders (the lower one considerably taller) and three bays, all defined by single Corinthian columns. The large pedimented portal is also Corinthian. The upper order is a little more Baroque than the lower, with an unusual Palladian window and fielded panelling; on the skyline: a central pediment and five large statues.

The unusual, imposing interior is designed to mathematical ratios, all based on the simple proportion of 2:1. The plan is a Latin cross, with central nave, two aisles, transepts and an E end terminating with three apses. The nave width is twice that of the aisles, while longitudinally the nave has three large square bays alternating with

San Salvador: upper part of façade, by Sardi, *circa* 1663

half-bays. Each of the square nave bays, and the two to the transepts, is covered by a plain cupola on pendentives. The general vocabulary is restrained and monumental, with only two materials: grey stone and white plaster. The main, giant order is again Corinthian, the secondary order Ionic.

Inside: a number of important altars and monuments. Right aisle: the second altar is by Campagna; the tomb of Francesco Venier is by Sansovino; the third altar is again by Sansovino, with an altarpiece (the *Annunciation*) by Titian. Off the right transept is Spavento's sacristy, originally frescoed by Francesco Vecellio.

In the chancel, the high altar is by Guglielmo de' Grigi, 1534. In front of the silver reredos is the *Transfiguration*, another late work by Titian. In the left apse: *Supper at Emmaus* by Giovanni Bellini. In the left aisle: altar of the Scuola dei Luganegheri (sausage-makers), by Vittoria, and altarpiece by Palma il Giovane. The organ was designed by Sansovino, with doors decorated by Francesco Vecellio. Adjacent to the left transept is a doorway into the Marzaria, formed by Tullio Lombardo in 1532; externally: a large stone arch and a long flight of steps.

The monastic buildings are ranged around two cloisters, both simply detailed in stone. The first is rectangular, Doric, with two floors of accommodation above. The second is larger, again Doric and rectangular, but with colonnades on three sides and the refectory on the fourth; the detailing is a little richer.

From the square, turn right down the Marzaria San Salvador. At the end on the left, at SM 4983, is the fine **Palazzo Giustinian Faccanon**; water façade to Rio de la Fava. Substantial *gotico fiorito*, probably late 1450s or 1460s, with tripartite plan and water façade. The façade is richly detailed, with refined carving, two watergates and two *piani nobili*, each with a six-light window to the *portego*. The second is richer than the first; tracery modelled on the Doge's Palace. The statues on the skyline were added by the Faccanon in the eighteenth century, as well as a roof terrace and astronomical observatory.

Take Calle de le Acque in front of the palace, and at the end, turn right along the quay, towards Ponte dei Barrettieri. At SM 4939 is the **Ridotto Venier**, one of the rare surviving *ridotti* that flourished in the eighteenth century, serving the nobility as gambling houses and for social, musical and literary gatherings. The surviving upper-floor apartments are beautifully decorated; four small rooms, and a dining room and kitchen, reached by a staircase and lobby. The stucco, primarily pink, green and gold, is probably by Pietro Castelli, Giuseppe Ferrari and perhaps Jacopo Guarana.

11 SAN BARTOLOMEO, THE FONDACO DEI TEDESCHI AND THE RIALTO BRIDGE

To complete the itinerary, return northwards up the Marzaria, then right along the Marzarieta Due Aprile into the busy, crowded Campo San Bartolomeo. The square was enlarged by demolition at the N end in 1855, after which the attractive statue of Goldoni (by Antonio dal Zotto) was added.

On the E side of the square is **Palazzo Moro** (SM 5282 and 5308), a significant early Gothic house, very late thirteenth or early fourteenth century; the façade is transitional, with windows of different dates. The *piano nobile* has a six-light window with inflected extrados (Ruskin's 'third order'), and stone *plutei* between the columns. **San Bartolomeo** itself is adjacent to the w side of the square, partly surrounded by other structures. It was founded in 840, but rebuilt several times. For a long time it was the church of the German community, based at the adjacent Fondaco dei Tedeschi (q.v.). The present modest structure is the result of radical restoration

The Fondaco dei Tedeschi, 1505–8, by Giorgio Spavento and Scarpagnino

(by Scalfarotto?) in 1723. The plan is a Latin cross, with a small central cupola. Several interesting paintings: organ doors of two saints by Sebastiano del Piombo; others by Sante Peranda, Palma il Giovane and Morleiter.

The campanile was demolished in 1747 but rebuilt by Scalfarotto in 1754, based on Tirali's bell-tower for Santi Apostoli, with rusticated base and onion dome.

The church's surroundings were radically altered when the new Rialto Bridge was built in the late sixteenth century. A new street, Salizada Pio X, was cut to improve access to the bridge, while much of the church fabric 'disappeared' behind new commercial premises. The **Fondaco (Fontego) dei Tedeschi** (SM 5346, 5554): the large square pile of the Fondaco stands just N of the Rialto Bridge. The German trading community was already established in the city by the 1200s, an important element in the Republic's international trade. The first Fondaco consisted of a heterogeneous collection of buildings, incorporating warehouse space and lodgings for traders. In 1505 the entire complex was destroyed by fire. A competition was held for a new Fondaco; Spavento (who was probably also the architect) was appointed to execute the work, but was soon replaced by Scarpagnino, who saw it to rapid completion in only three years. Generous funding was provided by the Republic, since it was vital to minimise disruption to trade. The design was intentionally simple, rational and repetitive.

The plan is a simple rectangle, with a large central courtyard and accommodation around it on all sides. The principal landward approach was from the s, with a fine stone portal; this façade was frescoed by Titian. On both landward façades, the ground floor was occupied by small outward-facing shops.

The broad, impressive Grand Canal façade was the most important; its present severe appearance was originally enlivened by frescoes by Giorgione. It has a generous central five-bay waterfront loggia for unloading goods; the three upper levels are simple and repetitive, with none of the traditional Venetian central emphasis; instead, the simple paired rectangular windows reflect the repetitive cellular accommodation inside. On the first *piano nobile*, balconies near the corners indicate the locations of two halls, the summer and winter dining rooms. The roofline has also changed; the two corner turrets have now gone, as has the row of Venetian chimneys, although the decorative crenellation remains.

The courtyard was originally open; the glass roof was added in 1937. Its façades are again regular, repetitive and simply but elegantly detailed. In the centre is a fine original well-head. Since the 1930s, the Fontego has been the city's central post office, although it is to be relocated elsewhere.

The **Ponte de Rialto**: the date of construction of the first bridge is unknown, perhaps in the twelfth century, but for centuries it was the only fixed crossing on the Grand Canal. It was the natural location for such a bridge: in the centre of the Venetian archipelago, and at a point where the Grand Canal is at its narrowest. The first bridge, like its many later reconstructions, was of timber, with two

Rialto and the timber bridge, from de' Barbari's engraving of 1500

The Ponte di Rialto by Antonio da Ponte, 1588–91

inclined ramps and a central drawbridge to permit the passage of ships. It was supported on numerous timber piers and piles. In 1458 a major reconstruction incorporated shops for the first time, providing rent towards its upkeep.

Discussion of a permanent stone bridge began in 1507, but only in 1554 was a famous design competition held, attracting proposals from Vignola, Michelangelo, Scamozzi, Sansovino and Palladio. Sansovino's was preferred, but the cost of the Turkish wars delayed commencement, and the idea was revived only in 1587. New designs were submitted by Scamozzi, Antonio da Ponte and others. In 1588 da Ponte's daring single-arch span was chosen, and the work was completed within three years, at a cost of 245,000 ducats. Da Ponte's scheme is said to be closely based on a lost proposal by Michelangelo.

The bridge remains a remarkable feat of engineering in the difficult Venetian terrain, its arch spanning approximately 30 metres, and supported by 12,000 elm piles, half on each side. Its plan is ingenious and very successful; the broad central route is flanked by four structures, each containing six small shops, which yielded substantial revenue to maintain the bridge. In the centre at the top is a spacious arched rusticated classical loggia, while the central axis itself is continued almost seamlessly into Salizada Pio x at one end

The Ponte di Rialto: detail of the central crowning arch

and Ruga dei Oresi on the other. Down the two outer flanks are secondary routes, less encumbered by commerce, but providing fine views down the Grand Canal in both directions.

The principal visible structure is the great stone arch, capped by a robust continuous balcony on corbels. On the outer spandrels: four relief sculptures; on the NE side the Republic's patrons, *St Mark* and *St Theodore*, on the other the *Annunciation*. Adjacent are commemorative plaques of the incumbent doge, Pasquale Cicogna; all were carved by Agostino Rubini, 1589–90. Above are the banks of shops; on their outer faces is a series of shallow rusticated arches; they have lead barrel-vaulted roofs.

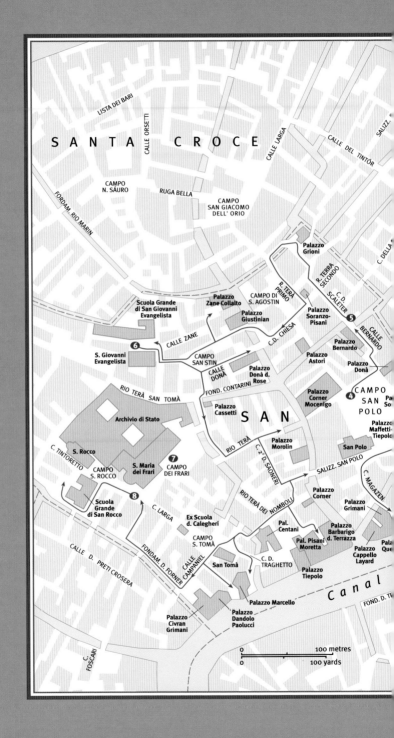

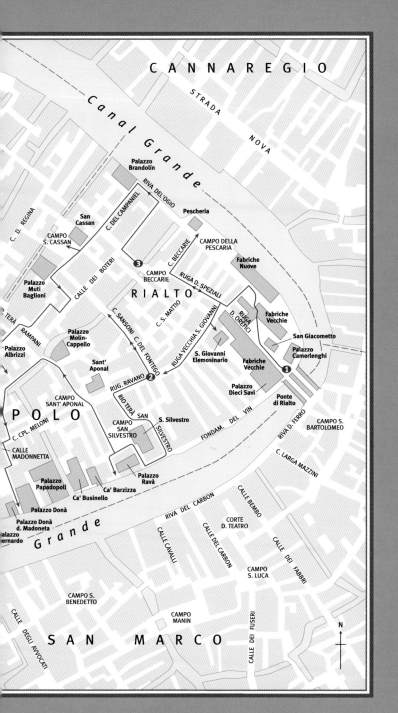

CANNAREGIO

STRADA NOVA

Canal Grande

Palazzo
Brandolín

RIVA DEL OGIO

C. D. REGINA

San
Cassan

C. DEL CAMPANIEL

Pescheria

CAMPO
S. CASSAN

C. BECCARIE

CAMPO DELLA
PESCARIA

Palazzo
Muti
Baglioni

CALLE DEI BOTERI

③

CAMPO
BECCARIE

Fabriche
Nuove

RUGA D. SPEZIALI

RIALTO

RUGA
D. OREFICI

Fabriche
Vecchie

San Giacometto

TERÀ

RAMPANI

C. SANSONI

C. S. MATTIO

RUGA VECCHIA S. GIOVANNI

Palazzo
Camerlenghi

Palazzo
Albrizzi

Palazzo
Molin-
Cappello

C. DEL FONTEGO

RUGA VECCHIA S. GIOVANNI

S. Giovanni
Elemosinario

Fabriche
Vecchie

Sant'
Aponal

RUG. RAVANO

②

POLO

CAMPO
SANT' APONAL

RIO TERÀ SAN

Palazzo
Dieci Savi

Ponte
di Rialto

①

C. CPL. MELONI

CAMPO
SAN
SILVESTRO

S. Silvestro

SILVESTRO

FONDAM. DEL VIN

RIVA D. FERRO

CAMPO S.
BARTOLOMEO

CALLE
MADONNETTA

C. LARGA MAZZINI

Palazzo
Papadopoli

Palazzo
Ravà

CALLE BEMBO

Palazzo Donà

Ca' Businello

Ca' Barzizza

RIVA DEL CARBON

CORTE
D. TEATRO

CALLE DEI FABBRI

Palazzo Donà
d. Madoneta

Grande

CALLE CAVALLI

CALLE DEL CARBON

Palazzo
ernardo

CAMPO
S. LUCA

CAMPO S.
BENEDETTO

CAMPO
MANIN

CALLE DEI FUSERI

CALLE DEGLI AVOCATI

SAN MARCO

N

San Polo

Sestiere of San Polo

THE ISLAND AND MARKETS OF RIALTO

The densely developed *sestiere* of San Polo is dominated by the
activities in its eastern part: the market district of Rialto, which has
formed the business heart of the city since the early medieval period.
The *sestiere* is defined by the Grand Canal to the NE and SE, and
abuts Dorsoduro and Santa Croce to the NW and SW. The large firm
islet at the sharp bend in the Grand Canal's course, Rivo Alto itself,
adjacent to the present bridge, was one of the earliest to be settled.
Rialto had the further natural advantage of being in the centre of the
city's archipelago, and at the natural confluence of several routes: the
Grand Canal itself; the route NE via the Rio de Noal to Murano; and
routes SW towards Dorsoduro, and SE into Castello. Rialto's history is
thus dominated by the activities associated with the markets, and the
complementary ones of banking and insurance. The early commercial
importance of the district is attested by the notable group of early
palazzi-fonteghi that survive here: the two Donà palaces, Ca' Barzizza
and Ca' Businello, and the former flour warehouse at San Silvestro.
Many government departments were also based here, particularly
those concerned with the administration of the city itself, as distinct
from the larger Republic. The principal quay, the Riva del Vin,
formed the commercial focus for water-borne goods, together with
the quays of the Erbaria, Pescheria and the Riva de l'Ogio, serving

Facing page: Palazzo Goldoni: canal façade

the markets themselves. This commercial concentration led to development at extremely high densities, and eventually the loss of much of the resident population in favour of these activities.

The character of the rest of the *sestiere* varies considerably; further w, the spacious *campo* of San Polo has always been a major social focus. Further w again is the extensive area occupied by the Franciscan church of the Frari, with its former monastic buildings (today the Archivio di Stato), dominating the surrounding area. Between these major foci are smaller, more typical island parishes: San Silvestro, Sant'Aponal and San Tomà along the Grand Canal, San Stin and Sant'Agostin further inland. The *sestiere* also contains the *scuole grandi* of San Rocco and San Giovanni Evangelista.

The market district focuses on the tiny, ancient church of San Giacometto; it has a long, complex history. The most important single event was a devastating fire in 1514, which destroyed almost all the buildings on the island of Rialto itself, the subsequent reconstruction of which resulted in the district that we see today. Although this reconstruction (completed in the late sixteenth century) resulted in some rationalisation of functions, most of the original street pattern survived intact. The market has always contained specialist 'sub-zones' within it; historically, the more 'noble' activities were located closest to the bridge, and the more popular ones further away, a distinction that has survived to some degree today. Thus, around the bridgehead were goldsmiths' and jewellers' workshops, around the *campiELLo* of San Giacometto were the nobles' banks and insurance offices; while along the Grand Canal itself were specialist food markets, whose names also still survive. From E to w we have the Naranzeria (oranges and other fruit), Erbaria (vegetables), Casaria (dairy produce), Beccarie (meat) and finally the Pescaria (fish market).

I THE ISLAND OF RIALTO

Palazzo dei Camerlenghi (SP 1): at the N foot of the Rialto Bridge, adjacent to the Grand Canal. The richly decorated palace is the result of a modernisation of older structures in 1526–8, under Doge Andrea Gritti. They consisted of a nobles' loggia, the offices of the *camerlenghi* (city treasurers) and the Razon Vecchie and Nove, government finance departments. The modernisation resulted in the loss of the loggia and the consolidation of the remaining two into

Rialto: detail of the façade of the Palazzo dei
Camerlenghi, probably by Guglielmo de' Grigi, 1526–8

one building, although of irregular shape. A new stone façade was
wrapped around both elements; it is usually attributed to Guglielmo
de' Grigi, although the portal is probably by Scarpagnino, since it
closely resembles that on the Fondaco dei Tedeschi.

The plan thus has two elements; the larger, facing the Ruga, has a
tripartite form, with a central hall, while the other, towards the Grand
Canal, has an irregular trapezoidal plan. The palace is unusual in that
it is completely free-standing; its complex, ornate façades have three
orders, each defined by a frieze with garlands and *tondi*. Articulation is
by an irregular distribution of flat Corinthian pilasters, and similarly
complex, irregular fenestration, with single and paired lights to the
upper floors. The interior was once richly decorated with paintings,
but the collection was dispersed after 1797; some are in the Doge's
Palace, others at San Giorgio. At present, the palace houses the Corte
dei Conti, continuing its historic use by fiscal magistracies.

Across the Ruga to the w is the **Palazzo dei Dieci Savii** (SP 19),
façade towards the Grand Canal. It forms part of Scarpagnino's
reconstruction programme following the fire of 1514, and terminates

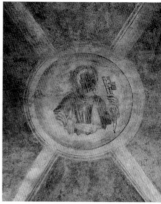

Rialto: the Palazzo dei Dieci Savii, by Scarpagnino, *circa* 1519–30, with the bridge to the right

Rialto: fresco detail from the vaults of the Fabbriche Vecchie, *circa* 1520s

the long block known as the Fabbriche Vecchie, occupying the NW side of the Ruga dei Oresi (Orefici = goldsmiths). The Dieci Savii were magistrates responsible for collecting tithes; later, the building became the seat of the Magistrato alle Acque, responsible for the lagoon and sea defences, whose offices remain there today. The simple, refined Grand Canal façade has a five-bay ground-floor colonnade and two upper floors lit by paired rectangular windows. A plaque records its construction under Doge Leonardo Loredan (1521). On the corner towards the bridge: a late sixteenth-century figure of Justice.

The contiguous **Fabbriche Vecchie** consist not only of the long block down the SW side of the Ruga, but also those that bound Campo San Giacometto to the NW and NE. They all have two floors of accommodation above ground-floor colonnades. The ground floor of the SW block was originally occupied by jewellers and fabric merchants (some remain today), while those to the NW and NE were occupied by money-changers, insurance offices and private banks. The SW block consists of two long, parallel buildings with a service alley (Parangon) between the two. The NW block is similar, with the narrow Calle de la Sicurtà down the centre. Their appearance is very simple, with minimal stone detailing; the colonnade has elegant stone arches, and the vaults were frescoed; many in the SW block survive. Construction began in 1519–21; the SW block was complete by 1532, the others *circa* 1537.

San Giacometto: the fifteenth-century portico

San Giacomo (Giacometto) di Rialto: the tiny church of San Giacometto (usually in the diminutive) stands on the se side of the square. According to tradition, it is the oldest foundation in the city, established in 421; other dates proposed are 428 and 540. The core of the present building is eleventh or early twelfth century, the period when the market itself was established. It was re-consecrated in 1177, the year of the 'peace conference' here between the pope and the Holy Roman Emperor; the former gave a number of privileges and indulgences to the city's churches. San Giacometto has great historic and symbolic importance, both for the city and the market district in particular. It was once patronised by the Querini and Tiepolo, but later came under the direct patronage of the doge, who processed here in Holy Week every year. It remained a rectory or parish church until 1810, when it was attached to San Silvestro.

San Giacometto survived the 1514 fire, but was altered in 1531 and 1601, when the façade was raised and the present vaulted ceiling installed. The simple brick façade has a fifteenth-century portico, with marble columns supporting a timber trabeation with *barbacani*. The central upper part, with its bell-frame, was rebuilt in 1792; the original free-standing campanile was lost in the 1514 fire. The internal plan (altered) is now a Greek cross, with four arms and a central crossing. The nave has only two bays, with flanking aisles of almost equal width; at the crossing is a little cupola on pendentives. The principal original elements are the six Greek marble columns, with fine foliage capitals; the earliest are almost certainly Venetian-Byzantine, reused from an earlier structure. Trade guilds had altars here, including the goldsmiths (left side chapel) and the dairy produce sellers.

Leave the square by the N corner, through the colonnade into Campo de la Corderia (Bella Vienna).

The **Fabbriche Nuove** (SP 148–84) formed the second stage of reconstruction after the 1514 fire. The long, narrow building flanking the Grand Canal was commissioned in 1554 from Sansovino; it was to house a fruit market on the ground floor, in sixteen shops, with two floors of storage above, much like the Fabbriche Vecchie. It is of fireproof construction, with vaulted floors of brick, and no timber other than the roof structure. Funding was generous, and the work was complete in just over a year. A further wing was then added at the SE end, to link the Fabbriche Nuove to the earlier Scarpagnino blocks, thus also enclosing the NW side of the Erbaria; this wing was complete *circa* 1558.

The design is based on Falconetto's Monte di Pietà in Padua (1531–5), but with an additional storey. The ground floor has a tall rusticated stone colonnade, while the upper floors have flat pilasters, each bay having a single window capped by a stone pediment, of alternating radiused and triangular profile. The long façade is simple and repetitive; since the upper floors were warehouses, there was no need for heating, and thus no fireplaces or chimneys.

Cross Campo de la Bella Vienna and take Calle dei Varotari into Ruga Vecchia; a short distance along on the left is the discreet entrance to **San Giovanni Elemosinario**, surrounded by other structures and with almost no external presence. It is first recorded in 1051 as a parish foundation. It was rebuilt in 1167, reconstructed again in the fifteenth century, but destroyed in the 1514 fire. The campanile (1410) survived, and still stands. The church was rebuilt in 1527–9 by Scarpagnino; the plan is a Greek cross, with a square plan, and roofed with simple plaster cross-vaults and barrel vaults. At the crossing is a cupola on a drum, supported by pendentives. The rectangular chancel has a square E end, and is raised five steps above the nave floor, with a low crypt beneath. The detailing is simple and classical, in a stylised Corinthian manner. All the light derives from high-level *oci* and a thermal window. Several works of art, most in the chancel; on the high altar is Titian's fine *St John the Almsgiver*, *circa* 1545. Other works are by Pordenone, Palma il Giovane and Corona. The organ doors are painted by Marco Vecellio.

From the corner of the Ruga Vecchia and Ruga dei Oresi, continue NW along Ruga dei Spezieri into Campo de la Becaria. On the right is the famous **Pescheria** (Pescaria), the fish market. It was first established in 1332, much closer to the bridge, and transferred to the present site in 1459. The first modern permanent structure was a cast-iron and glass covered hall (1884); it stood SE of the two present neo-Gothic market halls (1902–7) by Domenico Ruspolo and Cesare Laurenti. In both structures, the tall open colonnaded ground floor supports a single upper floor. Remains of the former Palazzo Querini (destroyed after the notorious plot of 1310) are incorporated into the buildings.

2   SAN SILVESTRO AND SANT'APONAL

Return to Ruga Vecchia and continue SW; it becomes Rugheta del Ravano. Turn right down Calle del Fontego del Curame. Under the *sotoportego*, the *calle* widens into Campielo dei Sansoni. Nearby was the lost church of **San Matteo**, founded in the twelfth century, but suppressed in 1805 and demolished in 1818. At the far end of the Campielo on the left, next to the bridge, is **Palazzetto Sansoni** (SP 898–9), with a canal façade incorporating various elements from Venetian-Byzantine to fourteenth-century Gothic and Renaissance. The citizen family Sansoni lived here from the fifteenth century until their extinction in 1678 (see plaque). Returning to the busy Rugheta del Ravano, turn right, then left down the Rio Terà to reach the **Chiesa de San Silvestro**, said to have been founded in the ninth century, but rebuilt in 1422 when it absorbed the adjacent oratory of Ognissanti (All Saints). It was restored again in the seventeenth century, but rebuilt in 1837–43 by Lorenzo Santi and Giambattista Meduna. The façade was completed only in 1909. Its parochial status has survived since its foundation; after the Napoleonic closures, it absorbed the adjacent parishes of San Giovanni Elemosinario and San Matteo. The north façade is a classical stone composition, with two superimposed orders of Ionic pilasters surmounted by a pediment. In the centre of the upper order is the titular saint, set into a niche. The longer w flank faces the square.

Interior: a single, large, spacious nave, with a semicircular eastern apse, all in a simple, impressive Neo-classical style; side altars down both flanks. A few paintings survived the nineteenth-century reconstruction, including the *Baptism of Christ*, a good late Tintoretto (first right altar). The high altar is a Neo-classical work by Luigi Ferrari.

Directly opposite the façade is **Palazzo Valier** (SP 1022), sixteenth century, with a large *quadrifora* with balcony. The façade was once frescoed by Taddeo Longhi (seventeenth century). On the w side of the quiet square: small Gothic houses. Take the wide Rio Terà down the E side of the church to reach the w end of the Riva del Vin; good views of the palaces across the Grand Canal, including (L to R) Palazzo Dolfin Manin, Palazzo Bembo, Ca' Loredan and Ca' Farsetti; further right: Palazzo Grimani.

At the w end of the Riva del Vin is **Palazzo Ravà** (SP 1099), with a front garden; by Giovanni Sardi, *circa* 1906, in a picturesque neo-Gothic manner. It stands on the site of the ancient **Ca' del Papà**, fragments of which survive. To reach them we return to Campo San Silvestro, leave by the SW corner (Sotoportego del Pasina) and continue left under a second *sotoportego* to the *vaporetto* stop. On the little quay is a row of fine thirteenth-century Byzantine arches (SP 1113–14). This once imposing palace was the Venetian home of the

patriarch of Grado, but in 1451 the patriarchate was subsumed into that of Venice (at San Pietro in Castello); the house thereby lost its function, and by 1653 most was demolished.

Immediately w of the quay is **Ca' Barzizza** (SP 1172–3), a small but noteworthy early thirteenth-century Venetian-Byzantine house; the plan is regular, with a spacious waterfront loggia, behind which

Ca' del Papà: thirteenth-century fragments of arches and capitals

is the long axial hall. The façade is much altered; the right wing was added later. Its chief original elements are the fine portal and the *quadrifore* to the upper halls. The left side was altered in the sixteenth century; the attic and *abbaino* are also later.

Return to Campo San Silvestro; take Calle del Luganegher (NW corner), into **Campo Sant'Aponal**. The dedication is to the first bishop of Ravenna, and the church was founded in the early eleventh century. It was rebuilt in the fifteenth century, and this fabric survives today. It was modernised internally in the sixteenth century, when much of the Gothic interior was lost. In 1810 it was closed and its parish function transferred to San Silvestro. Thereafter, it was used for secular functions, but restored and reopened for worship in 1851, then closed again. The characteristic tripartite Gothic *campo* façade has an exuberant skyline, ornamented with stone aedicules. Above the portal is a collection of sculptures from elsewhere, including a large crucifix (above the *ocio*), a relief of the Virgin (top) and a large group including the Crucifixion, two large fifteenth-century relief panels and flanking pinnacles.

The interior has a flat panelled ceiling; down the side walls are four altars by Vittoria; the fine Baroque high altar comes from Santa Giustina. The adjacent campanile is a good Venetian-Byzantine survivor, probably eleventh century; all brick, with shallow pilasters,

and surmounted by an octagonal tambour, added in 1467. Next to the campanile: the former **Scuola dei Taiapiera** (SP 1252), the stonemasons' guildhall; high-level relief panel (1652).

Out of the SW corner of the square, Calle del Todeschini and Calle de Ca' Businello bring us to the land entrance of **Ca' Businello**, similar in date to Ca' Barzizza, but with a broader, tripartite canal façade. Probably built by the Morosini, it passed to the Businello only in the

Sant'Aponal; sculptures on the façade, mostly fourteenth and fifteenth centuries, assembled from elsewhere eighteenth century. The central transverse loggia is flanked by small side rooms, but, despite the early date, the overall plan is close to the classic mature tripartite form. The ground floor retains part of the original nine-bay colonnaded portico; the two upper floors have central six-light windows, although the outer flanks are altered.

Returning to Campo Sant'Aponal, take Calle del Ponte Storto out of the N side. At the end on the right is the attractive **Palazzo Molin Cappello** (SP 1279–80), an early Lombard Renaissance palace, probably very late fifteenth century. The asymmetrical canal façade has refined detailing, with two *quadrifore*. The house was the home of Bianca Cappello, born here in 1548. She had an affair with a Florentine, and they eloped to Florence together; later she began a relationship with Francesco de' Medici, grand duke of Tuscany, and after his wife's death she married him. Her transgressions were later pardoned by the Venetian Republic, which made extensive use of her new title in its diplomatic relations with the Grand Duchy of Tuscany.

Cross Ponte Storto and continue w along the *fondamenta*, much of it colonnaded. On the other bank (SP 1296) is the early sixteenth-century **Palazzo Molin**, again Lombard Renaissance. Further w is **Palazzo Bernardi** (SP 1319), originally Gothic but modernised in the sixteenth century. Cross Ponte de la Furatola and continue down the street and its continuation, Calle del Luganegher. We enter Campiello dei Meloni. Both *calli* off the s side lead to the garden of **Palazzo Coccina Tiepolo Papadopoli** (SP 1364). The palace was built *circa* 1560, and is often attributed to Giangiacomo de' Grigi. It is traditional and tripartite, with two superimposed apartments on the upper floors, each one originally reached by a separate stair on each side of the *androne*. After 1864 the palace was extended towards the w, and the interior was extensively modernised in an eighteenth-century manner by Gerolamo Levi.

Palazzo Coccina Tiepolo Papadopoli (left), *circa* 1560, by Giangiacomo de' Grigi; and the thirteenth-century Ca' Businello

Palazzo Donà; later thirteenth century

The Grand Canal façade is elegant and refined, clad with stone and marble; three orders: Doric, Ionic and Corinthian. The first contains the imposing central watergate in the form of a Serliana, while the two *piani nobili* are very similar; both also with a central Serliana, but the first floor has a prominent stone balcony as well, and is given further prominence by two large Coccina *scudi*. Above the bold cornice are two stone obelisk-chimneys.

Take Calle Papadopoli, Calle del Brusà and then Calle del Tragheto; we reach the Grand Canal again. Just to the E is **Palazzo Donà** (SP 1426), another early Venetian-Byzantine house. Although altered considerably later, it retains the original structure and fenestration pattern, as well as the fine five-light window to the *piano nobile*; probably second half of the thirteenth century, since it evinces a further development from Ca' Businello towards the mature tripartite *palazzo* form, with three equal elements. The house was altered in the fifteenth century, when many earlier features were lost; the top floor and *abbaino* were added in the eighteenth century.

On the W side of the *calle* is another Donà house, **Palazzo Donà de la Madoneta** (SP 1429–30), perhaps *circa* 1230, but considerably smaller. The name derives from a small frieze on the façade, between the mezzanine windows. The narrow frontage precluded a tripartite plan, and the plan is L-shaped, with a narrow courtyard in the internal angle. The Grand Canal façade retains the original off-centre portal, and a fine eight-light window across the full width of the *piano nobile*, with stilted arches and refined capitals. Unusually, the top floor *liagò* has survived.

This concludes the first section of the itinerary; for the next, we return to the fish market.

3 FROM SAN CASSAN TO SAN POLO (1)

From Campo de le Becarie, take Ponte de le Becarie and continue into the busy Calle dei Boteri. Turn right and continue to the Riva de l'Ogio at the end; a fine view of the Grand Canal and the Ca' d'Oro. Continue NW to the end of the quay. On the corner is **Palazzo Morosini Brandolin** (SP 1789), late Gothic, *circa* 1460. The chief feature is the Grand Canal façade, altered in 1850, when the top floor was removed, giving the whole an unfortunately squat appearance. It is, however, finely detailed, with two *piani nobili*; the lower has a *gotico fiorito* six-light window, while the upper also has an *esafora*, modelled on the Doge's Palace, with high-level quatrefoils in stone circles. Continue down Calle del Campaniel into Campo San Cassan. **San Cassan (Cassiano)**: originally a small oratory dedicated to St Cecilia; by 1069 it had parochial status, and was patronised by the Michiel and Miani families. It was rebuilt after a devastating fire in 1105, and again in 1350. The thirteenth-century campanile was increased in height in 1350, and has survived. The church interior was modernised in 1611, with nave and side aisles, and square apses. The nave has cross-vaults frescoed by Costantino Cedini. The high altarpiece is a *Resurrection* by Tintoretto, 1565, while the altar is a rich Baroque work by Meyring, 1680s. On the chancel walls: two further works by Tintoretto, 1568. The church's external appearance is nineteenth century, when the W portico was demolished and the *campo* façade simplified and classicised; very plain, with three high-level thermal windows.

Take Calle de Ca' Muti out of the S corner of the square. On the right (SP 1866) is the massive **Palazzo Muti Baglioni**, 1602, badly damaged by fire in 1737 and restored. Most of the sumptuous internal decoration dates from this period. Since 1919 it has been owned by the ancient da Mosto family. The plan and façades are tripartite and traditional, with a long central hall. Two stairs give access to the two superimposed *piani nobili*. The façades, almost identical, are imposing but difficult to see. Both have three superimposed Serliane, the lowermost incorporating the land and watergates, the upper pairs the main halls.

Turn left back into Calle dei Boteri, then take Calesela and Rio Terà Rampani, then the short Ramo Albrizzi into Campielo Albrizzi. The NW side is occupied by **Palazzo Albrizzi** (SP 1940), whose restrained exterior conceals perhaps the richest Baroque and Rococo interiors in the city. Built by the Bonomo towards the end of the sixteenth century, it has characteristic superimposed Serliane; the tripartite façade may have been frescoed. After 1648 it was acquired in stages by the Albrizzi, who spent many years decorating the interior. In 1771 they bought some adjacent cottages and extended the palace towards the SW. This extension is connected by a high-level bridge to a garden across the canal. The palace is still owned by a descendant of the Albrizzi. Its interior may have been planned by Gaspari; much of the rich stucco is by Abbondio Stazio. The *portego*, in particular, has extraordinarily lavish decoration, with inset paintings by Liberi and Giovanni Antonio Pellegrini. One of the square halls has a ceiling of tent-like stucco drapery, with numerous 'flying' *putti* attached to it.

From the *campielo*, take Calle Stretta out of the SW corner, cross the bridge, then take Calle dei Cavalli on the right. **Palazzo Cavalli** (SP 1952) is sixteenth-century Renaissance, with an elegant *trifora* to the upper hall. Continue over the bridge into **Campo San Polo**; said to be the largest parish square in Venice. A spacious rectangle, the church projecting into the SW corner; the NE side is defined by fine palaces, all once separated from the square by a narrow canal, with access by small private bridges; it was reclaimed *circa* 1760. Historically, the square was used extensively for public events, from bullfights to military parades. Near the SE corner is **Palazzo Maffetti Tiepolo** (SP 1957), extensively modernised *circa* 1690 on the structure of a much older house, probably by Domenico Rossi. The plan and façades are conventional, tripartite and symmetrical. Flat rustication to the lower order of the lively façade, and a grand entrance portal, in the form of a Serliana, rising through the mezzanine. The first *piano nobile* is more prominent than the second, with a balcony on large stone brackets, integrated with the Serliana below. Inside: rich stucco decoration and the remains of frescoes, perhaps by Abbondio Stazio. We return to the square shortly.

The next group of palaces all have façades to the Grand Canal. From the SE corner of the square, take Calle and Ramo de la Madona. At the far end is the land gate of the fine Gothic **Palazzo**

Bernardo (SP 1978), built perhaps by the Giustinian, before 1442. In 1651 it was bought by the Bellotto, who in turn sold it to the Bernardo in 1694. The palace deteriorated in the nineteenth century, but was restored in 1948, and today is occupied by Ca' Foscari university. The plan is complex, the two watergates representing two upper apartments, each reached by their own land gate, courtyard and external staircase. The overall plan is an L, with the larger courtyard, with its splendid external stair, in the internal angle. This stair rises to the second, more important, *piano nobile*. The impressive Grand Canal façade has four storeys, a generous ground floor, two *piani nobili* and an attic. On the first floor: a fine six-light window to the *portego*, but that to the second, slightly later, is more complex, with tracery based on that at the Doge's Palace. The outer windows have prominent balconies and refined pendant-tracery, based on Bon's at the Ca' d'Oro (1424); possibly by Bon himself.

The next three palaces, although almost adjacent to Ca' Bernardo, are reached by a different route. **Palazzo Giustinian Querini Dubois** (SP 2004) is immediately w, reached from Campielo del Librer, and then Campielo de le Erbe, off the SE corner of Campo San Polo. Originally fifteenth-century Gothic, radically modernised *circa* 1560 by the Zane, with a new façade and an extra floor. The plan is conventional, the façade large and impressive; it was originally frescoed. Five storeys and two *piani nobili*; both have central arched *quadrifore*. Inside, the palace conserves a fine portal to the stairs, and some rooms retain eighteenth-century stucco decoration.

Back in Campo San Polo, Calle del Magazen, again off the s side, leads to the land entrance of **Palazzo Grimani Giustinian Marcello** (SP 2033), one of the most beautiful smaller Renaissance palaces in the city. Its Grand Canal façade is best seen from Sant'Angelo *vaporetto* stop. Probably from the 1520s, and has been attributed to various Lombard masters, and to Giovanni Buora; there are similarities to Palazzo Malipiero Trevisan at Santa Maria Formosa. It remained in Grimani ownership for a considerable time, and was modernised internally in the early eighteenth century by Pietro Grimani (doge 1741–52). In 1825 it was modernised again by Carlo Bevilacqua; more recently it has been the property of the Sorlini.

The elegant Grand Canal façade is clad in stone and marble, with refined proportions and detailing; three orders of nearly equal importance, and three bays defined by Corinthian pilasters with rich capitals. On the lowest storey, the outer bays have single lights with triangular pediments, an early use of the form. In the centre of the

Palazzo Grimani Giustinian Marcello at San Polo: Grand Canal façade, *circa* 1520s, perhaps by Giovanni Buora

two upper floors is an arched *trifora*; each order is defined by a rich, broad cornice and fascia, while between the window groups are inset marble paterae and stone relief decoration.

The final house in this small group is **Palazzo Cappello Layard** (SP 2035), immediately w of Palazzo Grimani, and reached from the same quay. Built in the sixteenth century by the Cappello, with an irregular plan and appearance, turning the corner of Rio di San Polo. A broad, fairly simple Grand Canal façade, with unusual paired windows; originally frescoed by Zelotti and Veronese.

We return to Campo San Polo.

4 SAN POLO (2): THE CHURCH, CA' CORNER AND PALAZZI SORANZO

San Polo (Paolo) is an important parish foundation, reputedly founded in 837 by Doge Pietro Tradonico. The first church was extensively modernised *circa* 1400; some surviving fabric dates from this period, including the rich Gothic side portal. In 1804 the church was modernised again by Davide Rossi; much medieval material was lost. The nave columns were replaced, old windows filled in and new ones formed; the rich semicircular apse was replaced by the present faceted structure. The church was now largely Neo-classical.

San Polo: detail of the main (side) portal;
rich *gotico fiorito*, *circa* 1420s

The interior was restored after 1927, when the original medieval roof structure was exposed. The nave retains a basilica form, with seven bays, Ionic columns supporting a continuous entablature, and two lower side aisles, with mono-pitch timber roofs. The central apse has a hemispherical cupola with Ionic pilasters and entablature; the right chancel chapel is a good early sixteenth-century Lombard work; a barrel-vaulted ceiling and a hemispherical cupola. In the chancel: two bronzes by Vittoria and five works by Palma il Giovane. In the left apse chapel: *Marriage of the Virgin* by Veronese. At the w end of the nave, the chapel of the confraternity of the Sacro Cuore di Gesù; an attractive little Corinthian Neo-classical stone façade.

The campanile stands across the *salizada* to the s; it bears the date 1362, but is certainly earlier. The brick tower is capped by a tiled 'pine-cone' roof. At the base: two thirteenth-century stone lions, from the original church portico.

At the NW corner of the square looms the imposing **Palazzo Corner Mocenigo** (SP 2128), with water façade onto Rio di San Polo (best seen from Corte Amaltea); a majestically impressive work by Michele Sanmicheli for the Corner, begun in 1545. An earlier house was destroyed by fire in 1535, and its replacement was commissioned by Zane, son of the immensely wealthy Zorzi (Giorgio) Corner. It was completed in 1564, four years after his death. Zane and his descendants occupied one of the two *piani nobili*; the other was rented, initially to the Querini. In 1799 the palace passed by marriage to the Mocenigo; today much is occupied by the Guardia di Finanza.

The plan is fairly conventional and tripartite, but with a very long (36 m) and narrow central hall. The land gate is in the corner of the square, leading first to an atrium, from which the main staircase rises. Across the atrium a colonnade gives access to an internal courtyard. The second internal staircase, giving access to the other *piano nobile*,

Palazzo Corner Mocenigo, San Polo: detail of *campo*
façade, by Michele Sanmicheli, begun 1545

is across the *androne*. The palace is extremely tall, with six storeys:
three principal floors (ground and two *piani nobili*), alternating with
mezzanines or 'service' floors. The canal façade is imposing but
restrained compared with Sanmicheli's typically robust 'military' style.
Rusticated stonework is confined to the water storey, with three
watergates. The *piani nobili* are defined by Serliane, ingeniously
incorporating the windows of the adjacent mezzanines. The classical
orders are applied correctly: Doric to the ground floor, Ionic and
Corinthian to the upper ones. The land façade to the square is less
important, but impressively detailed, with two tall, grand *trifore* to the
piani nobili.

Off the N side of the square is Calle Pezzana; at the end, on the
right, is **Palazzo Sanudo** (SP 2165), fifteenth-century *gotico fiorito*,
with tripartite symmetrical plan and water façade. On the rear
façade, towards the courtyard, are vestiges of an earlier Venetian-
Byzantine *fondaco*.

Back in the square, the most notable palaces on the E side are the
two contiguous **Palazzi Soranzo** (SP 2169 and 2170–71), that on the

Palazzi Soranzo, Campo San Polo, *circa* 1380–1420

left, the *casa vecchia*, earlier than the other. The refined façades follow
the gentle curve of the *rio* that formerly edged the square.
Interesting differences of detail between the two: the first house is
late fourteenth century, and has a narrower plan and façade than the
other, with a courtyard on the right side and a long, narrow *androne*;
the internal stair rises adjacent to the courtyard. On the *piano nobile*
the *portego* widens towards the façade, to form an ∟-shaped plan,
with a generous loggia lit by a *quadrifora*. Two square portals give
access to the two *piani nobili*; above their architraves are two
Romanesque stone animals. The upper façade has transitional
elements marking the beginning of the final *gotico fiorito* stage, like
the roundels and square outer frames to the main widows.

The right palace has a shallower plan but is much broader, with a
generous central *androne* and *portego*, widening towards the canal at
the rear. The main stair follows the medieval tradition, and rises
in two long flights on two sides of the courtyard. This palace is
probably *circa* 1420, fully *gotico fiorito*. Its single entrance has a curved
lunette above the square portal, flanked by rectangular *bifore*. On the
piano nobile: a fine six-light window to the main hall, attached to

two flanking single lights, giving the appearance of an eight-light window. The decorative paterae are more disciplined than those in the left house, and the capitals are particularly rich. In the centre of the *polifora* are the Soranzo arms. The upper floor is much more modest, with a central *quadrifora*. The façade is said to have been frescoed by Giorgione. Both rear façades to Rio de la Madoneta were modernised in the sixteenth century, with a Lombard Renaissance appearance. The interiors are richly decorated, with paintings by Amigoni, Fontebasso and Gregorio Lazzarini. The palaces are still owned by the Soranzo.

Immediately N is **Palazzo Balbi** (SP 2172), Gothic, with a narrow four-storey *campo* façade. The offset *quadrifora* represents the long, very narrow *portego*. Immediate N again is **Palazzo Donà** (SP 2177); an unusual Gothic portal (early fourteenth century), incorporating a frieze depicting animals. The attractive courtyard has a colonnade and *barbacani* supporting the upper floors, and a fine four-light window, probably late thirteenth century; an open Gothic stair.

Taking the short Rio Terà out of the NE corner of the square, follow the *calle* to Ponte de Ca' Bernardo. On the left is the fine late Gothic **Palazzo Bernardo** (SP 2184 and 2195), with a long flank façade to the *calle* and water façade to the NW. Built by Alvise Bernardo *circa* 1450, the *rio* façade is good *gotico fiorito*, with a splendid watergate. Two land gates, one along the *calle*, the other on the bridge. The plan is tripartite and conventional, with a generous central hall; at the rear is a large square courtyard. Both *piani nobili* are lit by fine multi-light windows on the canal façade, richly detailed. In the centre of the lower *quadrifora* is the family arms.

5 FROM CAMPO SAN BOLDÙ TO SAN GIOVANNI EVANGELISTA

Just across the bridge on the right is **Palazzetto Contarini Querini** (SP 2196), also fifteenth-century Gothic, with two *quadrifore* to the main halls; the return façade to Rio de San Boldù is sixteenth-century Renaissance. Continue NW along Calle del Scaleter, then turn right (Rio Terà Secondo) and then left into Campo San Boldù. On the E side is the seventeenth-century **Palazzo Grioni** (SP 2271), modernised in the eighteenth century, with two *trifore* to the main halls. To the right is a campanile, all that survives of San Boldù, founded in the eleventh century, but closed in 1805 and demolished shortly thereafter. Nearby, at Ponte del Parucheta (SP 2281), is a garden marking the site of the former **Palazzo Grimani**, modernised by Francesco Contin in the seventeenth century, but demolished in the early nineteenth; part of the water façade survives. Take Rio Terà Primo southwards; at the corner of Rio Terà Secondo is **Palazzo Soranzo Pisani** (SP 2278), Gothic, although little remains visible other than the unusual chamfered corner façade, with the portal and a tall Gothic window above, incorporating a high-level quatrefoil. Above the doorway: fourteenth-century Soranzo and Pisani arms. Opposite, on Ramo Astori, is **Palazzo Astori** (SP 2313), Gothic but modernised in the Baroque era; the birthplace of Daniele Manin. Continuing SW, we enter Campo Sant'Agostin. The church was founded in 959, and was rebuilt on several occasions; it survived as a parish foundation until 1808; it was later deconsecrated and in 1873 was demolished.

Continue down Calle de la Chiesa, and cross the Campielo diagonally towards the NW; from the bridge, looking N, is the imposing canal façade of **Palazzo Morosini Zane Venier Collalto** (SP 2360). Immediately adjacent to the bridge (right) is **Palazzo Cicogna Loredan Giustinian** (SP 2351); sixteenth century, using an earlier structure. By the early nineteenth century it was owned by the Loredan, who still own part of the palace. The interior contains rich stucco decoration and *terrazzo* floors. Cross the bridge; continue under the *sotoportego* into Calle de la Vida, then right into Calle Collalto; at the N end is the land gate to Palazzo Collalto. It was begun in 1665 by Longhena for Domenico Zane. After Longhena's death in 1682, work continued on the interior under Gaspari. There are two canal façades, one to Rio de San Giacomo, the other to Rio de Sant'Agostin. The house had a large garden, in which a *casinò* was also built by Gaspari; a second garden building was then built to house the Zane's extensive library. The *casinò* was completed by Domenico Rossi in 1695–7. The house passed to the Collalto in 1784; for the last century or so it has been used as a technical institute.

Longhena retained much of an earlier structure; the *androne* is very broad, with a colonnade down the centre, supporting the equally broad *portego* above. The imposing canal façades are both richly detailed, all clad in stone; two *piani nobili*. The main façade has paired watergates and a rusticated basement, while tall Ionic pilasters frame the *portego* windows. Today the garden is lost, but the library fabric survives (SP 2368), with a *trifora* to the canal façade.

Return down Calle Collato, and turn right along Calle de la Vida, into **Campo San Stin**. The title is a corruption of Steffanino, in the diminutive, to distinguish the former church from the monastery of Santo Stefano. San Stin was founded in the tenth century, but was closed in 1810, and soon demolished. Around the square are typical vernacular houses and apartments. Leave by Calle del Tabacco near the NW corner; turn right into Calle del Magazen. After a few metres we reach Campielo San Giovanni Evangelista, flanked by the eponymous church and Scuola Grande.

San Giovanni Evangelista was founded by the Badoer in 970; largely rebuilt 1443–64, but partially modernised in the late sixteenth century under Simon Sorella, and again in 1759 by Maccaruzzi. The latter retained the Gothic chancel, with its cross-vaulted apse, but opened the nave by removing the side aisles to create a single large rectangular space, with a flat compartmented ceiling. Off the right side of the nave are two deep chapels. That dedicated to San Carlo (St Charles Borromeo) was originally the Cappella de la Croce, when a relic of the Cross was kept here; today it is in the adjacent Scuola. The high altarpiece is by Liberi. The modest adjacent campanile is also by Maccaruzzi.

Between the church and the Scuola Grande is a broad *campielo*, which was transformed *circa* 1481 to achieve its present rich appearance. The work is almost always attributed to Pietro Lombardo, and consisted of the insertion of a richly decorated transverse marble screen, dividing the *campielo* into two parts, and the cladding of the adjacent flank walls with an applied order of rich pilasters and cornices. The screen is a remarkable example of urban intervention, creating a formal approach to the Scuola, and a civic sense of arrival. It has three bays, the larger central one with an open portal, flanked by two rectangular 'windows'. The portal is capped by a radiused pediment originally containing a relief of the titular saint (today in the Berlin Museum). In its place is an eagle, symbol of St John the Evangelist. On the outer corners of the screen: two kneeling angels.

The **Scuola Grande de San Giovanni Evangelista** was founded in 1261, and originally based at Sant'Aponal. It was relocated here in 1301, and was first based within the adjacent church. In the fourteenth century the confraternity built its own accommodation on this long, narrow site. It was suppressed by Napoleon in 1797, but in 1857 a new confraternity was established here, and in 1929 it became an *arciconfraternità*, incorporating a society of building crafts; it thrives today.

Scuola Grande di San Giovanni
Evangelista: detail of the central arch of
the entrance screen; generally attributed
to Pietro Lombardo, *circa* 1481

Scuola Grande di San Giovanni
Evangelista: detail of flanking 'window'
in the entrance screen

The entrance is a richly detailed portal in the NW corner of the
campielo, often said to be by Codussi. The main lower hall was
remodelled in 1415–21, when a row of columns was inserted down
the centre to support the floor of the upper hall; it survives mostly
unaltered. The splendid staircase rising along the back wall was
begun by Codussi in 1498, based on his earlier stair for the Scuola
Grande di San Marco. It is more grandiose, although the plan is
similar, with two long flights rising from each end of the lower halls
to meet in the middle at the top landing. The intermediate landings
and the top landing all have cupolas on pendentives; at the top a
grand portal to the upper *sala capitolare*. The detailing is rich but
disciplined, with fluted Corinthian pilasters and square coffering to
the arch soffits.

The upper hall may also have been remodelled by Codussi, but
was modernised again by Massari in 1727, who later installed a rich
marble floor (1752) and an equally rich coffered and gilded ceiling.
The ceiling paintings are by Guarana, Marieschi and Diziani, with

two by G.D. Tiepolo. On the walls: paintings of the life of John the Baptist, including three by Domenico Tintoretto. In the E wall a doorway leads to the Hall of the Cross, where the sacred relic is kept. The original cycle of paintings that decorated the walls, by Gentile Bellini, Carpaccio and Mansueti, is today in the Accademia. Leading from this hall is the *albergo*, also remodelled by Massari, in 1732. The walls have four paintings by Palma il Giovane; the ceiling was decorated by Titian, but the works are now dispersed.

6   FROM CAMPO SAN STIN TO SAN TOMÀ

Return to Campo San Stin, and take Calle del Spezier out of the E side. To the right are Ramo and Calle Soranzo, at the end of which is **Palazzo Soranzo** (SP 2521 and 2542), fifteenth-century Gothic, with a *quadrifora* and rather archaic windows to the second floor. Returning to Calle del Spezier, turn right; at the E end, left side, just before the bridge, is **Palazzo Molin** (SP 2514), rebuilt in 1806 on the remains of a thirteenth-century house; the façade incorporates eclectic detailing in different styles. Immediately S of the bridge is **Palazzo Donà da le Rose** (SP 2515), with a traditional Renaissance canal façade; the family arms above the watergate.

Return to Campo San Stin, and now take Calle de la Chiesa out of the S side. Directly in front, next to the bridge, is **Palazzo Cassetti** (SP 2557), an impressive seventeenth-century house; the second-floor windows are composed as a Serliana. Immediately to its left is **Palazzo Zen** (SP 2580), *gotico fiorito*, with superimposed *quadrifore*; the rear façade, to Campiello Zen, is sixteenth century. It was the home of Carlo Zeno, the famous admiral, who defeated the Genoese at Chioggia in 1380.

Crossing the bridge, take Fondamenta dei Frari, and at the end, turn left down the Rio Terà. At the far end, a narrow gap leads into Corte Amalteo. **Palazzo Amalteo** (SP 2646) is early seventeenth century, with two water façades and hints of the Baroque. From Corte Amaltea we see the noble canal façade of Sanmicheli's Palazzo Corner. Back in the Rio Terà, turn left down Calle Seconda dei Saoneri to reach Calle dei Saoneri. Turn left to Ponte San Polo; from the bridge (NW) we see the canal façade of **Palazzo Moro Lin** (SP 2672), an interesting transitional work, with late Gothic and early Renaissance features together. The main Renaissance element is the elegant *quadrifora*, surrounded by late Gothic windows. The single

The *sestiere* of San Polo, lining the Grand Canal from Palazzo Pisani Moretta (left) to Ca' Businello (right)

window facing the bridge has a complex stone balcony, a Renaissance version of the Gothic ones at Palazzetto Contarini Fasan.

Returning w along Calle dei Saoneri, turn left down Rio Terà dei Nomboli. Ramo Pisani leads to the land gate of **Palazzo Barbarigo de la Terrazza** (sp 2765), by Bernardino Contin, 1568–9, for Daniele Barbarigo. In 1793 the palace was joined to the adjacent Palazzo Pisani Moretta, when the two clans intermarried. Palazzo Barbarigo has an unusual plan and façade; the narrow Grand Canal façade has a large terrace at the corner of Rio di San Polo. A large watergate in the form of a Serliana, and two *quadrifore*.

Palazzo Pisani Moretta (sp 2766) stands immediately to the w. A fine, harmonious late Gothic canal façade, tripartite and rigorously symmetrical. It was built *circa* 1470 for the Bembo, passing to the Pisani Moretta in 1629. In 1737 the interior was modernised by Tirali, who added a grand staircase; the *portego* became a ballroom, decorated by G. B. Tiepolo, Guarana and Giambattista Piazzetta; further modernisations followed in 1770–73. Today the palace remains the property of the Pisani Giusti. The plan is tripartite and conventional, the superimposed *piani nobili* represented by the two watergates. The canal façade is largely intact, with two fine six-light

Palazzo Pisani Moretta: multi-light windows to the
upper halls, *circa* 1470

windows to the upper halls. The lower has tracery in the Doge's
Palace manner, while the upper has intersecting semicircular arches,
above which are quatrefoils in stone circles.

Inside, Tirali's monumental three-flight stair rises at the N end of
the *androne*; at the top is an impressive portal into the ballroom.
Other halls contain paintings by G. B. Tiepolo and Piazzetta, many
commissioned by Chiara Pisani Moretta in the 1740s.

Immediately w is the sixteenth-century **Palazzo Tiepolo** (SP
2774); a sober, symmetrical façade, originally frescoed by Schiavone.
It was built on the foundations of an earlier house; again
superimposed *piani nobili*, each with a central *quadrifora*. Adjacent to
the w is **Palazzetto Tiepolo** (SP 2781), originally fifteenth-century
Gothic (first *piano nobile*) but modernised in the sixteenth century
(second *piano nobile*). The last of this group is **Palazzo Giustinian
Persico** (SP 2788), reached by land from Campielo Centani, off Calle
dei Nomboli. A large, early Renaissance palace, with a rigorously
symmetrical tripartite canal façade. All these canal façades are best
seen from Sant'Angelo *vaporetto* stop.

At the w end of Calle dei Nomboli, left, is **Palazzetto Centani** (SP 2793–4), generally known as Casa Goldoni, because the famous playwright was born here in 1707. A good medium-sized Gothic house, *circa* 1440, although its plan is unusual, and the façade follows the curve of the canal. It was built by the Rizzo, passing to the Centani, then to the Goldoni. Its condition deteriorated in the nineteenth century, but in 1914 it was bought by a group of citizens to establish a theatre museum here, as it remains today. The canal façade is almost symmetrical, with a single *piano nobile*. The L-shaped plan wraps around the attractive internal courtyard, with its open stair rising on two sides; the original well-head has the Rizzo arms. The land gate gives directly into this courtyard.

Nearby: some interesting early fragments. At SP 2802 is **Palazzo Bosso** or **Bosco**, just across the *calle*, with water façade next to the bridge. A good early thirteenth-century watergate, and a long frieze. The house was altered and extended in the fourteenth century, from which period dates the splendid portal on the bridge, with a high-level quatrefoil. On the left part of the water façade are fourteenth-century windows; an open stair in the courtyard.

Cross Ponte San Tomà and the *campiello*; on the flank wall of the church is a fine Gothic lunette containing a *Madonna de la Misericordia* (*circa* 1345), formerly at the Carità nunnery. Turn left down Calle del Tragheto. **Palazzo Morosini** (SP 2812) is an impressive seventeenth-century house, with a powerfully articulated stone façade in the manner of Longhena, although the architect is not known. At SP 2810 is **Palazzo Marcello dei Leoni**, with Grand Canal façade by the ferry stop. Sixteenth century, but modernised in the seventeenth, with two façades at an obtuse angle. The plan reflects the awkward shape of the site. Its name derives from two Romanesque stone lions on the façade, perhaps from the old church of San Tomà.

Return to Campielo San Tomà, and turn NW into the small, attractive square. The church occupies the SE end.

San Tomà (Tommaso) was founded in 917, funded by the Miani family. It underwent many restorations before reconstruction in 1395. It was enlarged in 1508 and modernised again in 1652, when a façade was added by Sardi, perhaps to a design by Longhena; it was a variant of the Palladian temple front. By 1742, however, the church itself had deteriorated, and was completely rebuilt by Francesco Bognolo, including the present façade, 1755. In 1807 its parish status was withdrawn and it became dependent on San Silvestro; in 1810 it was re-established as an oratory.

The rather heavy stone façade has two orders and three bays, the larger central bay defined by paired Corinthian columns, the outer bays by pilasters. The large doorway is surmounted by a radiused pediment, while the flanking bays have niches with statues. The façade is crowned by a small pediment, with statues on the skyline. The interior: a broad nave without aisles, and a vaulted ceiling. In the centre is a fresco of the martyrdom of St Thomas by Guarana. In the chancel: a collection of relics; flanking the altar are *St Peter* and *St Thomas* by Campagna.

On the sw side of the square are attractive vernacular houses. Opposite the church, at the nw end, is the **Scuola dei Calegheri** (SP 2857), the former shoemakers' guildhall (1478); a symmetrical façade, capped by a pitched roof. The principal feature is the fine relief sculpture above the central doorway, generally believed to be an early work by Pietro Lombardo; it depicts St Mark healing the cobbler Anianus, and retains some original colouring. The upper hall has two large Renaissance windows; in the centre is a fourteenth-century *Madonna de la Misericordia*, from the lost Servi church.

Take Calle del Campaniel next to the sw corner of the church, and then Calle del Tragheto Vecchio. At the end on the left is **Palazzetto Dolfin** (SP 2878), a modest house with Gothic and Renaissance elements. On the other side of the calle, by the *vaporetto* stop, is the seventeenth-century **Palazzo Dandolo Paolucci** (SP 2879), with a markedly asymmetrical Grand Canal façade. Immediate to the sw (reached by Calle Civran, off Calle del Campaniel) is **Palazzo Civran Grimani** (SP 2896), an imposing house with a rear garden. It was rebuilt *circa* 1709, but extensively modernised in 1720–40. The fine stone Neo-classical façade has been attributed to Massari. Its lower two floors are rusticated, while the *piano nobile* has seven single-light windows, divided by pilasters, and a full-width stone balcony.

At the sw end of Calle del Campaniel is Ponte de la Frescada. Next to the bridge, at SP 2901, is **Palazzetto Madona**, an attractive sixteenth-century house, with a first-floor *quadrifora*. On the same quay, at SP 2925: another house of similar date and appearance. At the nw end of Fondamenta del Forner is Ponte de la Dona Onesta. On the corner (SP 2933–4) is **Palazzetto Lipoli**, again sixteenth century, whose carved stone figure of a woman's head (the honest woman) gives its name to the bridge.

Continue along the Fondamenta de la Dona Onesta and turn right along Calle de Ca' Lipoli, into the s corner of Campo dei Frari.

The square is really a series of linked spaces, wrapped around the enormous form of the Frari church. Walk NE down the length of the church towards Ponte dei Frari at the far end. The bridge was built by the Franciscans in 1428, but rebuilt in the nineteenth century. On the right, SP 2999, is the former **Scuola de la Passione.** The foundation date is unknown, but the Scuola moved here in 1572, when it bought the hall formerly used by the Mercanti. Badly damaged by fire in 1587, it was rebuilt on a larger scale. The Palladian *campo* façade is a robust symmetrical composition, with a central doorway; on the *piano nobile* are three large pedimented windows. The ceiling of the first-floor hall was decorated with nine panels of the Resurrection by Palma il Giovane. The Scuola was suppressed in 1806 and the paintings dispersed. Today it is a private house.

Together with the contemporary Santi Giovanni e Paolo, the **Frari (Santa Maria Gloriosa dei Frari)** is the greatest Gothic church in the city. The Friars Minor or Franciscans arrived in Venice *circa* 1222; St Francis (1182–1226) is popularly believed to have founded the friary of San Francesco del Deserto, in the northern lagoon. In 1236 Doge Jacopo Tiepolo arranged the donation of a large area of low-lying land (including a pond, the Lago Badoer), and the first church was begun in 1250; it was consecrated in 1280, and had a reverse orientation to the present church. It soon became too small, and in 1330 a much larger church was planned, patronised by wealthy nobles such as the Gradenigo and Giustinian. Construction began with the apses at the W end, while the old church continued in use at the E end. The apses were complete *circa* 1360, and in 1361 the massive campanile was begun, the tallest in Venice other than that of San Marco; it was complete in 1396.

By the 1390s the transepts were under construction and the nave was begun. By 1415 the old church was demolished to complete the E end of the nave, structurally complete by *circa* 1440. The Corner Chapel was added in 1417, the Miani Chapel in 1432–4. In 1468 the rich, complex, wooden choir was complete. In the following year the high altar was consecrated, and in 1475 the rich marble choirscreen was finished. Only in 1492 was the entire church consecrated; it has remained almost unaltered.

The plan is a Latin cross, with a six-bay nave flanked by lower, narrower aisles. At the crossing are the transepts, each two bays long. The nave width continues into the chancel, which has a square plan; beyond is the apse, with six facets. Flanking the chancel are three smaller faceted chapels on each side. The campanile stands adjacent to the left transept. The overall external length of the church is approximately 102 metres (335 ft), the width across the transepts is 51 metres (158 ft), and the height of the nave vault is 30 metres (91 ft).

The exterior appears homogeneous, despite the century-long construction period, typically late Venetian Gothic, all brick, with stone detailing. The main façade was the last element to be completed, and its tripartite form reflects the church behind; the pilasters terminate with stone pinnacled aedicules, with a taller one in the centre. The Istrian stone portal is *gotico fiorito*, with Christ at the top (by Vittoria), and the Virgin and St Francis on each side, perhaps by Bartolomeo Bon. The left flank to the square has a tall traceried window to each bay, and a much shorter one to each clerestory bay. Attached to the left aisle is the Miani Chapel, with a fine façade, a smaller version of that of the church itself. The beautiful portal has a relief of St Peter in the lunette, with the Redeemer at the top; attributed to the Bon or the dalle Masegne. At the end of the Miani Chapel rises the majestic brick campanile, 90 metres (280 ft) high, with three orders; above the three-light bell-chamber is an octagonal tambour. Beyond the campanile is the *St Ambrose* portal, giving access to the left transept. Adjacent again is the small projecting Corner Chapel, with a fine portal, that of St Mark, with luxuriant wave decoration and an exceptional relief of the Virgin enthroned, attributed variously to Jacopo della Quercia, Niccolò Lamberti and Bartolomeo Bon; at the apex is the Eternal Father.

Rounding the sw corner we reach the imposing apses; each of the smaller apse chapels has two facets; in the centre is the six-faceted central apse. It has two orders, divided by a bold cornice; both have tall lancets to each facet, with traceried heads.

The interior is vast, simple and imposing, designed to accommodate large numbers of worshippers attending the mendicant friars' sermons. Its structure is very simple: huge, plain, stone cylindrical piers with foliage capitals and octagonal cornices. Above the pointed arches rises the plain brick clerestory. Stability is reinforced by longitudinal timber tie beams above the capitals, and lateral ties at two levels. The ceilings throughout are simple cross-vaults; above them, massive timber trusses support the outer roof. The only more elaborate ceiling is that to the chancel, with its radiating ribs. The last one-and-a-half bays of the nave are occupied by the choir (see below).

The Frari: exterior of the Miani Chapel, 1432–4;
the portal has sculptures attributed to Bartolomeo
Bon and the dalle Masegne

The church contains many notable monuments and works of art.
From the inner face of the main façade: above the portal: Baroque
monument to Girolamo Grimani (+1668); left side: monument to
Alvise Pasqualigo (+1528), perhaps by Lorenzo Bregno. Right side:
monument to Pietro Bernardo (+1538), very rich, perhaps by Tullio
Lombardo.

Right aisle, first bay: altar of St Anthony of Padua, a complex
Baroque work by Longhena, *circa* 1663. Second bay: monument to
Titian, a cold, ponderous work by Luigi and Pietro Zandomenighi
(1838–52), in the form of a triumphal arch on four Corinthian

The Frari: detail of the *St Mark* portal to the Corner Chapel, *circa* 1417; exceptionally fine sculptures, attributed variously to Jacopo della Quercia, Niccolò Lamberti and Bartolomeo Bon

columns. Titian himself is flanked by figures representing Painting, Writing, Sculpture and Architecture. Third bay: Zeno Valier altar; altarpiece by Giuseppe Salviati (1548). Fourth bay: Zane family altar, by Vittoria. Fifth bay: Pesaro family altar; altarpiece: *St Catherine of Alexandria* by Palma il Giovane. Sixth bay: above the cloister door is a sarcophagus once containing the remains of Carmagnola, the famous *condottiere*, executed for treason in 1432.

Right transept, right wall: monument to Jacopo Marcello (+1434), a refined work attributed to Pietro Lombardo. On the same wall: fresco by Bernardo Licinio (fifteenth century) of five early Franciscan martyrs. End wall: monument to Fra Pacifico, 1437, a rich late Gothic work attributed to Rosso Fiorentino, with the *Baptism of Christ* in the lunette, and sumptuous wave decoration to the extrados. Around the sacristy doorway: monument to Benedetto Pesaro (+1503); a refined classical work, with Lorenzo Bregno's figure above the doorway. At high level, left side: wooden equestrian monument to Paolo Savelli (+1405), the oldest in Venice, attributed to Jacopo della Quercia.

The sacristy (*circa* 1478) has a faceted apse onto Campo San Rocco. Right wall: marble tabernacle brought from Constantinople in 1479, probably by Tullio Lombardo. In the apse: Pesaro Chapel, with an exceptionally fine triptych of the Virgin and Child flanked by *SS Nicholas, Peter, Benedict and Mark*, by Giovanni Bellini, 1488. The original frame is by Jacopo da Faenza. Opposite the entrance: an extraordinarily complex Baroque altar of reliquaries by Andrea Brustolon, 1711. On the left wall: a seventeenth-century clock by Francesco Pianta.

The large simple chapter hall, late fourteenth century, encloses part of the first cloister. Inside: tomb of Doge Francesco Dandolo (+1339).

Back in the church: right apse, right chapel: of the Bernardo family; altarpiece: *Virgin and Child with Saints* by Bartolomeo Vivarini, 1482, in its rich original frame. Right wall: monument to Girolamo and Lorenzo Bernardo, attributed to the dalle Masegne.

Second chapel (of the Sacrament): right wall: monument to Duccio Alberti (+1336). Third chapel: that of the Florentines: on the altar: the remarkably haunting painted and gilded *John the Baptist* by Donatello (1451), his only surviving work in Venice.

Main chancel: the chancel is an imposing composition, with tall lancet windows. Right side wall: monument to Doge Francesco Foscari (+1457), a rich, complex, late Gothic work, with Renaissance influences, often attributed to Antonio and Paolo Bregno. The high altar: the altarpiece is Titian's magnificent *Assumption*, 1516–18, one of his most famous and remarkable works. Its dramatic and unusual composition was initially highly controversial, but is perfectly integrated into its context, terminating the axis down the choir with its powerful *chiaroscuro*. It has three orders or zones, the lowermost containing the Apostles, the central one the Virgin surrounded by angels; at the top is the Eternal Father. Its Corinthian frame has outer figures by Lorenzo Bregno. Left wall: monument to Doge Niccolò Tron (+1473), a refined early Renaissance masterpiece by Antonio Rizzo; the complex composition has four orders above a plinth, surmounted by a lunette. The flanking pilasters have niches with figures of warriors, while the doge stands in the centre of the lower order. His bier is in the upper centre, above which is a row of five niches containing figures of the Virtues.

Chapels left of the chancel: first chapel, that of St Francis, with altarpiece by Bernardo Licinio, 1524. At the sides: marble figures of St Francis and St Helena by Vittoria, 1585. Right wall: *St Francis* by

Palma il Giovane, 1598. Second chapel, that of St Michael: on the altar are gilded wooded statues of saints, fifteenth century. Third chapel, of the Milanesi, established here in 1361: painted and gilded altarpiece begun by Alvise Vivarini (+1503), completed by Marco Basaiti; it represents St Ambrose, patron of Milan. In the floor: modern plaque to the composer Claudio Monteverdi (+1643).

Corner Chapel: opposite the entrance: elegant early Renaissance monument to Federico Corner. Baptismal font: figure of St John the Baptist, a fine work by Jacopo Sansovino. On the high altar: triptych by Bartolomeo Vivarini, 1474: *St Mark Flanked by Saints*, set in a rich complex frame. On the façade inner wall: *Descent of Christ into Limbo* by Palma il Giovane.

Left transept: fourteenth-century wooded carved dossal in twenty-one panels.

Left aisle, sixth bay: a huge painting of Franciscan saints by Pietro Negri, 1670. Fifth bay: entrance to the Miani Chapel. In the chapel: late Gothic sarcophagus of Pietro Miani, perhaps by the dalle Masegne workshop. The marble altarpiece is another fine late Gothic work, with two rows each of five niches, with statues set into them. Above the *campo* doorway is a *Crucifixion*, occasionally attributed to Titian.

Left aisle, fourth bay: the Pesaro family altar, with a splendid altarpiece by Titian, commissioned in 1519. The composition is dramatic and dynamic, with the Virgin and Child below right, St Peter in the centre and the Pesaro family in the lower corners; the background is dominated by two huge painted columns. The altar itself is a Renaissance work, perhaps by Pietro Lombardo's shop.

Left aisle, third bay: massive monument to Doge Giovanni Pesaro (+1659), by Longhena, *circa* 1669. It has two orders and three bays; the lower order has four huge figures of Moors supporting the massive central architrave, while the upper order has the doge enthroned, flanked by black marble columns and figures of Virtues.

Left aisle, second bay: extraordinary pyramidal monument to Canova (+1822), designed by Canova himself and originally intended to be dedicated to Titian. It was carved by Canova's own students. The Neo-classical figures represent Painting, Sculpture and Architecture, accompanied by a large winged Venetian lion.

Left aisle, first bay: altar of the *Crucifixion*, by Longhena, 1672, with sculpture by Giusto Le Court.

The friars' choir: consists of two discrete elements, the choirstalls and the marble screen across the front. The magnificent carved wooden stalls are the finest in the city, 124 stalls in three rows, on each side of the central aisle. They were carved by the Cozzi family, completed in 1468. On the back wall are intarsia relief panels, two in each stall, 100 in all, set into scalloped niches, while the stalls are divided by complex brackets. The marble screen was completed *circa* 1475; the first stage is sometimes attributed to Bartolomeo Bon (+*circa* 1464), and it is generally believed to have been completed by the Lombardo shop. The style is transitional Gothic/Renaissance, and the screen has a large central arched opening, flanked by four bays on each side. The panels contain figures of the Prophets. Above the parapet on each side of the arch are the Apostles, and in the centre at high level is a bronze Crucifixion. Above the outer corners are small marble pulpits.

The conventual buildings: an extensive complex NW of the church, built around two large cloisters. That adjacent to the church is the Chiostro della Santissima Trinità, comprehensively modernised in the seventeenth century, with a new colonnaded cloister, eleven bays to each face. It is surmounted by a terrace. The monumental Baroque well-head is from 1713. The second cloister, of St Anthony, has a simple Renaissance appearance, again eleven bays square, with square stone piers supporting semicircular arches. Two floors of accommodation above, originally containing the friars' cells. The other monastic accommodation is located in a block between the two cloisters, and another E of the first one, where the main refectory is located; a large, spacious, late Gothic six-bay hall, with a central colonnade, today the reading room of the Archivio di Stato.

The friary was suppressed by Napoleon, and the church 'relegated' to parish status. In 1815 it was decided to house the State Archives of the Republic here, and a new block was built along Rio Terà di San Tomà to provide further accommodation. Today this unique, priceless archive occupies most of the huge monastic complex, with several million documents in its 300 rooms. The present entrance is on the square at SP 3002.

8 SAN ROCCO: THE CHURCH AND SCUOLA GRANDE

To complete the itinerary of the *sestiere*, return to the western apses of the great church, and continue into Campo San Rocco. The titular church is at the NW end, and the monumental Scuola Grande is on the left side. On the right is the modest, original **Scuola**

San Rocco: façade by Giorgio Fossati and Bernardino Maccaruzzi, 1771

Vecchia de San Rocco, 1478; a simple structure that remained the Scuola's meeting hall until the new one was completed. Adjacent is the church, established in 1489 on land acquired from the adjacent friary. Four years earlier the body of the saint, the patron of plague sufferers, had been brought here from Lombardy; the church was built by Bon the Bergamasco to house his remains. It was completed *circa* 1508, but was largely rebuilt by Scalfarotto after 1725, by which date it was in a ruinous condition. The only part unaffected was the eastern apse. The façade was dismantled and Bon's portal reassembled on the left flank, where it remains. The new façade is by Giorgio Fossati and Bernardino Maccaruzzi, 1771. It is strongly articulated, all in stone, and relates to the two orders of the adjacent Scuola. Its three bays are defined by free-standing Corinthian columns, the outer bays containing niches with statues of saints. More statues in the upper order and three on the skyline, all by Morleiter. Scalfarotto's interior has a single broad nave; Corinthian pilasters articulate the side walls, and the vaulted plastered ceiling has high-level thermal windows. The fine high altar survives from Bon's church, a form of triumphal arch, with rich porphyry and *verde antico* marble. In the centre is the sarcophagus with the venerated remains of the saint. The church contains a number of notable paintings by Tintoretto, Sebastiano Ricci and Pordenone.

The **Scuola Grande de San Rocco** is one of the most impressive of the *scuole grandi*, renowned for the prodigious cycles of paintings by Tintoretto with which it is decorated. The purchase of the site was completed in 1516; shortly afterwards Pietro Bon was appointed *proto*. The construction process, however, was complex and highly contentious. The plan is similar to those of the earlier *scuole grandi*, with two large superimposed halls. One end faces the square, while at the other is a loggia facing Rio de la Frescada. The stair rises on the NW side. The small *albergo* wing is at one end, also facing the square. The lower hall was built 1517–24; by 1524 the lower order of the *campo* façade was also complete. The design of the stair was a long, complex process, culminating in Bon's dismissal (or resignation) in 1524, and his replacement by Sante Lombardo, assisted by his father, Tullio. The *portegal* towards the canal was designed by yet another master, Zuanne Celestro, a Tuscan, until his dismissal in 1425; the upper part of the canal façade (1526–7) is by Sante Lombardo, who was dismissed in turn in 1527. Five months later, Scarpagnino was employed to complete the remaining works, including the upper windows. By 1537 the *albergo* was completed, but the Scuola decided that the *campo* façade was insufficiently impressive, and yet another master, Guglielmo de' Grigi, added eight free-standing columns in front of the completed façade. In 1534 the Scuola acquired additional land on the W side, thus allowing a completely new staircase design to be developed. In 1541 a model was made of Scarpagnino's proposal, a design never seen in the city before: two parallel, outer, lower flights, meeting at a broad half-landing, from which a central flight continued up between the lower ones, to the top landing. In 1545 the earlier staircase was demolished and the new one begun. Completion of the interior of the *sala capitolare* took place at the same time; the *albergo* doorway was completed *circa* 1547, the last element before Scarpagnino's death two years later. By 1557 the stairs were complete and the high altar was installed. Finally, in 1559–60 the chapter hall and stair block were roofed.

The impressive façade dominates the square, the three left bays representing the larger wing, with the *androne* and *sala capitolare*, the two right-hand bays the *albergo*. A fine portal in the centre of the left wing, decorated with rare marbles, gives direct access into the *androne*; it is framed by Corinthian columns supporting a triangular

Scuola Grande di San Rocco: detail of
first-floor window to the main façade;
by Scarpagnino, *circa* 1527

Scuola Grande di San Rocco: upper
canal façade by Sante Lombardo,
1526–7

pediment. The lower order, with Codussian windows, is by Bon, the
upper by Scarpagnino. The smaller right portal gives access to the
albergo wing. The first-floor fenestration is different, with paired
arched windows, framed by Corinthian columns and surmounted by
pediments. De' Grigi's eight outer columns have rich capitals,
supporting a boldly overhanging roof cornice. The rear, canal façade
has a tall, spacious three-bay ground-floor loggia, through which
passes a public street; the refined upper order (by Sante Lombardo) is
again all in stone, with three bays defined by fluted Corinthian
pilasters. In the centre an aedicule indicates the location of the high
altar in the chapter hall inside.

The plan has three elements: the large rectangular chapter hall
block; the block containing the stairs; and the *albergo* wing. The
androne is divided into three aisles by two rows of tall stone columns
on plinths, with six bays. The capitals support timber *barbacani*, which,
in turn, carry a massive continuous timber architrave supporting the
chapter hall floor. On the right side, two triumphal arches lead to

the grand processional staircase. At the far end is the altar by
Campagna, 1587. The *androne* is decorated with eight large canvases
by Tintoretto, 1581–7. Left wall: the *Annunciation, Epiphany, Flight to
Egypt, Slaughter of the Innocents, Mary Magdalene*. Right wall: *St Mary of
Egypt*, the *Circumcision*, the *Assumption*. All are late works in his
characteristic style, with free, fluid brushwork and dramatic lighting.

The main staircase has a plain barrel-vaulted ceiling; above the
half-landing is a small cupola. On the walls of the broad upper flight:
large canvases by Zanchi (*The Plague of 1630*, 1666) and Negri (1673).

The magnificent chapter hall is almost entirely decorated by
Tintoretto; around the walls are twelve New Testament scenes, with
thirteen Old Testament scenes in the richly carved gilded and
coffered ceiling. The ceiling cycle was painted first (1575–8), followed
by those to the walls (complete in 1581). Both exhibit extraordinarily
inventive and expressive techniques. Ceiling paintings (facing the
high altar): right side: the *Crossing of the Red Sea, Jacob's Ladder, Elijah
Distributing Bread*. Central row: *Adam and Eve (Original Sin), Moses
Striking Water from the Rock, Jonah Escaping the Belly of the Whale,
Moses and the Bronze Serpent*, the *Sacrifice of Isaac*, the *Delivery of
Manna from the Sky, Passover*. Left side: *God Appearing to Moses*, the
Vision of Ezekiel, Elijah Saved from Famine.

The wall paintings, clockwise, from the NW corner, near the *albergo*
entrance: NE wall: *St Roch, St Sebastian*. SE wall: *Christ in the Manger,
Christ's Baptism*, the *Resurrection, Sermon in the Garden*, the *Last Supper*.
SW wall: the high altar (see below). NW wall: the *Miracles of Loaves and
Fishes, Resurrection of Lazarus*, the *Ascension*, the *Pool at Bethesda, Christ
Tempted by Satan*. Below this last is Tintoretto's self-portrait, 1573.

The high altar is by Francesco di Bernardino, 1588; in the centre:
the *Glory of St Roch* by Tintoretto, flanked by *St Sebastian* and *St
John the Baptist*, both by Campagna. In the sanctuary are several
pictures on easels, including Titian's *Annunciation*, Tintoretto's
Visitation and two youthful works by G. B. Tiepolo.

Around the hall walls are richly carved seventeenth-century timber
dossals by Francesco Pianta; one represents a famous caricature of
Tintoretto.

The *albergo* has a square plan, with a grand entrance portal. In
1564 the board decided on a competition for the ceiling decoration,
St Roch in Glory. The competitors were Veronese, Salviati, Zuccari
and Tintoretto; the last won – notoriously – by producing a
completed painting instead of the preliminary sketches that had been
stipulated; he offered it to the board free. Despite the others'

Castelforte San Rocco, by Scarpagnino, 1547–*circa* 1550

protestations, Tintoretto was then commissioned to complete the *albergo*'s decoration. The back wall is filled by the huge, imposing *Crucifixion*, 1565; on the side walls are *Prophets*; on the entrance wall, facing the *Crucifixion*, are: *Christ before Pilate,* the *Crown of Thorns* and *Christ Going to Calvary.* The rich ceiling has allegorical figures of the *scuole grandi* surrounding the central *St Roch in Glory.* On an easel, usually in the *albergo*, is the famous *Christ Carrying the Cross*, attributed to either Titian or Giorgione.

Immediately NW of the Scuola Grande is the impressive apartment block known as **Castelforte San Rocco** (SP 3105–8). It was designed by Scarpagnino for the Scuola, following a competition, to contain large apartments for commercial rent; it was begun in 1547. The block has a ground floor, mezzanine, two *piani nobili* and an attic. The ingenious plan contains four sizeable apartments, each with half of a *piano nobile* and half a mezzanine, either above or below the main floor. The ground floor contains four independent entrance halls and staircases. Each principal storey has a long *portego*, indicated on the façade by *trifore.* The Scuola became immensely wealthy, and developed many commercial housing schemes such as this (as well as charitable almshouses), all distinguished by a plaque with the monogram 'SR' set into a frame.

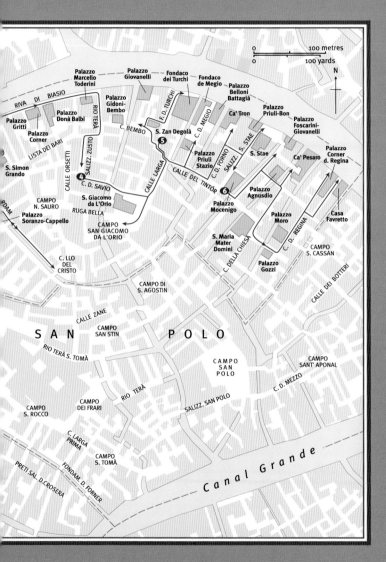

Palazzo
Marcello
Toderini

Palazzo
Giovanelli

Fondaco
dei Turchi

Fondaco
de Megio

Palazzo
Belloni
Battagià

Palazzo
Gidoni-
Bembo

Ca' Tron

Palazzo
Priuli-Bon

Palazzo
Foscarini-
Giovanelli

RIVA   DI   BIASIO

Palazzo
Donà Balbi

RIO TERÀ

F. D. TURCHI

C. D. MEGIO

Palazzo
Gritti

Palazzo
Corner

C. BEMBO

S. Zan Degolà

S. STAE

Palazzo
Corner
d. Regina

Ca' Pesaro

S. Stae

LISTA DEI BARI

CALLE ORSETTI

SALIZZ. JUSTO

❺

Palazzo
Priuli
Stazio

C. D. FORNO

SALIZZ.

S. Simon
Grando

❹

C. D. SAVIO

CALLE DEL TINTÒR

❻

Palazzo
Agnusdio

S. Giacomo
da L'Orio

CALLE LARGA

Palazzo
Mocenigo

CAMPO
N. SAURO

RUGA BELLA

Palazzo
Moro

Casa
Favretto

Palazzo
Soranzo-Cappello

CAMPO
SAN GIACOMO
DA L'ORIO

C. D. REGINA

CAMPO
S. CASSAN

C. LLO
DEL
CRISTO

S. Maria
Mater
Domini

CALLE DEI BOTTERI

CAMPO DI
S. AGOSTIN

C. DELLA CHIESA

Palazzo
Gozzi

CALLE ZANE

CAMPO
SAN STIN

S A N   P O L O

RIO TERÀ S. TOMÀ

CAMPO
SANT' APONAL

CAMPO
SAN
POLO

C. D. MEZZO

RIO TERÀ

CAMPO
DEI FRARI

SALIZZ. SAN POLO

CAMPO
S. ROCCO

C. LARGA
PRIMA

CAMPO
S. TOMÀ

FONDAM. D. FORNER

PRETI SAL. D. CROSERA

C a n a l   G r a n d e

0   100 metres

0   100 yards

N

Santa Croce

Sestiere of Santa Croce

The smallest *sestiere*, and one of extreme contrasts. The E part is bordered by the Grand Canal to the N, and to the S and SE by the *sestiere* of San Polo. Its general 'grain' is typical of the historic centre as a whole, with island parishes (San Simon Piccolo, San Simon Grando, San Zan Degolà, San Stae) along the S bank of the Grand Canal, and one larger hub, San Giacomo da l'Orio, in the centre of the district. This historic zone extends as far W as the Papadopoli Gardens. The area further W is quite different, dominated by the modern transport interchange of Piazzale Roma, the bridgehead to the Terraferma, and the docks, the Stazione Marittima. Beyond the docks is the large reclaimed island of Tronchetto, where wholesale markets are located. In the SW corner are the Tereni Nuovi, a zone reclaimed in the late fifteenth and early sixteenth centuries, and developed with a rational plan of rectangular blocks divided by parallel canals. Stranded among the modern developments around Piazzale Roma are the remains of much earlier isolated religious houses: Santa Chiara, Santa Croce (the lost nunnery that gives its name to the *sestiere*) and Sant'Andrea de la Zirada.

The tour begins in the SE corner, at its junction with Dorsoduro.

Facing page: Ca' Pesaro; flank façade, mostly by Gaspari, *circa* 1730

Medieval house on Rio del Gaffaro, with Byzantine arches

I THE TOLENTINI AND THE TERENI NUOVI

The numeration starts at Ponte San Pantalon, and then into
Campielo Mosca, from which the busy Calle dei Vinanti leads w
towards Rio del Malcanton. At sc 34–5 is the seventeenth-century
Palazzo Arnaldi, with land access from Salizada San Pantalon. The
house at the end of the Salizada, on the left, sc 42–50, has a façade
to Rio del Gaffaro incorporating three large Byzantine arches. The
upper parts are mainly fourteenth-century Gothic. On the Salizada
opposite (sc 133) is the former **Scuola dei Laneri**, the wool-
workers' guildhall; an unusual stone façade, rebuilt by Longhena in
1633, after fire damage. The lower order has a six-arch colonnade, in
two groups of three, with original metal grilles. Upstairs: large paired
lights to left and right, with a plain central section, broken by a
small aedicule once containing an image of St Bernardino, the
patron. The attic has Longhena's typical oval windows.

Continuing w, at sc 134a is the notable Gothic **Palazzo Marcello**;
a broad, asymmetrical façade, *circa* 1460. Two elements, with the
portal to the right, and the main *portego*, with a fine *quadrifora*, to the
left. Further w again, at sc 143 is the seventeenth-century **Palazzo
Minotto**, and at sc 151 the fifteenth-century Gothic **Palazzo Odoni**,
again with a good *quadrifora* and balcony. The façade was once
frescoed; in the sixteenth century it was owned by Andrea Odoni, an
antiquarian and friend of Titian and Aretino.

Scuola dei Laneri, remodelled by Longhena, 1631–3

At the w end of Fondamenta Minotto, turn right along Fondamenta dei Tolentini into the square.

San Niccolò da Tolentino (I Tolentini): the regular Theatines were established in Rome in 1524, but following the sack of the city three years later, they sought refuge in Venice. After several moves, they were given a small oratory here. By 1591 funds were amassed to build a larger church and an extensive monastery. Scamozzi was appointed architect, but his relationship with the order deteriorated, culminating in litigation. The Theatines completed the church themselves, consecrated in 1602. The monastery was built at the same time, centred on a large, elegant cloister. In 1671 the church interior was finally complete; in 1701 a bequest from Alvise da Mosto gave funds for the *campo* façade, by Tirali (1706–14), a notable Neo-classical work: an imposing pronaos, based on the temple of Antoninus and Faustina in the Roman Forum.

The façade is raised on steps, with a portico of six giant fluted Corinthian columns, above which is a large pediment. Inside, the nave has a single volume, flanked by chapels, three down each side, divided by cross-walls; large arches join the chapels to the nave. The articulation of Corinthian pilasters supports a bold, continuous trabeation; at high level are large thermal windows. The spacious crossing was originally surmounted by a cupola, removed in the eighteenth century for safety reasons; the pendentives and drum survive. On each side are short square transepts; beyond is a deep chancel, with the free-standing altar towards the front and the choir behind. The altar is by Longhena, 1661.

The interior was elaborated in the eighteenth century, when stucco decoration was added. Right side, first chapel: altarpiece by Sante Peranda. Second chapel, of the Pisani, dedicated to St Charles Borromeo. Third chapel, of the Soranzo: altarpiece again by Peranda. Right transept: Corner family chapel: altarpiece: *Virgin in Glory* by Palma il Giovane. Chancel: high altar: sculpted decoration by Giusto le Court. Right wall: *Annunciation* by Luca Giordano. Left transept: chapel of San Gaetano, richly decorated, again by le Court.

Left aisle, first and second chapels: both decorated by Palma il Giovane and his workshop. Third chapel: decorated by Peranda; altarpiece by Camillo Procaccini.

The conventual buildings are built around the large central cloister, with an additional wing to the SE, formerly containing the refectory below and the library above. The buildings are now the principal base for the IUAV (Istituto Universitario di Architettura di Venezia), the University Institute of Architecture, one of the most prestigious in Europe; its entrance is in Campazzo dei Tolentini. It was extensively modernised and converted by Daniele Calabi (1961–3), with an idiosyncratic new entrance by Carlo Scarpa, 1984.

Opposite the church, across the canal, are the eighteenth-century **Palazzo Papadopoli** (SC 250) and **Palazzo Loredan Condulmer** (SC 251). Return s down the quay, cross Ponte del Gaffaro and continue down Calle de la Cereria. At the end, cross the first and second bridges onto Fondamenta del Pagan. The zone bounded by the parallel canals of Rio de le Burchiele and Rio de Santa Maria Maggiore is the **Tereni Nuovi**, reclaimed from the lagoon *circa* 1480–1500; it covers around 6.5 hectares. The rectangular islets are planned with quays around their perimeter; one, Rio Terà dei Pensieri, was later reclaimed. Despite some early construction, the Tereni were not fully built up until the eighteenth century. The chief developments are:

Apartment block on the w side of Rio Novo (SC 271, etc.); four storeys, late sixteenth century, with ground-floor shops.

Apartment block on Fondamenta de Ca' Rizzi (SC 304–15): a long, substantial development by the Rizzi family, *circa* 1711. Five units or

Left: The Tereni Nuovi: Palazzo Rizzi,
probably *circa* 1720

Above: The Tereni Nuovi: cottages on Rio
de le Burchiele, *circa* 1678

'houses', each identical, and each with a large upper and lower
apartment. **Palazzo Rizzi** (sc 316) stands at the w end of the
terrace; seventeenth century, by the same clan, with a broad,
impressive, symmetrical façade, reminiscent of Longhena.

On the s side of Rio de le Burchiele (sc 390–415) is a long
terrace of simple two-storey cottages, built by the Bernardo before
1678; eleven of the original fourteen survive.

At the w end of the Tereni Nuovi is a square islet containing the
former church of **Santa Maria Maggiore** in the sw corner. It was
begun in 1497 by Franciscans from Sant'Agnese, and complete *circa*
1504. The conventual buildings stood to the n and e. In 1806 the
nunnery was deconsecrated and consigned to the military. In 1914
the monastic buildings were demolished and the present **women's
prison** built (1920–30). By 1961 the church was derelict; a
comprehensive, sensitive restoration was concluded in 1965.

Its basilica plan has a long six-bay nave and lower side aisles; the
square chancel is flanked by chapels. The w façade is of brick, with
two orders divided by a broad stone architrave. In the upper order,
above the Corinthian stone portal, is a large *ocio*. The interior has
long since lost its altars and fittings, which included paintings by
Veronese, Titian and the Bellini, some now in the Accademia. It is

simple but refined: Ionic nave colonnades on plinths, supporting semicircular stone arches. Today it has an open timber truss roof. The chancel is reached by a large stone arch. The late Gothic campanile stands NE of the church.

2   PIAZZALE ROMA AND SAN SIMON PICCOLO

Return E along Rio Terà dei Pensieri, reclaimed in 1840, with seventeenth- and eighteenth-century vernacular terraced housing; turn left down Calle dei Pensieri. Across the canal is the extensive former **Manifattura Tabacchi**, with annexes to both N and S. The original building is by Maccaruzzi, begun 1786, but altered in the nineteenth century; early cast-iron structures within the masonry envelopes. The complex has been converted for the new Cittadella della Giustizia, bringing to one location various judicial functions (courts, tribunals, administration) scattered around the city.

Cross Ponte de le Burchiele onto Fondamenta dei Tabacchi, and continue E and then N on Calle Nova dei Tabacchi; we enter Piazzale Roma. On the NW side is the large **Autorimessa**, multi-storey car park (Eugenio Miozzi, 1933), an important example of 'white modern' architecture; one of the earliest such buildings in Europe. Down its left flank, at the end (left) is **Sant'Andrea de la Zirada**, established as an oratory in 1329; rebuilt in 1475, but the interior was elaborated in the seventeenth century, when a flat ceiling and stucco decoration were added to the nave. It was closed by Napoleon and the monastic buildings demolished; the church façade is typically late Venetian Gothic, tripartite, and capped by a semicircular gable and paired quadrants, like those at Bragora and San Michele. The *fiorito* portal has a relief of St Peter and St Andrew.

The interior retains the *barco*, supported on two Gothic columns with *barbacani*; the face towards the altar was richly decorated in the seventeenth century, with stucco, decorative grilles and paintings. The nave has four side altars, with eighteenth-century marble statues on each. First right altar: *St Nicholas*; second altar: *St Mary Cleophas*. In the chancel: altarpieces by Paris Bordone (right) and Veronese (left). Left side, first altar: *St Andrew*; second altar: *Crucifixion*. The adjacent campanile is also fifteenth century, with a Baroque cupola.

A short distance NE along the quay is the **Chiesa del Nome di Gesù**, a rare nineteenth-century *ospizio* foundation, begun by G. A. Selva in 1815; after his death, it was completed by Antonio Diedo. In

Piazzale Roma: the almost completed new bridge by Santiago Calatrava (2008): beyond: Eugenio Miozzi's Autorimessa, 1933

1846 it became a nunnery. The façade is restrained and Neo-classical; inside, a single nave, with the Apostles in niches around the walls. The side altars have altarpieces by Querena; the tabernacle on the high altar is also by Diedo. Take the adjacent steps up onto the road bridge, and continue NW over Canale Santa Chiara. On the right, towards the Grand Canal, is the former nunnery of **Santa Chiara**. This was the farthest extremity of the city to be settled, and in 1236 a nunnery of Poor Clares (Franciscans) was established here. In 1807 it was suppressed, and in 1819 it became a military hospital. The church was demolished but the seventeenth-century monastic buildings survive, housing the Red Cross and the Guardie di Pubblica Sicurezza; three storeys around a large square cloister, with ground-floor colonnades.

Return to Piazzale Roma. The square was formed on completion of the Terraferma road bridge, opened on 25 April 1933. At the NE corner, Calatrava's new bridge (2006–8): see Cannaregio. Near the E side is the site of the lost nunnery of **Santa Croce**, an ancient foundation (eighth century), which in 1109 became a Benedictine house. The church itself was rebuilt in 1583, but in 1810 it was suppressed, and demolished three years later. The land was acquired by Spiridione Papadopoli, whose private garden it became; it was set out in 1834, but is now a public park. At the corner of the Rio

Novo are remains of what was perhaps an early medieval defensive structure, later incorporated into the nunnery, today a hotel.

Walk along Fondamenta de la Croce in front of the Gardens, and cross Ponte de la Croce; at SC 561, facing the station, is **Palazzo Emo Diedo**, late seventeenth century, attributed to Tirali. The broad façade has an unusual *portego* window: three large single lights divided by fine stone columns and surmounted by a pediment. Continuing along the quay, we reach the distinctive **San Simon Piccolo (Santi Simeone e Giuda Apostoli)**. The 'piccolo' refers to the modest size of the original church. Founded in the ninth century, it was rebuilt several times; the present church is by Scalfarotto, 1718–38. It remained a parish foundation until 1810, when it was joined with the other San Simon (see below). Scalfarotto's only major work in Venice, it is loosely modelled on the Pantheon in Rome; the interior is indebted to Longhena's Salute. The church is raised on a tall stylobate, with prominent steps up to the Neo-classical pronaos: four Corinthian columns framed by a cluster of pilasters. In the pediment: a relief of the martyrdom of the titular saints. The picturesque, copper-clad cupola makes a prominent landmark, although its proportions are imperfect. The plan is circular, the interior articulated by a tall lower order of Corinthian pilasters; at the mid-point on each side is a group of three niches defined by free-standing Corinthian columns. The upper order, again Corinthian, forms the drum for the cupola, with alternating aedicules and niches with statues. Above the inner hemispherical cupola is a timber structure supporting the outer one. The chancel is approached by a semicircular arch, with a transverse plan and semicircular apses at each end; the free-standing high altar is richly decorated. Four side altars and four pulpits. Below the nave is a vault containing numerous monuments.

Immediately NE, facing the Grand Canal, at SC 712, is **Palazzetto Adoldo**, sixteenth-century Renaissance, with superimposed arched *bifore*; next door, at SC 713–15, is **Palazzetto Foscari Contarini**, in fact two houses, built around a courtyard. The SW wing has an elegant five-bay window to the first floor and a *liagò* across the top; the other element has a simple canal façade but a richer one to the internal courtyard. Take Calle Longa Bergama inland, turn left and cross Ponte Bergama.

To the sw is the imposing **Palazzo Gradenigo** (sc 767–8); the initial design was probably by Longhena, but it was completed by Domenico Margutti, a close follower, in the late seventeenth or early eighteenth century. The main façade is onto the picturesque Rio Marin, with two superimposed *piani nobili*; like the plan, it is highly asymmetrical, the multi-light windows to the *portego* being at the left side, near the land gate. On the right side: a long row of windows, some single and some paired. The façade returns at the sw end; near the sw corner is the grand stair, lit by a large *bifora*. Adjacent is the land access, with an impressive outer gate giving onto a small courtyard and a short quay, then a second rusticated portal to the house itself.

Inside: some rich stucco decoration, and frescoes by Guarana. Although subdivided, parts are still owned by the Gradenigo. The palace had a famous garden, extending almost to San Simon Piccolo; some remains, although much was lost to housing in the 1920s.

Palazzo Gradenigo, Rio Marin; probably by Longhena, completed by Domenico Margutti, late seventeenth or early eighteenth century

Continue SE along Fondamenta dei Garzoti. A little further, on the other bank, is **Palazzo Bragadin Priuli Cappello** (SC 770), late sixteenth or very early seventeenth century; originally owned by the Priuli; the design is influenced by Sanmicheli's Palazzo Corner at San Polo. A tall, imposing, four-storey façade; the impressive *piano nobile* has a large Serliana. The façade terminates with a prominent *abbaino*. Its plan is tripartite and traditional; at the far end of the *androne* is a three-bay loggia towards the extensive garden, which contained three elements: a rectangular courtyard surrounded by statuary; then, on axis, a large rectangular garden; to the side was an orchard; parts survive today.

A little further along is **Palazzo Contarini** (SC 802–3), another substantial seventeenth-century house, with superimposed *trifore*. At SC 837, just before Ponte del Cristo, is **Palazzo Malipiero**, eighteenth century, with unusual details; on the balcony corners are figures of harpies, while all the head keystones are oriented towards the centre of the façade.

Return NW along the quay to the small Campo Santo in front of **San Simon Grando (San Simeon Profeta)**. Founded in 967, and rebuilt in the early medieval period; a major restoration/modernisation in the early eighteenth century by Margutti, and *circa* 1750 by Massari. The tripartite basilica form was retained, and Massari designed a new façade, but the present simple Neo-classical temple front is from a further modernisation in 1861.

Inside: a Latin-cross plan, with transepts. A five-bay nave, with early medieval material, notably the column capitals; above are Renaissance arches, with sculptures of the Apostles above the arch spandrels. On the inner face of the façade is the eighteenth-century marble choir gallery, on four Corinthian columns. The nave has a shallow cross-vaulted ceiling. Baroque side altars: first right aisle altar: altarpiece by Palma il Giovane. The right chancel chapel has Baroque frescoed vaults. Left aisle, first altar: altarpiece by Corona; nearby, a *Last Supper* by Tintoretto. Second altar: that of the guild of wool-carders (*garzoti*): the *Annunciation*, a relief, perhaps by Vittoria.

Outside, the modest campanile is eighteenth century. To the N is a *sotoportego* on *barbacani*, containing an early fourteenth-century tomb monument to a bishop, once inside the church. Beyond the *sotoportego*, the square extends N to the Grand Canal. Continue NE into Salizada de la Chiesa, and turn left. At the end is a long quay, Riva di Biasio. Near the SW end is **Palazzetto Gritti** (SC 1303), a small sixteenth-century Renaissance house; a symmetrical façade with a *trifora*. Next door is **Palazzo Corner** (SC 1302), seventeenth century, with a tall, asymmetrical façade, lacking one wing. Further NE again (SC 1299a) is the substantial **Palazzo Donà Balbi**, again seventeenth century, built over an older Gothic house, with an odd asymmetrical plan and façade. The *portego* is at the extreme SW end, with two refined *quadrifore*, with balconies. Finally, near the NE end is **Palazzo Marcello** (SC 1289), an attractive, smallish, seventeenth-century house, with a well-balanced façade incorporating a Serliana.

Take the broad Rio Terà inland and turn right and then left into Salizada de Ca' Zusto. This small district is known as **Bari**, and is bounded by Lista Vecia del Bari to the N and Campo Nazario Sauro to the S. It was developed in the early medieval period, and contains small vernacular houses and apartments. At SC 1361 (corner of the Salizada): a good medium-sized Gothic house, **Ca' Zusto**.

4 SAN GIACOMO DA L'ORIO AND SAN ZAN DEGOLÀ

From the S end of the *salizada*, take Calle del Savio towards San Giacomo da l'Orio. Over the bridge is Campielo del Piovan, one of several spaces that wrap around the church; **Campo San Giacomo** itself is on the E side. The church apses project into the square, one of the largest and most attractive in this part of the city, and which remained grassed until 1711, when it was finally paved.

San Giacomo da l'Orio is formally dedicated to St James the Greater, the Apostle; despite various claims, the popular affix is of uncertain origin. An early foundation, probably tenth century, the church was largely rebuilt in 1225 by the Badoer and da Mula families. The campanile is from the same period. The church was radically restored in the late fourteenth and early fifteenth centuries, when transepts were inserted into the original basilica form; they also have aisles, producing a full Latin-cross plan. The Byzantine colonnades were replaced with Gothic ones, and the present splendid 'ship's-keel' roof was installed. More modernisation took place in the early sixteenth century, when the nave walls were further embellished. In 1549 the Sacrament Chapel was built.

The exterior is very simple, with the main façade to the W. On the E side, the three radiused apses are equally plain. The Sacrament Chapel is identified by large arched windows, and is surmounted by a low pyramidal roof with lantern.

San Giacomo da l'Orio: the apses projecting into the square

Inside, the Gothic nave arcades retain columns and capitals from the earlier basilica; the arches of the open timber roof are supported on elaborate *barbacani*. The soffit is decorated with coffered panels. Above the entrance façade: organ decorated by Schiavone (sixteenth century). Big Gothic arches between the transepts and the chancel. Right transept: fourteenth-century monument to Clara Priuli. In the new sacristy: ceiling by Veronese, *circa* 1577. On the walls: works by Veronese, Marescalco, Bonifacio de' Pitati and Palma il Giovane. Sacrament Chapel: paintings by Padovanino, Tizianello, Palma il Giovane; in the cupola: fresco by Guarana.

Chancel: the high altarpiece is the *Virgin and Child* by Lorenzo Lotto, 1546. Left of the left apse chapel: the old sacristy, late sixteenth century, with a cycle of paintings by Palma il Giovane. In the left nave aisle and baptistery: further works by Palma.

Outside, in the square: in the SW corner (SC 1507) is the former college of medicine, containing the remains of the **Teatro Anatomico**, built by the Republic and the nobleman Lorenzo Loredan, 1669–71. Above the ground-floor theatre were three tiers of galleries. It was badly damaged by fire in 1800, and extensively rebuilt.

Take Calle Larga out on the NE corner of the square. Nearby, at SC 1639, is **Palazzo Colombo**, fifteenth-century Gothic with water façade to Rio del Megio. At SC 1661–5 is the Gothic **Palazzo**

San Zan Degolà: façade to the square

Badoer, with a second, Renaissance wing on one side. Continuing along the Fondamenta, at sc 1666 is **Palazzo Mutti**, seventeenth century, with two *quadrifore*.

At Ponte del Megio, turn left down the narrow Calle del Spezier, then Calle del Capitello, into Campo San Zan Degolà. On the NE side of this quiet square is **San Zan Degolà (San Giovanni Decollato)**: literally, St John the Beheaded, to distinguish this church from others with a similar dedication. Its origins lie in the seventh century, but it was rebuilt in the early eleventh century and restored by the Pesaro in the early thirteenth; alterations in 1703 included the present simple Neo-classical façade. It was closed by Napoleon, but reopened in 1818. Its parish status was removed, and it became an oratory under San Giacomo. The early medieval basilica has survived almost unaltered, and the façade reflects the tripartite structure behind it. From the square, the thirteenth-century clerestory windows can be seen. The campanile was demolished in the early eighteenth century, when the present short solid bell-tower replaced it.

The interesting interior is defined by two rows of Greek marble columns, with eleventh-century Venetian-Byzantine capitals, reused in the thirteenth-century rebuilding. Above are painted Gothic brick arches (traces of fresco over), while the roof is a simplified ship's-keel type. Right chancel chapel: fourteenth-century fresco, *St Michael Trampling on the Devil*. Left chancel chapel: valuable thirteenth-century frescoes, rediscovered in a restoration in 1945. In the ceiling: a cross, with the four Evangelists in the vault spandrels; on the right wall, St Helena, below which are four saints (John, Peter, Thomas and Mark?). On the left wall: thirteenth-century *Annunciation* fresco.

Off the N side of the square, Calle Giovanelli leads to **Palazzo Giovanelli** (sc 1681a). A substantial Gothic palace, with a broad, symmetrical Grand Canal façade; perhaps as late as 1480, since the lower windows are Renaissance. Three watergates grouped in the centre of the façade, which has *quadrifore* to the two principal storeys.

Return and take Calle dei Preti along the N side of the church, then left down the broad Salizada del Fontego. On the right is the **Fondaco dei Turchi (Museo di Storia Naturale)**. A remarkable building, with a long, complex history. The *palazzo* was built *circa* 1225 by Giacomo Palmieri from Pesaro; in 1381 the family sold it to the Republic, which thereafter leased it to several notable figures, including the marquis of Ferrara; it was also used to house illustrious visitors. In 1621 it was rented as the base for Turkish traders in the city, but its condition deteriorated; by the mid-nineteenth century it was half ruined; in 1858 it was radically restored by the Comune. In 1865 the Correr Museum was located here, but since 1923 it has housed the Museo di Storia Naturale; recently, a further protracted restoration.

The present distinctive appearance is really a nineteenth-century replica, since little original material survived, other than some columns, capitals and relief decorations. Nevertheless, the Grand Canal façade is a reminder of the original appearance of a great thirteenth century *palazzo-fontego*. The long façade has three-storey *toresele* or turrets at each end, and a broad two-storey central section, containing a spacious ten-bay loggia to the canal, with stilted arches, and a first floor with eighteen narrower bays. The façade is capped by an unusual crenellation and is clad with sheets of marble.

The present long, deep plan, with its rectangular central courtyard, is radically different from the historic extent, and is largely nineteenth century. The original plan was approximately square, the landward façade having a colonnaded loggia to a rear courtyard, and two open stairs. On the *piano nobile* the long waterfront loggia was 'matched' by a similar transverse hall across the rear, onto the courtyard.

Facing page: Contrasting styles: foreground: the Venetian-Byzantine Fondaco dei Turchi (originally *circa* 1225), then the fourteenth-century Fondaco del Megio, and beyond, Palazzo Belloni Battagia, 1648–*circa* 1663

Return s down the Salizada, and continue down Calle del Spezier. At SC 1740 and 1757 is **Palazzo Sanudo**; the canal façade is mainly Lombard Renaissance, although the street façade is late Gothic, so is perhaps *circa* 1480–90. For many years thereafter it was owned by Marin Sanudo, the diarist. Continue to Ponte del Megio; cross the bridge and take Calle del Megio (left). At SC 1777 is **Palazzo Surian Stazio Priuli**, early sixteenth century, built by the Surian, but rebuilt in 1584 by the Prezzato. Sometimes attributed to Sansovino, today it houses a school. At the end, on the right, is **Palazzo Belloni Battagia** (SC 1783), with façade to the Grand Canal. Begun in 1648 by Longhena; completed *circa* 1663. A rich stone canal façade, with fine detailing to the *piano nobile*, all of whose windows are treated as aedicules, with split pediments and Corinthian pilasters. The plan is tripartite and conventional; much of the interior is from after 1804, when it was owned by Antonio Capovilla, who enlarged and modernised the palace, adding decoration by Giambattista Canal, Borsato and others.

On the other side of the *calle* is the fourteenth-century **Fondaco de Megio** (SC 1779 and 1790), the Republic's former millet warehouse. An L-shaped plan, the shorter wing facing the Grand Canal, the longer the Rio del Megio at the side; a simple brick structure with rectangular windows, although the canal façade has decorative crenellation.

Return down Calle del Megio, and turn left into Ramo and Calle del Tintor, then left again into Calle del Forno and Calle Dandolo. At the end is **Ca' Tron** (SC 1957), with Grand Canal façade. Built by the Tron, who owned an earlier Gothic house on the site; it was reconstructed in the late sixteenth century, and is sometimes attributed to Sansovino. *Circa* 1710 it was extended by Gaspari with two narrow wings towards the rear garden. He also modernised the interior; the *portego*, with paintings by Dorigny, has survived. Gaspari added a *casinò* at the end of the garden, with a first-floor ballroom decorated by Guarana, demolished in 1828. Today, the palace houses one of the faculties of IUAV.

The stone Grand Canal façade is well proportioned, with superimposed *quadrifore*, the lower Ionic, the upper Corinthian; the watergate forms the central element of a Serliana. The garden façade is framed by Gaspari's later wings, but the earlier central section is mostly glazed, with a five-light window to both upper halls; the ground floor has an open loggia, with two large Verona marble columns supporting the upper façade. The internal plan is entirely traditional.

Immediately E is **Palazzo Duodo** (SC 1958), a smallish, attractive fifteenth-century Gothic house, with a well-proportioned, symmetrical canal façade. The single *piano nobile* has a *gotico fiorito* four-light window.

Return along Calle Dandolo, and turn left into Calle de Ca' Tron. At Salizada San Stae, turn left, back towards the Grand Canal. At the end is Campo San Stae. On the left corner is **Palazzo Priuli Bon Dandolo** (SC 1979), a house with a complex history. The low, broad façade includes a water loggia with narrow, highly stilted arches, probably early thirteenth century. Above is a refined *pentafora* to the main hall, with stilted, inflected arches, originally mid-thirteenth century, but perhaps rebuilt when the Gothic balcony was added. The rest of the façade is plain and much later.

San Stae (Eustachio) stands on the S side of the square, facing the Grand Canal. An early parish foundation, perhaps from the tenth century. Following successive reconstructions, the church was rapidly rebuilt after 1678, to a design by Giovanni Grassi, his only known work. It lacked a façade until 1709, when Doge Alvise Mocenigo left a legacy in his will. A competition was held, with twelve entries from Rossi, Gaspari and others; Rossi's was chosen, and was complete within a year; he also designed the internal lateral chapels.

The Palladian façade has a giant order of four Corinthian columns on tall plinths, supporting a pediment. In the large central bay is a flamboyant Baroque portal, flanked by colonnettes and capped by a broken pediment. Above is a complex group of statues, with more enlivening the skyline. The narrower outer bays contain niches with statues; the figures are by Torretto, Corradini and others.

The interior is also Palladian. The single broad nave has three lateral chapels down each side. The flanks

San Stae: detail of the Baroque portal, begun 1709, by Domenico Rossi are articulated by robust columns on tall bases, carrying a prominent trabeation. In the chancel: a deep apse containing the high altar. Light is provided by large thermal windows down each side and in the chancel. Among the works of art are: right side, first altar: altarpiece by Bambini. Chancel: ceiling by Sebastiano Ricci, 1708. The high altar is a rich, complex work, also by Rossi. Chancel walls: paintings by G. B. Tiepolo, Lazzarini, Giovanni Antonio Pellegrini, Piazzetta and Ricci.

The campanile was also rebuilt, its Baroque portal bearing the date 1702. Immediately SE of the church is the **Scuola dei Battjoro** (SC 1980), the guildhall of the gold-workers. Rebuilt in 1711, with an attractive little Baroque façade, overwhelmed by the adjacent church. Three bays, with a central doorway; the façade is crowned by a curvilinear parapet. Inside: the usual two superimposed halls, but here they are linked by a central double-branch staircase with a mezzanine floor at the half-landing.

Return SW down Salizada San Stae; at SC 1992 is the imposing **Palazzo Mocenigo**, begun in the late sixteenth century and completed in the early seventeenth; today it houses the Museum of Costume, part of the Correr Collections. The monumental palace has two component parts: a smaller element to the N (four storeys) and the main palace to the S, with seven storeys.

The principal palace has two main façades, this one and the other (almost identical) to the canal to the SE. Both are symmetrical and tripartite, with three superimposed Serliane, the lowermost incorporating the water and land gates, the upper two the superimposed *piani nobili*. The plan is traditional, with the main staircase to the right of the *androne*. The smaller N wing may have been used for accommodating guests; it is less monumental, with only one *piano nobile*; its façade and plan are again regular and tripartite.

The interior of the main palace achieved its present appearance in the late eighteenth century, when Alvise Mocenigo had the main halls decorated by Guarana, Mengozzi Colonna and Zanetti. The interior survives almost unchanged, with contemporary furniture, fittings and Murano chandeliers. The *portego* has an impressive double portal onto the staircase. In 1954 the last Mocenigo bequeathed the palace to the city, and the museum was established.

Take Ramo de la Ruoda at the sw end of the palace, and cross the bridge into Campielo del Spezier. **Palazzo Zanetti** (sc 2047 and 2052) is a group of houses on the NE side, between two canals. There are fourteenth-century Gothic elements, as well as later Renaissance modernisations. Down Fondamenta Rimpeto, at sc 2055, is a fine Gothic doorway with a steep gable and a coat of arms. Continue down the *fondamenta*; at the end is **Palazzo Foscarini Giovanelli** (sc 2070), *circa* 1570, with two large Serliane on the Grand Canal façade. The land façade was once frescoed by Zelotti.

Return a short distance along the quay and turn left along Calle va al Forno. At the bridge is **Palazzetto Agnusdio** (sc 2060), with canal façade. An interesting small late fourteenth-century house, noted for the rich detailing of the *pentafora*, with carved symbols of the Evangelists in the spandrels between the arch heads. At the outer corners are the figures of the Annunciation, while below, directly above the watergate, is the Mystic Lamb, from which the name derives. The land gate has thirteenth-century reliefs and a fifteenth-century angel and shield.

Cross Ponte del Forner and turn left along the short quay to the land gate of **Ca' Pesaro**, together with the equally monumental Ca' Rezzonico, the largest, most opulent Baroque palace in the city; also

Palazzetto Agnusdio: detail of the portal to the bridge

Ca' Pesaro: Grand Canal façade; begun by Longhena, 1628; completed by Gaspari, *circa* 1730

designed by Longhena but completed by others. The Pesaro acquired the site in stages, starting in 1558, but work began only in 1628. Construction commenced at the rear, while the family continued living in an older Contarini house on the Grand Canal frontage. Work was still in progress when Giovanni Pesaro (by now doge) died in 1659; in 1682 both Longhena and Leonardo Pesaro died, with only the first and second orders of the Grand Canal façade completed. Longhena, however, had also completed the *androne*, the courtyard façade, the rusticated land gate and perhaps the great staircase.

In 1703 work re-commenced under Gaspari; the second *piano nobile* was completed *circa* 1710, but the long side façade to the *rio* was not finished until the 1730s; Gaspari also altered the stair and courtyard. In 1830 the Pesaro became extinct, and the palace was bought by the Gradenigo; in 1889 it was given to the city, and since 1902 it has housed the Gallery of Modern and Contemporary Art, as well as the Correr oriental collection.

Ca' Pesaro: detail of the courtyard façade, begun by
Longhena, but altered by Gaspari

The majestic Grand Canal façade (seen from Calle del Tragheto at
San Felice) is a fairly radical reinterpretation of the traditional
tripartite composition; there is little central emphasis, despite the
tripartite plan behind it. The first order contains two impressive
watergates and is boldly rusticated. Above is a stone balcony across
the full width of the façade. The first *piano nobile* has seven bays, with
the central three (representing the *portego*) divided from the outer
pairs by paired Ionic columns; this is the only subtle, centralising
emphasis. The outer corners are again reinforced by paired columns.

A broad entablature divides the two upper orders; again, a
continuous stone balcony. The third order is Corinthian, and follows
the design of the second. The façade terminates with a broad, rich
trabeation, without Longhena's usual oval attic windows. The long
side façade to Rio de le Due Torri is also (unusually) richly detailed
in stonework. Other than Longhena's first two bays, Gaspari devised
a refined, simplified version for this flank elevation, but with the
same orders and similar windows.

The plan is axial and traditional, with the watergates giving onto a broad loggia, before the impressively rusticated *androne* is reached by a triple portal. Longhena's original staircase terminated this axis at its s end, but Gaspari relocated it to one side, which, while opening the s end to the courtyard, is not entirely satisfactory. The square, impressive courtyard is on axis, with a well-head originally at the Zecca.

The plans of both upper floors are almost identical and traditional, with a long enfilade of rooms down the e side. Several rooms on the first *piano nobile* retain their original decoration, including rooms 1 and 3, decorated by Bambini and Pittoni.

The present collection of twentieth-century art originated with the first International Art Biennale in 1895, but the collection was reordered in 1938. It contains a good representation of Italian art of the nineteenth and twentieth centuries, as well as works by (*inter alia*) Bonnard, Utrillo, Matisse, Klimt, Nolde, Klee, Kandisky, Ernst, Roualt and Dufy.

Return along the quay, then take Calle del Tiozzi. At sc 2084 is **Palazzo Tron**, fifteenth-century Gothic, with a good *quadrifora* to the upper hall; on the *calle*: an equally good portal. The water façade was partly modernised in the early Renaissance. Take Ramo and Corte del Tiozzi, and continue straight on to **Santa Maria Mater Domini**, on a restricted site, bounded to the NW by a canal. Founded in 960 by the Zane and Cappello families, it was established as a parish by the eleventh century. By the early sixteenth century the Byzantine structure was in poor condition; it was rebuilt by *circa* 1510; altars were installed in 1512–24. The architect is not known, but the church is strongly Codussian in appearance and was probably designed by him, perhaps completed by his sons after his death in 1504.

The plan is a form of Greek cross, with a two-bay nave flanked by side aisles (or chapels), and a cupola on pendentives at the crossing. The chancel projects towards the canal, with a deep semicircular apse flanked by small shallower apsidal side chapels. The façade faces a narrow *calle*, and is difficult to see; two orders, the lower one with three broad bays, the upper with just the central bay, flanked by curved volutes; in the centre is an *ocio*.

The interior is typical of Codussi, with the articulation all in grey Paduan stone, and the planar surfaces simple white plaster. The crossing is defined by Composite attached columns at the corners, supporting a deep architrave, above which spring the arches. The transepts are roofed by barrel vaults, while the side chapels have plastered cross-vaults. The thermal windows were cut later to improve a very dark interior.

Palazzo Viaro Zane: fourteenth-century Gothic
pentafora, with a sixteenth-century Renaissance
one above

Nave, right side, first altar: Trevisan family altar, begun by Lorenzo
Bregno, *circa* 1520. Second altar: altarpiece by Catena. Right chancel
chapel: a very fine, richly carved altar, perhaps by Lorenzo Bregno.
Left chancel chapel: *St Mark and St John*, again by Bregno. Left
transept: the *Finding of the Cross* by Tintoretto. Nave, left side, first
altar: by Sansovino, 1536. Second altar: of the Contarini family.

Adjacent is the attractive little square, surrounded by interesting
smaller houses. At the NW end, next to the church, is **Palazzo Viaro
Zane** (SC 2120–23), with canal façade to the rear. The narrow *campo*
façade has an elegant fourteenth-century *pentafora*, above which is a
later, second one from the sixteenth century. To the left is the
courtyard, within which rises an open Gothic staircase. The canal
façade repeats the two superimposed *pentafore* to those on the square.

On the SW side of the square are houses once also owned by the
Zane (SC 2172–4). That towards the NW has been extensively altered,
with a collection of large Gothic single windows and other later
ones. The left house has a good late thirteenth-century *quadrifora*,
with stilted inflected arches; the façade has several contemporary
paterae and crosses set into it. A boldly overhanging eaves.

Palazzo Corner de la Regina; lower part of the Grand Canal façade, by Domenico Rossi, 1724–7

On the NE side of the square is **Palazzo Barbaro** (SC 2177), with a fourteenth-century Gothic *campo* façade (including a quadrifora), and a mostly Renaissance canal façade to the right. Cross Ponte Santa Maria, then turn left down Calle de la Regina. Continue down Calle de Ca' Corner to the Grand Canal. On the right is **Palazzo Corner de la Regina** (SC 2214); the imposing palace takes its name from the branch of the Corner that included Caterina, queen of Cyprus, born in an earlier house on this site in 1454. This house was modernised in 1602–25 by Tommaso Contin, who extended it towards the SW. An adjacent house to the SE, facing the Grand Canal, was acquired in 1678, and in 1700 the Corner decided on complete reconstruction. The family's *proto*, Tremignon, was now too old, so Rossi was appointed instead. Early intentions to build a palace to rival Ca' Pesaro were thwarted when a further plot could not be bought, but work began in 1724; within three years it was complete. It remained in Corner ownership until 1800; after further ownership changes, in 1971 it became the property of the Cassa di Risparmio (savings bank); for some time after 1975 it housed the library and archive of the Biennale.

The imposing Grand Canal façade is rich, but more restrained and Neo-classical than Ca' Pesaro. The very tall first order incorporates the *androne* and a mezzanine, faced with rusticated stonework; the tall central watergate is flanked by two smaller ones. Above are two generous *piani nobili*, each different, although both have full-width balconies. On the first, a row of five tall arched windows is articulated by Ionic half-columns, with single windows towards the outer corners. The upper order, Corinthian, repeats the pattern, but with rectangular pedimented windows.

The plan is unusual. The *androne* and the upper halls are exceptionally long, terminating at the courtyard, while the rear part of the palace wraps around the courtyard on all sides. Much of the interior was decorated in 1773–83 by Cedini and Domenico Fossati; the length of the *portego* was subdivided by the insertion of shallow arched bays, and rich coffered ceilings were added. Further paintings were added in 1793 by Giuseppe Montanari, with stucco decoration; most survives.

Immediately NW of Ca' Corner are two small houses facing the Grand Canal: **Palazzetto Donà** (SC 2211), a small eighteenth-century house with a large watergate; and **Palazzo Corregio** (SC 2219), larger, but of similar date. Return down Calle de Ca' Corner, and then take Ramo and Calle del Rosa, back to the Grand Canal. On the right is the small but interesting **Palazzetto Bragadin Favretto** (SC 2232); the Grand Canal façade has a mid-thirteenth-century *quadrifora*. The façade, regular and tripartite, also has four fifteenth-century Gothic single windows. Return along Calle del Rosa, and then back along Calle de la Regina. At SC 2265 is **Palazzo Moro**, good fifteenth-century Gothic, with superimposed *quadrifore*; the courtyard contains a contemporary open staircase. Next door is **Palazzo Manzoni** (SC 2267), seventeenth century, with a prominent watergate; just across the *calle*, at SC 2260–68 is the sixteenth-century **Palazzo Gozzi**, with two watergates and two principal upper apartments.

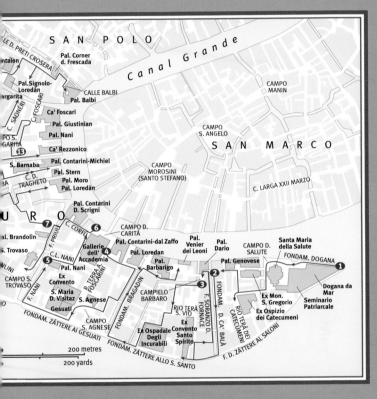

SAN POLO

Pal. Corner
d. Frescada

CALLE D. PRETI CROSERA

ntalon

Pal. Signolo-
Loredan

argarita

CALLE BALBI

Pal. Balbi

Ca' Foscari

Pal. Giustinian

Pal. Nani

Ca' Rezzonico

Pal. Contarini-Michiel

Pal. Stern

Pal. Moro

Pal. Loredàn

Pal. Contarini
D. Scrigni

Canal Grande

SAN MARCO

CAMPO
MANIN

CAMPO
S. ANGELO

CAMPO
MOROSINI
(SANTO STEFANO)

C. LARGA XXII MARZO

S. Barnaba

C. D.
TRAVASO

BA

U R O

al. Brandolin

S. Trovaso

NLINI

CAMPO S.
TROVASO

Ex
Convento
S. Maria
D. Visitaz

7

C. CORFU

6

CAMPO D.
CARITÀ

Gallerie
dell'
Accademia

4

Pal. Contarini-dal Zaffo

Pal. Loredan

Pal.
Barbarigo

Pal.
Venier
dei Leoni

Pal.
Dario

CAMPO D.
SALUTE

Santa Maria
della Salute

FONDAM. DOGANA

1

Dogana da
Mar

Pal. Genovese

2

3

Ex Mon.
S. Gregorio

Ex Ospizio
dei Catecumeni

Seminario
Patriarcale

S. Agnese

CAMPIELLO
BARBARO

RIO TERÀ
S. VIO

Ex
Convento
Santo
Spirito

Gesuati

FONDAM. ZÀTTERE AI GESUATI

CAMPO
S. AGNESE

Ex Ospadale
Degli
Incurabili

FONDAM. ZÀTTERE ALLO S. SANTO

F. D. ZÀTTERE AL SALONI

200 metres

200 yards

Dorsoduro

Sestiere of Dorsoduro

Dorsoduro takes the form of a large, sweeping arc, covering all the southernmost historic centre. It is defined to the NE by the Grand Canal, while its long southern boundary is the broad Giudecca Canal; its N and W confines are a very short boundary with the *sestiere* of San Polo and a longer one with Santa Croce. Its name – 'hard back' – derives from the chain of firm islets that formed its original core. This chain begins at the Punta de la Dogana and runs NW to include the islets of San Gregorio, San Vio, the Carità, San Barnaba, Santa Margherita and San Pantaleon. A little further S is the early parish foundation of San Trovaso, while a second chain of islets running westwards includes the important early settlement of Anzolo Rafael (Angelo Raffaele), terminating at the former peninsula of San Niccolò dei Mendicoli. The eastern part of the *sestiere* has a fairly regular pattern of settlement, with a series of roughly parallel canals linking the Grand Canal to the Giudecca Canal. The E end is dominated by the mass of Longhena's Salute church, just W of the Customs House point, where the two canals meet.

In the N centre of Dorsoduro is the large, attractive *campo* of Santa Margarita, an important social and commercial focus, while the W end has a markedly different character. Formerly isolated and impoverished, much was reclaimed in the nineteenth century, and developed with industrial zones and (later) social housing, notably at

Facing page: Santa Maria de la Salute from the colonnades of the Doge's Palace; by Baldassare Longhena, begun 1631

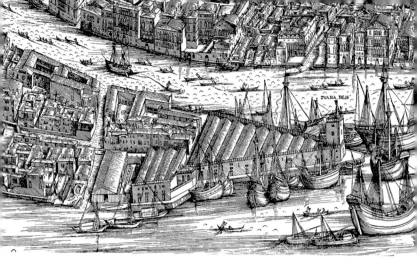

The Punta de la Dogana in 1500, from de' Barbari's engraving of 1500

Santa Marta. In the NW corner, the *sestiere* includes part of the Tereni Nuovi, an earlier, fifteenth-century reclamation zone, most of which lies within Santa Croce (q.v.).

The itinerary starts at the Punta de la Dogana, and proceeds N and W, terminating at Palazzo Balbi.

I THE DOGANA, THE SALUTE AND SAN GREGORIO

The Dogana da Mar (DD 2–11): the large triangular plan of the Customs House occupies the E tip of the *sestiere*. It was established *circa* 1315 for evaluating and taxing goods arriving into the city by sea. The medieval building occupied a similar extent to the present one, but in 1677 a competition was held for its replacement. Designs were submitted by Longhena, Cominelli, Sardi and Giuseppe Benoni; despite his success at the adjacent Salute, Longhena was rejected in favour of Benoni, whose proposal was built rapidly. The site was highly vulnerable to tides and currents, and the western part was largely rebuilt by Alvise Pigazzi in 1835–8, because it was in danger of collapse.

Other than the E tower, these simple façades are each broken by six large doorways to long, narrow warehouses inside. The 'Punta' itself is more monumental, all in Istrian stone, with a colonnade of free-standing rusticated piers, set in pairs. The square tower above is also rusticated, and surmounted by a golden sphere (the Earth), carried by two figures of Atlas; on top is a gilded bronze figure of Fortune, which was a beacon for shipping. The sculptures are all by Bernardo Falcone. After many years of abandonment, the Dogana has been restored and converted by Tadao Ando (2007–9) as a centre of contemporary art, based on the collections of the French industrialist François Pinault.

Immediately w, facing the Grand Canal, is the **Seminario Patriarcale** (DD 1), begun by Longhena in 1670, but completed after his death by Domenico Mazzoni. It originally housed a monastic order, the Somaschi, which, like the others, was suppressed by Napoleon. In 1817 Emperor Franz I of Austria established the patriarchal seminary here, where it remains. It also collected works of art and artefacts from suppressed churches and monasteries, which form the basis of its present collection.

The sober, restrained exterior forms a square four-storey block around a central courtyard; the latter has elegant stone colonnades on all sides. The main staircase is imposing, with two long straight flights of steps and a rich, heavy, stone balustrade. Its decoration is by Giusto le Court, a long-term collaborator of Longhena.

Immediately w of the seminary is the imposing pile of Longhena's Salute church, on the site of a lost monastic house, the **Santissima Trinità**, founded *circa* 1256, but demolished in 1631. Further s, towards the Zattere, was **Santa Maria dell'Umiltà**, built by the Jesuits in 1578–89. They were expelled from Venice in 1606, and it was then occupied by Benedictines, until 1806, when it was suppressed. In 1824 church and monastery were demolished to provide gardens for the patriarchal seminary.

Santa Maria de la Salute is the largest and most important Baroque church in Venice, and Longhena's ecclesiastical masterpiece. It was built by the Republic as a votive church, following the devastating plague of 1629–30, which killed more than 46,000 people, around one-third of the population. The decision was taken by the Senate on 22 October 1630, and the church was the subject of a competition. Although the site was defined, there were no conditions as to the design itself; eleven proposals were submitted, which were then reduced to two, one a traditional axial design by Smeraldi, the other a radical, centralised proposal by Longhena. He was selected in June 1631, after a Senate secret ballot, and the project took more than thirty years to complete. In 1681 the square in front was laid out, but Longhena died the following year; the church was completed by Gaspari, his close associate, and consecrated on 9

November 1687. Thereafter, every year on 21 November, the feast of the Presentation of the Virgin, the doge and Senate processed to the church across a temporary bridge of boats across the Grand Canal; the ceremony continues today, with the procession led by the Cardinal Patriarch.

Both the plan and the appearance were revolutionary. The former is based on a centralised octagonal nave, with eight piers supporting two orders, and surmounted by a huge cupola, the largest in the city. The octagon is surrounded by an ambulatory, also with eight sides; this ingenious arrangement allowed the congregation a clear view of the sanctuary, while the peripheral ambulatory was used by the ducal procession; the procession divided inside the main entrance and reunited in front of the high altar. The plan is not wholly centralised; it has a great portico towards the Grand Canal, while on the opposite side is the sanctuary. This has its axis at right angles to that from the entrance, and terminates at each end with semicircular apses.

The exterior dominates the E end of the Grand Canal, raised high above the square on sixteen steps: two superimposed orders, the lower ones with high-level thermal windows, and capped by pediments. The Grand Canal facet is a triumphal arch, with paired Corinthian columns on tall bases. Between the columns are two orders of statues in niches, while the wide central bay is capped by a pediment. The upper order is set inside the lower one, and is carried by the piers of the octagon. Each facet has a pair of arched windows, and at each angle large volutes are capped by statues. The cupola itself is crowned by a rich stone lantern, itself decorated with statues and capped by a miniature cupola. Behind the central cupola, a second, smaller one denotes the sanctuary below, flanked by the curved walls of the lateral apses.

In contrast to the exuberant Baroque exterior, the interior is cool, restrained and monumental, strongly influenced by Palladio. Only two materials are used: stone and plain white plaster. The octagon is defined by massive Corinthian composite columns on tall plinths, supporting an elegant continuous corbelled entablature. The nave is defined by an arched colonnade set below this giant order, again with Corinthian pilasters. In the upper order, each facet of the octagon is defined by a statue, while the interior of the cupola, although hemispherical externally, also has eight internal facets. The vocabulary of the sanctuary continues that to the nave, on a reduced scale, its rich entablature set at the same level. A circular drum carries the hemispherical cupola.

The free-standing high altar, also by Longhena, has pairs of Corinthian Greek marble columns and a central semicircular arch; the sculpture is by Giusto le Court. Behind is the rectangular choir, also oriented left–right, like the sanctuary.

Around the perimeter are two groups, each of three side chapels, all similarly detailed. Right side, first altar: altarpiece: *Presentation of the Virgin* by Luca Giordano. Second altar: *Assumption*, also by Giordano. Third altar: *Birth of the Virgin*, again by Giordano. Left side, first altar: *Descent of the Holy Spirit* by Titian, *circa* 1555. Second altar: *St Anthony* by Pietro Liberi. Third altar: *Annunciation*, also by Liberi.

In the main sacristy, reached from the retrochoir: many art works, including works by Titian, Rizzo and others.

Walk down the W flank of the church, crossing the bridge into Rio Terà dei Catecumeni. On the left: the **Pio Loco dei Catecumeni** (DD 108), established at San Marcuola in 1557, transferred here in 1571. The Pio Loco housed prisoners of war and former slaves brought to Venice after foreign campaigns. It was rebuilt by Massari after 1727, following the model of Palladio's Zitelle, with a central church flanked by two blocks of accommodation. The exterior is very simple, but the church is clad with stone: a single order of Corinthian pilasters and a large pediment. Turning left at the end, halfway down Rio Terà ai Saloni, at DD 70–74, is **Palazzetto Costantini**, a small Gothic house, modernised in the sixteenth century. The façade stands on a six-bay colonnade with timber *barbacani*. Take Calle de Mezo N into the little Campo San Gregorio. On the E side: the Gothic façade of **San Gregorio**. Of ancient foundation, perhaps from AD 806; *circa* 1140 it passed to the Benedictines, and was rebuilt in the early fifteenth century. The façade is *circa* 1445–60, with a typical *gotico fiorito* portal. In 1805 it was suppressed, its interior stripped. After 1969 it was restored radically internally and became a centre for the restoration of works of art and artefacts. The church has a single tall aisle-less nave, with an open timber roof. At the E end: three polygonal apses, with tall, thin lancets and good decorative brickwork. The surviving monastic buildings are to the N, facing the Grand Canal; half were demolished to build Palazzo Genovese. The attractive E cloister survives, with colonnettes supporting a continuous double row of *barbacani*; the attractively asymmetrical Grand Canal façade has a fine, rich, square Gothic portal.

Immediately W is the imposing neo-Gothic **Palazzo Genovese** (DD 173), by Edoardo Trigomi Mattei, 1892. The Grand Canal façade is broad and impressive, if rather mechanical; its central tracery is based on that at the Ca' d'Oro. The *campo* façade is similar. A little further w, along Calle del Bastion, is **Palazzo Salviati** (DD 195), 1903–6, by Giacomo dell'Olivo, for the famous Murano glass-making family. The neo-Renaissance Grand Canal façade (best seen from Santa Maria del Giglio) is clad with glass mosaic, added in 1924 to advertise the skills of the owners.

2 THE ZATTERE (1), RIO DE LA FORNACE AND CA' DARIO

At Ponte San Gregorio, turn left along Fondamenta de Ca' Balà, flanking the attractive Rio de la Fornace. Halfway down (DD 222) is the sixteenth-century **Palazzo Morosini**, today a hotel; a little further, at DD 244, is **Palazzo Querini**, also sixteenth century, an impressive five-storey house, whose façade was once frescoed by Pordenone. At the far end of the quay, on the left, are the imposing sixteenth-century **Maggazini del Sale** (DD 258–66), the Republic's former salt warehouses. The Zattere façade is simple and functional; the warehouses consist of nine long, narrow sheds, each with an open timber trussed roof, and with massive brick cross-walls. Cross Ponte de Ca' Balà and continue w along the Zattere.

The **Zattere** form a continuous quay along the s edge of Dorsoduro, from the Dogana to San Basegio. They were reclaimed from the lagoon and paved in 1519, greatly improving communications

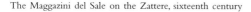

The Maggazini del Sale on the Zattere, sixteenth century

along this hitherto remote shoreline; a fine view of the Giudecca from the quay, whose name derives from the rafts (*zattere*) of timber that were brought ashore here for the construction industry.

Scuola del Spirito Santo (DD 275): founded in 1506, it survived until the Napoleonic suppression in 1806. The attractive façade has two orders, both tripartite and symmetrical, with flat Ionic pilasters defining the bays. The large central portal has an arched head, capped by a shallow pediment; the side bays each have a large single light; the upper order is capped by a pediment. The interior was once richly decorated, with two superimposed halls. Immediately w is the larger façade of the **Chiesa del Spirito Santo**, founded in 1483 for Augustinian nuns. The conventual buildings are to the rear, on a long, narrow site, with a courtyard garden down the centre. The church was rebuilt in the early sixteenth century, after the Zattere were reclaimed, and its orientation was reversed, with the façade now to the s; the nunnery was suppressed in 1806. The church façade is a larger version of that of the adjacent Scuola, but with rather squat proportions; again two superimposed orders, here with fluted Corinthian pilasters to the lower order, plain ones above. The lower order is richer than the upper; the impressive portal has a semicircular head. In the upper order: a large central *ocio*. Inside: a single aisle-less nave, with seventeenth-century altars down the sides. The high altar is Baroque, richly detailed, with 'corkscrew' columns. Several notable paintings, including altarpieces by Guarana, Palma il Giovane and Jacopo Bassano, mostly from other closed churches.

Immediately w of the church: apartment block by Ignazio Gardella (DD 402), 1954–8, with eclectic detailing and self-indulgent asymmetry.

Take Calle de la Scuola inland, and turn right along Calle de la Crea; we are now on Fondamenta Soranzo, w side of Rio de la Fornace. Turn left. The canal is lined by attractive vernacular houses. At DD 299 is **Palazzo Soranzo**, Gothic, modernised in the sixteenth century. At Ponte San Gregorio, turn left onto Ramo Barbaro. In front is the rear façade of **Palazzo Barbaro** (DD 348), with a quirky, asymmetrical façade to the Grand Canal; *gotico fiorito*, *circa* 1440. On the *piano nobile* is a fine *esafora*, on the second floor neo-Byzantine windows, inserted much later. Turn left into the attractive little Campielo Barbaro. On the north side: the garden of **Ca' Dario** (DD 352). Main façade to the Grand Canal; its modest size belies its fame, which partly derives from the rich façade, partly from the biographies of its successive owners. An earlier Gothic house (elements of which survive at the rear) was extensively modernised by Giovanni Dario, *circa* 1487. On Dario's death, it passed to his daughter, who married Vincenzo Barbaro, owner of the palace next door. In 1838 it was bought by the historian Rawdon Brown, who undertook an urgent restoration; further restoration was necessary in 1904. A series of later owners met with tragic ends, giving rise to its reputation as a house of 'ill fortune'. They included Charles Briggs, an American, who committed suicide, Filippo Giordano delle Lanze (assassinated), Christopher Lambert (suicide), Fabrizio Ferrari (bankrupted) and Raul Gardini (suicide).

The Grand Canal façade is richly detailed and clad with marble, in the early Lombard Renaissance manner; it is often attributed to Pietro Lombardo, although without documentary evidence. The site is narrow, and the asymmetrical façade lacks the left wing. The four storeys are all of similar importance, with two *piani nobili* and a generous water storey. Unlike the upper levels, this is symmetrical, probably altered in the nineteenth-century restorations. An inscription reads: 'GENIO URBIS JOANNES DARIO', i.e., the work was dedicated to the 'spirit of the city'. The upper floors all have four windows on the left side and a single light on the right. The panel between them is decorated with inset paterae of marble and porphyry. On the skyline: an array of 'traditional' Venetian chimneys, all nineteenth-century inventions.

3   THE ZATTERE (2), THE INCURABILI AND
PALAZZO VENIER DEI LEONI

From Campielo Barbaro, take Fondamenta Ospedaleto along the s bank of Rio de la Toresela. At DD 375 is the site of the former **Ospizio de la Frescada**; the fourteenth-century Gothic portal survives. Take Corte del Sabion s, then follow Calle drio gl'Incurabili, turning right and then left, down Calle degli Incurabili, to reach the Zattere again.

The former **Ospedale degli Incurabili** occupies a large square site facing the quay. Like the other *ospedali*, it was established (in 1522) by the Republic, at the instigation of Gaetano of Thiene (later canonised). It housed women with incurable diseases, particularly syphilis; in 1524 it also began to take in orphans. By 1565 the *ospedale* had 300–400 occupants, and was now far too small. The present building (completed 1591) is sometimes attributed to Antonio da Ponte. In the centre is a large cloister, in the middle of which was the church; it has been attributed to Sansovino, although he died in 1570, long before the church was completed (*circa* 1600). Like the other *ospedali*, the Incurabili developed a famous reputation for music; the church was designed principally with musical and acoustic functions in mind. The Incurabili was suppressed in 1806, and a civic hospital established. In 1819 it became a barracks, and deteriorated; the church was demolished in 1831. Thereafter the Incurabili was a prison, until its recent restoration; the Accademia delle Belle Arti was transferred here in 2004–5.

The regular plan has an entrance in the centre of the Zattere façade, which is massive, simple and imposing, with three storeys. Inside is a loggia, formerly leading to the church. To the left and right are flank wings, with colonnades supporting the upper floors. Down each side of the cloister were two colonnaded infirmaries, each 65 metres long, divided into three aisles by double colonnades; boys on one side and girls on the other. On the upper floors was the residential accommodation. With the church gone, the large empty cloister can be seen in its entirety: very simple, seven bays by eleven, with rectangular windows to the upper floors. The church had an unusual plan, with straight sides and a large semicircular apse at each end. The choir was in galleries down the sides, with access by bridges from the surrounding dormitories.

Continue w along the Zattere, then take Fondamenta de Ca' Bragadin along the e bank of Rio de San Vio. At the n end it opens into Campo San Vio. The church, **Santi Vito e Modesto**, stood on the s side; founded in 912, it survived until 1808, when it was closed, and demolished five years later. On its site is a small oratory (1864–5) built by Pietro Crovato, with materials from the demolished church; Gothic Revival style, with striped marble to the lower façade, the rest in brickwork.

Take Calle de la Chiesa e, and continue along Fondamenta Venier dei Leoni. At DD 699–701 is the notable **Palazzo Venier dei Leoni**. In 1749 Lorenzo Boschetti was commissioned by the Venier to design a new palace, based on Longhena's Ca' Rezzonico, to extend from the Grand Canal to the Rio de le Toresele; it was extraordinarily ambitious, and only a fragment was ever completed. Boschetti's wooden model survives in the Correr collection. The plan was broad and symmetrical, with a grand enfilade of spaces down the central axis, from a spacious Grand Canal loggia to a transverse hall forming the land access from the quay to the s. The only element completed was the single-storey Grand Canal wing, with a central terrace, a three-bay loggia and a double row of fairly small rooms on each side. The basement and heavy central columns are rusticated, but all stops abruptly at what was to have been the first mezzanine floor level.

The modern history of this fragment begins with Peggy Guggenheim, a wealthy American heiress, who amassed an outstanding collection of twentieth-century art. In 1949 she bought Palazzo Venier; she died in 1979, but the foundation remains. It contains notable works by Klee, De Chirico, Chagall, Giacometti, Mondrian, Braque and others. Much of the site is an attractive sculpture garden.

West of Palazzo Venier is **Palazzo Centani (Zantani) Morosini** (DD 716), with Grand Canal façade; a tall, narrow, four-storey eighteenth-century house. Next to it again is the fifteenth-century *gotico fiorito* **Palazzo Da Mula Morosini** (DD 725); land access from Ramo da Mula. The original canal façade survives; four storeys, with paired watergates and two *piani nobili*. Next again, with flank wall to Campo San Vio, is **Palazzo Barbarigo** (DD 730), originally sixteenth-century Renaissance, but transformed in the late nineteenth century, when it was bought by the Compagnia Venezia e Murano, which produced glass and mosaics. In 1887 the façade was clad with mosaics, designed by Giulio Carlini.

Directly W of Campo San Vio, facing the Grand Canal, is the sixteenth-century **Palazzo Molin Loredan Cini** (DD 732); a narrow N façade, but a long principal façade to the *rio* at the side. The portal is reached by a private bridge. In the mid-twentieth century it was bought by the industrialist Vittorio Cini, together with the adjacent seventeenth-century **Palazzo Caldagno Cini Valmarana** (DD 864), immediately S; the Piscina façade has a large Serliana. Continuing W along the Piscina we reach the seventeenth-century **Palazzo Molin Balbi Valier della Tressa** (DD 866), built on the structure of an earlier Gothic house. To the W is a large garden The plan and Grand Canal façade are tripartite and symmetrical, with three orders. On the façade: two projecting side wings, added in the eighteenth century, clad with rusticated stone and framing the waterfront loggia.

To the W of the garden is the important early Renaissance **Palazzo Contarini dal Zaffo** (DD 875); land access from Cale Rota. The fine, rich façade is best seen from the Accademia bridge. The original owners are unknown; the Contarini modernised the interior comprehensively in 1562–82, but the exterior remains unaltered.

Palazzo Contarini dal Zaffo, sometimes attributed to Giovanni Buora, very late fifteenth century

During the eighteenth and nineteenth centuries, it underwent a series of ownerships; today it is owned by the duc de Polignac-Decazes.

The canal façade, sometimes given to Giovanni Buora, is influenced by both Codussi and Lombardo, the former in its refined proportions, the latter in its decoration: three superimposed orders, with no mezzanines or basement, thus resembling Palazzo Malipiero Trevisan at Santa Maria Formosa. The façade is clad with stone and marble, the three bays defined by fluted Corinthian pilasters. Between the first and second order is a broad, refined frieze, with reliefs of garlands and eagles. The *piani nobili* have elegant five-light windows to the *portego*, with stone balconies; the panels between the central and side wings are decorated with porphyry and marble *tondi*, with further *tondi* above and between the window heads. The plan is regular and tripartite, with a broad *androne*; the stairs are at the rear on the w side. At the s end of the *androne*: a three-bay loggia onto the rear courtyard.

Immediately w is **Palazzo Rota Brandolin** (DD 878), flank wall towards the Accademia bridge; a substantial seventeenth-century palace on the site of a Gothic house. The plan and façades are conventional, with five-light windows to the *piani nobili* and a prominent *abbaino*.

4 SANT'AGNESE, THE ZATTERE (3), GESUATI AND LA VISITAZIONE

Return E along the Calle Nova and Piscina, then take Fondamenta Venier down the W side of Rio de San Vio. At DD 737 is the site of the seventeenth-century **Palazzo Venier**, perhaps by Longhena; fragments of the portals and rusticated quoins survive. At DD 741: a surviving **Palazzo Venier**, also seventeenth century, with refined windows and a stone balcony. Turn right on Calle de Mezo, then left down Piscina Sant'Agnese. Turn right at the end to enter Campo Sant'Agnese. On the S side is the fifteenth-century Gothic **Palazzo Trevisan degli Ulivi** (DD 789 and 809); its broad Zattere façade has an elegant *quadrifora* to both *piani nobili*. The small garden contains the olives that give the house its name.

Sant'Agnese: the church defines the N side of the quiet, leafy square, its façade to the Rio Terà; founded perhaps in the tenth century, but rebuilt after 1105, again a century later. It was re-consecrated in 1321, and its exterior remains largely unchanged. A basilica plan, with a central nave and two lower side aisles; the W narthex is lost. The parish was suppressed in 1810, after which the church was used as a warehouse; all the interior fittings were lost or destroyed. In 1839 it was acquired by Marcantonio and Antonangelo Cavanis, who established an oratory here and a church school nearby. It was heavily restored, and again in 1939. The simple exterior is all of brick, with a tripartite façade, a square portal and an *ocio*. The nave has small paired clerestory windows, survivors from the early medieval construction.

Return to the Zattere, passing the imposing flank wall of the church of the **Gesuati (Santa Maria del Rosario)**. The Gesuati were followers of St John Colombini, and established this house in 1392. In 1493 the original oratory was rebuilt as a church, dedicated to the Visitation (see below). In 1668 the order was suppressed, and the site was given to the Dominicans. In 1726 a new church, by Massari, was begun to the E of the earlier one, together with the conventual buildings, begun in 1751. In the same period, Massari adapted the earlier church to become a library. After the Napoleonic suppression, the monastery became an orphanage managed by the Padri Somaschi, and the church was given parish status following the suppression of San Vio and San Gregorio.

It was Massari's first important commission in Venice; its heavy Palladian stone façade has a giant order of four Corinthian pilasters, with the central bay larger than the flanks. Above the deep architrave

The Gesuati church from the Giudecca; façade by Massari,
begun 1726

is a large pediment on corbels. The central portal is also Corinthian,
its columns supporting a segmental arched pediment. In the niches:
four large statues of Virtues by Giuseppe Torretti and others.

The plan is modelled on Palladio's Redentore, with three large
nave bays, alternating with narrower cross-bays, with paired columns;
down each side are three interconnecting chapels. The corners of the
nave plan are chamfered, those at the N end defining the grandiose
chancel arch. The chancel has a square plan, surmounted by a cupola
on pendentives; in the centre is Massari's rich marble altar, with an
impressive *baldacchino*. Beyond again is the choir, set at right angles to
the nave axis, and terminating with radiused apses.

The interior is rich and monumental, although the constructional
materials are limited to grey stone and white plaster; again
Corinthian, the nave columns supporting a deep, rich, continuous
trabeation that defines and encloses the space. On the walls between
the paired nave columns: sculptures of the life of Christ by
Morleiter. The barrel-vaulted ceiling is broken by cross-vaults with
large clerestory windows. Set into the nave ceiling are stucco reliefs
by Antonio Pelle, three framing notable frescoes by G. B. Tiepolo,

1737–9: the *Glory of St Dominic*, the *Institution of the Rosary* and *St Dominic Blessing a Dominican Friar*.

Nave flank walls and altars: first right chapel: the *Virgin and Child with Saints*, another fine work by Tiepolo, *circa* 1740. Second chapel: marble altarpiece by Morleiter, framing *St Dominic* by Giambattista Piazzetta, *circa* 1743. Third chapel: altarpiece of *St Vincent Ferrer* and other Dominican saints by Piazzetta, *circa* 1739. Left side chapels: first chapel: a good *Crucifixion* by Tintoretto, *circa* 1555. Second chapel: *Virgin and Child* by Antonio Rosa. Third chapel: altarpiece by Sebastiano Ricci, *circa* 1734.

The conventual buildings have two elements. The first, N, adjacent to the apses, and built around a small square cloister, was completed by Massari; the second, larger range to the NW, is incomplete.

Immediately w is the former church and monastery of **Santa Maria de la Visitazione**. The tripartite church façade is an attractive early Renaissance work, begun *circa* 1493; two orders, the taller lower one with a fine Lombard Renaissance portal, similar to Pietro Lombardo's at San Giobbe. Above the flat stone pilasters is a broad trabeation, while the richer upper order has a large central *ocio*, and single arched lights to the flanking bays. The crowning pediment contains a relief of two angels holding a monogrammed *scudo*; on the skyline: the Saviour flanked by two saints.

The interior is a simple rectangle, with a coffered timber ceiling, but bereft of all original fittings and decoration. A rare frescoed

frieze survives around the walls at high level, while the chancel has a small cupola on pendentives. The modest monastic buildings to the E were built after 1423, around a small rectangular cloister, with stone columns supporting brick arches.

Continue w along the Zattere; at DD 929: an attractive late Gothic house with a colonnade, modernised in the sixteenth century. Turn N along

Santa Maria de la Visitazione: fine early Renaissance portal to the Zattere, *circa* 1493

Fondamenta Nani. Opposite: the well-known *squero* (boatyard: see below). At DD 960 is the fine fifteenth-century *gotico fiorito* **Palazzo Barbarigo Nani Mocenigo**. Built *circa* 1460–70 by the Barbarigo, it passed to the Nani in 1501, and is still partly occupied by the family today. In the late sixteenth century the interior was modernised by Sansovino, with decoration by Vittoria. The tripartite façade is almost unaltered and nearly symmetrical, with a slightly wider left wing containing a second, small portal. Two *piani nobili*, of which the lower is more important; both have a refined *quadrifora* to the central hall, with later Baroque balconies. On the first *piano nobile* are two Barbarigo arms. The garden façade is similar, again with superimposed *quadrifore*, and a large arch from the *androne* into the garden.

5 THE CARITÀ CHURCH, THE SCUOLA GRANDE AND THE GALLERIE DE L'ACCADEMIA

Turn right along Calle Larga Nani, then left along Rio Terà de la Carità; at the end we reach Campo de la Carità and the Accademia. This important complex consists of three elements: the former monastic church of Santa Maria de la Carità, its (extended) monastic buildings and the former Scuola Grande de la Carità. Collectively they form the Gallerie de l'Accademia, with probably the world's finest collection of Venetian painting.

Santa Maria de la Carità: the first church was built in the early twelfth century, but in 1446 was rebuilt by regular Lateran canons from Lucca. Reconstruction took ten years, and the fabric of this late Gothic church survives, although radically altered internally and externally. Most of the decorative stonework was carved by Bartolomeo Bon; a single, broad, aisle-less nave, with a painted, decorated, open timber truss roof. Almost all the E end survives: three polygonal chapels, the larger central one forming the chancel, and all three with stone vaults. Some frescoes also survive. The *campo* façade had a rich Gothic portal, a large central *ocio* and three tall pointed gables; the skyline was enriched with aedicules with statues. All are now gone. The interior was also richly decorated, with paintings by the Vivarini and sculpture by Donatello. In the late 1480s the huge double monument to doges Agostin and Marco Barbarigo was installed, but was destroyed in 1807 when the church was deconsecrated.

The medieval monastic buildings survived until the later sixteenth century. By now the monastery was extremely wealthy, and in 1548–55 Palladio was appointed to redesign it. Work began in 1561, but in 1630 a fire destroyed most of Palladio's completed work. The only element surviving is the E wing, with its adjacent sacristy and staircase. In 1768 the order was suppressed, and in 1807 the Accademia delle Belle Arti was established here. Most of the other monastic buildings were destroyed when Selva and Lazzari built the present S picture galleries after 1820 (see below).

Palladio's E wing is simple but refined, the principal element being the three-storey, seven-bay, cloister façade, all in fine brickwork. The orders are Doric, Ionic and Corinthian, with rich terracotta entablatures, although the colonnades are now filled by modern glazed timber screens. The little Doric sacristy is at the N end on the ground floor, and is designed like a Roman *tablinium*, with an exedra containing two niches. The elegant helical stair also rises at the N end, with cantilevered stone steps and a large oval void in the centre; its design was highly influential, notably in Georgian Britain.

The former **Scuola Grande de la Carità** stands immediately W of the former church. It was founded in 1260, and moved here in 1294. In 1345 the Scuola bought a plot from the Carità monastery and construction began; it took several decades to complete. The small *albergo* wing was rebuilt in the 1440s, and survives today. Its ornate gilded ceiling is from 1496, while the W wall is still occupied by Titian's *Presentation of the Virgin*, commissioned in 1534. The much larger chapter-hall wing was altered in the eighteenth century by Massari, when the new paired curved staircase was built, and the lower hall was modernised. The upper hall retains its late medieval appearance (1461–84), when the rich, coffered, gilded ceiling was added by Marco Cozzi. Fragments of fresco wall decoration also survive. In 1760 the Gothic *campo* façade was replaced by the present heavy stone façade by Maccaruzzi, to a design by Massari; a giant order of four half-columns, set in pairs on a tall plinth; above the entablature is a low, plain attic.

The **Accademia delle Belle Arti** was founded in 1807 by Napoleonic decree; it grew from an earlier Accademia founded in 1750 under the presidency of the artist Giambattista Piazzetta, which met at the Fontego de la Farina. The Carità church was radically altered by the insertion of a mezzanine floor, dividing it into two, the lower hall for teaching studios, the upper one for display. In 1821 the massive new S wing was begun, to a design by Selva (who died in 1819) and executed by Lazzari. Several notable bequests were made in the nineteenth century. Modernisations of the galleries took place in 1920 under the director, Gino Fogolari, and in 1945 under Vittorio Moschini. The latter, including the displays, furniture and fittings, was by Carlo Scarpa.

In 2003–4 the Incurabili on the Zattere was vacated, and the teaching activities of the Accademia transferred there. This gave the galleries considerable space for expansion, and a major programme of restoration, enlargement and modernisation, begun in 2005, is still in progress.

6 FROM THE ACCADEMIA TO SAN TROVASO

In the Campo de l'Accademia: to the left, facing the Grand Canal, is **Palazzetto Querini Vianello** (DD 1051), a modest eighteenth-century house, until recently the British consulate. Continuing w along Calle Gambara, at DD 1056 is the substantial late seventeenth-century **Palazzo Mocenigo Gambara**, with a broad asymmetrical façade to the Grand Canal. The main hall is offset to the w, with a Serliana to the *piano nobile*. The s façade was once frescoed by Pordenone, while the interior has fine decoration, including frescoes by Giambattista Canal, 1796.

Continuing along Calle Contarini Corfù, we reach **Palazzo Contarini degli Scrigni** (DD 1057), again with a Grand Canal façade. The affix is said to derive from the numerous *scrigni* (caskets) that the extremely wealthy family possessed. It was begun by Scamozzi in 1608, as an extension to the adjacent Palazzo Contarini Corfù (see below), that the family already owned. Scamozzi also altered the other house, so that the floors all interconnected, although its Gothic façade remained unchanged. It remained in Contarini ownership until the death of Giacomo in 1838, who left his fine art collection to the nearby Accademia; his furniture went to Ca' Rezzonico. The stone canal façade has flat rustication to the lowermost order, and two generous upper orders. Unusually, neither has a central emphasis; instead, five large single lights, divided by paired pilasters, Ionic to the lower, Corinthian to the upper floor; an elegant crowning *abbaino*. The façade's design influenced Manopola, the Contin and Longhena. The rear façade has superimposed *logge* to the upper floors.

The adjacent **Palazzo Contarini Corfù** (DD 1057) is *gotico fiorito*, *circa* 1440–50, with a regular, symmetrical, tripartite canal façade, in the centre of which are *quadrifore* to the two principal floors; the lower has tracery based on that at the Doge's Palace. The affix may derive from a family member who was governor of the island. The flank façade to Rio de San Trovaso has an early Renaissance portico.

Turn left onto Fondamenta Priuli. Just past the bridge, on the left, is the imposing seventeenth-century **Palazzo Basadonna Priuli Giustinian Recanati** (DD 1012). Its last owners, the Giustinian Recanati, gave the palace to the Comune, and since 1975 it has been the Liceo d'Arte. The impressive façade is attributed to Francesco Contin, and has a large first-floor Serliana. The plan is conventional and tripartite, incorporating remains of an earlier Gothic house. The principal rooms have lavish decoration, dating from Priuli ownership after 1768. The large surviving garden, perhaps by Giuseppe Jappelli, was laid out in the English Romantic manner, with winding paths and small hills. Across Ponte de le Maravegie, on the right is **Palazzo Maravegia** (DD 1071), an attractive asymmetrical *gotico fiorito* house with two good superimposed *quadrifore, circa* 1470.

Opposite Palazzo Basadonna is the equally impressive, slightly later **Palazzo Bollani** (DD 1073), early eighteenth century, on the structure of another Gothic house; attributed to Tirali, but detailing more typical of the seventeenth century and Longhena. Today it houses the Liceo Classico Marco Polo. The broad façade is slightly asymmetrical, partly reflecting the trapezoidal plan, with a narrow extra left bay; it was originally capped by unusual chimney-obelisks. The plan is conventional, and the house conserves some fine stuccoed interiors. At the rear was a large garden, today occupied by a school.

Continuing down Fondamenta Toffetti, we reach **Palazzo Marcello Foscarini Sangiantoffetti Brandolin** (DD 1075). Modernised *circa* 1570, built over an earlier, probably fifteenth-century structure. In 1577 the façade was frescoed by Tintoretto, but no trace survives. It was badly damaged by fire in 1763. The palace is conventional, tripartite and symmetrical. Its rear garden was one of the largest in the city, and much remains undeveloped today. Adjacent, at DD 1097, is **Casa Brass**, built by the artist Italico Brass (1925) in a simple neo-Renaissance manner; the façade is decorated with numerous historic paterae. We reach Campo San Trovaso, which has two elements, one E of the church, the other to the SW. In front of us, between the two, is the well-known historic *squero* or boatyard (DD 1097), where gondolas are made and repaired; said to be one of only two surviving in the city; probably established in the seventeenth century. Restored several times; a picturesque

The boatyard and church of San Trovaso, the latter *circa* 1585–92

composition, best seen from Fondamenta Nani, with an L-shaped block of housing enclosing the timber boatsheds and slipways.

San Trovaso (Santi Gervasio e Protasio) is universally known by its popular contraction, one of the oldest parish foundations in Venice, perhaps ninth century. It was rebuilt by the Barbarigo and others in 1028, and was one of the largest parish churches in the city; its definitive reconstruction dates from 1585–92, after part of the nave collapsed; although of Palladian inspiration, it is usually attributed to Smeraldi, a close follower. In 1810, following the Napoleonic closures, the parish was extended to include San Basegio and part of Anzolo Rafael.

The church's form is rather obscured by residential accretions to the SE and W, but remains impressive. The campanile, from the same period, stands to the NE, near the bridge. The two façades represent the Latin cross of the plan; both are simple and monumental. The principal one is to the SW; the side façade, masking the E transept, is very similar. Both are of rendered brick, with stonework confined to the Corinthian pilaster capitals, corbels and the portal. In the upper order: huge thermal windows.

The spacious interior is lit by high-level windows. A broad three-bay nave is flanked by chapels, and has a barrel-vaulted ceiling;

Corinthian pilasters terminate with a heavy trabeation. The piers are all finished in pink *marmorino*. The right chancel chapel is that of the Molin family; the altarpiece is *Christ on the Cross, with the Three Marys*, by Domenico Tintoretto. In the chancel: two large canvases also by Domenico and his shop. To the left of the chancel: the Milledonne Chapel: the altarpiece is the *Temptation of St Anthony*, by Tintoretto, restored but impressive.

Outside, across the canal (sw), at DD 1372–4, is a block of apartments, built by Jacopo Sansovino after 1552, as a commercial venture for rental income; there were many such developments in the sixteenth century.

7 TOLETA, LE EREMITE AND THE ZATTERE (4)

We retrace our steps as far as Ponte de le Meravegie; this time, turn left along Calle de la Toleta, following it around to the narrow canal. Cross Ponte del Squero, take the short Fondamenta, then turn right down Calle de' Cerchieri. At the end are three houses with their façades to the Grand Canal; they are best seen from San Samuele, on the far side. The first is **Palazzo Marioni Mainella** (DD 1259), reached from Ramo dell'Ambasciatore. Built in 1858 by the artist Ludovico Cadorin; a rather eclectic neo-Renaissance façade, broad and low, returning down the *rio* at the side. The upper parts are clad with decorative brickwork. Immediately adjacent is the Gothic **Palazzo Loredan dell'Ambasciatore** (DD 1261), with a noble, symmetrical canal façade. Built *circa* 1450–70, it incorporates early Renaissance details, notably the two niches set into the canal façade. It was built by the Loredan; the affix derives from the Austrian embassy based here after 1754. The palace was badly damaged by fire in 1891, but immediately restored. The fine façade has two tall *piani nobili*, with *quadrifore* to the two upper halls; they have rich capitals. The lower has tracery modelled on the Doge's Palace, the upper is simpler *gotico fiorito*. In the niches are Renaissance figures of soldiers carrying the Barbarigo family arms, sometimes attributed to Pietro Lombardo. The third in this group is **Palazzo Diedo Moro Dolfin Barbini** (DD 1263a), just north of the Loredan. A substantial early sixteenth-century house, extensively modernised in the nineteenth century, with a broad canal façade.

Return to Fondamenta de la Toleta, and turn left at the N end, along Fondamenta Lombardo; at the end, turn left again onto

Palazzo Loredan dell'Ambasciatore: detail of Grand Canal façade

Fondamenta del Borgo. The attractive Rio de le Romite is lined with vernacular houses. On the other side is **Le Eremite (Convento di Gesù, Giuseppe e Maria)**, founded by Augustinian nuns in 1693. The little church (1693–4) has a simple canal façade, although the interior is richly decorated, divided into two spaces by the monumental high altar. The conventual buildings lie to the w and s of the church, built around two large cloisters; their appearance is equally simple. The nunnery was suppressed by Napoleon, but in 1863 the Cavanis brothers established a girls' school here, run by Canossian nuns, who remain there today. Continue down Fondamenta de le Romite, cross both bridges at the s end; down Calle Trevisan we reach the w section of the Zattere.

Towards Ponte Longo, at DD 1381 is **Palazzo Moro**, probably fourteenth century, with six trilobate windows and a Gothic figure of a saint. At DD 1397 is the sixteenth-century **Palazzo Priuli Bon**, with a *quadrifora* to the main upper hall; today the French consulate. Further w, at DD 1402, is **Palazzo Giustinian Recanati**, also from the sixteenth century, but extensively modernised in the early eighteenth century by Giovanni Battista Recanati, a noted bibliophile and art collector; on his death his library was left to the Biblioteca Marciana. The palace is still owned by his family. Its severe exterior masks a rich, opulent, eighteenth-century interior. At DD 1410 is **Palazzo**

Part of the western section of the Zattere, with the sixteenth-century Palazzi Priuli Bon (right) and Giustinian Recanati (left centre)

Molin: fifteenth-century Gothic, with a *quadrifora* to the *piano nobile*; in recent times the offices of the Società Adriatica. **Palazzo Zorzi** (DD 1416) is also fifteenth-century Gothic, with reliefs set into the façade, including a Gothic *scudo* and a twelfth-century cross.

Diverting briefly, take Calle Corteloto inland, and cross the bridge at the end. To the right is the church and monastery of **Ognissanti**. Established in 1472 by Cistercian nuns from Torcello; by 1505 they had begun reconstruction of the original small chapel, in a rather Codussian manner, completed *circa* 1520. The monastic complex was completed only *circa* 1586. It survived until the Napoleonic closure of 1806; in 1820 it reopened as a girls' school, and later became a geriatric hospital, when parts of the monastic buildings were demolished. The church has a tall, tripartite façade, with a good Lombard portal, incorporating the Priuli arms.

Return to the Zattere and continue w towards San Basegio. At DD 1473 is the former **Scuola dei Luganegheri**, the guildhall of the sausage-makers, late seventeenth century, in the style of Longhena. The façade has two orders, the simpler lower one with four doorways, the upper richer, with three tall arched bays. In the centre is *St Anthony Abbot*, the patron, flanked by large windows. At the end of the quay, at DD 1514–20, is **Palazzo Molin**, in fact a large apartment block with rear façade to Campo San Basegio. Built *circa* 1560 by the Molin as a commercial development, it contains eight apartments over four storeys, each apartment comprising one-quarter of the two *piani nobili*, with ancillary accommodation in the

San Sebastiano: façade by Scarpagnino, 1506–48

mezzanines above and below. The ground floor contained stores.
Entering the square, the former church of **San Basegio (San Basilio)** stood on the E side; founded in the tenth century, it was closed in 1810, and demolished fourteen years later. Walk N along Fondamenta San Basegio to Ponte San Sebastiano.

8 SAN SEBASTIANO AND THE ANZOLO RAFAEL (ANGELO RAFFAELE)

San Sebastiano: originated in the late fourteenth century as a hospital for the poor and an oratory, occupied by the congregation of San Girolamo. The church was rebuilt by Scarpagnino (1506–48), who altered its orientation, with a new façade to the E. An elegant all-stone composition, with two superimposed orders and a crowning pediment. Three bays, defined by paired Corinthian columns on tall plinths: two narrow outer ones, and a broad central one, containing the portal. In the upper order is an *ocio*, while the outer bays of both orders have large rectangular windows.

The single nave is preceded by a lobby, above which is the choir gallery or *barco*, which continues down the two sides of the nave. Below it are three small chapels on each side. Between the chapels are arches supported by refined pilasters and crowned by a balustrade. A large arch leads into the deep chancel, lit by windows set into the drum that carries a cupola. In the centre is the imposing free-standing high altar, screening the semicircular apse.

The church is noted for a remarkable series of frescoes and canvases by Veronese, begun in 1555. The first were those to the sacristy ceiling, with the crowned Virgin in the centre, surrounded by the Evangelists. He then began the compartments of the coffered nave ceiling, depicting the life of Esther; these were followed by a fresco of the Assumption in the cupola (later replaced by a work by Sebastiano Ricci, also now lost). Veronese's next work was the frescoed frieze around the upper nave walls, with the Fathers of the Church and episodes from the life of St Sebastian, *circa* 1558; in 1559–61 he painted the high altarpiece, the *Virgin and Child and Saints*. From the same period are the organ doors, and from 1565 the large canvases to the chancel side walls. In 1570 Veronese painted a *Last Supper* for the adjacent refectory (now at the Brera, Milan). After his death in 1588, he was buried in the church, with a monument adjacent to the organ.

Other works of art include: nave, right side, first altar: *Virgin and Child*, an early work by Veronese; third altar: *Christ on the Cross*, a late Veronese. Right chancel chapel: altarpiece by Palma il Giovane. Nave side chapels, left side: first chapel, of the Grimani: marble portrait of Marcantonio Grimani by Vittoria. Second chapel: *Baptism of Christ* by Veronese's studio.

Outside, the free-standing campanile was built in 1544–7; we continue NW across the Campazzo and into Campo de l'Anzolo Rafael.

L'Anzolo Rafael (Angelo Raffaele) is one of the city's oldest parish foundations, said to date from AD 416; others claim AD 640. It was rebuilt two or three times before the present reconstruction by Francesco Contin, *circa* 1618–40. Further modernisations followed in 1676 and 1685; in 1735 the façade was rebuilt. Contin's essential structure survives; the plan is a Greek cross, almost a square, with the façade to the N and the chancel at the S end. The three simple external façades (N, W and E) have two orders and three broad bays divided by pilasters; above the stone N portal is *Raphael with Tobias*, perhaps by Sebastiano Mariani. The interior is tall, spacious and harmonious, with a large square central bay. The chancel is also square, flanked by smaller chapels. Articulation consists of a giant order of Corinthian pilasters supporting a rich, complex trabeation; by contrast, the arches defining the nave bays are very simple. The central bay has an equally simple barrel-vaulted ceiling; the square corner bays have cross-vaults.

Inside the N façade the organ has notable parapet paintings by Francesco or Gianantonio Guardi. Other paintings include works by Fontebasso, Palma il Giovane, Morleiter and Bonifacio de' Pitati.

9   MENDIGOLA AND SANTA MARTA

From the church's N façade, cross the bridge and walk W along Fondamenta Barbarigo and Fondamenta Lizza Fusina. This is the former peninsula of Mendigola, historically one of the poorest, most remote parts of the city. At the end, turn right into Campo de l'Oratorio. The eighteenth-century Baroque **Oratorio di Maria Vergine e San Filippo Neri** (DD 1838) has an elegant portal surmounted by a blind window. Immediately N is the ancient parish foundation of **San Niccolò dei Mendicoli**, established in the seventh century. The affix is said to derive from the poverty of the inhabitants: *mendicità* = begging. The church was rebuilt in the 1100s; part of this basilica survives, with a long central nave, two lower side aisles and a semicircular eastern apse. The characteristic W narthex, although rebuilt in the 1920s, probably resembles its original appearance, and is the only survivor other than that at San Giacometto. It has a four-bay timber colonnade supporting a continuous architrave and a lean-to roof. The church was partly rebuilt in the early 1300s, when the nave capitals were replaced by the present ones, and the roof was reconstructed; the transepts were also formed in this period.

Further modernisation took place *circa* 1580, when the upper nave walls were clad with decorated timber panelling, statues and paintings. A flat, coffered ceiling was added, and an iconostasis erected in front of the chancel. The final alterations, *circa* 1760, comprised a new stone N façade, an attractive little Baroque work, perhaps by the Roman Paolo Posi, who may also have designed the adjacent oratory. Its central portal has a curved pediment, and is flanked by niches with statues; at the top: a broken pediment, with a third niche containing a statue. A long programme of restoration of the church took place after 1971.

San Niccolò dei Mendicoli: interior of nave

The interior is a modified axial basilica, with transepts. Its six-bay nave colonnade retains its twelfth-century marble columns, now with fourteenth-century capitals (three are dated: 1361, 1364 and 1366). The semicircular arches have decorative keystones, above which is a rich trabeation, continuing across the E end to form the iconostasis. Above the nave trabeation, the clerestory has Corinthian pilasters, with paintings of the life of Christ between them. Those on the right: school of Veronese and Palma il Giovane; those on the left by Alvise dal Friso. The flat ceiling contains several large paintings. All is richly decorated and gilded. The three-bay iconostasis is supported by paired marble columns, and above is a painted and gilded sixteenth-century *Crucifixion*, perhaps by Campagna. Defining the transepts are two large fifteenth-century Gothic arches, with contemporary fresco decoration. In the chancel: a polychrome wooden statue of St Nicholas, 1457, attributed to the Bon workshop.

Adjacent to the SW is the stocky twelfth-century brick campanile, one of the oldest in the city.

The zone N and W of Mendigola was transformed in the nineteenth century by extensive reclamations. Immediately W, across the *rio*, is part of the large former **Cotonificio Veneziano** cotton factory (*circa* 1882–1900), restored and now used by IUAV. Further W again is an area of mid-twentieth-century housing. To the S is the Stazione Marittima, with docks and warehouses. Further N is a large triangular site, reclaimed in 1815 as a military parade ground, later an industrial zone (Veneziana Gas). The historic limit of this district was a narrow peninsula ending at the w at the former church of **Santa Marta**, founded in 1315 as a hospital and chapel for the poor; later a Benedictine nunnery was established, and in 1466 the church was rebuilt. This fabric survives, stripped of all internal fittings. The order was suppressed in 1805; soon afterwards, the monastic buildings were demolished. The church has been recently restored for community uses.

10 FROM LE TERESE TO THE TERENI NUOVI

Return to San Nicolò, and walk e along Fondamenta de le Terese. The **Convento de le Terese** was founded by Carmelites in 1647. The present buildings are by Cominelli, *circa* 1688. The nunnery survived until the Napoleonic suppression in 1810; it was then converted into an orphanage; today, part is used as a school, and the church is restored. The plan derives from Palladio's Zitelle, the church framed by two wings of conventual buildings. At the rear, the former nunnery wraps around a large central courtyard. The church has a broad, plain façade, with two orders, but no articulation. Its interior is spatially simple but tall, rich and imposing. The plan is almost square, uninterrupted by columns or piers, with a square n projection for the chancel. Perimeter articulation is a giant order of flat Corinthian pilasters, supporting a deep, rich entablature. The chancel is approached by a large semicircular arch on fluted Corinthian columns. Around the nave perimeter are side altars, above which are large clerestory windows. The flat coffered ceiling is also richly carved and decorated, while the complex high altar is finished with decorative marble. The many paintings include works by Francesco Ruschi, Guarana and Niccolò Renieri.

Immediately e is the **Ospizio Contarini** (DD 2209), probably late fourteenth or early fifteenth century, with a first-floor *trifora*. Cross Ponte de le Terese and turn s down Corte Maggiore, to reach Fondamenta Barbarigo; turn left. At DD 2356 is **Palazzo Barbarigo**, late seventeenth century, with a *bifora* to the upper hall. Next door, at DD 2364: the enclosing wall and fifteenth-century portal, all that remains of the former **Convento de le Pizzochere de San Francesco**. Continue e along Fondamenta Briati. At DD 2376–8 is **Palazzo Ariani**, built in the fourteenth century on the structure of an

Palazzo Ariani; tracery detail

earlier house. In 1650 it passed to the Pasqualigo; in 1849 it was acquired by the city and today houses the Istituto Tecnico Vendramin Corner. Both plan and façade are asymmetrical, lacking the left wing. The pièce de résistance is the six-light window to the upper hall, with complex geometrical interlocking tracery. The inspiration perhaps came from Spain or France, where such tracery was prevalent in the period; there are no precedents in the city. Within the small side *cortile* rises an external stair to the colonnaded *liagò* on the upper floor.

Continue E and cross Ponte del Soccorso. The **Chiesa del Soccorso (Santa Maria Assunta)** was founded by the famous courtesan, poet and benefactor Veronica Franco in 1593, as a home for 'traduced' women. An oratory was established, consecrated in 1609. It flourished until the Napoleonic closures (1807), but was later reoccupied by a religious order. A simple façade, with two orders, Doric and Ionic. Along the quay is **Palazzo Zenobio** (DD 2597), designed by Gaspari for the Zenobio in the late seventeenth century; behind the restrained façade are some of the most splendid Baroque interiors in the city. Following the extinction of the Zenobio, in the mid-nineteenth century the palace was acquired by the Mechitarist order, and it became an important seat of Armenian learning. Today it is used for cultural events.

The broad quay façade is imposing but reticent, with the exception of the central bays: a Serliana to the *piano nobile*, and a long stone balcony; six further bays on each side. The garden façade is similar, with a Palladian window to the *piano nobile*.

The house has an exceptionally wide plan in the form of a C, with two rear wings enclosing a paved courtyard, leading into a substantial garden. The front canal block is symmetrical, the portal giving access to a square colonnaded atrium, at the far side of which is a narrower, more conventional *androne* leading to the rear façade. The atrium is flanked by narrower hallways giving access to two rows of side rooms.

The *piano nobile* is richly finished. Above the atrium is a large rectangular ballroom, linked to the *portego* by a Palladian archway, the T-shaped plan repeating that below; the arch supports a musicians' gallery. The sumptuous white and gold decoration, with numerous

Palazzo Zenobio: interior of the first-floor ballroom, by Gaspari, late seventeenth century; decoration by Louis Dorigny

mirrors, is by Louis Dorigny, G. B. Tiepolo and Carlevarijs. The illusionistic decoration inspired the ballroom at Ca' Rezzonico.

The formal garden survives, divided from the courtyard by a wrought-iron screen and gates. At the far end, on axis with the house, is a library pavilion, by Temanza, *circa* 1767; a large central loggia to the symmetrical façade.

Continue E along Fondamenta del Soccorso, into Campo dei Carmini. We divert briefly northwards; cross Ponte dei Carmini, follow the quay W and then N along Fondamenta Rossa. At the far end is Ponte Rosso onto Fondamenta dei Cereri. This is the S part of the Tereni Nuovi, a marshy area reclaimed from the lagoon at the end of the fifteenth century (see also Santa Croce). At the E end is **Corte San Marco** (DD 2478–504), 1529–42, built by the Scuola Grande di San Marco as almshouses for poor members: twenty-four cottages around a central courtyard, all originally on two floors, now mostly with three. Further W on the same islet, at DD 2410–30, are two long four-storey apartment blocks, built in 1555–7 by Paolo d'Ana, as a speculative rental development. They are all regularly and repetitively planned. Return down Fondamenta Rossa to the Carmini.

11 THE CHURCH AND SCUOLA GRANDE DEI CARMINI

Chiesa e monastero dei Carmini (Santa Maria Assunta del Carmelo): the Carmelites arrived in Venice in the thirteenth century; the present church was begun in 1286, consecrated in 1348. It was restored several times thereafter; in 1515 a major modernisation of the interior and the *campo* façade was begun by Sebastiano da Lugano. Towards the end of the century, further internal works included the addition of high-level nave panelling, resembling that at San Niccolò dei Mendicoli; the aisles were also raised in height. The adjacent monastic buildings (W) were all rebuilt in the early sixteenth century; the campanile, one of the tallest in the city, was also reconstructed. It was restored by Sardi in 1688. In 1810 the house was suppressed, and the monastery today houses an art college. The church was given parish status, absorbing those of San Barnaba and Santa Margarita.

The N façade is a simple Codussian composition, all brick with stone articulation. The three bays are defined by pilasters, and the façade terminates with quadrants to the side aisles and a larger

Rio de San Barnaba, towards the campanile of the Carmini

semicircular pediment to the nave. The portal has an unusual double pediment; an octagonal *ocio* in the centre of the upper order, and five statues on the skyline. On the long E flank wall: an unusual fourteenth-century portico, with a boldly projecting brick arched canopy, capped by a double-pitched tiled roof, and supported by marble columns and rich stone corbels.

The basilica plan has survived the numerous interventions; it is very long, with a twelve-bay nave, beyond which is a square crossing and two short transepts. Beyond again is the chancel, terminating in a polygonal apse. The aisles also end with polygonal apses.

The interior is solemnly imposing, its strong linear emphasis dominated by the close-set rhythm of the nave colonnades. The capitals are linked by tie beams, while the sixteenth-century semicircular arches have gilded wooden statues in the spandrels. Directly above are timber panels in which paintings are set. Above again, thermal windows define the clerestory, while the nave ceiling is a simple plastered cross-vault. The Gothic chancel apse is largely subsumed by the modernisations of 1507.

The church contains several significant works of art. Right side aisle: first altar: *Deposition*, school of Tintoretto. Second altar: *Nativity* by Cima, *circa* 1509. Third altar: the *Virgin in Glory*, school of Titian.

Fourth altar: *Circumcision*, once attributed to Tintoretto, 1548. The end bays of the nave are occupied by the organ gallery (left) and the choir gallery (right). Their late sixteenth-century decoration is by Marco Vicentino and Andrea Schiavone. In the chancel: paintings by Querena, Palma il Giovane, Diziani and Vicentino. The high-level paintings down the nave flanks are scenes from the history of the Carmelites, some attributed to Luca Giordano. The sacristy, reached from the right aisle, retains some original fifteenth-century decoration.

The conventual buildings to the w centre on the large, square, seven-bay cloister, with simple arched colonnades. On the N side is the Gothic chapter house, three bays long, with two *trifore*.

Immediately NE is the **Scuola Grande dei Carmini**, established by a confraternity from the church in 1594. In 1625 most of the restricted site was acquired and cleared of existing buildings. The Scuola was designed by Franco Cantello, and inaugurated in 1638, although not complete until 1663. Decoration of the upper chapter hall was begun by Domenico Bruni in 1664. In 1668 a further adjacent plot at the s corner was acquired; it was now possible to complete and unite the two main façades, to the sw and SE. Longhena had the difficult task of reconciling the façades with the completed fabric behind them; both were begun *circa* 1668.

Between 1740 and 1749 G. B. Tiepolo decorated the chapter hall, while the *albergo* was decorated by Gaetano Zompini in 1751; the rich staircase is by Gaspari, Longhena's pupil. In 1767 the Scuola was elevated to a *scuola grande*, the last to be thus recognised. It was suppressed in 1806, and many art works removed, but was reconstituted in 1840 and survives today.

Both façades are clad with fine stonework, although different in character. The shorter SE façade is more strongly articulated, with five bays defined by paired fluted Corinthian columns, and two orders, the lower having two portals alternating with three windows. The similar upper order has larger, prominent windows above the portals. The longer sw façade has a tall lower order with flat rustication, again with two prominent doorways. The two upper orders are not identical, the first floor having two large lights above the portals, detailed as aedicules, while the upper order has ten identical lights.

The plan is a compact rectangle, the lower hall having a tripartite plan, three bays long. At the N end is the fine staircase, rising in two flights to a long transverse intermediate landing, richly stuccoed, and from which a further central flight rises to the upper hall.

Scuola Grande dei Carmini: detail of south-east façade, by
Longhena, *circa* 1668

Inside, the small ground-floor sacristy has rich stucco decoration,
while the *androne* has an open timber ceiling. The upper chapter hall
is noted for Tiepolo's famous ceiling, 1739–44. The nine pictures
form a unified composition, with the *Virgin in Glory* in the centre,
surrounded by angels in flight and the Virtues. On the walls:
paintings by Zanchi and Lazzarini. Adjacent is the Sala de l'Archivio,
whose lower walls are clad in rich timber panelling and figures,
probably by Francesco Pianta. The coffered ceiling has nine
compartments, with paintings by Menescardi, a follower of Tiepolo.
Adjacent to the fine Palladian doorway into the *albergo* is *Judith and
Holofernes* by Giambattista Piazzetta. The *albergo* ceiling contains an
Assumption by Padovanino.

Take Calle de le Pazienze down the long E flank of the Carmini church, cross the bridge and continue to the junction with Calle Longa San Barnaba; turn left. This long, straight *calle* has characteristic small vernacular housing. Continue into Campo San Barnaba.

San Barnaba: the heavy stone Palladian façade dominates the small, lively square. Said to have been founded in 809 and reconstructed two or three times, the present church is by Lorenzo Boschetti, a follower of Massari, 1749–76. The façade is based on Massari's nearby Gesuati, with giant Corinthian semi-columns and a large pediment. The broad central bay contains the over-sized portal, itself Corinthian; the outer bays are much narrower, with niches for statues. The outer corners are defined by a complex massing of Corinthian pilasters and half-columns.

Inside: a broad, spacious aisle-less nave, with a giant order of Corinthian half-columns down the flanks and three altars down each side. The chancel has a rectangular plan, covered with a cross-vault frescoed by Costantino Cedini. On the chancel flank walls: two works by Palma il Giovane. The first left altar has an altarpiece perhaps by Veronese.

The ancient campanile stands on the edge of the canal towards the NE; one of the oldest in the city, probably twelfth century, with a conical tiled 'pine cone' roof. Diverting briefly down Calle del Tragheto (right side of church), at DD 2784 is a good small fourteenth-century Gothic house, with a first-floor *quadrifora*; restored, today a hotel. At the end, by the *vaporetto* stop (right) is **Palazzetto Stern** (DD 2792a), with Grand Canal façade. Designed by Giuseppe Berti, and built 1909–12 for a Madame Stern, in an eclectic neo-Gothic manner, asymmetrical and romantic. In front is a terrace garden. On the N side of the little quay are the two small **Palazzi Contarini Michiel** (DD 2793–4), both seventeenth century, with asymmetrical façades.

Return to Campo San Barnaba. Take Fondamenta Gherardini (W) and then Ponte dei Pugni, scene of historic fist fights between the two popular factions of Castellani and Nicolotti. Continue up the broad Rio Terà Canal, then left into **Campo Santa Margarita**: one of the largest parish squares in Venice, with a spacious trapezoidal form; it has always been associated with the poor and artisan classes, and was frequently the scene of popular entertainments. It contains a small market, and remains the social hub of the district. There are

San Barnaba: Palladian façade by Lorenzo Boschetti, 1749–76;
twelfth-century campanile

several historic buildings, most on the NW side. At DD 2927–35 is
Palazzetto Foscolo Corner, built in the 1380s for the Corner,
although some elements are earlier. The broad façade has only two
storeys, the ground floor probably always occupied by commercial
activities, and a single spacious *piano nobile*. The unusual portal
(probably thirteenth century) has a brick arched head with rich
terracotta decoration; the tympanum contains the Corner arms, with
an angel above (fourteenth century). On the *piano nobile*: random
fenestration, with a *quadrifora* lighting the main hall, all fourteenth
century. The façade is crowned by boldly projecting eaves on
barbacani. The complex plan reflects numerous alterations over the
centuries; behind the shallow right wing is a courtyard, containing
an open stair to the first floor.

Immediately left are two other Gothic houses, at DD 2980–85;
both late fourteenth century, again with a low ground floor used
for commercial activity, and a single *piano nobile* above. The left

Palazzetto Foscolo Corner, thirteenth-century portal, fourteenth-century first floor

house is roughly symmetrical and tripartite; the other is bipartite, lacking the left wing. Their fenestration reflects this, with a *trifora* in the centre of the left house's façade, and an off-centre *trifora* to the right house. All the windows are trilobate, similar to those at Palazzetto Corner.

To the NE of Palazzetto Corner, at DD 2945 and 2961: two more interesting medieval houses. That on the right (DD 2961) is older, originally thirteenth century, with a large *trifora*; the façade is again capped by overhanging eaves in the Tuscan manner. The left house also has a tall *piano nobile* above shops and workshops, with a Corner *stemma* and a large *bifora*; the early fourteenth-century windows have inflected heads.

Towards the s end of the square is the free-standing former **Scuola dei Varotari** (DD 3020), the tanners' guildhall, 1725, in a neo-medieval style. A simple rectangle, with two superimposed halls, the upper one used for assemblies and services. The main façade is symmetrical, with a simple portal and windows. In the centre: a niche containing the *Madonna de la Misericordia* (1502), from their old hall at the Gesuiti. Since its closure by Napoleon, the hall has been used for many functions, including local council meetings.

We return to the N end of the square shortly. Next, take the Rio Terà Canal back towards San Barnaba, and then turn left along Fondamenta Alberti and Fondamenta Rezzonico. The quay

Ca' Rezzonico: Grand Canal façade, begun by Longhena, 1667; third order completed by Massari, 1756

terminates at the vast, imposing **Ca' Rezzonico** (DD 3136), one of Longhena's masterpieces and perhaps the greatest Baroque palace in the city. It was commissioned by Filippo Bon in 1667, and constructed until Longhena's death in 1682, when it was still incomplete. Work continued under Gaspari, but in 1712 Bon died, and his descendants had insufficient funds to construct the upper *piano nobile*. It remained in this condition for fifty years, until in 1750 it was bought by Giambattista Rezzonico, who employed Massari to build the second *piano nobile* (1756), the ballroom and ceremonial staircase. In 1758 Rezzonico's son was elected pope (Clement XIII). The palace remained Rezzonico property until 1810; it then passed to the Widmann, and several other successive owners. In 1934 it was sold to the city, which then established the Museo del Settecento, inaugurated in 1936, and which remains here today. In 1979 a twenty-year restoration programme began.

The plan is tripartite, although departing from tradition in some respects. The central *androne* is flanked by two rows of minor rooms; at the Grand Canal façade is a three-bay portico. The principal private stair rises halfway down one side. At the other end is a loggia onto a central courtyard; at the back of the palace the two rear wings are linked by the ballroom wing, with its axis orthogonal to the *androne*. The ballroom is reached by the grand staircase from the rear vestibule. Both *piani nobili* are traditionally planned, with a central *portego* and smaller rooms down each side.

The Grand Canal façade (best seen from San Samuele) is one of the most monumental in the city. It rises from a massive socle, with three orders, Doric, Ionic and Corinthian, capped by a low attic. The first is clad with powerfully rusticated stonework, with a central three-bay loggia, defined by rusticated Doric half-columns and reached by a broad sweep of steps. The same articulation defines the side bays, two on each flank. The *piano nobile* departs from the traditional tripartite division, and derives from Sansovino's Ca' Corner, with a continuous row of seven equal bays across the façade, only the double columns at the corners providing local emphasis. The windows are framed by smaller Ionic colonnettes, with carved figures in the arch spandrels, and a full-width stone balcony. The order terminates with a broad trabeation. Massari's third order is a little less rich, but with the same basic articulation. Above is a much thinner trabeation, and finally the attic, lit by seven oval windows, and capped by a bold cornice. The long flank façade to Rio de San Barnaba is less monumentally detailed, with tall, arched, single-light windows, each with a stone balcony.

Land access is by a rusticated stone portal, inside which is a fountain set into a niche, with the Rezzonico arms. The *androne* is simple but imposing, with portals at intervals down the sides. Massari's Corinthian stair of honour rises to the ballroom in two long straight flights and a half-landing. The ballroom, measuring 24 by 14 metres and 12 metres in height, is richly decorated with frescoes and illusionistic paintings. In the ceiling is an allegory by Giambattista Crosato, the *Four Regions of the World*; most of the other decoration is by Pietro Visconti. Other than the portal, almost all the wall decoration is fictive.

The following brief notes describe the main features of the principal rooms:

Room 2: of the *Allegory of Marriage*: ceiling fresco by G. B. Tiepolo.

From the corner, stairs lead to a small suite of mezzanine rooms, with eighteenth-century stucco decoration, once occupied by Robert Browning.

Room 3: Chapel: original gilded stucco decoration.

Room 4 (of the pastels): ceiling by Giambattista Crosato; a collection of pastels by Rosalba Carriera.

Room 5 (of the tapestries): ceiling: *Allegory of Virtue* by Guarana.

Room 6 (throne room): ceiling: *Allegory of Merit* by G. B. Tiepolo; the room is sumptuously decorated.

Room 7 (Tiepolo room): ceiling: *Fortitude* and *Wisdom* by G. B. Tiepolo; other paintings by G. D. Tiepolo

Room 8: passageway with display cases.

Room 9 (library): fine original bookcases; ceiling paintings by Francesco Maffei.

Room 10 (Lazzarini room): three mythological paintings by Gregorio Lazzarini.

Room 11 (Brustolon room): fine furniture by the Brustolon workshop. Ceiling decoration by Maffei.

Room 12 (main *portego*): an imposing hall with a fine central doorway, flanked by figures of Atlas by Vittoria. Family busts and portraits.

Second *piano nobile*:

Room 13 (upper *portego*): paintings from the Correr collection: Giambattista Piazzetta, Diziani, Guardi, Carlevarijs, Zuccarelli and G. D. Tiepolo.

Room 14 (Guardi room): three good frescoes by Francesco Guardi.

Room 15 (alcove room): reassembled from Palazzo Carminati; contemporary furniture.

Room 16 (Cabinet of the Hawk): ceiling fresco by G. D. Tiepolo.

Room 17 (Stucco room): stucco from Palazzo Calbo Crotta.

Room 18 (Green drawing room): Chinoiserie furniture; ceiling by Francesco Guardi.

Room 19 (Longhi room): ceiling by G. B. Tiepolo; a collection of genre paintings by Pietro Longhi.

Room 20 (*ridotto*): paintings by the Guardi, Longhi, G. B. Tiepolo; the Guardi paintings depict a *ridotto*, giving the room its name.

Room 21 (passageway): paintings by Marco Ricci and others.

Room 22 (Spinet room): Rezzonico family portraits.

Off this room: a small suite of rooms (23–6) decorated with frescoes by G. B. Tiepolo, from his own villa at Zianigo; delightful scenes of rural life.

Room 27 (chapel): fresco by G. D. Tiepolo.

Rooms 28 and 29: both decorated with frescoes by G. D. Tiepolo; some highly skilful monochrome works.

13   CA' GIUSTINIAN, CA' FOSCARI AND SANTA MARGARITA (2)

Return along the Fondamenta; turn right into Calle de le Botteghe, Calle del Fabro and Calle Bernardo. At DD 3197 is **Palazzo Nani Bernardo**, with Grand Canal façade; a modest, late sixteenth-century house. Immediately to the N is the seventeenth-century **Palazzo Giustinian Bernardo** (DD 3199), with an asymmetrical façade and unusual paired windows; two watergates. Return down Calle Bernardo and turn right into Calle del Capeler, which opens into the attractive Campielo dei Squelini. To the E are three exceptionally fine late Gothic palaces, the two **Ca' Giustinian** (DD 3228 and 3232) and the famous **Ca' Foscari** (DD 3246). Their splendid Grand Canal façades are best seen from Ramo Grassi, next to Palazzo Grassi.

The two Giustinian palaces (1450s) are a 'matching pair', each a mirror of the other, both in plan and in their contiguous façades. They have been attributed to Bartolomeo Bon, chiefly because the refined pendant tracery is modelled on Bon's tracery for the Ca' d'Oro (1420s). Today one of the palaces is owned by the Brandolini d'Adda family, the other by Ca' Foscari university.

The plans are essentially tripartite and symmetrical, both taking the form of a C, with the small central courtyards abutting each other on each side of the 'party wall'; two larger courtyards at the rear have land access from Calle Giustinian. Both palaces have two superimposed *piani nobili*, the lower one reached from the smaller inner courtyard, the upper from open staircases in the larger rear courtyards. The Grand Canal façades are noble and impressive; the central watergate terminates the narrow Calle Giustinan, while each palace has its own central watergate. The *piani nobili* are treated a little differently, the upper one having a six-light window with richer tracery modelled on that at the Doge's Palace. Above the *piani*

Palazzi Giustinian (left and centre) and Ca' Foscari (right); all *circa* 1450–60

nobili the attic storey has a central *quadrifora*; all the detailing is rich
gotico fiorito.

Immediately N is the even more imposing **Ca' Foscari**,
approached by land though a fine late Gothic portal into a large
square courtyard. One of the most notable medieval palaces in
Venice, although much altered internally and to the rear in the
seventeenth and nineteenth centuries. The site was originally
occupied by a third Giustinian house, acquired by the Republic and
auctioned in 1452; it was bought by Doge Francesco Foscari, who
demolished the older house and began the present one. It was
intended to be one of the finest in the city, commanding the view
up the Grand Canal to Rialto. Foscari was forced to abdicate in
1457 and died shortly thereafter, but the palace remained in Foscari
hands until after the fall of the Republic. Many notable foreign
visitors were accommodated here, including the king of France,
Henri III, in 1574. In 1847 it was acquired by the city, restored, and
became the nucleus of the new university. Radical works were

Ca' Foscari: façade detail, with the Foscari arms in the
frieze above the windows

undertaken in 1844–6, when the palace was extended towards the
rear and a new landward façade added; the Grand Canal façade was
restored in 2003–6.

The plan is traditional and tripartite, with the central axis
widening towards the Grand Canal, to form a spacious L-shaped
loggia. The principal element is the harmonious canal façade, almost
exactly square, with four generous orders. The water storey has a
large central gate, flanked by six individual windows; the first *piano
nobile* has a splendid eight-light window in the centre, flanked by the
usual single windows; the upper *piano nobile* is the more prominent,
though, with another fine eight-light window, with rich tracery.
Directly above is a broad frieze, with pairs of early Renaissance *putti*
holding the Foscari arms. The attic is unusually richly detailed, too,
with a central *quadrifora*.

Little remains of the palace's historic interiors. In the 1950s Carlo
Scarpa modernised some of the internal rooms for the university,
including the great hall on the upper *piano nobile*.

From Ca' Foscari, return to Campiello dei Squelini; take Calle and Corte de la Madona into Calle and Campielo de la Vida. At the far NE end of Calle dei Saoneri, at DD 3368, are the thirteenth-century remains of the **Fontego Foscolo**: traces of a colonnade.

From Campielo de la Vida, take Calle de l'Aseo and then Calle del Magazen to return to Campo Santa Margarita. Near the NE corner of the square, a *sotoportego* leads to **Corte del Fontego**: remains of another early thirteenth-century Venetian-Byzantine colonnade (DD 3413–25). At the N end of the square is the **Scuola de Santa Margarita** (DD 3429), built into the S flank of the former church; now apartments. At high level: a stone aedicule with a late fifteenth-century figure of the saint. Behind is the former church of **Santa Margarita**; façade to the W. Founded in the ninth century by Doge Pietro Tradonico, the present fabric is a reconstruction of 1647 by the parish priest, Giovanni Battista Lambranzi. It was closed in 1810, and its parish functions transferred to the Carmini. Thereafter it had a variety of profane uses, including (1921) a cinema; today it is used for cultural events. The interior, once richly decorated, is now devoid of fittings; three Tintoretto paintings are now at Santo Stefano. The exterior is very plain; the campanile, formerly twice the present height, survives as a brick stump.

Take Calle del Forno out of the NW side of the square, and cross the bridge onto the *fondamenta*; turning left, at DD 3462, is the eighteenth-century **Palazzo Vendramin**; an unusual configuration with two narrow wings facing the quay, a central courtyard and the central section of the palace set further back. Next door is the imposing **Palazzo Foscarini** (DD 3463), late sixteenth century. A double palace, with impressive superimposed Serliane, three to each of the two main wings. The unusual plan has paired central halls, but only one side wing, to the right. In the seventeenth century the interiors were richly decorated, and further enriched by Pietro Foscarini in the 1740s. In 1797 the owner, Giacomo, made a highly inflammatory speech to the Maggior Consiglio, as a result of which the palace was comprehensively sacked by the people. Thereafter, it declined radically, its famous library transferred to Vienna (where it remains); recently, it has been semi-derelict The garden was once one of the most famous in Venice, with rare and exotic species; at the N end, Doge Marco Foscarini (1762–3) built a pavilion to house his remarkable library. The two-storey structure survives, a simple Neo-classical work, with Ionic pilasters.

Return to Santa Margarita and cross the adjacent bridge into the *campo* of **San Pantalon**. Probably founded in the ninth or tenth century, it was rebuilt several times before the present structure was begun in 1668–86 by the Trevisan architect Francesco Comino. The façade was never completed. The plan has a single broad aisle-less nave, with three linked lateral chapels down each side. A deep chancel projects at the N end, based on Scamozzi's at the Tolentini. The nave interior has a Composite order, roofed by a vaulted ceiling. It is dominated by the vast painted decoration of forty works by Antonio Fumiani, covering the entire ceiling, and which took twenty-four years to complete (1680–1704). All in *trompe l'œil* perspective, they represent the life and martyrdom of the patron saint; in the centre is the saint himself. Nave, right side, first chapel: *St Philip and St Bartholomew* by Guarana. Second chapel: altarpiece: a late work by Veronese. Third chapel, of San Bernardino: another late Veronese. In the chancel: very rich high altar by Giuseppe Sardi, 1671. To the left: chapel of the Sacred Nail: a richly decorated Gothic altar (1427–58) containing a reliquary of a nail from the Cross. Right wall: *Coronation of the Virgin* by Antonio Vivarini, 1444.

Nave, left side, first altar: vault by Fumiani; altarpiece by Lazzarini. Second chapel: in the spandrels: *James the Greater* and *James the Less* by Guarana. Third chapel: altarpiece by Niccolò Bambini.

The adjacent campanile was rebuilt in the eighteenth century by Scafarotto; a tall, elaborate bell-chamber. Take Calle San Pantalon down the right flank of the church, into the busy Crosera. Turn right and right again down the broad Calle Larga Foscari. Standing on the bridge at the end, facing NW, beyond a garden, is the canal façade of the seventeenth-century **Palazzo Secco Dolfin** (DD 3833). Built in the manner of Longhena, the tall second floor was added in the eighteenth century by Domenico Rossi. The interior was decorated by G. B. Tiepolo; today it houses part of Ca' Foscari university. The water façade has a tall *piano nobile*, lit by five large single windows, with arched heads; a continuous stone balcony across the façade. The upper floor repeats the fenestration pattern but with square windows.

Looking E from the bridge, on the N side of the canal is Brenno del Giudice's **Fire Station**, begun in 1932, in a heavy modernist, rather neo-Fascist manner.

Palazzo Balbi: Grand Canal façade by Alessandro Vittoria, 1582–90

Return to the Crosera and continue SE. At the end on the left is
Palazzo Corner de la Frescada Loredan (DD 3908–11), a good
mid-fifteenth-century Gothic palace. The water façade, with paired
watergates and a fine *quadrifora*, is seen from Fondamenta del Forner.
Today it is also occupied by Ca' Foscari university. The plan is
traditional and tripartite, with a small, attractive courtyard on the
landward side; the *androne* is reached through a large archway.

Taking Calle and Fondamenta de la Frescada, continue into Calle
Venier or Balbi. At the end is **Palazzo Balbi** (DD 3901). Its
prominent Grand Canal façade (1582–90) is best seen from Calle
Mocenigo on the far side. Designed for Niccolò Balbi, and usually
attributed to Vittoria, it evinces early Baroque features in its refined,
elegant façade. The interior was modernised several times; frescoes
by Guarana were added in the eighteenth century, but in the 1920s
the interior was badly damaged and 'modernised' before it was
acquired by the Veneto regional government in 1971 and carefully
restored.

The plan is tripartite and traditional, with a grand stair at the side
of the *androne*; two superimposed *piani nobili*. The canal façade has
flat rustication to the two lowermost storeys, with a rich central

watergate capped by a bold pediment, and two flanking watergates. The *piani nobili* have flat pilasters, Ionic and then Corinthian, and are differentiated by the large florid *stemme* on the first one; on both floors is a rich central *trifora* with a prominent balcony. The flanking windows have Baroque curved broken pediments, while two stone obelisks enliven the skyline.

The Grand Canal

Facing page: The Grand Canal

Chiesa de San Geremia

Begun *circa* 1753 by Carlo Corbellini; façades completed 1871; campanile: twelfth century but with later bell-chamber
Canale di Cannaregio

Palazzo Emo

Narrow eighteenth-century façade at the junction with the Cannaregio Canal

Palazzo Querini

The original structure is Byzantine; a long, plain, nineteenth-century façade
Campielo del Remer

Palazzo Correr Contarini

A substantial seventeenth-century palace with two *piani nobili*

Palazzo Gritti

A simple but refined seventeenth-century façade

Palazzo Martinengo Mandelli

Rebuilt late eighteenth century; asymmetrical, partly rusticated façade

Chiesa de San Marcuola

By Antonio Gaspari and then Giorgio Massari, 1728-36; Grand Canal façade never completed

Case Gatti Casazza

Two small Gothic houses, one modernised in the eighteenth century
Rio de San Marcuola

Palazzo Loredan Vendramin Calergi

Masterwork by Mauro Codussi, completed *circa* 1508; a massive stone façade screen with three orders; to the right is the 'white wing', rebuilt in 1660

Palazzo Marcello

Rebuilt *circa* 1700; a refined, simple, symmetrical façade

Palazzo Erizzo

Fifteenth-century Gothic, with an asymmetrical façade

Palazzo Soranzo Piovene

Early sixteenth-century Renaissance; attributed to Sante Lombardo

Palazzo Emo
Seventeenth century; the façade is 'bent' to follow the course of the canal

Palazzo Molin
Also seventeenth century, with façade at the junction of Rio de la Maddalena
Rio de la Madalena

Palazzo Barbarigo
Late sixteenth century, with surviving fresco fragments; asymmetrical façade

Palazzo Zulian
Seventeenth century, symmetrical façade

Palazzo Ruoda
Also seventeenth century; slightly larger symmetrical façade

Palazzo Gussoni Grimani de la Vida
A refined sixteenth-century façade, attributed to Sanmicheli, once frescoed by Tintoretto
Rio de Noal

Palazzo da Lezze
A small fifteenth-century Gothic house with a garden in front

Palazzo Boldù
Seventeenth century; a tall, asymmetrical façade

Palazzo Contarini Pisani
Seventeenth-century reconstruction of a much older house; a tall colonnade to the quay
Rio de San Felice

Palazzo Fontana
Late sixteenth and early seventeenth century; a large palace with an asymmetrical façade; an additional wing on the right side

Palazzo Giusti
By Antonio Visentini, *circa* 1776; interesting façade with niches on the lowermost order

The Ca' d'Oro (Palazzo Contarini)
Gothic masterpiece by Bartolomeo and Zane Bon, Matteo Raverti

and others; built for Marin Contarini *circa* 1422–34. The finest medieval façade in Venice, complex and asymmetrical, clad with marble and richly decorated

Palazzo Pesaro Ravà
Fifteenth-century Gothic; narrow, asymmetrical façade and an L-shaped plan

Palazzo Morosini Sagredo
Originally thirteenth century, but modernised in the fifteenth, and again in the eighteenth century; a broad, asymmetrical façade
Campo Santa Sofia

Palazzetto Foscari
A small fifteenth-century Gothic house with asymmetrical façade

Palazzo Michiel da le Colonne
Substantial palace modernised in the late seventeenth century by Gaspari; a prominent colonnade and two *piani nobili*

Palazzo Michiel dal Brusà
Fifteenth-century Gothic, but badly damaged by fire in 1774 and partially rebuilt

Palazzo Mangilli Valmarana
Elegant façade begun by Visentini in 1751; two top storeys added by Gianantonio Selva after 1784
Rio dei Santi Apostoli

Ca' da Mosto
Important twelfth- to thirteenth-century palace, much altered later; the two lower orders are original. In very poor condition

Palazzetti Dolfin
Two small adjacent fifteenth-century Gothic houses

Palazzo Bollani Erizzo
A small late sixteenth-century house, once occupied by Pietro Aretino
Rio de San Giovanni Grisostomo
Campielo del Remer
At the back of the *campielo* is the façade of **Palazzo Lion**, originally thirteenth century

Palazzo Sernagiotto

A substantial palace rebuilt in the nineteenth century; colonnade to the quay

Palazzo Civran

A tall, refined, seventeenth-century façade, the lower part rusticated

Palazzetto Perducci

A small attractive fifteenth-century Gothic house

Palazzo Ruzzini

A late nineteenth-century reconstruction; site of the ancient Fontego dei Persiani
Rio del Fontego

Fontego (Fondaco) dei Tedeschi

A massive structure, rebuilt in 1505–8 after a fire, under the direction of Spavento and Scarpagnino. A broad symmetrical façade with a spacious waterfront loggia; three upper floors

Ponte de Rialto

By Antonio da Ponte, 1588–91. The oldest and most important of the Grand Canal bridges, all of Istrian stone, with a single large arch spanning 28 metres. On top are four groups of shops
Riva del Ferro

Palazzo Dolfin Manin

By Jacopo Sansovino, 1536–75. Imposing stone façade, with a continuous ground-floor colonnade and two upper orders
Rio de San Salvador
Riva del Carbon

Palazzo Bembo

An impressive late fifteenth-century Gothic 'double *palazzo*', with a broad, symmetrical façade

Palazzetto Dandolo

A tiny narrow fifteenth-century Gothic façade; next to it is a larger, contemporary, Dandolo house

Ca' Loredan

An important early thirteenth-century palace, modernised in the eighteenth century, with a spacious colonnaded façade

Ca' Farsetti

Built at the same time as Ca' Loredan, and of similar appearance, with full-width colonnades and fenestration

Palazzo Corner Martinengo Ravà

Eighteenth century, with a broad, fairly low, façade

Palazzo Corner Valmarana

Seventeenth century, with a richly decorated façade partly from the nineteenth century

Palazzo Grimani

By Michele Sanmicheli; begun in 1556, completed in 1575 by Giangiacomo de' Grigi. A massively imposing stone and marble Renaissance façade with three orders; decorated by Vittoria
Rio de San Luca

Palazzo Corner Contarini dei Cavalli

Fifteenth-century Gothic (*circa* 1445), with rich tracery to the *portego* window

Palazzetto and Palazzo Tron

A tiny, rich 'infill' building in nineteenth-century Gothic; the palace itself is fifteenth-century Gothic

Palazzo Martinengo

Mid-sixteenth century; a broad façade partly clad with stone, once frescoed by Pordenone

Palazzo Benzon

Eighteenth century, modernised in the nineteenth. A broad, symmetrical, fairly simple façade

Palazzo Tornielli

A small nineteenth-century house, partly rusticated, with pedimented windows

Palazzo Curti Valmarana

Seventeenth century; a tall façade with five storeys; a plain, symmetrical façade
Rio de l'Albero

Palazzo Lando Corner Spinelli

A significant early Renaissance work by Mauro Codussi, *circa* 1490; stone façade with partial rustication and characteristic paired windows
Campielo del Teatro

Casa Barocci
Nineteenth century, by Pellegrino Oreffice

Palazzo Tito
By Angelo Scattolin, 1954; a reticent modern interpretation of the
traditional palace façade
Rio de Sant'Angelo

Palazzo Garzoni
Fifteenth-century Gothic, with symmetrical façade and two
superimposed *quadrifore*

Palazzo Corner Gheltoff
Originally Gothic, rebuilt in the sixteenth century; simple refined
façade

Palazzo Mocenigo 'Casa Nuova'
Impressive stone façade, built in the 1570s, attributed variously to
Guglielmo de' Grigi, Vittoria and Rusconi. Rigorously symmetrical,
with three superimposed Serliane, and two large family arms

Palazzi Mocenigo
Immediately adjacent to the above; two identical conjoined houses,
smaller and less ostentatious. Late sixteenth century; the façades were
once frescoed by Benedetto Caliari

Palazzo Mocenigo 'Casa Vecchia'
The other 'book-end' palace; originally Gothic, but comprehensively
modernised in 1623–5 by Francesco Contin

Palazzo Contarini da le Figure
An important sixteenth-century Renaissance palace, with an elegant
stone façade, often attributed to Scarpagnino. Palladio lived here in
the 1570s

Palazzo Erizzo Nani Mocenigo
Fifteenth-century Gothic, with a symmetrical façade and
superimposed *quadrifore*

Palazzo da Lezze
A smaller Gothic house, early fifteenth century

Palazzo Moro Lin
Rebuilt in the mid-seventeenth century by Sebastiano Mazzoni for
the painter Pietro Liberi. An unusual broad façade with thirteen bays
and a continuous waterfront colonnade

Palazzo Grassi

A massive and imposing edifice begun by Giorgio Massari in 1749, completed after his death. The last great noble palace built in Venice, with a symmetrical Neo-classical façade, two *piani nobili* and partly rusticated

Campo San Samuele; at the back: the façade of San Samuele and its twelfth-century campanile

Palazzo Cappello Malipiero

Originally Gothic but modernised at various dates thereafter; the early seventeenth-century work is attributed to Longhena. Two large watergates and a *pentafora*. Garden at the side

Ca' del Duca

Fragmentary remains of the grandiose palace begun by Bon for the Corner *circa* 1459; two sections of a massively rusticated stone base

Rio del Duca

Palazzetto Falier

Picturesque small fourteenth-century Gothic house with two flanking *logge*

Palazzo Giustinian Lolin

A refined stone façade, 1620–30, an early work by Longhena; partially rusticated, with superimposed Serliane

Palazzetto Civran Badoer

Late seventeenth century with a simple, symmetrical façade; garden at the side

Rio de San Vidal

Ponte de l'Accademia

By Eugenio Miozzi, 1934, built of iron and timber; intended to be temporary, but still there today

Palazzo Cavalli Franchetti

Mid-fifteenth-century Gothic, but extensively modernised by Camillo Boito, *circa* 1898. A rich symmetrical façade, with complex tracery to the *portego* windows; garden at the side

Rio de l'Orso

Palazzo Barbaro

Built by Bartolomeo and Zane Bon, *circa* 1440; *gotico fiorito* façade, with a later Renaissance watergate. Adjacent is a narrow later wing, added in the seventeenth century

Palazzetto Benzon Foscolo

A small seventeenth-century house with a central *trifora*

Palazzetto Pisani

A narrow façade, completed 1751, with paired windows
Rio del Santissimo
Fondamenta San Maurizio

Casina de le Rose (Casetta Rossa)

A small eighteenth-century *casinò*; Canova's first studio; adjacent is
the garden of Ca' Corner

Ca' Corner (Palazzo Corner de la Ca' Granda)

A massively impressive palace, one of Sansovino's masterpieces. Begun
in 1533, completed *circa* 1560. The façade is a great stone screen, with
the lower orders rusticated and two *piani nobili*. The rich detailing
relates to the Marciana Library
Rio de San Maurizio

Palazzo Minotto

A small asymmetrical fifteenth-century Gothic house

Palazzo Barbarigo

Seventeenth century; a markedly asymmetrical façade, with
superimposed Serliane on the left side
Rio de Santa Maria Zobenigo

Palazzo Marin Contarini

Fifteenth-century Gothic, with sixteenth-century modernisations;
asymmetrical façade

Palazzo Venier Contarini

Attractive small seventeenth-century house, with a simple refined
façade
Campo Santa Maria del Giglio

Palazzo Pisani Gritti (Gritti Palace Hotel)

Originally fifteenth-century Gothic; the top floor was added in the
nineteenth century; an exceptionally broad façade, once frescoed by
Giorgione
Rio de le Ostreghe

Palazzo Flangini Fini

Attributed to Tremignon, *circa* 1688. An impressive 'double *palazzo*'
with two watergates and two parallel halls

Palazzo Manolesso Ferro
Very late Gothic, with early Renaissance elements; an impressive six-storey façade

Palazzetto Contarini Fasan
A small but exquisitely decorated late Gothic façade; the balconies are particularly refined

Palazzo Venier Contarini
A small, well-proportioned fifteenth-century Gothic house; two superimposed *quadrifore*

Palazzo Gaggia
A modest seventeenth-century façade with a central Serliana

Albergo Regina
A nineteenth-century hotel

Palazzo Tiepolo (Hotel Europa)
A tall, fairly narrow, asymmetrical seventeenth-century façade

Palazzo Treves de' Bonfili
Seventeenth century, sometimes attributed to Manopola; modernised in the early nineteenth century. Superimposed Serliane on the markedly asymmetrical façade
Rio de San Moisè

Albergo Bauer Grünwald
Nineteenth-century neo-Gothic façade by Giovanni Sardi; later side wing by Marino Meo, 1946–9

Ca' Giustinian
Notable fifteenth-century Gothic palace, *circa* 1474, one of the last Gothic *palazzi* built in the city. A symmetrical façade; attached is a narrow side wing of similar date

Albergo Monaco Grand Canal
A simple nineteenth-century façade

Fontegheto de la Farina (Capitaneria del Porto)
Early sixteenth-century Lombard Renaissance, with a five-bay loggia to the quay
Rio de la Luna

Coffee House
A small stone Neo-classical pavilion by Lorenzo Santi, 1815–17

Giardinetti Reali
At the back of the gardens is the rear façade of the **Procuratie Nuove (ex Palazzo Reale)**
Rio de la Zecca

Palazzo de la Zecca
Impressive stone façade begun by Jacopo Sansovino in 1537. The third order was added in 1558–66. The façade is powerfully rusticated, with nine bays of large single-light windows

Biblioteca Nazionale Marciana
Begun by Sansovino in 1537; the last bays towards the Molo were added by Scamozzi in 1583–8. The s end has only three bays, but is exceptionally richly detailed

The Molo
The two monolithic columns of San Todaro (w) and San Marco (e) were erected by Doge Sebastiano Ziani in 1172.

The Doge's Palace
See pp. 211–24

2 WEST AND SOUTH BANKS FROM PIAZZALE ROMA TO THE PUNTA DE LA DOGANA

Fondamenta Santa Chiara
Palaces from the sixteenth and seventeenth centuries

Albergo Santa Chiara
Seventeenth century, incorporating fragments of the lost nunnery of the same name
Ponte del Monastero; Rio Novo

Giardini Papadopoli
Set out in the early nineteenth century on the site of the Convento de la Croce
Ponte de la Croce; Rio de la Croce
Fondamenta San Simon Piccolo

Palazzo Diedo Emo
Late seventeenth century; attributed to Tirali. The central bay is clad with stone, and pedimented

Chiesa di San Simon Piccolo
Rebuilt by Giovanni Scalfarotto, 1718–38. A Corinthian pronaos above a long flight of steps; a prominent copper cupola

Casa Adoldo
Early sixteenth century, with a symmetrical façade

Palazzo Foscari Contarini
Two linked sixteenth-century houses, the first with a large *pentafora*, the second with its façade to the side

Ponte degli Scalzi
By Eugenio Miozzi, 1934, all in Istrian stone

Palazzo Foscari
Rebuilt by Marino Meo, 1951–4; the original Gothic house was partly reconstructed, with new modern elements
Rio Marin

Palazzetto Nigra
With garden in front; by Giovanni Sardi, 1904, in Venetian-Byzantine style
Campo San Simon Grando; with the church at the far end
Riva di Biasio: several modern buildings with ground-floor colonnades

Palazzetto Gritti
A small sixteenth-century Renaissance house, with central *trifora*

Palazzo Corner
Seventeenth century, with an asymmetrical façade and a prominent *quadrifora*

Palazzo Donà Balbi
A substantial seventeenth-century house, with a notably asymmetrical façade

Palazzo Marcello Toderini
A smallish seventeenth-century house with a central Serliana
Rio de San Zan Degolà

Palazzo Giovanelli
A fairly large fifteenth-century Gothic palace with a symmetrical façade and two central *quadrifore*

Casa Correr
A modest seventeenth-century house, once owned by Teodoro

Correr, whose collections formed the basis for the Museo Civico Correr

Fondaco dei Turchi

Originally a *palazzo-fontego* from the twelfth century to the thirteenth; radically restored in 1858–69. A broad two-storey façade with a generous waterfront loggia, and flanked by two short towers (*toresele*); decorative crenellation
Rio del Fontego del Megio

Deposito (fontego) di Megio

Former millet warehouse of the Republic; a simple fifteenth-century brick structure, with rectangular windows and decorative crenellation

Palazzo Belloni Battagia

Impressive mid-seventeenth-century palace by Longhena, all clad with stone, and with rich Baroque decoration, notably to the *piano nobile*
Rio Tron

Palazzo Tron

Second half of the sixteenth century; stone-clad façade, with two *piani nobili*

Palazzo Duodo

A fairly small fifteenth-century Gothic house, with a symmetrical façade and a central *quadrifora*
Garden: site of the former Palazzo Contarini

Palazzo Priuli Bon

Originally thirteenth-century Venetian-Byzantine, modernised in the fifteenth century and again in the modern era
Campo San Stae

Chiesa de San Stae

The rich Palladian Baroque stone façade is by Domenico Rossi, 1709

Scoleta dei Tiraoro

Former guildhall of the gold-workers; attractive little Baroque façade, 1711, attributed to Giacomo Gaspari
Rio Mocenigo

Palazzo Foscarini Giovanelli

Late sixteenth or early seventeenth century, attributed to Giuseppe Sardi; the symmetrical façade has two superimposed Serliane
Rio de la Pergola

Ca' Pesaro

A Baroque masterpiece begun by Longhena in 1628, but completed in 1703 by Antonio Gaspari. The massive stone façade has a rusticated lower order, with paired watergates, and two superimposed *piani nobili*
Rio Pesaro

Palazzetto Donà Sangiantoffetti

A very small eighteenth-century house

Palazzo Correggio

Also from the eighteenth century, but larger; a symmetrical tripartite façade

Palazzo Corner de la Regina

An imposing work by Domenico Rossi, begun in 1724. The tall stone façade has a two-storey rusticated base, above which are two *piani nobili*

Casa Bragadin Favretto

An interesting small house, originally fourteenth century, but with later Gothic elements
Rio de San Cassan

Palazzetto Jona

Early twentieth-century neo-Gothic by Guido Sullam

Palazzo Brandolin Morosini

Fifteenth-century Gothic, with two *piani nobili*, both with fine tracery; the upper floor was removed
Riva de l'Ogio
Ponte de Pescaria; Rio de le Beccarie

Pescaria

A substantial neo-Gothic structure by Domenico Rupolo and Cesare Laurenti, 1907. The colonnaded lower floor contains the fish market; above is a single storey with a *liagò* towards the Grand Canal
Campo de la Pescaria

Fabbriche Nuove di Rialto

A long three-storey block by Sansovino, 1554–6; the twenty-five-bay façade follows the bend in the canal. The lower storey has a stone colonnade, the upper floors single pedimented windows between pilasters

Erbaria

At the back of the Erbaria:

Fabbriche Vecchie di Rialto

By Scarpagnino, 1520–22; three storeys, with a simple stone ground-floor colonnade

Palazzo dei Camerlenghi

At the corner immediately before the Ponte di Rialto. Remodelling of an earlier structure by Guglielmo de' Grigi and Scarpagnino, 1525–8; clad with richly detailed stonework, with two *piani nobili*

Ponte de Rialto

Palazzo dei Dieci Savi

By Scarpagnino, 1520s, part of the Fabbriche Vecchie reconstruction after the 1514 fire; three storeys, with stone colonnade and paired upper windows

Riva del Vin: lined with a collection of medium-sized palaces and houses, mostly sixteenth and seventeenth century

Palazzo Ravà

Neo-Gothic, by Giovanni Sardi, 1906, on the site of the lost Ca' del Papà

Campielo Pasina

Palazzo Barzizza

Originally thirteenth-century Venetian-Byzantine, but much altered

Ca' Businello

Mid-thirteenth century but much altered; part of the water loggia and the two upper-floor multi-light windows survive

Rio dei Meloni

Palazzo Coccina Papadopoli

An impressive and elegant mid-sixteenth-century palace, attributed to Giangiacomo de' Grigi; the stone and marble façade has superimposed Serliane to the *piani nobili*, and is capped by two obelisks. Garden at the side

Palazzo Donà

A notable thirteenth-century palace with a symmetrical tripartite façade; the original *pentafora* survives

Palazzo Donà de la Madoneta

Originally thirteenth century; a narrow façade with a full-width eight-bay window across the *piano nobile*
Rio de la Madoneta

Palazzo Bernardo

An impressive fifteenth-century Gothic palace, with a nearly symmetrical façade; paired watergates and two *piani nobili*, the upper with rich tracery. The side windows also have fine tracery

Palazzo Querini Dubois

Late sixteenth or early seventeenth century; a large palace with a simple refined, symmetrical façade

Palazzo Grimani Marcello

A medium-sized early sixteenth-century Renaissance palace, with a refined, symmetrical, tripartite, stone and marble façade; attributed to Giovanni Buora

Palazzo Cappello Layard

Sixteenth century; the unusual asymmetrical façade was once frescoed by Veronese and Giambattista Zelotti
Rio de San Polo

Palazzo Barbarigo de la Terrazza

Begun 1568–9 by Bernardino Contin; an unusual l-shaped plan with a large terrace in the internal angle

Palazzo Pisani Moretta

A fine early fifteenth-century Gothic palace; a symmetrical tripartite façade with twin watergates and two *piani nobili*, both with rich window tracery

Palazzo Tiepolo

Sixteenth century, with a well-proportioned tripartite symmetrical façade, once frescoed by Andrea Schiavone

Palazzo Tiepolo (Tiepoletto)

Late fifteenth-century Gothic, with sixteenth-century modernisations; the Gothic first-floor windows all survive

Palazzo Giustinian Persico

Sixteenth century, with attractive Lombard Renaissance façade, tripartite with superimposed *quadrifore*
Rio de San Tomà

Palazzo Marcello dei Leoni

A simple but asymmetrical sixteenth-century façade

Palazzo Dolfin

A small, fifteenth-century Gothic house, partly modernised later

Palazzo Dandolo Paolucci

Seventeenth century, with an asymmetrical façade

Palazzo Civran Grimani

Seventeenth century, but rebuilt in the early eighteenth, perhaps by Giorgio Massari; a four-storey stone façade, the lower two rusticated
Rio de la Frescada

Palazzo Caotorta Angaran

A fairly small seventeenth-century house, rebuilt in 1956 by Angelo Scattolin

Palazzo Balbi

An impressive late sixteenth-century palace, 1582–90, generally attributed to Vittoria. The rich stone façade has early Baroque elements such as the broken pediments; a rusticated lower order, two *piani nobili* and obelisks
Rio de Ca' Foscari (Rio Novo)

Ca' Foscari

An imposing Gothic palace, begun in 1453 by Doge Francesco Foscari. The grandiose façade has four orders; above the central watergate the *piani nobili* both have splendid multi-light windows with rich tracery

Palazzi Giustiniani

Very fine 'twin' Gothic palaces of the same date as Ca' Foscari; they have mirrored plans and façades, with four orders and richly traceried six-light windows to the *piani nobili*

Palazzo Giustinian Bernardo

A fairly small seventeenth-century house with unusual paired fenestration; one wing was never completed

Palazzo Bernardo Nani

An attractive small sixteenth-century palace, with superimposed *trifore*

Ca' Rezzonico

A Baroque masterpiece by Longhena, begun in 1649, but completed by Massari in 1750. The massive, richly decorated stone façade has

three orders, with a triple watergate and seven bays to the upper floors
Rio de San Barnaba

Palazzzi Contarini Michiel
Two small asymmetrical seventeenth-century houses

Palazzetto Stern
A neo-Gothic late nineteenth-century villa by Giuseppe Berti, eclectic and asymmetrical
Rio Malpaga

Palazzo Moro
Early sixteenth century; a broad façade with three orders; simple detailing

Palazzo Loredan de l'Ambasciatore
An important late Gothic palace, with a fine tripartite façade; the *piano nobile* has rich tracery

Casa Mainella
Built in 1858 by Ludovico Cadorin; asymmetrical, with Lombard Renaissance detailing
Rio de San Trovaso

Palazzo Contarini Corfù
Fifteenth-century Gothic, with a symmetrical façade and superimposed *quadrifore*

Palazzo Contarini degli Scrigni
By Vincenzo Scamozzi, begun in 1609; the stone façade has three orders, the lowermost rusticated, the upper ones with five bays

Palazzo Mocenigo Gambara
Originally Gothic, remodelled in the seventeenth century; asymmetrical façade with a Serliana to one side

Palazzetto Querini
A small sixteenth-century house, remodelled in the eighteenth century
Campo de la Carità

Gallerie dell'Accademia
To the right, the stone façade of the former Scuola Grande de la Carità, by Massari and Maccaruzzi, 1756–65. To the left, the former church of Santa Maria de la Carità, *circa* 1440–55, now part of the Accademia

Facing page: The Grand Canal and Santa Maria de la Salute

Ponte de l'Accademia

Palazzo Brandolin Rota
Late seventeenth century; tripartite symmetrical façade with
superimposed five-light windows

Palazzo Contarini dal Zaffo
Important early Renaissance palace, late fifteenth century, probably
by Giovanni Buora; an elegant tripartite stone façade with a five-
light window to the *piano nobile*, and rich decoration

Palazzo Molin Balbi Valier
Seventeenth century, with central terrace and side wings added in
1750

Palazzo Loredan Cini
Sixteenth century, with a narrow Grand Canal façade; main façade to
Rio de San Vio
Rio de San Vio
Campo San Vio

Palazzo Barbarigo
Early sixteenth century, but with mosaic decoration added *circa* 1880
by Giulio Carlini

Palazzo da Mula
Fifteenth-century Gothic, with a symmetrical façade and two *piani
nobili*

Palazzo Centani
A tall, narrow, eighteenth-century façade

Palazzo Venier dei Leoni (Fondazione Guggenheim)
The only completed fragment of the proposed vast Palazzo Venier,
begun by Lorenzo Boschetti, 1749
Rio de le Toresele

Palazzo Dario
Built *circa* 1487; the early Renaissance façade is narrow and
asymmetrical, but has four orders and is richly decorated with
marble cladding

Palazzo Barbaro
A tall, narrow, late fifteenth-century Gothic façade, with irregular
fenestration
Rio de la Fornace

Palazzo Salviati

A small nineteenth-century house with mosaic decoration

Palazzo Benzon

A small fifteenth-century Gothic house with irregular fenestration

Palazzo Genovese

Grandiose neo-Gothic palace by Tricomi-Mattei, 1892; a broad, symmetrical, façade with three orders

Former Abbazia di San Gregorio

Mostly fourteenth- and fifteenth-century Gothic; an attractively irregular façade with a fine square watergate
Campo de la Salute

Chiesa di Santa Maria de la Salute

Magnificent Baroque masterpiece by Longhena, begun in 1631, completed in 1687; all clad with stone and marble and surmounted by the largest cupola in the city

Seminario Patriarcale

A sober façade, also by Longhena, 1671; four storeys, with rustication at the base

Dogana da Mar

By Giuseppe Benoni, begun in 1677; partially rebuilt 1835–8. A long, simple, rusticated façade terminating at the Punta with a powerfully rusticated open loggia and a stone tower.

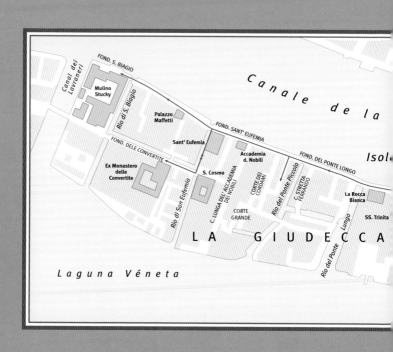

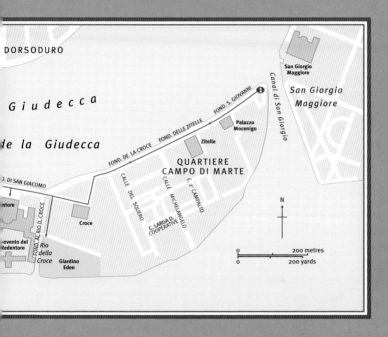

DORSODURO

Giudecca

de la Giudecca

FOND. DI SAN GIACOMO

FOND. DE LA CROCE   FOND. DELLE ZITELLE   FOND. S. GIOVANNI

Zitelle

Palazzo Mocenigo

San Giorgio Maggiore

San Giorgio Maggiore

Canal di San Giorgio

QUARTIERE CAMPO DI MARTE

CALLE DEL SQUERO

CALLE MICHELANGELO

C. 2ª CAMPALTO

C. LARGA D. COOPERATIVE

entore

Convento del Redentore

FOND. AL RIO D. CROCE

Rio della Croce

Croce

Giardino Eden

N

0   200 metres
0   200 yards

La Giudecca

La Giudecca

The Giudecca consists of a long arc of islets directly south of the city centre, from which it is divided by the broad, deep, Giudecca Canal. This chain extends from San Giorgio Maggiore in the E (see below) to a modern reclaimed group of islets, Sacca Fisola, in the W. The historic extent of the Giudecca was smaller than it is today, originally consisting of a chain of six square or rectangular islets, all bordering the Giudecca Canal. Much of the southern shore is the result of later reclamation.

The origin of the name has been debated for centuries, although it was first called Vigonovo ('new suburb') or Spinalonga, reflecting its physical form. There is no evidence for the popular derivation from *Giudei*, that is, Jews, who were established at Mestre on the Terraferma, and later in the Gheto in the city itself.

The Giudecca's slightly detached nature has resulted in a distinctive pattern of development that differs in several respects from that of the historic centre. Several religious houses were established here, taking advantage of the space for orchards and vineyards, much like northern Cannaregio and eastern Castello. Its lay settlement remained confined to a linear village along the N shore until the sixteenth century, when, for some decades, the island became popular among the nobility for building suburban villas, again with gardens extending as far as the lagoon to the S. This popularity was short-

Facing page: The Redentore by Andrea Palladio, completed by Antonio da Ponte, 1576–92

lived, since many nobles later acquired much larger mainland estates, and built correspondingly more impressive villas; by the seventeenth century the Giudecca was a quiet backwater again, as it remained until the nineteenth. Its backland was then developed for industrial functions, and most of the nobles' gardens were lost. More recently again, as the industrial zones have declined in turn, the backland sites have been redeveloped with several modern housing projects. Although technically the Giudecca is annexed to the *sestiere* of Dorsoduro, it has its own civic numeration, beginning at the eastern tip and proceeding westwards.

At the E end of the main quay, Fondamenta San Giovanni Battista, stood the eponymous monastery, founded in the early fourteenth century. The order was suppressed by the Republic in 1767, and the whole complex was demolished in the mid-nineteenth century. On Campo Nani was **Palazzo Nani** (GD 10), a Renaissance villa with gardens, and a centre of intellectual life in the sixteenth century.

Further W along the quay is **Palazzo Mocenigo** (GD 19–22), one of the few surviving sixteenth-century villas. In 1570 it was owned by Alvise Mocenigo, elected doge in that year. The present fabric, attributed to Manopola or Francesco Contin, was completed just after Mocenigo's death in 1577. A long, broad façade, with ground floor, a generous *piano nobile* and a low attic with later windows – a second principal floor may have been intended. The façade is clad with lightly rusticated stonework; eight bays and a square central portal. The *piano nobile* is lit by tall, elegant, single lights, with none of the usual emphasis on the central hall. The plan had a U-shape, with two rear wings enclosing a courtyard, beyond which was the garden. The canal façade was restored in 1976, although the garden wings were demolished and the palace converted into apartments.

Next door, at GD 23, is **Palazzetto da Mosto**, a small fourteenth-century Gothic house with trilobate windows. A little further is the former **Chiesa e convento de Santa Maria de la Presentazione (Le Zitelle)**, founded in 1561 by Benedetto Palmi, a Jesuit priest, to house and educate poor young girls. The overall concept is by Palladio, but construction of the church (1582–6) was directed by Jacopo Bozzetto. The site has a restricted width, and Palladio's influential layout places the church façade in the centre, flanked on both sides by symmetrical wings of accommodation, which extend back to the s to enclose three sides of a rear courtyard. A similar layout was to be used later at the Penitenti, the Catecumeni, the Mendicanti and the Pietà.

The canal façade is very simple, the flanking wings particularly plain; the church façade has two orders, divided by a broad trabeation, a restrained, compact version of Palladio's other Venetian church façades. The order is Corinthian, with paired pilasters to the outer bays and a broad central bay containing a pedimented portal. The upper order is dominated by a large thermal window, and the façade is capped by a triangular pediment, above which rise two stocky turrets at the outer corners. The cupola, on a very low drum, is seen clearly only from a distance.

Inside: a small barrel-vaulted vestibule, beyond which is the square nave, with radiused corners; these radii extend upwards to form the pendentives that carry the drum of the cupola. The nave is articulated with Corinthian pilasters echoing those on the façade. At high level on both sides are choir galleries, reached directly from the upper floors of the flanking accommodation.

At GD 42–7 is the eclectic **Casa Mario de Maria** (the *casa de' tre oci,* 'house of three eyes'), designed for himself by the artist in 1912. The canal façade is an imaginative reinterpretation of fifteenth-century Gothic, dominated by the three huge windows of the main floor, and clad with diaper patterned brickwork after the Doge's Palace. The façade is capped by a fanciful stone crenellation.

Next door is the sixteenth-century **Palazzo Minelli da Ponte** (GD 50), and then the former granary building, at GD 55–65. Take Calle Michelangelo inland, right across to the far side of the island. Adjacent: two fairly recent housing developments: the former ice-factory conversion by Valeriano Pastor (1993) and the Zaggia development by Luca Rossi (1994–9), incorporating a former bakery. At the far s end of Calle Michelangelo (E side) is Villa Heriott, an eclectic neo-Gothic/Byzantine villa, with an H-shaped plan, centred on a full-height atrium.

Back on the main quay, two further former granaries stand further w, at GD 77–82 and 84–8. At GD 105–15 are the former **Maggazini Mocenigo**, originally Gothic, today used by the Archivio di Stato for storage. Take the narrow calle just E of the Magazzini to reach the **Chiesa de la Croce**, originally a Benedictine nunnery, the first record of which dates from 1328, although its origins are obscure. The church was rebuilt in the Gothic era, but modernised in 1508–11, when the pediment was added to the façade and high-level thermal windows inserted. The monastic buildings were rebuilt and enlarged in the succeeding centuries, but it was suppressed in 1806, when the nunnery became a prison; the church was mutilated and most fittings dispersed or destroyed. The basic fabric survives, recently restored, with a simple brick façade, including a high-level *ocio*.

Further s, down Rio de la Croce, is the extensive **Giardino Eden**, created by a British expatriate, Francis Eden, who settled here in 1884; in 1930 it passed to the Greek royal family. On the w bank of Rio de la Croce, on the s corner towards the lagoon, is **Ca' de' Leoni** (GD 140), on the site of the gardens of the former Villa Corner. We return to the main waterfront, and continue w.

Immediately before the Redentore church, the narrow Calle dei Frati leads to the **Convento dei Padri Cappuccini**. Established in the early sixteenth century, with a small chapel dedicated to Santa Maria degli Angeli, in 1541 it was given to the Franciscans, but in 1548 it passed to the Capuchins, who continued to use the chapel until completion of the Redentore itself.

Santissimo Redentore: in 1575–6 the city was afflicted by one of the worst epidemics of plague in its history, claiming around 50,000 lives, including that of Titian. On its conclusion, the Senate decided to construct a votive temple, dedicated to the Holy Redeemer, partly on land occupied by the Capuchins; the doge and Signoria were to process there every year on the third Sunday in July, when a temporary bridge of boats was constructed across the Giudecca Canal from the Zattere. The ceremony still takes place today, with a great celebration in the Bacino on Saturday evening and a solemn procession on Sunday morning led by the Cardinal Patriarch of the city. The church is one of Palladio's masterpieces, completed in 1592 by Antonio da Ponte.

The long, axial approach across the canal and the need for a generous square in front to accommodate crowds were central considerations in the design. The church is also raised high above the quay, approached by a grand flight of steps, ensuring visibility for the participants. The façade marks a stage in Palladio's refinement of the 'temple front', a giant order of classical columns supporting a pediment, and flanked by secondary elements. Here, the narrow side wings represent lateral chapels, because the church has no aisles. The imposing façade is clad with stone, with giant Corinthian outer pilasters and inner columns supporting a massive triangular pediment; the large central portal replicates these features on a smaller scale, while the outer bays have niches containing statues of St Mark and St Francis by Campagna. These outer bays are capped by half-pediments, while above and behind the main pediment rises a square cornice, behind which is the hipped gable of the main roof. Down the flank walls paired raked buttresses support the upper nave flank walls, and the composition is completed by the lead-clad cupola on a drum.

The interior was designed specifically for the annual rites and processions; the language is refined and monumental, Corinthian throughout. The rectangular nave has three main bays, with smaller bays between them, containing niches and statues. Down each side are three lateral chapels, linked together and approached by large arches from the nave. The nave columns support a powerful continuous entablature, which defines and encloses the space, and is broken only by the chancel arch. Above the entablature is a plain barrel-vaulted ceiling, with cross-vaults for thermal windows.

The chancel forms a cross-axis to the nave, with semicircular transepts on each side and a free-standing high altar in the centre (by Giuseppe Mazza, 1679). Above is a circular gallery, and the drum carrying the cupola. Beyond the chancel is an unusual semicircular colonnade, beyond which is a deep choir. Each space had a clear function: the large open nave for the crowds of worshippers; the two transepts for the procession to conclude on each side of the altar; and the choir beyond, audible but not visible.

Principal monuments and altars: right side, first chapel: altarpiece by Francesco Bassano; second chapel: altarpiece by Veronese; third chapel: altarpiece from the workshop of Tintoretto.

Sacristy (right of the choir): paintings by Alvise Vivarini, Veronese, Bastiani and the Bellini school.

Nave left side, first chapel: altarpiece by Palma il Giovane; second chapel: altarpiece by Francesco Bassano; third chapel: altarpiece attributed to Tintoretto.

Immediately w of the Redentore stood the monastery of **San Giacomo**, founded in 1338 by Marsilio da Carrara, lord of Padua. It survived until the Napoleonic dissolution of 1806; by 1821 the entire complex had been demolished. On the site is a modern Franciscan nunnery, founded in 1827. A little further w, at GD 218, before the Ponte Longo, is **La Rocca Bianca**, the remains of the villa of the Visconti, lords of Milan. Very early sixteenth century, with a *pentafora* on the first floor. The Ponte Longo was first built in 1340; the present bridge is a mid-nineteenth-century iron structure.

Walking left down Fondamenta del Ponte Longo, across the canal on the w side is a modern residential development on the site of

Giudecca: modern housing on the Junghans site by Boris Podrecca,
Cino Zucchi and others, 1997–2006

the former Junghans industrial complex; apartment blocks by Cino
Zucchi, Luciano Parenti, Boris Podrecca and others, 1998–2006.

Return to Ponte Longo; across the bridge, at GD 322 is the
Ospizio di San Pietro, founded in 1316, but rebuilt in 1568, as the
inscription records. Continue across the Ponte Piccolo and along
Fondamenta Sant'Eufemia. Taking Calle del Forno, left, we reach
Corte dei Cordami; good small vernacular housing, including (on
the E side) a row of seven seventeenth-century cottages (GD 530–38
and 499–506). Identical plans, each with one apartment above
another, fourteen in all; several fine traditional chimneys survive.
Back on the main quay, at GD 607–8 is the former **Accademia dei
Nobili**, fifteenth century, but modernised in the sixteenth. A Gothic
quadrifora and four single lights on the first floor; a second *quadrifora*
above. The name dates from 1619, when the Accademia was founded

here, to educate sons of poor nobles; it survived until 1797. At the W end of the quay is the small *campo* of the parish church of **Sant'Eufemia**. One of the oldest foundations on the Giudecca, established in 865 by Doge Orso Partecipazio. Restored on numerous occasions, although the basic basilica plan survives. Modernised in 1371 (plaque), and again in the mid-eighteenth century, when the interior was transformed, incorporating elaborate stucco decoration to the upper nave walls and ceilings. In the 1880s the stone colonnade was added along the N flank wall. The W façade is very simple; above the portal: a fourteenth-century *Crucifixion*, originally at the lost Santi Biagio e Cataldo.

The stout granite columns and fine eleventh-century capitals of the nave colonnade support semicircular arches, above which are rows of panels with paintings. Above again is the Baroque ceiling. The right aisle ceiling contains paintings by Giambattista Canal; the first right side altar has two paintings from a triptych by Bartolomeo Vivarini.

Turn left outside the church façade, along Fondamenta del Rio de Sant'Eufemia, to the **Chiesa de San Cosmo (Santi Cosmo e Damiano)**; founded in 1481 by Benedictines from Murano, and complete *circa* 1492. The house survived until the Napoleonic dissolution, when its fittings and art works were dispersed. The church was then used as a warehouse, while the monastic buildings were converted into housing. The exterior remains quite imposing, with a three-bay façade and a pedimented stone portal. The extensive monastic buildings are all to the S, centred on a large rectangular cloister; a simple but refined stone colonnade with brick arches.

Cross the bridge in front of the church and continue W along Fondamenta de le Convertite. At GD 690–93 is a Renaissance villa with a broad, two-storey façade, capped by a central pediment. It is said to be a reconstruction of the so-called Rotonda, built by Palladio for the Vendramin. A little further W is **Le Convertite (Santa Maria Madalena)**, founded in the sixteenth century to house penitent and reformed prostitutes, who followed the rule of St Augustine. It survived until the Napoleonic dissolution of 1806, when it became a hospital. In 1856 it became a women's prison. The original nucleus is the small chapel facing the canal, with its simple façade, and the accommodation behind centred on a small square cloister. It was later extended to the W and SW. We return to the main waterfront.

Molino Stucky by Ernst Wullekopf, begun 1896, enlarged 1907–25; restored and converted 2000–06

At GD 785–7 is **Palazzo Maffetti**, a substantial fifteenth-century Gothic house, with superimposed *quadrifore*; at GD 795 is **Palazzetto Foscari**, also Gothic. Next door are the remains of **Palazzo Vendramin** (GD 796–7), once one of the most notable villas on the Giudecca; only three stone portals survive. Down the *calle* adjacent to GD 801, the former Dreher brewery, ingeniously converted for housing by G. Gambirasio, 1995. At GD 805 is the Fortuny textile works (1919, enlarged 1927). Cross Ponte San Biagio, named after the lost church, founded perhaps as early as the tenth century, but closed in 1809. In 1882 the complex was demolished to build the towering mass of the **Molino Stucky**, a vast flour-mill complex in a Hanseatic Gothic style, all in brick, designed by Ernst Wullekopf (begun 1896) for Giovanni Stucky. The buildings occupy the whole block between Rio de San Biagio and Rio dei Lavraneri; they were extended in 1907–25. The mills remained in use until 1954, after which they were abandoned for many years; they have recently been converted into a luxury hotel and conference centre, with housing. The most imposing building is that on the NE corner, with eight storeys, and a tower with a steeply pitched roof. The two adjacent blocks facing N also have Nordic Gothic brick detailing. Directly behind the Molino, facing the Canale dei Lavraneri: high-density housing by Gino Valle (1980–86), rising forbiddingly sheer out of the water. The landward approach is more successful.

Beyond the Molino is the reclaimed island of Sacca Fisola, occupied by public housing. On the SE corner, facing the Valle scheme, recent housing by Pietro Mainardi, Valeriano Pastor and Iginio Cappai; rather mannerist detailing, but successful external spaces.

The Island of
San Giorgio Maggiore

San Giorgio defines the s side of the Bacino of San Marco; its memorable location, together with Palladio's famous church, render it one of the iconic images of the city. Its origins date from 982, when a Benedictine monastery was established here. It grew and flourished, patronised by doges, popes and nobles. The monastery was rebuilt in the early 1200s, followed by a long process of further modernisation and enlargement. Michelozzo's famous library was added in the 1430s, but was destroyed by fire in 1614. The monastery was closed in the Napoleonic suppression of 1806, but reopened two years later. The church was begun in 1566 and completed in 1589. It continues to be occupied by Benedictines, although the monastery and most of the island were ceded by the state in 1951 to the Fondazione Giorgio Cini, established by Vittorio Cini, the wealthy industrialist, in memory of his son. It forms the nucleus for an extensive programme of artistic and cultural activities, research and conferences.

Palladio's church façade is one of his most successful compositions, a development from those at San Francesco and the Redentore. The plan has side aisles rather than chapels, and this is reflected in the broader façade, with more emphasis on the side wings. It consists of

Facing page: San Giorgio Maggiore from the Molo; by Andrea Palladio, *circa* 1560–80; campanile rebuilt in 1774–91 by Benedetto Buratti

San Giorgio Maggiore: façade

two apparently 'interlocking' or overlapping elements: a dominant tall, central one, with four giant Corinthian columns supporting a pediment; and a second, broader, lower one, framed at the outer corners by Corinthian pilasters, and with its own very broad, lower, triangular pediment broken by the insertion of the first element. The façade was completed in 1607–10 after Palladio's death by Simon Sorella, who, it is believed, made some alterations to his intentions; the statuary in the niches is by Giulio del Moro. The façade, intended to be seen on axis from a distance (like the Redentore), is framed by the two projecting wings of the brick transepts beyond, while the whole is capped by a lead cupola. The tall campanile, based on that of San Marco, forms a contrasting, strongly vertical element. The ancient tower collapsed in 1774 and was rebuilt by Benedetto Buratti, completed in 1791; fine views from the bell-chamber.

The plan also derives from the Redentore, but the scale is more monumental, the features more pronounced. The core is a Latin cross, with a nave of three-and-a-half bays, and broad side aisles. The

San Giorgio Maggiore: nave interior

square central crossing supports a drum and the cupola, but the transepts here are larger, extending beyond the width of the aisles, and terminating with radiused apses. Beyond the crossing there is one further nave bay and then the square chancel; beyond this is a three-bay screen, the lower order of which is open, with the organ loft above. Beyond again is a deep choir, again with a radiused apse.

The interior is grandiose and self-confident; the order is Corinthian throughout, but the rich monumentality stops at the trabeation, and the upper surfaces and vaults are all simple plaster. The nave bays are defined by attached columns, clustered at the crossing; the trabeation is continuous, but breaks forward at the column capitals. Light comes from high-level thermal windows. The aisles have simple cross-vaults, and are linked to the nave by semicircular arches on pilasters.

Principal art works: right nave aisle: first altar: altarpiece by Jacopo Bassano; second altar: wooden Crucifixion, early fifteenth century; third altar: altarpiece perhaps by Tintoretto. Right transept, fourth altar: altarpiece also attributed to Tintoretto. To the right of the high altar: altarpiece by Ricci, 1708. The high altar: by Aliense. In the centre: bronze of the four Evangelists by Campagna, 1591–3. On the flank walls: two important works by Tintoretto, the *Last Supper* and the *Fall of Manna*. The choir: around the perimeter are forty-eight stalls, decorated with panels of the life of St Benedict, by Albrecht van der Brulle, 1594–8. In the sacristy: works by Palma il Giovane and Lombardo. Back in the church: altar to the left of the high altar: altarpiece by Tintoretto, but completed by his son. Left transept: fifth altar: another Tintoretto, completed by his son; sixth altar: altarpiece by Matteo Ponzone; seventh altar: marble altarpiece by Campagna; eighth altar: altarpiece by Leandro Bassano.

The monastic buildings

The **manica lunga** ('long sleeve') is an exceptionally long narrow wing, containing monks' cells, down the se side of the complex, and with a short end façade onto the little enclosed harbour; designed by Giovanni Buora, 1494–1513, in a simple, early Renaissance style. The **Chiostro degli Allori** or **degli Cipressi** (cloister of the laurels, now that of the cypresses) was also begun by Buora, but completed by his son Andrea, 1516–40. It measures thirteen bays by eleven, and has a simple, elegant, Renaissance arcade on all four sides. The first-floor fenestration differs according to the internal functions; abutting the *manica lunga* there are simple paired windows; two other sides have large arched paired lights, while on the fourth side (containing the library) there are tall single windows. The second cloister is generally known as the **Chiostro Palladiano**, but was once (until the eighteenth century) also known as that of the cypresses. It stands adjacent to the right flank of the church itself, and is entered directly from the square; begun by Palladio *circa* 1579, but completed only in 1614, many years after his death. The lower order has a tall arcade, with Ionic stone columns supporting stone arches. The first floor has rows of tall rectangular single windows, with alternating triangular and radiused pediments. On the e side is a three-bay loggia linking the two cloisters together. In the centre of the w wing: the monumental **staircase of honour**, added in 1641–3 by Longhena, in the location intended by Palladio. An impressive composition, with paired flights of steps meeting at the top landing in a spacious colonnaded loggia. All richly detailed in stone, and framed by Corinthian pilasters. Longhena also designed the **library**, which occupies the upper floor of the wing between the two cloisters. The impressive hall has a simple barrel-vaulted ceiling, with high-level thermal windows. The richly carved wooded bookcases are also by Longhena. The **refectory** was completed by Palladio on the basis of a pre-existing structure. Its stands s of the two cloisters, extending into the gardens, another simple, impressive barrel-vaulted hall, approached by a ceremonial staircase. The lobby was completed *circa* 1540, the refectory itself in 1562. On the end wall was Veronese's vast canvas, the *Marriage at Cana*, today in the Louvre.

Most of the rest of the island is occupied by extensive gardens, as well as an open-air Greek theatre.

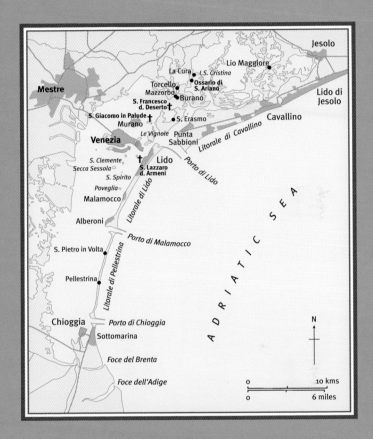

The Venetian Lagoon

The Venetian Lagoon

1 SAN MICHELE AND MURANO

San Michele

Immediately N of the city, and easily reached from the Fondamente Nove, is the cemetery island of San Michele. Historically, it consisted of two much smaller islets, San Michele itself and San Cristoforo de la Pace. In 1807 it was designated the city cemetery by Napoleon, and the islets were joined together in 1837, when the intervening canal was reclaimed; the cemetery was then enlarged considerably by the Comune, and surrounded by neo-Gothic red brick walls, with stone detailing.

The monastery was founded in 1212 by the Camaldolesi, who remained until the Napoleonic suppression. The principal monument is the church, Mauro Codussi's first major work in Venice, 1469–*circa* 1478. Its gleaming Istrian stone façade was remarkable in its time: although its overall composition developed from the Venetian Gothic tradition, it was revolutionary in that no church in the city had yet been given an all-stone façade, and in the new Renaissance style. Its three bays represent the nave and aisles inside; the central bay, tallest and broadest, is capped by a large radiused pediment, while the side bays have smaller quadrants. The façade is clad with flat rustication, the first time it had been used on a Venetian church.

Facing page: Chioggia: Santissima Trinità and the Vena canal

San Michele in Isola: church by Mauro Codussi, 1469–78; the adjacent Miani Chapel by Guglielmo de' Grigi, 1529–35

The interior: a basilica plan, with a five-bay nave and lower, flanking aisles; across the second bay of the nave is a richly detailed free-standing *barco*, with an arched colonnade supporting the gallery. The nave interior is restrained but refined, with ingenious capitals. Its ceiling is flat and coffered; at the east end is a shallow cupola on pendentives. Inside the vestibule: a modest monument with the ashes of Paolo Sarpi (+1623), the noted theologian and adviser to the Republic. Right aisle: first chapel: of the Zorzi family. In the chancel: monument to Andrea Loredan (+1513), one of the church's benefactors. The Baroque high altar dates from 1686. Left aisle, first chapel: of the Priuli family. Off the left aisle: sixteenth-century Cappella de la Croce.

The **Miani Chapel** (usually erroneously called the Emiliani Chapel) stands at the NW corner of the church, to which it is linked; a prominent octagonal form, all clad in rich stone and marble and surmounted by a unique stone-clad cupola. Funded by the will of Margherita Vitturi, widow of Giovanni Miani, it was begun by Guglielmo de' Grigi in 1529; completed *circa* 1535. Inside: three contemporary altars, with marble relief altarpieces: the *Annunciation*,

Adoration of the Magi and the *Shepherds Worshipping*, by Giovanni Antonio Carona.

The fine late Gothic brick campanile (1460) stands N of the chancel; it is capped by a balcony and an octagonal drum surmounted by a tiled cupola.

Immediately s of the church façade is the late Gothic entrance to the monastic buildings, fifteenth century, transitional in style, built around a quadrilateral cloister with simple arched colonnades. The cemetery itself extends s and se, and is monumentally, formally planned in a series of large square enclosures (by Annibale Forcellini, completed in 1872). At the e side is the 1908 extension, including a zone for non-Catholics, in which are buried several notable figures, including Diaghilev, Stravinsky, Ezra Pound, Josif Brodsky and Sir Ashley Clarke, former ambassador to Rome and founder of Venice in Peril. Immediately beyond this 'quarter' is the large new extension by David Chipperfield, partly completed in 2007.

Murano

Venice's largest, closest and most important satellite. Although of ancient foundation (the Roman Amurianum), its history is fairly obscure until the late thirteenth century; in 1275 a Venetian governor was established, but Murano retained considerable independence, with its own council and ruling citizenry. In 1291 the Republic transferred the city's glass furnaces here, to remove the danger of fire; despite vicissitudes over the centuries, Murano has lived on its famous glass industry ever since. Its period of greatest fame and

Murano in 1500, from de' Barbari's engraving

Murano: Rio dei Vetrai, with the fourteenth-century Palazzetto Corner on colonnades

prosperity was the fifteenth and early sixteenth centuries, when not only was the industry flourishing but also many Venetian nobles built villas here, with extensive gardens. A handful survives today. By the later sixteenth century, the nobility were investing in much larger estates on the Terraferma, where they also built numerous villas; Murano declined, and became a backwater again. In the nineteenth century the glass industry was modernised; today the island produces large quantities of glass of widely varying artistic quality, although the best is work of great skill and creative craftsmanship.

Murano (population approximately 7,000) spreads over five principal islets, and is divided in half by its own Grand Canal, broad but less grand than its Venetian namesake. The heart of the community is the Rio dei Vetrai, with a narrow quay down both banks; this itinerary starts at the Colonna *vaporetto* stop at the s end.

Walking NE along Fondamenta dei Vetrai, at no. 6 is the first of two Contarini houses, both of similar date and refined sixteenth-century appearance. At no. 27–8 is the second **Palazzo Contarini**. Both are substantial *palazzetti* rather than villas, with tripartite symmetrical façades. On the other bank, at Fondamenta Manin 24, is the tall, four-storey seventeenth-century **Palazzo Miotti**. A little further on the west bank, at no. 37, is the incomplete **Casa Andreotta**, late fifteenth-century *gotico fiorito*, with a fine *trifora* to

Murano: detail of the Baroque Ospizio Briati, 1752

the *piano nobile*. On the E bank: two attractive medieval houses: at no. 6 is the fourteenth-century **Palazzetto Obizzi e Sodeci**, with quayside colonnade and *barbacani*. The other, at no. 71, is **Palazzetto Corner**, trilobate Gothic, probably late fourteenth century, with a stone colonnade, a good *trifora* and five single lights. Halfway down Rio dei Vetrai, cross the Ponte de Mezo (Ballarin) and turn right down the avenue traditionally called Bressagio (Bersaglio), formally Viale Garibaldi. On the left near the end is the **Ospizio Briati**, established by the glass-maker Giuseppe Briati in 1752 as a charitable home for glass-workers' widows; an attractive little Baroque stone façade, with a curved pediment capped by sculptures. On the right is the former **Teatro Piave**, nineteenth century, named after the Muranese librettist Francesco Maria Piave, who worked with Verdi; now absorbed by adjacent glassworks. At the end is the imposing stone Faro (lighthouse). From the *vaporetto* stop, looking SW, we see the refined brick façade of the **Casinò Mocenigo** (1591–1617), today almost entirely surrounded by glassworks. The single-storey pavilion has Palladian windows, surmounted by alternating triangular and radiused pediments, divided by Doric pilasters; the architect was perhaps Scamozzi. Its interior contains three rooms elegantly frescoed

Murano: Casinò Mocenigo, 1591–1617

in the manner of Veronese (the themes are Music, Poetry and Love),
probably by Benedetto Caliari.

Turn left along Fondamenta San Giovanni dei Battuti. At no. 8 is
Palazzo Soranzo, an attractive early sixteenth-century house, in poor
condition. The quay continues as Fondamenta Antonio Colleoni,
forming the s bank of the Grand Canal. At no. 15–16 is a second
Soranzo villa, with a slightly asymmetrical but elegant façade; two
storeys, with a central *quadrifora*. Nearby were three more
Renaissance villas, all now lost: Palazzi Grimani, Giustinian and
Morosini. At the w end, turn left, inland into the picturesque
Campo Santo Stefano. The church was closed in 1813, and
demolished in 1835, but the *osteria* (no. 3) is said to contain twelfth-
century material. The neo-medieval brick clock tower (1890) stands
on the site of the lost campanile of Santo Stefano. Directly across
Rio dei Vetrai again is:

San Pietro Martire: originally a Dominican monastery, built in
1348–63, patronised by the Michiel. Consecrated in 1417, it suffered a
serious fire in 1474 and was extensively rebuilt; re-consecrated in
1511. Suppressed in 1806, it reopened as a parish church in 1813, as it
remains. A fine sixteenth-century Renaissance west portal. The
interior has a broad, spacious nave, with flanking aisles, the nave
colonnade of four large bays with semicircular arches. Both nave and
aisles have open timber truss roofs. At the E end is a large barrel-
vaulted chancel. Halfway down the right aisle is the fine *Virgin and
Child with Saints and Doge Agostin Barbarigo* (the 'pala Barbarigo',
1488), by Giovanni Bellini. Adjacent, to the right, is a second Bellini,
the *Assumption with Eight Saints*, 1510–13. Many of the church's

Murano: interior of San Pietro Martire, rebuilt
1474–1511

paintings were collected from suppressed monasteries. To the w of
the nave: a simple arched colonnade, remains of the lost house of
Santa Chiara, reassembled here in 1924. The adjacent campanile
(1498–1502) is capped by an 'onion' cupola.

Continue around the N end of the quay, to Ponte Longo
(Vivarini), the only bridge crossing the Grand Canal. Near the
bridge, on the left is the eclectic Gothic façade of **Palazzo da Mula**:
the most notable medieval house in Murano. Originally Venetian-
Byzantine, what we see is mostly fifteenth-century Gothic, partially
modernised in the sixteenth century, and elaborated with inset
decoration, mostly Venetian-Byzantine. The central *quadrifora* is
flanked by windows with unusual pendant tracery, *circa* 1480. To the
rear: remains of an enclosing garden wall, with twelfth-century
marble decoration. Adjacent to the N stood the lost monastery of
San Cipriano (founded 1108), and the seat of the patriarchal
seminary (1507–1807), then suppressed and demolished.

Crossing Ponte Longo (1866), turn left along Fondamenta
Sebastiano Venier. At no. 44: **Palazzo Correr Grimani**, mid-sixteenth

Murano: Palazzo Giustinian (right), modernised by Gaspari, 1707;
behind, the fourteenth-century campanile of Santi Maria e Donato

century, with four storeys and a large *bifora* to the upper hall. The
interior was once richly decorated with stucco and frescoes. At the
far end is **Santa Maria degli Angeli**, an ancient foundation,
re-established in 1187, and rebuilt in the early sixteenth century
(re-consecrated in 1529). An important Augustinian nunnery, it was
suppressed in 1810. A simple tripartite façade, with tall, arched, single
windows. The interior has a single nave; the nuns' *barco* is lost. The
nave ceiling is decorated with thirty-nine paintings by Piermaria
Pennacchi and others, *circa* 1520. The church had a notable collection
of paintings, including works by Palma il Giovane, Salviati,
Pordenone and Vittoria; some were transferred to San Pietro Martire.

Return to the foot of Ponte Longo, and continue E along
Fondamenta Cavour. At no. 37 is a Gothic house on colonnades,
with timber *barbacani*, modernised in the sixteenth century. Almost
next door, at no. 47, is **Palazzo Manolesso Seguso**, a substantial,
asymmetrical seventeenth-century house, lacking the left wing.
Changing direction, the quay becomes Fondamenta Marco
Giustinian. At no. 8 is the imposing **Palazzo Giustinian**, the largest
Baroque house in Murano, and since 1861 the seat of the Museo
Vetrario (glass museum), founded by the abbot and local historian
Vincenzo Zanetti. The palace was originally Gothic, owned by the

Murano: Santi Maria e Donato: the exterior; 1125–41, recently restored

Cappello, but in 1659 became the residence of the bishops of Torcello; after 1707 it was extensively modernised and refaced by Gaspari for the bishop, Marco Giustinian. The house has three storeys, and an L-shaped plan wrapped around a courtyard. The imposing *piano nobile* has a large central cluster of windows, crowned by the family arms and flanked by paired lights. The rear wing remains mainly Gothic, but supported on an elegant early Renaissance stone colonnade. The main upper hall has a ceiling frescoed by Francesco Zugno. The museum contains an exceptionally fine collection of glass, from the Roman period to the present, including some very rare medieval pieces and many refined works from the seventeenth and eighteenth centuries.

Further NW along the quay, we reach the spacious Campo San Donato, on which is the principal ecclesiastical monument of Murano, the cathedral of **Santi Maria e Donato**.

Probably founded in the seventh or eighth century, in 1125–41 the church was completely rebuilt as we see it today, an almost unique survivor, contemporary with San Marco. The new church was to house the remains of St Donato, patron of the island since 1400, and added to the earlier dedication to St Mary. The exterior is all of brickwork, the most prominent feature being the faceted hexagonal eastern end, with fine superimposed colonnades of decorative brickwork. Both orders have rich brick arches supported by paired stone columns, and a broad band of decorative brickwork between the two orders. The external composition directly reflects the internal plan, a hybrid between a centralised Greek cross and a Latin cross with transepts.

The w façade is very simple, other than the rich reliefs flanking the portal; originally Roman, second century AD, with an eighth-century inscription.

Internally, the central six-bay nave is flanked by two colonnades, each of five Greek marble columns, with rich Byzantine-Corinthian capitals supporting decorative brick arches. Nave, transepts and chancel are all covered with a fine open 'ship's-keel' timber roof. The transept extends as far as the width of the side aisles; the central radiused apse is flanked by smaller square side chapels. The floor is covered by extensive complex marble mosaics, contemporary with the church's reconstruction, dated 1140.

In the hemispherical chancel vault is the single mosaic figure of the Mother of God, on a gold background, early 1200s; at lower level are early fifteenth-century frescoes of the Evangelists by Niccolo di Pietro. In the centre of the chancel: monument to Bishop Marco Giustinian (+1735).

To the sw of the church is the tall fourteenth-century brick campanile, with three orders; three-light openings to the bell-chamber on each face. Immediately adjacent is the Monument to the Fallen of the First World War, by Napoleone Martinuzzi, a local sculptor, 1927.

Take Fondamenta San Lorenzo as far as Ponte Zanetti, cross the bridge and return along Fondamenta Sebastiano Santi. At no. 11 is the well-proportioned **Palazzo Foscari**, originally fourteenth-century Gothic, tripartite and symmetrical, with a central *bifora* to the *piano nobile*, flanked by pairs of single lights. At no. 5 is the broad façade of **Palazzo Marcello**, late sixteenth century, but much altered, since it later became the monastic church of San Giuseppe; from 1737 to 1810 it was occupied by Carmelite nuns. The façade has a central Serliana. At the s end of the quay is Ponte San Martino; along the quay towards the E (Rio di San Matteo), at Fondamenta Radi nos. 19–23, is the little Neo-classical façade of the oratory of **San Matteo**, all that survives of the former monastery, founded in 1280, but demolished in the 1830s.

South of Ponte San Martino, the main quay continues as Fondamenta Antonio Maschio, then Fondamenta Andrea Navagero.

Murano: Palazzo Trevisan, 1555–8, perhaps to an original design by Palladio or Daniele Barbaro

On this quay are three substantial houses. At no. 34 is **Palazzo Trevisan**, the most remarkable Renaissance palace on Murano: it may have been designed by Daniele Barbaro, the Renaissance humanist and philosopher. Barbaro was patron of Palladio at Maser at the time that Palazzo Trevisan was being built; it owes much to Palladio, who may have furnished initial ideas and plans. The house was built for Camillo Trevisan in 1555–8, and has an unusual plan. The front section, towards the quay, is traditional, symmetrical and tripartite, with the usual central *androne*; beyond is a transverse hall with apsidal ends, a feature never seen in Venice before. (Palladio's illustrations in *I quattro libri dell'architettura* incorporate such a hall, including that at Palazzo Chiericati, Vicenza.) Beyond again is a central three-bay colonnaded loggia, flanked by two large rooms, all looking eastwards onto a formerly extensive garden.

The quay façade is noble, severe and imposing, with four orders, the lower two representing the ground floor, with the *piano nobile* above; also a low attic. It was originally frescoed by Prospero Bresciano. The dominant feature is the central Serliana, with its balcony on huge stone corbels, and a pedimented central window. The quoins are rusticated and the façade is capped by a monumental cornice. Inside, the *androne* is flanked by rusticated stone pilasters, and leads to the transverse hall, with niches for statues. This hall has a richly decorated barrel-vaulted ceiling, with grotesques and landscapes.

The interior was decorated by Veronese, Zelotti and Vittoria, although Veronese's work was confined to one room on the ground floor and the transverse hall on the *piano nobile* (*circa* 1557), which survives in poor condition. It consists of four landscape scenes on the curved walls, and the Olympian Gods on the ceiling; Vittoria's stucco decoration has survived in part, although much is gone, including his fine fireplaces. The palace remains (2008) in very poor condition.

Next door, at no. 38, is the extensive **Palazzo Pesaro**; originally Gothic, but now of sixteenth-century appearance; an extremely broad canal façade, originally with ten bays; three large *monofore* grouped together, united by a balcony, to light the first-floor *portego*.

Next again, at no. 41, is **Palazzo Cappello**: originally Gothic but much altered; the rear façade retains a Gothic *trifora*.

At nos. 48–52 is a small fourteenth-century Gothic house with trilobate *pentafora*. Finally, at nos. 60–62, is **Palazzo Navagero**, with a colonnade along the quay; recently ruinous, now restored. The house is originally Gothic but extensively altered and modernised in the sixteenth century. Behind were famous, extensive gardens of the humanist and scientist Andrea Navagero, one of the first and most notable botanical gardens in Europe.

2 THE EASTERN LAGOON: LA CERTOSA, LE VIGNOLE, SANT'ERASMO, THE LAZZARETTO NUOVO

La Certosa, a short distance E of Sant'Elena, was probably first settled in the twelfth century, taking its name from a Carthusian monastery, established in 1424. It was suppressed by Napoleon in 1806, and thereafter abandoned. The church, Sant'Andrea (by Pietro Lombardo), was destroyed and its many art works dispersed, one of the gravest losses of post-Republican Venetian history. The island was later used as a military base, until 1968. In 1977 it was declared a public park and restored.

Le Vignole, a larger island, lies NE of La Certosa. Traditionally intensively cultivated with orchards and market gardens, and the vines from which its name derives; some are now abandoned. Settlement is scattered, chiefly traditional farmhouses. On the E side is a long, narrow, artificial canal, used by seaplanes during the Second World War. At the southern tip is the imposing **Forte di Sant'Andrea**, the historic fort defending the N side of the Porto di Lido. It is best seen either by boat or from the N end of the Lido. The nucleus is a brick medieval tower, but it was greatly extended (1543–71) by Sanmicheli, the Republic's military architect, to form the present structure. The principal (s) façade faces the fort of San Niccolò di Lido. Two long, low, side wings are faced with Istrian stone, with a series of openings for cannon; the central section projects forward, and is massively impressive, with three large arched Doric bays, heavily rusticated. On the face of the brick tower is the Marcian lion and an inscription recording the victory of Lepanto (1571).

Sant'Erasmo lies N of Le Vignole, and is the largest island in the lagoon after Venice. It has never been intensively settled, and today contains scattered farmhouses, mainly along the W (lee) shore. It is intensively cultivated with orchards and market gardens, providing much of the city's daily supplies. The island is subdivided by numerous small drainage channels.

In the s corner is the **Torre di Massimiliano**, a drum-shaped brick fortress, built in 1813 to improve the lagoon's sea defences, and recently restored. Halfway down the lagoon side of the island is the hamlet of Sant'Erasmo, with the parish church of Cristo Re (Christ the King) by Brenno del Giudice (1928–9) on the site of the ancient original church, founded in 1120 but demolished *circa* 1800.

The **Lazzaretto Nuovo** is adjacent to the W tip of Sant'Erasmo. Established in 1468 to house quarantine accommodation for people and goods arriving from abroad, it was later used as a plague and leper hospital. In the great plague of 1576, 10,000 people were accommodated here. It was later abandoned; in 1975 it became a military base. Extensive archaeological work continues, and a museum is being established. The principal surviving building is the Teson Grande (1562), a great warehouse, 100 metres long, in which incoming goods were stored and fumigated. There are also remains of a twelfth-century Benedictine church.

3   FROM MURANO TO THE NORTHERN LAGOON: SAN FRANCESCO DEL DESERTO, MAZZORBO, BURANO, TORCELLO AND BEYOND

In the early medieval period the northern lagoon was extensively settled; only one substantial settlement survives today – Burano – as well as a scattering of hamlets and isolated farms.

From Murano, the main channel NE passes two tiny islets. The first is **San Giacomo in Paludo** ('St James in the Marshes'), once housing a hostel for pilgrims to the Holy Land, established in the twelfth century. It was abandoned after 1797, then fortified by Napoleon, remaining a fort until 1964. Recently, some surviving buildings have been restored. Further towards Burano is **La Madona del Monte**, again fortified by Napoleon, and today with two ruined military buildings. In the fourteenth century a Benedictine monastic house was established here, San Niccolò de la Cavana. In the early eighteenth century it was re-established as the Vergine del Rosario, but suppressed by Napoleon.

To the E is the distinctive cypress-clad island of **San Francesco del Deserto**, reached by hiring a boat from Burano. According to legend, the island monastery was founded by St Francis in 1220, on a visit to Venice. Shortly after Francis's death, the owner of the island, Jacopo Michiel, built a church and in 1233 dedicated it to the Franciscans. It survived until 1420, when the island was abandoned for thirty years, following widespread silting and malaria; hence the affix 'del deserto'. In 1453 the friars returned; the church was restored, and a new cloister built. It was abandoned again at the Napoleonic suppression in 1806, but the friars returned in 1858, under the Austrian occupation; they remain there today.

The friary is surrounded by densely planted cypresses; annexed are gardens and orchards. It is centred on two small cloisters, one originally fourteenth century, the other from the 1450s. The church is small and very simple, with a rectangular nave; it was extensively restored after 1858. The campanile stands near the corner of the first cloister.

A little further N of Madonna del Monte, we reach **Mazzorbo**. This once prosperous settlement (the name derives from *maiurbium*, large town) is today a straggling hamlet on the E side of the Canale di Mazzorbo, which bisects the former settlement. It was one of the earliest islands to be settled from the Terraferma; in the Middle Ages it was wealthy, with five monasteries and five parishes. Its peak of prosperity was the fourteenth century, after which it began a long,

Mazzorbo; housing by Giancarlo de Carlo, 1985

slow decline, as its canals silted up and malaria became rife. On the NW side of the main canal are a couple of substantial farmhouses, one of them fourteenth-century Gothic. At the N end (left bank) is the so-called Ridotto, remains of the monastery of Sant'Eufemia, turned into a munitions base in 1838.

The main settlement, on the SE side of the channel, consists of a ribbon of traditional houses, mostly seventeenth and eighteenth centuries, built along the *fondamenta*. Towards the S, the Canale di **Santa Caterina** leads to the eponymous church, originally part of a Benedictine nunnery, founded in 783, together with an adjacent pilgrim hostel. It was rebuilt in the fourteenth century, and most survives today. The campanile and its bell are from 1318. The church has a rectangular, aisle-less nave, and preserves a *barco*, supported on columns and *barbacani*. The fourteenth-century nave roof is of the 'ship's-keel' type, with a double row of *barbacani*.

Return to the *vaporetto* stop, and continue NE along the quay; at the corner is the fifteenth-century campanile of the lost church of **Santa Maria in Valverde**, now set in an attractive small park. Continue along the quay towards Burano. On the E side of the island is a housing project by Giancarlo de Carlo (1985), a modern reinterpretation of the small vernacular housing of the lagoon, with courtyards off a central *calle*, and taking inspiration from the brightly coloured cottages of Burano. Cross the long timber bridge to Burano.

Burano: typical cottages on Rio de la Zuecca (Giudecca)

Burano

This is the largest settlement in the northern lagoon, a densely packed miniature archipelago, population approximately 5,300. In the medieval era, it never achieved the prominence or wealth of Mazzorbo or Torcello, and historically was inhabited chiefly by fishermen. It remained very poor until recent times, when the tourist industry revived the local economy, which remains partly based on fishing, boat-building, the traditional production of lace (now for tourists), and on the glass industry of Murano. The attractive village is completely pedestrianised. The bright colours of its cottages, though, are a comparatively recent phenomenon; historically, the colours were more subdued and traditional. The settlement has a distinctive urban 'grain', with dense settlement along the narrow canal quays, and the remaining cottages mainly built in parallel rows along narrow *calli*.

The centre of the village is the Rio dei Assassini, and its continuation, the reclaimed Via Galuppi, named after the Baroque composer Baldassare Galuppi (1706–1785), who was born here. At its SE end the street opens into the spacious Piazza Galuppi. On the SE side is Burano's only church, **San Martino Vescovo**, founded in 959, but rebuilt several times. The present large plain structure is sixteenth century; it has no façade, since its W end abuts a block of houses. The entrance is from the Piazza, on the N side. Its plan is a Latin cross, with side aisles and transepts; the nave is flanked by Corinthian colonnades, and has a barrel-vaulted ceiling. The aisles and transepts

Burano: the fourteenth-century Palazzo Comunale and monument
to Baldassare Galuppi

have simple cross-vaults. In the left aisle is a fine *Crucifixion* by G.B.
Tiepolo (1722); other paintings include works by Fontebasso, Zanchi
and the workshop of Palma il Giovane. Some have been relocated to
the adjacent **Oratorio di Santa Barbara**; the oratory was formerly
the Scuola dei Pescatori; a simple, symmetrical seventeenth-century
brick façade.

Near the S end of the church is the tall campanile, by Tirali,
1703–14; it has a remarkable inclination to the S.

On the NW side of the Piazza is the medieval **Palazzo Comunale**,
today housing the lace-making school and a small exhibition. Burano
was famous for lace-making during the sixteenth and seventeenth
centuries, after which it declined drastically. By the early nineteenth
century the craft was almost lost, until it was revived by Contessa
Adriana Marcello, who established a school here in 1872. The Palazzo
Comunale is fourteenth-century Gothic, on two storeys, although the
ground floor is altered; the first-floor *trifora* denotes the location of
the council room. Immediately to the right is another fourteenth-
century Gothic house, on three floors (the uppermost later), formerly
the **Palazzo del Podestà** or governor; the façade is tripartite and
symmetrical, with another *trifora* to the first-floor *portego*.

From the S end of Via Galuppi we can take the reclaimed Rio
Terà del Pizzo and Calle Tibaldon as far as the picturesque Rio de la
Zueca (Giudecca). At no. 386 is the **Villa Michiel Deste**, early

Torcello: general view from Burano, with Santa Fosca (left) and the cathedral and campanile (right)

seventeenth century, and by far the largest house on the island, although today divided into apartments. It has a remarkably broad plan and façade, with two storeys; in the centre: a prominent *abbaino*. A central main portal and two secondary entrances to the side wings; the detailing throughout is simple and restrained. All the remaining housing along the little canal is of the typical small-scale vernacular type.

Torcello

The most famous settlement of the northern lagoon, although today a hamlet, with only a couple of dozen inhabitants. Torcello lies a short distance N of Burano and consists of several islands, some now uninhabited. In the Roman era it was probably effectively a suburb of the nearby mainland town of Altino; it was re-settled in the period of the 'barbarian' invasions, and the cathedral was founded in 639. Torcello became wealthy, with several thousand inhabitants and a dozen churches and monasteries. It was the 'capital' of the northern lagoon, and the local governor (*podestà*) was based here. Its long decline began in the fourteenth century, as the modest size of the contemporary surviving council hall attests. By 1400 it was already a mere village, and, despite a modest revival in the seventeenth century, it has remained so ever since. All its monasteries are long gone, mostly pillaged for their building materials, and today only the handful of historic buildings around the village green records Torcello's lost importance.

Torcello: Santa Fosca: exterior of the apse, *circa* 1100–20

From the *vaporetto* stop, walk along the Fondamenta dei Borgognoni, the left bank of the Rio di Torcello, towards the hamlet. On the right is the Ponte del Diavolo, an almost unique survivor of a bridge without parapets. Just beyond the end of the canal is the main grassed square, around which are Santa Fosca, the cathedral and its campanile, and two small medieval buildings, the Palazzo dell'Archivio and the Palazzo del Consiglio.

Santa Fosca was built to house the remains of the titular saint, and was begun *circa* 1100. It has a centralised Greek-cross plan, surrounded on five sides by a colonnaded portico, with marble columns and capitals, and stilted brick arches; five bays to the N, S and W faces and three on each of the NW and SW faces. Two of the original marble *plutei* are still in place. The interior is simple but harmonious; the *cipollino* marble nave columns have fine marble capitals, supporting brick arches. At high level, brick squinches in the four corners support a circular drum, almost certainly intended to support a cupola. Today it has an open timber roof. The chancel projects a little towards the E, with a radiused apse, and is flanked by two tiny side chapels, also with radiused apses. The chancel has a simple barrel vault. The exterior of the church has fine decorative brickwork, similar to that at Santi Maria e Donato, Murano, wrapping around the eastern apses.

Santa Fosca is linked by a covered colonnade to the portico of the cathedral of **Santa Maria Assunta**, the outstanding monument of the island. Founded in 639, it was enlarged in 824, and extensively reconstructed by Bishop Orso Orseolo in 1008; much of this fabric survives. The tall, austere, brick façade is preceded by a lower narthex, first built in the ninth century but enlarged in the fourteenth, when it was linked with Santa Fosca. In front of the narthex are the remains of a circular seventh-century baptistery, which had eight stone columns supporting the drum of the roof.

The cathedral is a basilica, with a long nave, two lower side aisles and an E end terminating with three radiused apses. The exterior is very plain; down the S side aisle, the windows are protected by heavy stone shutters, which could be closed in times of danger. We enter by the right lateral doorway off the narthex. The nave is defined by two rows, each of nine monolithic Greek *cipollino* marble columns, with rich Corinthian capitals, most from the 1008 reconstruction, although a few survive from the earlier church. The complex marble mosaic floor also dates from the 1008 rebuilding. Near the entrance is a marble eleventh-century holy water stoup, supported by four small figures.

On the inner face of the façade is the renowned mosaic of the Apotheosis of Christ and the Last Judgement, late twelfth or early thirteenth century. The scenes are as follows (from the top): *Christ Crucified between Mary and John the Evangelist*; second order: *Christ Descending into Limbo, Flanked by Archangels Gabriel and Michael*; third order: in the centre is *Christ in Glory*, flanked by the Virgin and John the Baptist, with Apostles and saints on each side; fourth order: *Preparation for the Last Judgement*, with *Angels Waking the Dead with Trumpets*; fifth order: left side: the *Blessed in Paradise*; right side: *Angels Pushing Sinners into the Fires of Hell*; sixth order, left side: *Abraham Receiving Souls*, and the *Virgin at the Door of Paradise*; right side: the *Fires of Hell, Skulls Attacked by Worms and Naked Sinners*.

Across the E end of the nave is the iconostasis; at low level: four fine eleventh-century marble *plutei*, with rich relief decoration. The iconostasis is supported by six marble columns and contains a series of fifteenth-century paintings of the Virgin flanked by the Apostles. Above is a large contemporary wooden crucifix.

Torcello: the cathedral (right), mostly after 1008; and the fourteenth-century Palazzo de l'Archivio (left)

To the left is the curious marble pulpit, made from pieces from the earlier church, or perhaps from the Roman ruins of Altino, and reassembled in the thirteenth century. In the chancel, the high altar again contains material from the original seventh-century altar; below it is a third-century sarcophagus with the remains of St Eliodorus, first bishop of Altino, brought here in 635.

The chancel is dominated by the superb mosaics of the central apse; in the spandrels of the outer face of the chancel arch are thirteenth-century mosaics of the Annunciation. In the centre of the apse, in a gold field, is the solitary image of the Virgin and Child; below: a series of mosaics of the Apostles; at low level in the centre is St Eliodorus. Around the semicircle of the apse are six stepped rows of seating, in brickwork, for the clergy; in the centre is the bishop's throne.

The south apse (the chapel of the Blessed Sacrament) also has exceptional mosaics; in the square vault are four figures of angels holding a crown, in the centre of which is the Mystic Lamb. The mosaics are the oldest in the church, twelfth/thirteenth century. In the centre of the semicircular vault: *Christ in Benediction, Flanked by Michael and Gabriel*. Below are four doctors of the early church: Gregory, Martin, Augustine and Ambrose.

Outside the cathedral, the massive eleventh-century brick campanile stands to the E, near the apses; it is 55 metres high. The

Torcello: the fourteenth-century Palazzo del Consiglio

bell-chamber has four small openings on each face. Nearby is a tiny oratory, dedicated to St Mark, and said to indicate the location where the first chapel was built to house the saint's body, when it was taken from Alexandria in 829.

Back in the Piazza, in the centre is a worn stone seat, the 'Throne of Attila', but probably once used for dispensing justice. On the N side, near the baptistery, is the **Palazzo dell'Archivio**, a modest fourteenth-century brick building, with an open staircase at one end and a colonnaded ground-floor loggia; the upper floor is supported by square stone columns and timber *barbacani*. Within the loggia is part of the archaeological collection of the Museo dell'Estuario, from Altino and Torcello itself. In the centre of the first floor is a *trifora*; the upper hall contains Roman, Etruscan and early Venetian finds from the vicinity.

On the w side of the grassy square is the **Palazzo del Consiglio**, a similarly modest building, also fourteenth century, with a small bell-tower on one corner, to summon citizens to meetings, and another open stair at the s end. On the ground floor are displayed medieval finds from the vicinity, as well as mosaic fragments from the cathedral; the centrepiece is the fine thirteenth- to fourteenth-century Pala d'Oro, of gilded silver, of which thirteen of the original twenty-nine pieces survive. On the upper floor: paintings, historic documents and sculpted fragments from the lost churches of Torcello.

Beyond Torcello

A short distance N of Torcello is a small cluster of islets, the remains of earlier settlements, now almost entirely disappeared. **Sant'Ariano** and **La Cura** are both fragments of the former town of Costanziaca, the former based on a monastery founded in 1160, but now disappeared. Sant'Ariano has a certain morbid fame as the island established by the Republic in 1565 as an 'overspill' for the city's cemeteries, from which its identification as an ossuary is derived. Today the islet, like La Cura, is deserted. Further NE is **Santa Cristina**, named after the saint whose remains were brought here in 1325, but transferred to San Francesco de la Vigna in 1453, by which time the island was effectively abandoned. It had formed part of the larger settlement of Ammiana. Today it is the centre of an extensive *valle da pesca* (enclosed basin for fish-farming).

4 THE SOUTHERN LAGOON: MONASTERIES AND LEPER HOSPITALS

This group of seven islands lies S and SE of the city; historically, none contained lay settlements; instead, they were all developed for specific Republican and religious institutions.

San Servolo

Halfway between San Giorgio and the Lido; accessible by *vaporetto*. First settled in 810 by Benedictine monks and then nuns until 1615; in 1725 they were replaced by hospitallers of St John of God, and in the same period (1733–66) the present church and conventual buildings were constructed. It then became a psychiatric hospital, until its closure in 1978. Since then, it has become a university centre for study and conservation. The church (1747) is by Tommaso Temanza; some of the hospital buildings (after 1733) are by Giovanni Scalfarotto, Temanza's pupil.

San Lazzaro degli Armeni

Just off the w shore of the Lido, and notable for the Armenian monastery founded by Senate decree in 1717. Much earlier, the island had housed a leper colony, already abandoned *circa* 1500. Construction of the present church and monastery under its founder, Padre Mechitar, was completed *circa* 1750. It was the only one not suppressed by Napoleon, and continues to function today; the monastery symbolises the international nature of scholarly study, contemplation and research, maintaining a generous hospitality to visitors. The monastic buildings centre on an attractively planted cloister, with a ground-floor colonnade and the monks' cells above; just beyond, on the e side, is the chapel, rebuilt after a fire in 1883. It has an attractive painted ceiling with stars. In the adjacent refectory: paintings by Sebastiano Ricci, Carlevarijs and Santacroce. The stair to the library is decorated with eighteenth-century stucco and frescoes by Zugno; adjacent is the Byron room, with his portrait and personal effects. The library, badly damaged by fire in 1975, contains approximately 50,000 volumes, an outstanding repository of Armenian culture. Down a short corridor to the s is the modern Rotonda (1967), containing an equally remarkable collection of approximately 2,000 manuscripts. The art collection occupies the corridors of the monastic buildings: paintings by Palma il Giovane, Jacopo Bassano, G. B. Tiepolo, Sebastiano Ricci, Canaletto, etc. The famous multi-lingual publishing house, Casa Editrice Armena, founded in 1796, has published in thirty-six languages, using its unique collection of fonts; it continues to do so, although the old press is now a museum, and the press is now at Punta Sabbioni.

Lazzaretto Vecchio

First settled by Eremitani Fathers in the twelfth century, with a hostel for pilgrims to the Holy Land. In 1423, at the request of Bernardino of Siena, it was acquired by the Republic as a quarantine island for plague victims. It was the first such isolation hospital in Europe; the name is a corruption of both Lazarus and Nazareth, and was later adopted for all leper hospitals. It was commandeered by Napoleon, who demolished the chapel, campanile and monastic buildings; it was abandoned in 1965, although several ward buildings survive: long, low, single-storey structures. They have been restored, and a museum of the lagoon is to be established here.

La Grazia (Santa Maria delle Grazie)

Also known as Cavanella, just s of the Giudecca. In 1264 a pilgrims'
hostel was established here, a dependency of the Ca' di Dio; in 1412
it passed to a group of monks from Fiesole, but was suppressed in
1668. Three years later, it reopened as a Capuchin nunnery, and
remained until its suppression in 1810. It was then used as a powder
store, but was blown up in the rebellion of 1848–9. More recently, it
has been an isolation hospital, but awaits a future use. A few hospital
buildings remain, but little of historic interest.

Sacca Sessola

A farly large islet about 1 kilometre s of the Giudecca. It was
created artificially, using material dredged from the lagoon to build
the Stazione Marittima, 1860–70. In 1914 a tuberculosis isolation
hospital was established here; the present hospital buildings, including
the neo-Romanesque church, were built in 1921–36. The hospital
was closed in 1979, and in 1992 a new international centre for
marine research was established.

Santo Spirito

The southernmost of this group, about 0.5 kilometres SE of Sacca
Sessola, towards the Lido. In 1140 an Augustinian monastery and
hospital were established, ceded in 1380 to nuns from Brondolo, near
Chioggia. In 1430 it was transferred to the Eremitani, and in the
sixteenth century a new church was built by Sansovino. In 1672 the
Friars Minor were transferred here, and remained until the
Napoleonic dissolution. In the early nineteenth century the monastic
buildings were destroyed, and by the early twentieth the islet had
been abandoned. It remains deserted today.

San Clemente

Between La Grazia and Sacca Sessola. First recorded in 1131; in 1160
a church and hospital were established by regular Augustinian canons.
In 1432 Lateran canons were transferred here, and in 1630 the island
was used as a temporary hospital for plague victims. In 1645 it was
occupied by Camaldolesi monks. After the Napoleonic suppression,
the island was militarised, and most of the monastery destroyed, but

in 1855 a psychiatric hospital was established here. A large complex of buildings was built in 1858–73, most of which survive. They are on three storeys, in a restrained Neo-classical style, built around three large courtyard gardens. In 1992 the hospital was closed; recently, the island was sold to become a luxury hotel. The surviving church has a complex seventeenth-century façade by Andrea Cominelli, incorporating monuments to Francesco (+1618) and Tommaso (+1647) Morosini, who funded the work. The interior is in a rich, typical seventeenth-century style, formerly with works by Lazzarini, Pittoni and Zanchi. In the chancel, there is no conventional altar, but a rich, Baroque version of the Santa Casa (Holy House) di Loreto, 1646.

5 LIDO DI VENEZIA

The most important of the long, narrow, barrier islands separating the lagoon from the Adriatic. Historically, there were more than there are today: Sant'Erasmo was once a lido, before the southward extension of the Cavallino peninsula; Pellestrina lido was once divided into two (see below).

The Lido formed a vital element in the lagoon's defences, both environmentally and militarily. Historically, it was sparsely settled, and was chiefly used for military exercises, and cultivated with orchards and vineyards. It was transformed after the late nineteenth century as a resort, by the establishment of notable hotels, chiefly the Excelsior and the Grand Hotel des Bains, followed by numerous smaller hotels, villas and apartments. Today the Lido is also a suburb, population approximately 20,000; the built-up area now extends s several kilometres towards Malamocco. These notes begin at San Niccolò at the N end and proceed southwards.

San Niccolò: at the N end of the island, in a crucial defensive location. Originally a Benedictine house, founded by Doge Domenico Contarini in 1043. The church was rebuilt on an adjacent site in 1626–9, but the plain brick façade was never completed; in the centre: monument to Doge Contarini (1640). The little Baroque campanile is contemporary with the church. The monastery was suppressed in 1770, but the church continued as a ducal chapel. In 1938 it was occupied by the Friars Minor of San Antonio. The church has a single nave, with six lateral chapels, three on each side; the high altar is of *pietre dure*, richly carved, coloured marble inlay. The surviving conventual buildings are now used for academic study and research; in the centre is the attractive cloister (1530). Adjacent are the remains of the earlier Romanesque church. On the quay nearby is the Palazzo del Consiglio dei Dieci, dated 1520, but modernised from an earlier building; it was used by the Republic to receive notable visitors arriving by sea.

San Niccolò was the location for the famous annual Sposalizio del Mare, on Ascension Day, when the doge 'married' the sea as a symbol of Venice's dominion over the Adriatic.

To the E, the small 'G. Nicelli' airfield was the earliest in Italy to be used for international flights (1918); the small terminal building (1932) is a rare survivor of the era.

Cimitero Ebraico: the Jewish cemetery was founded by the Republic in 1386. It was enlarged several times, and in 1774 a new cemetery was established nearby. A sensitive restoration took place in 1997–9, when many tombstones were salvaged and reordered. Adjacent is the Protestant cemetery (founded in 1684). Continuing S along the lagoon shore, we reach the **Tempio Votivo**: its imposing volume dominates the approach from the city. It was designed by Giuseppe Torres in 1921 as a 'temple of victory', but not completed until 1938. Today it is a memorial to the dead of both world wars, and contains the remains of more than 3,000 who died defending the city. The temple stands above an extensive crypt; it takes the form of a large cylinder, surrounded by a circular colonnade and surmounted by a copper cupola.

A little further along the waterfront is the tiny church of **Santa Maria Elizabetta**, founded in the sixteenth century, enlarged in 1627, since when it has been the island's parish church; comprehensively restored *circa* 1970. The interior has five altars, two on each side and the high altar. The little campanile is late nineteenth century.

The main avenue of the Lido, the Gran Viale, extends across the width of the island, terminating at the E end at Piazzale Bucintoro. On the right side, corner of Via Lepanto, is Guido Sullam's **Villa Mon Plaisir** (1906), a good example of the 'Liberty' (Art Nouveau) style. Halfway down on the right is the splendid tile-encrusted façade of the **Albergo Hungaria** (1906). At the E end of the Gran Viale is Piazzale Bucintoro; set back discreetly on the right is the looming mass of the **Grand Hotel des Bains** (Francesco Marsich, 1905), severely Neo-classical for a hotel dedicated to refinement and luxury. Directly in front, on the sea shore, is an exuberant 'folly', the **Blue Moon**, a restaurant/bar/club/shop serving the adjacent public beach, by Giancarlo de Carlo, 2001.

Lido di Venezia: detail of the Albergo Hungaria, 1906

Lido di Venezia: the Blue Moon, by Giancarlo de Carlo, 2001

Continuing s down Lungomare Marconi, we reach the **Casinò Municipale** (Eugenio Miozzi, 1936–8), a restrained exercise in symmetry in a 'white modern', rather fascistic style. Immediately adjacent is Miozzi's **Palazzo del Cinema** (1936, modernised in 1952), also 'white modern', but now to be rebuilt. A little further again, on the seaward side, is the magnificently self-indulgent but impressive **Excelsior Palace Hotel** (Giovanni Sardi, 1898–1908), a riotous collection of Moorish minarets and 'oriental' decoration.

South of the Excelsior, if we are travelling by bus, the route turns westwards and then runs down Via Sandro Gallo and Via Malamocco, along the lagoon shore, through the modern suburb of Ca' Bianca.

Malamocco: a small, attractive hamlet with an ancient history. The first Metamauco was one of the original 'confederation' of twelve settlements; it was the lagoon capital from 742 to 811, when it was definitively transferred to Rivo Alto (Venice); but Metamauco's site was to the E of the present hamlet, and is said to have been destroyed in an undersea earthquake in 1106. The 'new Malamocco' was then established on a pair of islets adjacent to the Lido, but separated from it (as we still see) by a narrow moat or canal.

It had its own *podestà* (governor), whose Gothic palace survives today (*circa* 1339) facing the lagoon waterfront; a substantial two-storey building, with a *trifora* on the first floor indicating the council hall, and numerous Gothic windows. The other monument is the church, **Santa Maria dell'Assunzione**, on its typically Venetian *campo*; originally fifteenth-century Gothic, modernised in 1557. It has a simple brick façade, with a Gothic portal and a large *ocio*. The interior has a single nave, with a vaulted roof. Inside: an altarpiece in the manner of Paolo dalle Masegne. The hamlet contains typical vernacular housing (sixteenth century to eighteenth).

Off the lee shore is the islet of **Poveglia**, a significant settlement in the medieval era. It was destroyed by the Genoese during the war of Chioggia (1379–80), and thereafter was fortified by the Republic, but few lay citizens remained. During the eighteenth century it was a *lazzaretto* (leper hospital), and in 1814 became an isolation hospital. At the Napoleonic dissolution, the church (San Vitale) was demolished, although its campanile survives. More recently it housed a sanatorium. It is being developed as a youth education, cultural and training centre.

Continuing down the littoral, we arrive at **Alberoni**, near the s tip. Alberoni guards the n bank of the important Porto di Malamocco, today intensively used by large commercial ships. Part of the land is a nature reserve.

6 LIDO DI PELLESTRINA

The ferry linking Alberoni with Santa Maria del Mare crosses the Porto di Malamocco to the littoral of Pellestrina, some 10 kilometres long, but extremely narrow, in places barely 150 metres across. Its settlement consists of a series of narrow, linear, street villages, all facing the lagoon and with their 'backs' towards the sea. Santa Maria del Mare is a small hamlet, but a little further s are the almost contiguous villages of **San Pietro in Volta** and Porto Secco. San Pietro is said to be named after the *volta* or curve in the lagoon channel at this point. The eponymous church was founded in the tenth century, but was destroyed by fire in 1567, and rebuilt in the early seventeenth century; the present structure is from 1777–1813, with a tripartite Palladian façade, capped by a large pediment. The village contains attractive

Pellestrina: general view from the lagoon

vernacular cottages, straggling along the lagoon quay, and with short, parallel lanes running inland at right angles. The same pattern of settlement is common to the whole littoral.

A little further s is **Porto Secco**, named after a gap in the littoral, reclaimed in the fifteenth century. It is thus recorded in 1425; its location can still be identified today. The church, Santo Stefano, was established *circa* 1488; the present church, from 1646 to 1684, has a Palladian façade similar to that of San Pietro.

To the s of Porto Secco there is a long stretch of littoral almost devoid of settlement, once intensively cultivated with orchards and vines, although recently much has been abandoned. Finally, **Pellestrina** itself, which extends along 3 kilometres of waterfront and is divided into three sections according to its churches, or four according to its unusual historic pattern of settlement. The churches are, from N to s: San Antonio, San Vio and Ognissanti, the last the principal parish of the island. Pellestrina was settled in the early medieval period, but was destroyed by the Genoese in 1379–80. After the Venetian victory, the Republic's first priority was rebuilding Chioggia; it then re-settled the littoral by offering the land to four of the principal clans of Chioggia; the Scarpa, Zennaro, Vianello and Busetti. These four clans still own most of the land today, and the

four zones, again still identifiable, became known (inappropriately) as *sestieri*; they are listed above from N to S.

San Antonio was founded in 1612 to serve the expanding population. It was enlarged in 1703, and has another bold stone Palladian façade with four pilasters supporting a crowning triangular pediment. Inside, the third right altar is by Longhena.

San Vio (properly Santi Vito e Modesto): the present church is by Tirali, 1718–23, and has an octagonal plan. It was built following an apparition of the Virgin in 1716, and is highly venerated. The church is partially clad with stone, with a principal order and an attic; the powerful entrance bay has a pair of bold Doric columns supporting an impressive pediment. Rising from the E face are two elegant *torreselle*. Adjacent is the former convent, 1723–6, again by Tirali.

Ognissanti: the original parish church of the island, first recorded in the twelfth century; enlarged in 1535 as the population grew, rebuilt in 1618 and enlarged again in 1684. Another Palladian façade, with two orders, divided into three bays by pilasters and with a triangular pediment. Most of the housing of Pellestrina is very similar to that of San Pietro and Portosecco, and to that at Burano: many small, cellular cottages, with a long continuous ribbon along the lagoon shore, and short alleys (locally called *carrizade*, carriageways) at right angles. The few larger houses, *case padronali*, are recognisable by their symmetrical façades, and represent the principal settler families; some are modelled on the contemporary Venetian noble villas of the seventeenth and eighteenth centuries.

The Murazzi: the littoral is protected from the sea by imposing sea-walls, formed of huge blocks of Istrian stone, and first built by the engineer Bernardino Zendrini in 1744, although they took thirty-eight years to complete. (The Murazzi also once protected the Lido itself.) At the south end of Pellestrina, just beyond the cemetery, the width of the littoral decreases to nothing, with only the wall between the lagoon and the sea. The littoral was severely damaged in the 1966 floods, and recently the Murazzi have been considerably strengthened.

At the s end is the hamlet of **Caroman** (or Ca' Roman), with surviving sixteenth-century fortifications. The ferry from Pellestrina cemetery continues s, crossing the Porto di Chioggia (with the sixteenth-century Lupa fort on the s side), as far as the little harbour at Vigo.

7   CHIOGGIA AND SOTTOMARINA

Chioggia is one of the principal fishing ports on the Adriatic, and the largest settlement in the lagoon after Venice, population approximately 55,000. The town's historic centre is built on islets, connected to the mainland by a causeway at its s end. It was a Roman settlement (Clodia Maiore), with its own satellite, Clodia Minore (modern Sottomarina), built on the lee shore of Chioggia's own lido, to the E. Sottomarina is today a holiday resort with sandy beaches, while Chioggia remains a working fishing town. It was a member of the original lagoon confederation, and received many migrants from Padua during the 'barbarian' invasions. Its history is inextricably linked to that of Venice, to which it was subject, with a Venetian governor (*podestà*), but it retained considerable autonomy, with its own statutes and council of leading citizens. Chioggia's early wealth derived from salt; until the sixteenth century the s end of the lagoon was covered with salt pans, a state monopoly from which the Republic derived a huge income. Its see was established in 1110, and the city flourished until the war with Genoa in 1379–80; Chioggia was besieged and then taken by the Genoese, who in turn were besieged by the Venetians themselves. Clodia Minore (Sottomarina) and Pellestrina were destroyed by the Genoese, and Chioggia itself was severely damaged before it was re-taken by the Venetians under Vettor Pisani and Carlo Zeno. Chioggia did not recover its pre-war prosperity, although it remained a major fishing port. Like Venice, it rose against foreign occupation, first in 1800 against Napoleon, then in 1848–9 against the Austrians. It finally joined united Italy in 1866, following a visit and rally from Garibaldi.

The city is built on two principal islands, both rectangular, oriented N–S, and divided by a narrow canal, the Vena. Just W of the Vena, and parallel to it, is the principal street, locally known as the Piazza (formally the Corso del Popolo), down which most major public buildings are distributed. The urban 'grain' consists of a large number of parallel *calli*, all at right angles to these two N–S axes, with one group to the W of the Piazza, and the other to the E of the Vena Canal. The whole town thus has a remarkably clear and consistent structure, much of which is perhaps of classical origin, but which was further 'regularised' after the 1379–80 war. To the W of the centre is the commercial Canale Lombardo; to the E is a small island containing the wholesale fish market, and then the Laguna di Lusenzo, on the E side of which is Sottomarina.

We start at Vigo, the traditional point of arrival. On the Piazzetta is a small column of Greek marble, with a twelfth-century capital and the winged Venetian lion. Cross **Ponte Vigo** (1685) to the left (E), across the Vena Canal. At the foot of the bridge: the former church of Santa Croce; a restrained Baroque tripartite façade with two orders. Continuing E (Calle Santa Croce), we reach another bridge to the monastery islet of **San Domenico**. Founded *circa* 1200, largely rebuilt 1745–62; it was later occupied by Jesuits, and restored *circa* 1800. A spacious single nave, with vaulted ceiling; three chapels down each side; a chancel flanked by two lateral chapels. Among the paintings are works by Carpaccio (*St Paul*, right side, 1520), Leandro Bassano and Tintoretto (attributed). The imposing eighteenth-century marble high altar has a remarkable wooden crucifix. The fourteenth-century campanile has survived the church's later modernisations.

Returning to the quay down the E side of the Vena; at no. 742: **Palazzo Grassi**, a significant early work by Tirali, 1703–14, with a colonnade along the quay and three upper floors. Rather fussily detailed, but impressive, among the largest palaces in the town. **Palazzo Lisatti** (no. 609) is more modest, again with a five-bay colonnade to the quay, two upper floors and a prominent *abbaino*; a tripartite façade with a first-floor *trifora*.

Continue s along the attractive *fondamenta*, with colonnaded houses and a lively street market. Just past the back of the Municipio, we reach the church of the **Filippini**, an impressive structure (1772), built at the expense of Conte Ludovico Manin, father of the last doge. The Neo-classical exterior is simple and restrained; the interior has a single nave with three chapels down each side and a barrel-vaulted ceiling. Paired pilasters down the flank walls, between which are reliefs of the story of St Filippo Neri by Giuseppe Maria Vianelli.

Continuing s: a little further, on the other bank, is the impressive **Santissima Trinità**, originally from 1528, but rebuilt by Tirali in 1703; a simple brick façade with a Renaissance portal. The imposing, spacious interior has a Greek-cross plan, with four short arms and a central cupola; several paintings of the school of Veronese and Tintoretto.

We continue down the quay, and cross Ponte Cuccagna (right) to meet the main street at the town gate.

Porta Garibaldi: a small, stocky, brick structure (1520), with a prominent Venetian lion on the outer face.

We enter the s end of the Piazza, a broad, animated thoroughfare, containing numerous shops, bars and restaurants, and flanked by civic monuments and *palazzetti*, chiefly sixteenth to eighteenth centuries.

The vast brick cathedral of **Santa Maria** was founded in the twelfth century, but destroyed by fire in 1623. It was rebuilt by Longhena, his first important ecclesiastical work, completed in 1674. The façade is plain, other than the stone portal (1633). On the right flank wall are fifteenth-century statues salvaged from the earlier church. Adjacent to the NW corner is the majestic free-standing campanile (1347–50), 64 metres tall, all brick, with *trifore* to the bell-chamber and an octagonal tambour. The cathedral interior is grandiose and monumental, of strongly Palladian inspiration; the nave is divided from the flanking aisles by Ionic pilasters with attached half-columns. The nave ceiling is a simple cross-vault, lit by large thermal windows. Marble lateral altars down both sides, and two fairly shallow transepts. The deep chancel has a rich free-standing marble high altar by Tremignon. Several paintings and altarpieces are relocated here from lost churches elsewhere, with works by Andrea Vicentino, Benedetto Caliari, G. B. Tiepolo, Giambattista Piazzetta and others. Between the cathedral and the Perottolo Canal to the s is an attractive small square, Piazza Vescovile, decorated with eighteenth-century sculptures.

Chioggia: side portal of San Martino, 1392

Immediately N of the cathedral, the little Gothic church of **San Martino** was built in 1392 to replace three churches destroyed by the Genoese during the 1379–80 war; all of brick, with an attractive s portal and decorative high-level blind arcading. Above the apse is an octagonal drum. The interior has a single nave with an open timber roof; above the altar is a small cupola. In the presbytery: two notable altarpieces (reassembled) from the school of Paolo Veneziano; one panel is dated 1349.

Continuing N up the Piazza, on the E side is the former chapel of **Santi Pietro e Paolo**, 1431; a small Romanesque-Gothic façade (restored).

A little further N (left side) is the little church of **San Francesco de le Muneghette**, rebuilt in 1454, and further restored and decorated in the eighteenth century. Inside: a single nave with barrel-vaulted ceiling; elegant stucco decoration (1743). Opposite, on the E side, is the former house of the artist Rosalba Carriera. The playwright Goldoni also lived here.

Next, on the W side: several prominent houses: **Palazzo Morari** (eighteenth century) has a rich, symmetrical façade balanced by

Chioggia: the west side of the Piazza, with eighteenth-century *palazzetti*

volutes at the outer corners; **Palazzo Nordio Marangoni** (seventeenth century) has a five-bay façade, in the centre of which is a majestically large archway, rising through two storeys; above is a continuous balcony and a central Serliana.

Directly opposite this last is the huge plain brick façade of **San Giacomo**; rebuilt in 1742–88 by Domenico Pelli, re-consecrated in 1790. The interior is a spacious rectangle, with Corinthian half-columns around the external walls and Neo-classical figures of the Virtues in niches set between the columns. The nave ceiling has a huge fresco by Antonio Marinetti (il Chiozzotto).

Immediately N is the **Monte di Pietà**, founded in 1485, but rebuilt in 1839 (Gothic tabernacle with sixteenth-century figure of the Virgin and Child); and then the **Loggia dei Bandi** (1537, restored *circa* 1800), the loggia from which public proclamations were made; it is faced by a simple Doric colonnade. Directly N again we reach the Neo-classical pile of the **Municipio** (Town Hall, 1840–50), restrained but impressive, if rather daunting in scale; it stands on the site of the medieval Palazzo Comunale, destroyed by fire in 1817. The symmetrical façade has a generous colonnaded ground floor, *piano nobile* and an attic. The lower façade is clad with stone, while the central section breaks forward slightly with a central first-floor loggia and a crowning pediment. Further N, on the same side, is the former **Granaio**, a long, low, two-storey structure, in the upper floor of which the town grain supplies were kept; built in 1321–2, modernised in 1864. The lower floor has a colonnade of stone piers and timber beams, the upper a row of simple Gothic windows. On the façade: *Virgin and Child*, said to be by Sansovino. Immediately N is **Palazzetto Rinavio**, late Gothic (1451), with a Renaissance *trifora* in the centre of the façade. Off the W side of the Piazza, Calle San Niccolò leads to the eponymous church; said to be the oldest in Chioggia, founded before 1320, although little survives.

Continuing northwards, still on the E side is the powerfully modelled Baroque façade of **Sant'Andrea**; of ancient foundation, rebuilt in 1743. The earlier stolid brick campanile (thirteenth century) survives nearby. The church has a Latin-cross plan, with side aisles and transepts; over the crossing: an octagonal cupola. The interior is rich and opulent. A little further N and we return to Piazzetta Vigo. On the W side is the impressive **Albergo Italia** (1912), formerly Palazzo Lissetto, a four-storey Neo-classical pile.

Sottomarina: reached by taking Calle San Giacomo eastwards and continuing across the causeway (1922) linking the two towns across the Laguna di Lusenzo. Sottomarina was destroyed in 1379–80, and was not re-settled until the seventeenth and eighteenth centuries. By tradition, the Marinanti are not fishermen, but cultivate the numerous orchards and market gardens to the S. The historic part of the town lies between the lagoon shore (W) and the Via San Marco to the E; here, the traditional pattern of *lido* settlement can be identified, with numerous parallel *calli* running down to the lagoon edge. The only monument of note is the large parish church of **San Martino**, rebuilt in 1830; an imposing building, with a single nave with lateral altars. The high altar was once attributed to Sansovino, and comes from the church of the Blessed Virgin of the Navicella, demolished by Napoleon. The modern resort town lies to the E and S of this small historic centre.

Appendix I

GLOSSARY OF TERMS

abbaino
A dormer in the roof of a palace, often faced with a pedimented aedicule

albergo
The small upper hall of a *scuola grande* (q.v.) where the governing board met

altana
A roof terrace, built of timber

androne
The principal ground-floor hall of a Venetian palace, usually with the land gate at one end and the watergate at the other; also the lower main hall of a *scuola grande* (q.v.)

Arsenale
The naval dockyards of the Venetian Republic, in eastern Castello; the name derives from the Arabic *darsina'a*, a place of industry

arte
A trade guild

Bacino
The Basin of San Marco, into which the Grand Canal flows

barbacane
An element of timber. The term is applied in two ways; first to the cantilever beams supporting an overhanging jetty of an upper storey; secondly, to the brackets that support a continuous beam above a colonnade

barco
A choir gallery in a church, generally located across the west end of the nave

Basilica
The term is applied in Venice only to the church of San Marco

bifora
A two-light window

botega
A shop or workshop

broccatello
A type of orange-pink marble from Verona

bugnato
Rustication, as applied to stonework

ca' (casa da stazio)
The principal residence of a Venetian noble family

calle (cale), callesella (calesela)
The usual Venetian name for a street, and its diminutive; a *cale larga* is a broad street, a *cale longa* a particularly long one

camin(o)
A chimney

campo, campiello
A public square, and its diminutive: they were originally grassed (*campo* = field)

canale
A major canal; all the minor canals are known as *rii*, singular *rio* (q.v.)

caneva (cantina)
A small storehouse

canton
The external corner or angle of a building

capitelo
A column capital; also a small external altar or tabernacle

casin(ò)
In a rural context, a small villa; in the city usually a garden pavilion attached to a palace, often used for entertaining

cason
A simple hut or shelter

cavana
A small boat shed, usually in the form of a wet dock

corte
A short, straight street, sometimes semi-private

cortile
An enclosed courtyard, usually to a private palace

cotto
Brickwork, from *pietra cotta*, literally 'cooked earth'

croxera, crosera
A simple cross-vault, resulting from the intersection of two barrel-vaults. The term is also used for a cross street, which links two other major streets

esafora
A six-light window

fenestra, fenestron
A window; a *fenestron* is a group of windows or a multi-light window

feramenta
Ironwork

fondaco, fontego
A warehouse, usually large in scale; also applied to the buildings used as trading bases by foreign communities in the city, e.g., dei Tedeschi (Germans), Turchi, Persiani

fondamenta
A quay along a canal; the other term is *riva* (q.v.)

formella
A decorative relief panel, in stone or marble, usually rectangular, with a cuved head

gotico fiorito
Literally florid Gothic; the final stage in the mature Venetian Gothic style, *circa* 1420–70, characterised by a large stylised stone *fiore* (flower) at the apex of the windows

granaio
A grain warehouse

liagò
A covered terrace on the top floor of a palace, with a colonnade to support the roof

Lido
One of the long narrow islands that divide the lagoons from the Adriatic Sea; thus Lido di Venezia, Lido di Pellestrina

Liston
The colonnade along the west side of the Doge's Palace; used as a meeting place for nobles

magazen
A store or warehouse; sometimes a tavern or wine-shop

Marzaria, merceria
A group of streets linking San Marco with Rialto, lined with shops, many originally mercers' shops

merlatura
Crenellation along the roofline of a building or wall; of eastern origin. Other than that at the Arsenale, it is decorative and not defensive

mezà (mezzanino)
A mezzanine floor of a building; usually for storage or ancillary accommodation

Molo
The quay directly in front of the Piazzetta of San Marco; the traditional point of arrival into the city for visitors

monofora
A single-light window

ocio (occhio)
A circular window (*ocio* = eye)

ospedal
A hospital, sometimes also a hospice

pala
An altarpiece

palazzo, palazzetto
In Italy, any substantial building, often for public offices. In Venice, the principal residence of a notable family, i.e. *casa da stazio* (q.v.)

pentafora
A five-light window

piano nobile
The principal floor of a Venetian palace; usually the first floor, but sometimes the second; sometimes palaces have two superimposed *piani nobili*. The most richly detailed floor, often with balconies

Piazza, Piazzetta
The terms are only applied to the squares at San Marco; all other Venetian squares are *campi*

piera, piera viva
Stonework, literally 'live stone'; *piera cotta*, however, is brickwork (see above)

piscina
A small pond, now often reclaimed

pluteo (plutei)
A decoratively carved panel of stone or marble, often forming part of a screen between the nave and chancel of a church

polifora
A multi-light window

portegal
A colonnaded entrance or atrium, with accommodation above

portego
The principal upper hall of a Venetian palace, standing directly above the *androne* (q.v.). Long and narrow, usually with multi-light windows at each end

proto(-maestro)
The chief master on a building site; often the architect as well. Many *proti* had permanent, salaried posts, either with the Republic or with important noble families

quadrifora
A four-light window

ramo
A short, narrow street (literally a 'branch); usually a cul-de-sac

rio, rielo, rio terà
The usual term for a canal and its diminutive; a *rio terà* (*rio interrato*) is a reclaimed canal

riva
A quay along a canal; the other term is *fondamenta* (q.v.)

ruga
A busy commercial street, lined with shops (said to derive from the French *rue*)

sacca
A body of water enclosed on two or three sides; a bay or inlet

sala capitolare
A chapter hall: the principal upper hall of a *scuola grande*, where Masses and assemblies of the membership were held

salizada
A paved street, that is, an important street that was paved at an early date

scudo, stemma
Coat of arms (literally a shield), or armorial bearing, of a noble family

scuola grande, scuola piccola
The *scuole grandi* were important voluntary lay confraternities, which built imposing accommodation for their assemblies and services; the *scuole piccole* are minor confraternities, often attached to a trade guild or *arte*. They also built much more modest halls in which to meet

Serliana
A type of window popularised by Sebastiano Serlio in the sixteenth century; it has a large central light (usually arched) flanked by two smaller lights, and often with square windows above the flanking lights

sofito
Ceiling or underside

soler
The storey of a building, usually an upper floor

sotoportego
A covered way, with accommodation above

squero
A small boatyard, where boats are made and repaired

tesa, teson
A shed; the larger *teson* is widely used for the sheds in the Arsenale

thermal window
A semicircular window, usually at high level; the term derives from its origins in the baths of classical Rome

tondo
A circular element used in decoration; sometimes with rare marble or a piece of sculpture set into it

tore (torre), toresela
A tower or (diminutive) a turret

travadura
The collective noun for the timber beams of a Venetian floor/ceiling construction; often exposed, painted and decorated

trifora
A three-light window

vera da pozzo
A well-head, of stone or marble; the 'well' is in fact a tank or cistern set into the ground, which collects rainwater from the surrounding roofs and pavements, and filters it through sand for domestic reuse

via, viale
The usual Italian terms for street and avenue; almost never used in Venice, but used on the Lido

Zattere, zattaron
Zattere: the quays along the city's south shore, where rafts of timber (*zattere*) were once brought ashore for the construction industry; a *zattaron* is the timber decking forming part of the foundations of a building

Appendix 2

THE SUCCESSION OF DOGES OF THE SERENISSIMA

Paoluccio Anafesto, 697–717

Marcello Tegalliano, 717–26

Orso Ipato, 726–37

Interregnum: Maestri delle Milizie, 737–42

Teodato Ipato, 742–55

Galla Gaulo, 755–56

Domenico Monegario, 756–64

Maurizio Galbaio, 764–87

Giovanni Galbaio, 787–804

Obelerio Antinorio, 804–11

Angelo Partecipazio, 811–27

Giustiniano Partecipazio, 827–29

Giovanni Partecipazio I, 829–36

Pietro Tradonico, 836–64

Orso Partecipazio I, 864–81

Giovanni Partecipazio II, 881–87

Pietro Candiano I, 887–88

Pietro Tribuno, 888–912

Orso Partecipazio II, 912–32

Pietro Candiano II, 932–39

Pietro Partecipazio, 939–42

Pietro Candiano III, 942–59

Pietro Candiano IV, 959–76

Pietro Orseolo I, 976–78

Vitale Candiano, 978–79

Tribuno Memmo, 979–91

Pietro Orseolo II, 991–1000

Ottone Orseolo, 1008–26

Pietro Centranico, 1026–32

Domenico Flabanico, 1032–43

Domenico Contarini, 1043–71

Domenico Selvo, 1071–85

Vitale Falier, 1085–96

Vitale Michiel I, 1096–1102

Ordelaffo Falier I, 1102–18

Domenico Michiel, 1118–30

Pietro Polani I, 1130–48

Domenico Morosini, 1148–56

Vitale Michiel II, 1156–72

Sebastiano Ziani, 1172–78

Orio Malipiero, 1178–92

Enrico Dandolo, 1192–1205

Pietro Ziani, 1205–29

Jacopo Tiepolo, 1229–49

Marino Morosini, 1249–53

Reniero Zen, 1253–68

Lorenzo Tiepolo, 1268–75

Jacopo Contarini, 1275–80

Giovanni Dandolo, 1280–89

Pietro Gradenigo, 1289–1311

Marino Zorzi, 1311–12

Giovanni Soranzo, 1312–28

Francesco Dandolo, 1329–39

Bartolomeo Gradenigo, 1339–42

Andrea Dandolo, 1343–54

Marin Falier, 1354–55

Giovanni Gradenigo, 1355–56

Giovanni Dolfin, 1356–61

Lorenzo Celsi, 1361–65

Marco Corner, 1365–68

Andrea Contarini, 1368–82

Michele Morosini, 1382

Antonio Venier, 1382–1400

Michele Steno, 1400–13

Tommaso Mocenigo, 1413–23

Francesco Foscari, 1423–57

Pasquale Malipiero, 1457–62

Cristoforo Moro, 1462–71

Niccolò Tron, 1471–73

Niccolò Marcello, 1473–74

Pietro Mocenigo, 1474–76

Andrea Vendramin, 1476–78

Giovanni Mocenigo, 1478–85

Marco Barbarigo, 1485–86

Agostin Barbarigo, 1486–1501

Leonardo Loredan, 1501–21

Antonio Grimani, 1521–23

Andrea Gritti, 1523–38

Pietro Lando, 1539–45

Francesco Donà, 1545–53

Marcantonio Trevisan, 1553–54

Francesco Venier, 1554–56

Lorenzo Priuli, 1556–59

Girolamo Priuli, 1559–67

Pietro Loredan, 1567–70

Alvise Mocenigo I, 1570–77

Sebastiano Venier, 1577–78

Niccolò da Ponte, 1578–85

Pasquale Cicogna, 1585–95

Marino Grimani, 1595–1605

Leonardo Donà, 1605–12

Marcantonio Memmo, 1612–15

Giovanni Bembo, 1615–18

Niccolo Donà, 1618

Antonio Priuli, 1618–23

Francesco Contarini, 1623–24

Giovanni Corner, 1625–29

Niccolò Contarini, 1630–31

Francesco Erizzo, 1631–46

Francesco Molin, 1646–55

Carlo Contarini, 1655–56

Francesco Corner, 1656

Bertuccio Valier, 1656–58

Giovanni Pesaro, 1658–59

Domenico Contarini, 1659–75

Niccolò Sagredo, 1675–76

Alvise Contarini, 1676–84

Marcantonio Giustinian, 1684–88

Francesco Morosini, 1688–94

Silvestro Valier, 1694–1700

Alvise Mocenigo II, 1700–09

Giovanni Corner II, 1709–22

Alvise Mocenigo III, 1722–32

Carlo Ruzzini, 1732–35

Alvise Pisani, 1735–41

Pietro Grimani, 1741–52

Francesco Loredan, 1752–62

Marco Foscarini, 1762–63

Alvise Mocenigo IV, 1763–78

Paolo Renier, 1778–89

Lodovico Manin, 1789–12 May 1797

Appendix 3

PRINCIPAL ARCHITECTS AND SCULPTORS
WORKING IN VENICE

Abbondi, Antonio ('lo Scarpagnino')
b. Milan, *circa* 1465–70; d. Venice, 1549. Architect. *Proto* of the Salt Office from 1505. Works and attributions: Fondaco dei Tedeschi; San Sebastiano; Doge's Palace; San Fantin; Scuola Grande di San Rocco; Castelforte San Rocco.

Benoni, Giuseppe
b. Trieste, 1618; d. Venice, 1684. Architect and engineer. Works: Dogana da Mar, from 1677.

Bon, Bartolomeo
b. Venice, ?*circa* 1400; d. Venice, *circa* 1464–7. Sculptor and mason. The principal master of the late Gothic period; many works and attributions: Ca' d'Oro; Porta della Carta; Scuola Vecchia de la Misericordia; portal of the Madonna de l'Orto; Carità church; west portal of Santi Giovanni e Paolo; portal of Santo Stefano; Ca' del Duca.

Bon, Bartolomeo ('il Bergamasco')
b. Bergamo, *circa* 1450; first recorded in Venice, 1463; d. ?1509. Architect and *proto*, often confused with Pietro Bon. Works and attributions: Campanile of San Marco; Torre dell'Orologio; Procuratie Vecchie.

Bon, Pietro
First recorded in Venice, 1496; d. Venice, 1529. Architect and mason. *Proto* of the Procurators of San Marco. Works and attributions: Scuola Grande di San Rocco.

Bon, Zane (Giovanni)

b. Venice, *circa* 1360; first recorded 1382; d. Venice, *circa* 1442. Sculptor and mason, established an important shop later managed by his son Bartolomeo. Works: Ca' d'Oro; Porta della Carta.

Bregno, Antonio

b. Osteno, Lugano; recorded in Venice, 1425–57. Mason and sculptor, member of a large extended family. Works and attributions: Francesco Foscari monument, Frari; Doge's Palace (Porta della Carta and Foscari Arch).

Bregno, Lorenzo

b. Verona, *circa* 1475; first recorded in Venice, 1500; d. Venice, 4 January 1525. Mason and sculptor from the same clan. Works and attributions: monuments to Bartolomeo Bragadin, Santi Giovanni e Paolo; and Benedetto Pesaro, Frari.

Buora, Giovanni

b. Osteno, Lugano, before 1450; first recorded in Venice, 1480; d. Venice, 1513. Early Renaissance sculptor and stonemason. Works and attributions: San Zaccaria; Scuola Grande di San Marco; Palazzo Michiel; Palazzo Contarini dal Zaffo; San Giorgio Maggiore (Manica lunga); sculptures at Frari, Santo Stefano.

Campagna, Girolamo

b. Verona, *circa* 1549; d. Venice, after 1626. Noted and prolific Renaissance sculptor. Works in many of the city's churches, e.g., Santa Maria Formosa; San Francesco de la Vigna; Santo Stefano; San Sebastiano.

Cattaneo, Danese

b. near Carrara, *circa* 1509; d. Padua, 1572. Renaissance sculptor. Trained under Sansovino and taught Campagna. Works and attributions: Loggetta San Marco; Biblioteca Marciana; monument to Leonardo Loredan, Santi Giovanni e Paolo; San Salvador; San Giovanni Evangelista.

Codussi, Mauro

b. Lenna, Bergamo, *circa* 1440; d. Venice, 1504. Architect and mason. Principal figure of the early Renaissance in Venice. Works and attrbutions: San Michele in Isola; Santa Maria Formosa; San Giovanni Grisostomo; Scuola Grande di San Marco; Scuola Grande di San Giovanni Evangelista; Palazzo Zorzi, San Severo; Palazzo Lando Corner Spinelli; Palazzo Loredan Vendramin Calergi.

Cominelli, Andrea

Active in Venice second half of the seventeenth century. Baroque architect and sculptor, a follower of Longhena. Works and attributions: Palazzo Labia, Le Terese.

Contin, Antonio, Bernardino, Francesco, Tommaso

Family of architects and sculptors, originally from Lugano. Antonio: b. *circa* 1566; d. Venice, 1600. Son of Bernardino. Works: Ponte dei Sospiri; Scuola di San Fantin. Bernardino: first recorded in Venice, 1568; d. before 1597. Works and attributions: San Salvador; Palazzo Barbarigo de la Terrazza. Tommaso (brother of Bernardino): active in Venice, 1600–18. Works: Palazzo delle Prigioni.

Donatello (Donato di Niccolò Bardi)
b. Florence, *circa* 1386; d. Florence, 13 December 1466. Sculptor. The greatest master of the early Renaissance. In Padua, 1443–53, and highly influential. His only surviving work in Venice is *St John the Baptist* in the Frari.

Gambello, Antonio
First recorded in Venice, 1458; d. 1481. Architect, mason and *proto*. Consultant on fortifications to the Republic. Works: San Zaccaria, perhaps San Giobbe.

Gaspari, Antonio
b. Venice, *circa* 1670; d. *circa* 1730. Baroque architect, notable follower of Longhena. Works and attributions: San Vidal; Palazzo Zenobio; Palazzo Michiel da le Colonne; Palazzo Morosini, Santo Stefano; Santa Maria de la Fava; Palazzo Giustinian, Murano. He also completed Ca' Pesaro.

Grigi, de', Guglielmo
b. Alzano, Bergmo, *circa* 1480; first recorded in Venice, *circa* 1515; d. Venice, ?1550. Architect and sculptor/mason. Works and attributions: Procuratie Vecchie(?); Palazzo dei Camerlenghi; Miani Chapel, San Michele; Palazzo Tasca; Palazzo Coccina Tiepolo.

Grigi, de', Giangiacomo
Active in Venice from *circa* 1549; d. Venice, 1572. Architect and mason, son of Guglielmo. Works and attributions: Scuola Grande di San Rocco; Palazzo Coccina Tiepolo; completed Palazzo Grimani, San Luca.

Leopardi, Alessandro
b. Venice; first recorded in 1482; d. Venice, *circa* 1522. Sculptor and bronze founder. His masterpiece is the equestrian statue of Colleoni in Campo Santi Giovanni e Paolo, begun by Verrocchio.

Lombardo (Solari), Pietro
b. Carona, Lombardy, *circa* 1435; d. Venice, 1515. Architect, mason and sculptor. A central figure of the early Renaissance, with a rich decorative style. Had a flourishing workshop in Venice with his sons Tullio (*circa* 1455–1532) and Antonio (*circa* 1458–1516). Works and attributions: San Giobbe; Santa Maria dei Miracoli; Scuola Grande di San Marco; Scuola Grande di San Giovanni Evangelista. *Proto* at the Doge's Palace from 1489 to *circa* 1505, building much of the east wing. Also made three notable ducal monuments, all at Santi Giovanni e Paolo: those of Pasquale Malipiero, Pietro Mocenigo and Niccolò Marcello. Tullio: work and attributions: San Salvador; monuments to Andrea Vendramin and Giovanni Mocenigo, Santi Giovanni e Paolo; the Arco del Santo at Padua.

Longhena, Baldassare
b. Venice, 1597; d. Venice, 1682. Architect. The central figure of the Venetian
Baroque, with a long and prolific career. Works and attributions: Chioggia
Cathedral; Palazzo Widmann; Palazzo Giustinian Lolin; Santa Maria de la
Salute; Spanish and Ponentine synagogues; library and staircase at San Giorgio
Maggiore; San Tomà; Palazzo da Lezze; Scalzi church; completed the
Procuratie Nuove; Ospedaleto; Ca' Rezzonico; Ca' Pesaro; Scuola Grande dei
Carmini; Collegio Flangini and Scuola San Niccolò dei Greci.

Maccaruzzi, Bernardino
b. Venice; d. 1798. Architect. Pupil of Massari. Works and attributions: San
Rocco (façade); San Giovanni Evangelista; Scuola de la Carità (façade).

Manopola (Monopola), Bartolomeo
Active in Venice, 1597–1623. *Proto* at the Doge's Palace from 1597. Works and
attributions: Clock-tower façade, Doge's Palace; Palazzo Ruzzini Priuli; part of
Palazzo Pisani, Santo Stefano.

Massari, Giorgio
b. Venice, 1687; d. Venice, 1766. Architect. The principal Neo-classical architect
in Venice; a follower of Tirali. Works and attributions: Gesuati church;
Catecumeni; San Marcuola; Oratorio del Cristo; Pietà church; La Fava; San
Zaninovo; Palazzo Grassi. Completed Ca' Rezzonico.

Miozzi, Eugenio
b. 16 September 1889; d. Venice, 10 April 1979. Architect and engineer.
Director of Public Works in Venice from 1931. Works: Ponte degli Scalzi;
Ponte de l'Accademia; Ponte della Libertà; Autorimessa, Piazzale Roma;
Palazzo del Casinò (Lido).

Palladio, Andrea ('della Gondola')
b. Padua, 8 November 1508; d. Maser(?), 19 August 1580. Architect, writer
and theorist. The most important architect of the High Renaissance; his
influence in Italy and abroad was enormous. *I quattro libri dell'architettura*
(1570) is probably the most notable treatise ever written. Works and
attributions: Redentore church; San Giorgio Maggiore (church, cloister,
refectory); San Francesco de la Vigna; Le Zitelle; monastic buildings of the
Carità monastic house; numerous villas on the Terraferma, and palaces, etc.,
in Vicenza.

Ponte, Antonio da
b. Venice, *circa* 1512; d. 20 March 1597. Architect and engineer. *Proto* of the
Salt Office from 1563, responsible for reconstruction at the Doge's Palace after
the 1574 fire. Works: Sala del Senato, Sale delle Quattro Porte, Sala del
Collegio, Sala del Maggior Consiglio (after the 1577 fire); Corderie at the
Arsenale; Ponte di Rialto; Palazzo delle Prigioni.

Rizzo, Antonio
b. Verona, before 1440; d. Cesena(?), 1499. Sculptor and architect. Earliest works are three altars at San Marco. Much of his œuvre remains contentious. Works and attributions: Niccolò Tron monument (Frari), east wing of the Doge's Palace and the Scala dei Giganti (after 1483); sculpted figures of *Adam* and *Eve* (Doge's Palace).

Rossi, Domenico
b. Lugano, 1657; d. Venice, 1737. Architect. Much influenced by Giuseppe Sardi; trained by Longhena. Works and attributions: San Girolamo; façade of San Stae; Gesuiti church; Palazzo Corner de la Regina.

Sanmicheli, Michele
b. Verona, *circa* 1487; d. Verona, 1559. Architect and engineer. A crucial figure of the High Renaissance, with a powerfully expressive style. Many works of fortification (city gates, etc.) on the Terraferma. Works and attributions: interior of Palazzo Corner Spinelli; Palazzo Corner, San Polo; Palazzo Grimani, San Luca; Forte di Sant'Andrea.

Santi, Lorenzo
b. Siena, 1783; d. Venice, 1839. Neo-classical architect. Works: Palazzo Patriarcale; interior of San Silvestro; coffee house in the Giardinetti Reali.

Sardi, Giovanni
b. Venice, 1863; d. early 1900s. Architect, mainly in the neo-Gothic manner. Works: Hotel Bauer; Palazzo Ravà; Hotel Excelsior, Lido.

Sardi, Giuseppe
b. Lugano, *circa* 1621; d. Venice, 1699. Baroque architect. Central figure of the later Venetian Baroque; probably trained under Longhena. Works and attributions: façade of Scuola di San Todaro; façade of San Salvador; Ospedaletto; façade of Scalzi church; façade of San Lazzaro dei Mendicanti; façade of Santa Maria del Giglio.

Scalfarotto, Giovanni
b. Venice, *circa* 1690; d. 1764. Architect. His only major known work is San Simon Piccolo; also modernised the interior of San Rocco.

Scamozzi, Vincenzo
b. Vicenza, 2 September 1548; d. Venice, 7 August 1616. Renaissance architect, theorist and writer. Author of the influential *L'idea dell'architettura universale* (1615). Works and attributions: Procuratie Nuove; completion of the Biblioteca Marciana; Tolentini church; Palazzo Contarini degli Scrigni.

Scarpa, Carlo
b. Venice, 2 June 1906; d. Sendai, Japan, 28 November 1978. Architect and designer. A multi-facetted modern master, noted for his profound understanding of materials and techniques. Many works in the Terraferma. Works in Venice: remodelling of the Accademia galleries; the Ca' d'Oro

galleries; the Museo Civico Correr; Palazzo Querini Stampalia; Olivetti showroom, Piazza San Marco; Venezuela Pavilion, Biennale Gardens.

Selva, Gianantonio
b. Venice, 1757; d. 1819. Neo-classical architect. Works: interior of Palazzo Dolfin Manin; La Fenice theatre; Nome di Gesù church; San Maurizio; extension of the Accademia galleries.

Spavento, Giorgio
Active from 1486; d. Venice, 17 April 1509. Architect. *Proto* of San Marco from 1486. Works and attributions: chapel of San Todaro, Doge's Palace; San Niccolò di Castello (lost); Fondaco dei Tedeschi; San Salvador.

Tatti, Jacopo ('il Sansovino')
b. Florence, 1486; d. Venice, 27 November 1570. Architect and sculptor. With Palladio, the central figure of the Venetian High Renaissance. Studied in Rome (1505–27), then moved to Venice; *proto* of San Marco from 1529 to his death. Works and attributions: Biblioteca Marciana; Zecca; Loggetta di San Marco; Palazzo Dolfin Manin; Palazzo Corner (San Maurizio); Santo Spirito (lost); Palazzo Moro, Cannaregio; San Francesco de la Vigna; Incurabili (lost); San Zulian; San Martino; San Gemignano (lost). Many sculptures, including the 'giganti' at the Doge's Palace.

Temanza, Tommaso
b. Venice, 1705; d. 1789. Neo-classical architect, engineer and writer. *Proto* to the Magistrato alle Acque. Works: Maddalena church; *casinò* at Palazzo Zenobio; San Servolo.

Tirali, Andrea
b. Venice, 1657; d. Monselice, 1737. Notable and prolific Neo-classical architect and engineer. *Proto* of the Magistrato alle Acque from 1694. Works and attributions: Ponte dei Tre Archi; Trinità church, Chioggia; Palazzo Grassi, Chioggia; Tolentini church (façade); Palazzo Diedo, Santa Fosca; *campanili* of San Martino, Burano, and Santi Apostoli; Scuola dell'Angelo Custode; paving of Piazza San Marco; San Giovanni Laterano; façade of San Vidal; Palazzo Priuli Manfrin; San Vio, Pellestrina.

Tremignon, Alessandro
b. Tremignon, Padua; active in Venice, late seventeenth century. Architect; *proto* to the Arsenale. Works and attributions: façade of San Moisè; Palazzo Flangini Fini; façade of Palazzo Labia.

Vittoria, Alessandro
b. Trento, ?1525; d. Venice, 27 May 1608. Sculptor and architect. An important, prolific figure of the High Renaissance; a pupil of Sansovino. Works and attributions: Doge's Palace (Scala d'Oro, Sala delle Quattro Porte). Sculpture in many churches, including San Giovanni in Bragora, Sant'Antonin, Santa Maria dei Miracoli, San Francesco de la Vigna, San Salvador, San Zulian.

Select Bibliography

GENERAL HISTORIES AND GUIDES

P. F. Brown, *Venice and Antiquity: The Venetian Sense of the Past*, New Haven and London, 1996

D. S. Chambers, *The Imperial Age of Venice, 1380–1580*, London, 1970

E. Concina, *A History of Venetian Architecture*, trans. J. Landry, Cambridge, 1998

R. J. Goy, *Venice: The City and its Architecture*, London and New York, 1997

C. Hibbert, *Venice: The Biography of a City*, London, 1988

D. Howard, *The Architectural History of Venice*, 2nd edn, New Haven and London, 2002

E. E. Kittell and T. F. Madden, *Medieval and Renaissance Venice*, Chicago, 1999

F. C. Lane, *Venice: A Maritime Empire*, Baltimore and London, 1973

G. Lorenzetti, *Venice and its Lagoon*, trans. J. Guthrie, Trieste, 1975

J. Martin and D. Romano, eds, *Venice Reconsidered: The History and Civilization of an Italian State, 1297–1797*, Baltimore, 2000

S. Muratori, *Studi per una operante storia urbana di Venezia*, Rome, 1959

J. J. Norwich, *A History of Venice*, Harmondsworth, 1982

G. Perocco and A. Salvadori, *Civiltà di Venezia*, 3 vols, Venice, 1973–6

G. Piamonte, *Venezia vista dall'acqua*, Venice, 1966

F. Sansovino, *Venetia, città nobilissima et singolare*, Venice, 1581; facsimile of the 3rd edn [1663], Venice, 1968

A. Zorzi, *Venezia scomparsa*, 2 vols, Milan, 1977

INDIVIDUAL HISTORIC PERIODS

The city's origins

W. Dorigo, *Venezia arigini: fondamenti, ipotesi, metodi*, 2 vols, Milan, 1983

Byzantine architecture and the medieval vernacular tradition

O. Demus, *The Church of San Marco in Venice: History, Architecture, Sculpture*, Washington, DC, 1960

G. Gianighian and P. Pavanini, *Dietro i palazzi: tre secoli di architettura minore a Venezia*, Venice, 1984

R. J. Goy, *Venetian Vernacular Architecture: Traditional Housing in the Venetian Lagoon*, Cambridge, 1989

E. R. Trincanato, *Venezia minore*, Milan, 1948; new enlarged edn, Verona, 2008

—, *La casa veneziana delle origini*, Venice, 1999

Gothic architecture

E. Arslan, *Gothic Architecture in Venice*, trans. A. Engel, London, 1971

R. J. Goy, *The House of Gold: Building a Palace in Medieval Venice*, Cambridge, 1992

D. Howard, *Venice and the East: The Impact of the Islamic World on the Architecture of Venice, 1100–1500*, New Haven and London, 2000

P. Maretto, *L'edilizia gotica veneziana*, 2nd edn, Venice, 1978

S. Quill, *Ruskin's Venice: The Stones Revisited*, Aldershot, 2000

J. Ruskin, *The Stones of Venice*, 3 vols, London, 1851–3

F. Valcanover and W. Wolters, eds, *L'architettura gotica veneziana: Atti del Convegno internazionale di Studio*, Venice, 2000

W. Wolters, *La scultura gotica veneziana, 1300–1400*, 2 vols, Venice, 1976

The Renaissance and Renaissance architecture

R. Lieberman, *Renaissance Architecture in Venice, 1450–1540*, London, 1982

P. F. Brown, *Art and Life in Renaissance Venice*, New York, 1997

J. R. Hale, ed., *Renaissance Venice*, London, 1973

N. Huse and W. Wolters, *The Art of Renaissance Venice: Architecture, Sculpture and Painting, 1460–1590*, trans. E. Jephcott, Chicago, 1990

J. McAndrew, *Venetian Architecture of the Early Renaissance*, Cambridge, MA, and London, 1980

M. Tafuri, *Venice and the Renaissance*, trans. J. Levine, Cambridge, MA, and London, 1989

—, *Interpreting the Renaissance: Princes, Cities, Architects*, New Haven and London, 2006

W. Wolters, *Architektur und Ornament: Venezianischer Bauschmuck der Renaissance*, Munich, 2000

Baroque and Neo-classical architecture

E. Bassi, *L'architettura del sei e settecento a Venezia*, Naples, 1962

E. Concina, *Venezia nell'età moderna: struttura e funzioni*, Padua, 1989

The nineteenth and twentieth centuries

P. Maretto, *Venezia: architettura del XX secolo in Italia*, Genoa, 1969

M. de' Michelis, ed., *Venezia: la nuova architettura*, Milan, 1999

M. Plant, *Venice: Fragile City, 1797–1997*, New Haven and London, 2002

G. Romanelli, *Venezia ottocento*, Rome, 1977

Monographs on individual architects

J. S. Ackerman, *Palladio*, Harmondsworth, 1966

E. Bassi, *Gianantonio Selva, architetto veneziano*, Padua, 1936

B. Boucher, *Andrea Palladio: The Architect in his Time*, New York and London, 1994

T. E. Cooper, *Palladio's Venice*, New Haven and London, 2005

F. Dal Co and G. Mazzariol, *Carlo Scarpa: The Complete Works*, trans. R. Sadleir, London, 1986

S. Frommel, *Sebastiano Serlio, architetto*, Milan, 1998

P. Gazzola et al., *Michele Sanmicheli: architetto veronese del Cinquecento*, Venice, 1960

L. E. Ghersi, *Alessandro Vittoria: architettura, scultura e decorazione nella Venezia del tardo Rinascimento*, Udine, 1998

A. Guerra, M. Morresi and R. Schofield, eds, *I Lombardo: architettura e scultura a Venezia tra '400 e '500*, Venice, 2006

A. Hopkins, *Baldassare Longhena, 1597–1682*, Milan, 2006

D. Howard, *Jacopo Sansovino: Architecture and Patronage in Renaissance Venice*, New Haven and London, 1975

A. Massari, *Giorgio Massari, architetto veneziano del settecento*, Vicenza, 1971

M. Morresi, *Jacopo Sansovino*, Milan, 2000

P. Piffaretti, *Giuseppe Sardi*, Bellinzona, 1996

L. Puppi, *Michele Sanmicheli, architetto di Verona*, Padua, 1971

—, *Andrea Palladio*, 2 vols, Milan, 1973

— and L. O. Puppi, *Mauro Codussi e l'architettura veneziana del primo Rinascimento*, Milan, 1977

A. M. Schulz, *Antonio Rizzo: Sculptor and Architect*, Princeton, 1983

Monographs on buildings and building types; other works

E. Bassi, *Palazzi di Venezia*, Venice, 1976

— and E. R. Trincanato, *Il Palazzo Ducale nella storia e nell'arte di Venezia*, Milan, 1960

M. Brusegan, *I palazzi di Venezia*, Rome 2005

D. Calabi and P. Morachiello, *Rialto: le fabbriche e il ponte, 1514–1591*, Turin, 1987

L. Ciacci, ed., *La Fenice ricostruita, 1996–2003: un cantiere in città*, Venice, 2007

A. Clark and P. Rylands, *The Church of the Madonna dell'Orto*, London, 1977

O. Demus, *The Mosaics of San Marco*, 4 vols, Chicago and London, 1984

U. Franzoi and D. di Stefano, *Le Chiese di Venezia*, Venice, 1976

—, T. Pignatti and W. Wolters, *Il Palazzo Ducale di Venezia*, Treviso, 1990

G. Guidarelli, *La Fabbrica della Scuola Grande di San Rocco in Venezia, 1517–1560*, Venice, 2002

A. Hopkins, *Santa Maria della Salute: Architecture and Ceremony in Baroque Venice*, Cambridge, 2000

P. Lauritzen and A. Zielcke, *Palaces of Venice*, Oxford, 1978

F. Mancini et al., *I teatri di Venezia*, 2 vols, Venice, 1995–6

P. Maretto, *La casa veneziana nella storia della città*, Venice, 1986

M. Morresi, *Piazza San Marco: istituzioni, poteri e architettura a venezia nel primo Cinquecento*, Milan, 1999

A. Palladio, *I quattro libri dell'architettura*, Venice, 1570; facsimile edn, Milan, 1969

M. Piana and W. Wolters, eds, *Santa Maria dei Miracoli a Venezia: la storia, la fabbrica, i restauri*, Venice, 2003

T. Pignatti, *Le Scuole di Venezia*, Milan, 1981

R. Polacco, *La cattedrale di Torcello*, Venice and Treviso, 1984

A. Rizzi, *Scultura esterna a Venezia*, Venice, 1987

G. Romanelli, *Ca' Corner della Ca' Granda*, Venice, 1993

G. Samonà et al., *Piazza San Marco: l'architettura, la storia, le funzioni*, Padua, 1970

P. Sohm, *The Scuola Grande di San Marco, 1437–1550: The Architecture of a Venetian Lay Confraternity*, New York and London, 1982

G. Tassini, *Curiosità Veneziane*, ed. L. Moretti, Venice, 1988

A. Zorzi, *Venetian Palaces*, New York, 1990

Index 1

CHURCHES AND RELIGIOUS HOUSES IN VENICE

Index 2

PALACES AND NAMED HOUSES IN VENICE

Note: Many palaces in Venice have several names, and their identification is by no means universal or standardised; they are therefore listed here under more than one name.

Marco, Corte San (DD 2490–503) 380

Marini (CN 2967) 140

Marioni Mainella (DD 1259) 370

Martinengo Mandelli Memmo
(CN 1756) 128, 400

Martinengo Pisani Volpi (SM 3947) 263,
404

Maruzzi Pellegrini (CS 3394) 60

Mastelli dal Cammello (CN 3381) 145–6

Mayer Grimani (CN 3024) 141

Memmo Cappello (CS 3698) 63

Memmo Martinengo Mandelli
(CN 1756) 128, 400

Merati Berlendis (CN 6293 and 6296)
188

Michiel (CN 3218) 143

Michiel, casinò (CN 3218) 143

Michiel (CN 2536) 139

Michiel Baffo Molin Piacentini
(CS 4391a–2a) 69–70

Michiel del Brusà (CN 4391) 166, 402

Michiel da le Colonne (CN 4314)
165–6, 402

Michiel Contarini (DD 2793–4) 384

Minelli Da Ponte (GD 48–52) 425

Minelli Spada (CN 3534–6) 148

Minio Gussoni Grimani (CN 2277) 134

Minotto (SC 143) 324

Mocenigo (GD 19–22) 424

Mocenigo (SC 1992) 340

Mocenigo Casa Vecchia (SM 3348) 258,
405

Mocenigo Casa Nova (SM 3349) 258,
405

Mocenigo Corner (SP 2128) 296–7

Mocenigo Corner Contarini (SM 3980)
263

Mocenigo Gambara (DD 1056) 367, 416

Modena Savorgnan (CN 349) 119

Molin (DD 1515–20) 372

Molin (SM 2757–8) 249

Molin (SP 1296) 290

Molin (SP 2514) 303

Molin [Adriatica della Navigazione]
(DD 1410–12) 371–2

Molin Balbi Valier de la Tressa
(DD 866) 360, 418

Molin Cappello (SP 1280) 290

Molin Cocco (SM 1659) 240

Molin Da Lezze (CN 3770–8) 158

Molin Erizzo Barzizza (CN 2139) 131,
288–9

Molin Loredan Cini (DD 732) 360

Molin Michiel Piacentini (CS 4391a–2a)
70

Molin Querini Gaspari (CN 2179) 132,
401

Moro (CN 3000) 140–1

Moro (SC 2265) 347

Moro (SM 5282 and 5308) 273

Moro (CN 2446) 138

Moro (DD 1381) 371, 416

Moro Diedo Dolfin (DD 1263) 370

Moro Lin (SM 3242) 257, 405

Moro Lin (SP 2672) 303–4

Morosini (CN 5825) 180

Morosini (CS 4391) 70

Morosini (DD 222–3) 356

Morosini (SP 2812) 306

Morosini Brandolin (SP 1789) 292

Morosini Cavagnis (CS 5171) 81

Morosini Da Mula (DD 725) 360

Morosini Gattemburg (SM 2803) 249

Morosini Gritti (SM 3832) 260–1

Morosini dal Pestrin (CS 6140) 91

Morosini Sagredo (CN 4199) 163–4, 402

Morosini da la Sbarra (CS 2842–5) 56

Morosini Strozzi (CN 4503) 168

Morosini da la Tressa (CN 233) 115

Morosini Valmarana dal Giardino
(CN 4636) (ex) 169

Morosini Zane Collalto (SP 2360) 300

Morosini Zane Collalto, casinò
(SP 2368) 300

Mosca Semenzi (CN 6270) 188

Muazzo (CS 6451–5) 92

Rizzi (SC 316) 327

Rizzo Patarol (CN 3499) 146

Rocca Bianca [Visconti] (GD 218–24)
     427

Roma (CN 923) 122

Rota Brandolin (DD 878) 361

Rota Campana (CS 4409 and 4421) 70

Rotonda (GD 690–3) 429

Rubini (CN 3554) 152

Ruoda (CN 2256–61) 134, 401

Ruzzini (CN 5783–5) 180, 403

Ruzzini Priuli Loredan (CS 5866) 88

Sagredo (CS 2720 and 3060) 53

Sagredo Morosini (CN 4199) 163–4, 402

Salamon (CN 3609) 155

Salviati (DD 195) 356, 419

Salvioni (CS 3463) 62

Sandi (SM 3870) 261

Sangiantoffetti Foscarini (DD 1075) 368

Sansoni (SP 898) 287

Sanudo (SP 2165) 297

Sanudo (SC 1740 and 1757) 338

Sanudo (SM 1626) 240

Sanudo Soranzo Van Axel (CN 6069–99)
     186–7

Savorgnan Galvagna (CN 349) 119

Scalfarotto (CS 5492) 85

Scarpon Priuli (CN 3709) 157

Sceriman Contarini Dolce (CN 4851a)
     169

Sceriman Zeno Manin (CN 168) 115

Secco Dolfin (DD 3833) 395

Selvadego (SM 1238) 238

Semenzi Mosca (CN 6270) 188

Sernagiotto (CN 5720) 178, 403

Simonetti (CS 6109) 91

Soderini (CS 3610) 63

Somachi Pisani Trevisan (SM 3831) 261

Soranzo (DD 299) 357

Soranzo (SP 2542) 303

Soranzo (SP 2169 and 2170–1) 297–9

Soranzo dell'Angelo (CS 4415–19) 70

Soranzo Bellavite Terzi Baffo (SM 2760)
     248–9

Soranzo Calbo Crotta (CN 122) 115,
     399

Soranzo Piovene (CN 2176) 131–2, 400

Soranzo Sanudo Van Axel
     (CN 6069–71 and 6099) 186–7

Spada Minelli (CN 3534) 148

Spinelli Lando Corner (SM 3877)
     261–2, 404

Stazio Priuli (SC 1777) 338

Stern Michiel Malpaga (DD 2792) 384,
     416

Superchio (CN 1295) 127

Surian (CN 336) 118

Surian Bellotto (CN 967–75) 122

Surian Stazio Priuli (SC 1777) 338

Tasca Papafava Veggia (CS 5402) 85

Terzi Bellavite Soranzo Baffo (SM 2760)
     248–9

Testa (CN 468) 120

Tetta (CS 6378–9) 91–2

Tiepolo (site of) (CN 3603) 155

Tiepolo (SP 2774) 305

Tiepolo Badoer (SM 2161) 243

Tiepolo Maffetti (SP 1957) 293, 414

Tiepolo Papadopoli Coccina (SP 1365)
     290–1, 413

Tiepolo Passati (SP 2781) 305

Tintoretto (CN 3399) 145

Tornielli (CN 2370) 136

Treves Bonfili (CS 3393) 60

Treves Emo Barozzi (SM 2156) 243, 408

Trevisan (CN 3584) 153

Trevisan Cappello in Canonica
     (CS 4328–30) 68, 75

Trevisan Malipiero (CS 4852 and 5250)
     75

Trevisan Pisani Somachi (SM 3831) 261

Trevisan dagli Ulivi (DD 789 and 809)
     362

Tron (SC 2084) 344

Index 3

SCUOLE GRANDI AND *SCUOLE PICCOLE* IN VENICE

Index 4

OTHER BUILDINGS AND FEATURES IN VENICE

Index 5

BUILDINGS ON THE LAGOON ISLANDS

Index 6

PROPER NAMES